Realist film theory and cinema

Manchester University Press

Realist film theory and cinema

The nineteenth-century Lukácsian and intuitionist realist traditions

IAN AITKEN

Manchester University Press

Manchester and New York

distributed exclusively in the USA by Palgrove

Published by Manchester University Press
Oxford Road, Manchester M13 9NR, UK
and Room 400, 175 Fifth Avenue, New York, NY 10010, USA
www.manchesteruniversitypress.co.uk

Distributed exclusively in the USA by
Palgrave, 175 Fifth Avenue, New York,
NY 10010, USA

Distributed exclusively in Canada by
UBC Press, University of British Columbia, 2029 West Mall,
Vancouver, BC, Canada V6T 1Z2

British Library Cataloguing-in-Publication Data
A catalogue record for this book is available from the British Library

Library of Congress Cataloging-in-Publication Data applied for

ISBN   0 7190 7000 7   *hardback*
EAN   978 0 7190 7000 6

ISBN   0 7190 7001 5   *paperback*
EAN   978 0 7190 7001 3

First published 2006

15 14 13 12 11 10 09 08 07 06   10 9 8 7 6 5 4 3 2 1

Typeset in 10.5 on 12.5 Minion
by Servis Filmsetting Ltd, Manchester
Printed in Great Britain
by CPI, Bath

FOR MY WIFE: HUA-FANG, LINDA

Contents

Acknowledgments

I would like to thank Vincent Porter and Robert Peck for helping to develop my interest in the subject of realism. I would also like to thank Dudley Andrew, Jack C. Ellis, Richard Abel, Deane Williams and others for their correspondence and advice during the course of this project. Thanks are also due to the staff of the John Grierson Archive, British Film Institute, Filmmuseum Amsterdam, Cinémathèque Française, Centre National du Cinéma, Cinématèca Brasileira, and the Cinematheque Royale, Belgium. I would also like to acknowledge the financial assistance of the Arts and Humanities Research Board, the Royal Mail Heritage Trust, the British Council, the British Academy and Hong Kong Baptist University. Thanks are also due to staff at the Universities of Westminster, West of England, De Montfort University and Hong Kong Baptist University. I would also like to thank Matthew Frost for his help in bringing this project to fruition. Finally, I would like to thank my family for their support, and my wife, Hua Fang, for her support during the particularly intense final stages of the project.

Introduction

Realist Film Theory and Cinema is the second in a planned trilogy. In the first part of the trilogy, entitled *European Film Theory and Cinema: The Intuitionist Realist and Modernist Tradition* (2001), an attempt was made to explore the relationship between two major traditions within European film theory and cinema. One of these was referred to as the 'intuitionist modernist and realist tradition', the other, the 'post-Saussurian'.[1] However, it will be more than apparent to the perceptive reader that the chief centre of attention of *European Film Theory and Cinema* was intuitionist modernist realism (rather than the post-Saussurian canon) and, in particular, 'intuitionist realism'. Of the book's nine chapters, only one covers the post-Saussurian legacy, whilst three (and, in part, four) are specifically concerned with realism, four with intuitionist modernism. *European Film Theory and Cinema* was, therefore, a book about intuitionist modernist realism, rather than a conventional 'introduction' to film theory.

In addition to this intuitionist modernist and realist orientation, *European Film Theory and Cinema* also attempted a twofold stratagem of recuperation and elision. The effort at recuperation was influenced by a conviction that, within a context of underscoring the latent consequence of a realist and intuitionist aesthetic, it appeared regrettable that some associated areas of European film theory and cinema (such as, for example, French cinematic impressionism and the film theory of Kracauer) had been relatively neglected within Anglo-American film studies. Of course, critical attention has been applied to these particular areas. However, it remains unclear, even after the intervention of scholars such as Richard Abel Alan Williams, David Bordwell, Dudley Andrew, Norman King and others, what real interest the general critical community retains in a movement such as cinematic impressionism; and to what extent the 'aesthetic' apparel of the movement continues to consign it to critical oblivion, despite the aesthetic and historical importance of films such as *Napoléon vu par Abel Gance,* and the achievements of directors such as Gance, Marcel L'Herbier, Louis Delluc, Jean Epstein and Germaine Dulac.[2] For example, a relatively recent intercession, such as that by Robert Ray, which endorses the value of impressionism, still seems to stand rather unaccompanied, and unlikely to spark a substantive critical reconsideration of the area.[3] Nevertheless, and albeit in necessarily schematic fashion, *European Film Theory and Cinema* did attempt such a reconsideration in terms of the book's over riding concern with intuitionist forms, through viewing French cinematic impressionism within a triple perspective of (1) a general tradition of intuitionist cinematic modernism, (2) a progressive French Romantic tradition critical of bourgeois capitalist culture, and (3) a shift towards the aesthetic and intuition as part of a more general rejoinder to the supposed misapplication of rationality within the societies and culture which had engineered the bloodbath of 1914–18.[4]

Much attention has also, again, relatively recently, been given to the work of Kracauer. However, here, once more, the presence of certain critical partialities requires that another process of recovery is initiated. Almost all of the attention paid to Kracauer in recent Anglo-American writing values the early Weimar work far more than Kracauer's major two works – *From Caligari to Hilter* and *Theory of Film* – whilst the posthumous *History: The Last Things Before the Last* is often disregarded. Here, it is supposed that an 'epistemological shift' can be detected between the superior 'early' Kracauer, 'the phenomenological observer of the everyday and the ephemeral' and the poorer 'late' Kracauer, the 'sociological reductionist' and 'unredeemed humanist'.[5] This distinction between early and late Kracauer is also reinforced in part in Miriam Bratu Hansen's 'Introduction' to the latest edition (1997) of *Theory of Film*, which uses primary sources in order to show that Kracauer's earlier conceptions of the book were superior to the final version (though Bratu Hansen does contend that these earlier conceptions also form a *link* between the Weimar writings and *Theory of Film*). Bratu Hansen's view, in particular, is that the completed book relinquishes the concern for historical specificity so evident in the Weimar and immediate post-Weimar writings and, in place of such a concern, adopts a more a historical focus on 'medium specificity'. In a highly detailed and illuminating process of research into primary sources, Bratu Hansen contends that the work which Kracauer carried out on the drafts of *Theory of Film* during the early 1940s, in particular, is of singular consequence:

> One might say that history disappears from *Theory of Film* in a double repression: on the level of theory, inasmuch as the specifically modern(ist) moment of film and cinema is transmuted into a medium-specific affinity with physical, external or visible reality; and, in the same move, on the level of intellectual biography, in that Kracauer seems to have cut himself off completely from his Weimar persona . . . Had it been completed at a time closer to the stage of its conception, Kracauer's virtual book on film aesthetics [Bratu Hansen is referring to the early 1940s drafts of *Theory of Film*] would have gone a long way to restoring the history that seems to have disappeared in the later book.[6]

Bratu Hansen may well be right on this point, and the argument is an important one because, as she, Gertrud Koch and Heide Schlüpmann have indicated, *Theory of Film* does not directly address important historical events such as the Shoah, and implications are attendant upon this.[7] However, *Theory of Film* must also be understood *in terms of* its focus on medium specificity and realism, rather than on the way that such a focus may exclude, or stand in for, a more historically specific account. The fact that *Theory of Film* is not directly concerned with concrete historical specificity does not necessarily mean that the 'late' Kracauer is not. In addition, whatever the value of the deleted 1940s drafts, it is the final version of *Theory of Film* which exists within the public domain, and that which must be addressed. In any case, the 1940s drafts of *Theory of Film* which Bratu Hansen has so profitably researched neither prove nor disprove her overall account, nor 'explain' the final perspective of *Theory of Film*, because, as will be argued in Chapter 6, evidence always 'underdetermines' theory.[8]

It can also be argued that much recent critical reassessment aspires to recover Kracauer against a backdrop advocacy of postmodernist criticism and phenomenology, rather than realism; and also that it is such theoretical allegiance which leads to the derogation of *Theory of Film* in favour of the Weimar writings, and to a raising up of a postmodernist phenomenological stance over and above the claims of realism. The work of Bratu Hansen, Levin, Koch, Schlüpmann and others is of considerable importance. However, this present book seeks to recover *Theory of Film* in terms of a realist, rather than phenomenological, backdrop advocacy. Like *European Film Theory and Cinema*, *Realist Film Theory and Cinema* also rejects the supposed distinction between a phenomenological and a realist Kracauer, arguing that phenomenology and realism can be discerned within *both* Kracauer's early and late writings, as part of a sustained critique of mainstream cinema as a force for both the reinforcement of abstraction and dominant ideology, and the liberation of the subject.

In addition to such Kracaurian dichotomies, both *European Film Theory and Cinema* and *Realist Film Theory and Cinema* also attempt to reconnect some more general fractures and, in particular, those which have emerged between categories such as 'realism', 'anti-realism' and 'modernism'. In place of such distinctions it is argued that early modernist intuitionist film culture and later practices of cinematic realism form part of one continuous tradition, and that there is, therefore, no abstract partition to be made between realism and modernism *here* (though of course, such partitions can be made elsewhere). Realism, in terms of *this* linked tradition, is as much modernism as realism, and what binds early intuitionist modernism and later intuitionist realism together is a shared *intuitionist* theory, or model, of knowledge. This shared approach to knowledge (an approach which is also, by the way, central to nineteenth-century naturalism and Lukácsian cinematic realism) transcends divergent endorsements of realist and 'non-realist' form within the tradition.

As already mentioned, the intuitionist realist tradition was the principal focus of realist interest in *European Film Theory and Cinema*. However, in the 'Introduction' to the book a number of other important areas of realist film theory and cinema were referred to which could not be accommodated within the remit of the book. These included nineteenth-century realism and naturalism, the realist cinema of Renoir, Visconti and others; and the work of Lukács. In addition, it was also suggested that a more detailed exploration of the relevance of philosophical conceptions of realism to elaborations of cinematic realism should be undertaken. *Realist Film Theory and Cinema* addresses these areas, whilst also attempting to carry out both a more substantive assessment of the shared ideas which link the three main theorists within the classical intuitionist realist tradition, and of the relationship between realist film theory and relevant aspects of contemporary film theory.

Realist Film Theory and Cinema explores two traditions of realist film theory and cinema, which will be referred to here as the 'intuitionist realist tradition' and the 'nineteenth-century Lukácsian tradition'. Chapter 1 begins by exploring the origins and characteristics of nineteenth-century realism and naturalism, including the influence of eighteenth- and nineteenth-century determinist philosophical discourses in the writings of Buffon, Maupertuis, Condillac, Helvétius, Saint-Hilaire and Darwin. The chapter then shows how this determinist tradition influenced nineteenth-century French literary realism and naturalism, and explores distinctions between realism and naturalism, focusing on conceptions of representation and human agency within the naturalist movement. The overall objective of the chapter is to elaborate a French nineteenth-century tradition of 'critical' naturalist-realism, distinguish that tradition from more normative forms of realism, and establish its themes, stylistic devices and historical consequence. Chapter 2 follows this tradition into the twentieth century, and explores the influence of the naturalist tradition on early French cinema, covering the pictorialist naturalist school of the 1920s, the cycles of Zola adaptations which appeared between 1902 and 1938 and the 'social realist' cinema of Renoir. The chapter concludes by returning to the model of critical realism elaborated in Chapter 1, and by accounting for Renoir's *La Bête humaine* in terms of that model.

Chapter 3 then establishes how Lukács appropriated the nineteenth-century realist tradition, and explores two central aspects of Lukács's theory: the notion of alienation, and the model of the intensive totality. Lukács's writing on cinematic realism is also considered, and it is argued that the inherent logic of Lukács's position on film leads him, however reluctantly, to espouse the type of naturalist/impressionist realism which, in his writings on literary realism, he largely rejected. Chapter 4 then applies Lukácsian models of literary and cinematic realism to an analysis of Wajda's *Danton* and Visconti's *Senso*, and it is argued that, whilst *Danton* is at variance with Lukács's models of 'classical' and 'democratic-humanist' realism, *Senso* can be considered as a work of 'inverse democratic humanist realism', rather than 'classical realism'. The chapter concludes by arguing that Lukács's theory of filmic realism can be associated philosophically with a naturalist, phenomenological model of cinematic realism.

Chapter 5 then explores intuitionist realism in the work of Grierson, Bazin and Kracauer, in relation to two key concepts: the 'problem of modernity', and 'totality'. Finally, Chapter 6 commences with a recapitulation of the key themes of nineteenth-century realism, and of Lukács's model of cinematic realism. The chapter then goes on to establish the central themes and characteristics of an intuitionist realist model of cinematic realism, and to relate intuitionist and Lukácsian cinematic realism to more general philosophical concerns of realism, and other forms of contemporary film theory which bear upon the question of realism. This study of cinematic realism concludes by assessing the significance of the nineteenth-century Lukácsian and intuitionist realist traditions in relation to the general and pressing question of the importance of realism, and by suggesting ways forward for the further development of studies into theories and practices of cinematic realism.

Notes

1 Aitken, Ian, *European Film Theory and Cinema: A Critical Introduction* (Edinburgh: Edinburgh University Press, 2001). The original title, 'European Film Theory and Cinema, the Intuitionist Realist and Modernist Tradition', was rejected by the publisher on the grounds that it would reduce the market for the book.

2 Bordwell, David, *French Impressionist Cinema: Film Culture, Film Theory and Film Style* (New York: Arno, 1980); King, Norman, *Abel Gance* (London: BFI, 1984); Abel, Richard, *French Cinema: The First Wave 1915–1929* (Princeton: Princeton University Press, 1984); Williams, Alan, *Republic of Images: A History of French Film-making* (Cambridge, MA, and London: Harvard University Press, 1992); Andrew, Dudley J., *Mists of Regret: Culture and Sensibility in Classic French Film* (Princeton: Princeton University Press, 1995).

3 Ray, Robert B., 'Impressionism, Surrealism and Film Theory: path dependence, or how a tradition in film theory gets lost', in Hill, John and Church Gibson, Pamela (eds), *The Oxford Guide to Film Studies* (Oxford: Oxford University Press, 1998), pp. 67–76.

4 Aitken, pp. 85–8.

5 Petro, Patrice, 'Kracauer's Epistemological Shift', in Ginsberg, Terri, and Thompson, Kirsten Moana (eds), *Perspectives on German Cinema* (New York: G. K. Hall & Co., 1996), p. 97.

6 Bratu Hansen, Miriam, 'Introduction', in Kracauer, Siegfried, *Theory of Film: The Redemption of Physical Reality* (Princeton: Princeton University Press, 1997), pp. xiii–xv.

7 Ibid., p. xiv.

8 The 'underdetermination of theory by evidence principle' argues that any theory can resist refutation by the test of evidence by reformatting its 'theoretical network', and that there are always a number of different theories which will fit any given 'fact'. The concept is derived from analytic philosophers such as Mary Hesse, W. V. O. Quine and F. Duhem, whose ideas will be discussed in Chapter 6.

1

From the 'true style' to the 'art-form of the bourgeoisie': the origins, characteristics, and theoretical foundation of the nineteenth-century French realist, and naturalist tradition

During the 1970s and 1980s, when anti-realist film theory dominated much of the critical agenda, the nineteenth-century realist tradition was habitually regarded with misgivings by those intent on the development of a progressive, critical film practice. This was partly as a consequence of the adoption of nineteenth-century realist aesthetic models by a totalitarian culture within the Soviet Union, and the emergence of state-endorsed 'realist' film cultures in fascist Italy and Germany between 1920 and 1945 – both of which could be associated with the nineteenth-century realist heritage. It was this perceived association between totalitarianism and realism, in conjunction with post-1968 post-structuralist, anti-realist partialities, which led some critics to renounce nineteenth-century realism on the grounds that, as an aesthetic practice, it was founded on implicitly directive, manipulative principles, and could not serve as a model for a progressive film practice in the twentieth century.

This sceptical attitude towards realism in general, and nineteenth-century realism in particular, was, in addition, also influenced by a belief that the latter could be considered as, in some way, the cultural and ideological correlative of a newly enthroned and hegemonic bourgeois capitalist order. For example, Fredric Jameson has characterised what he called the 'moment of realism' in the nineteenth-century in terms of the 'conquest of a kind of cultural, ideological and narrative literacy by a new group or class',[1] whilst, in similar vein, Colin MacCabe has argued that the nineteenth-century realist novel carried through 'ideological tasks . . . undertaken for the bourgeoisie'.[2] More recently, Brian Winston has criticised the British documentary film movement on the grounds that its advocacy of realism could be compared with the development of a conservative realist tradition in the nineteenth-century.[3] Arguments such as these can also be found in a number of other critical writings within media studies, and this, in turn, has led to the emergence of a substantial degree of accord over the issue. However, this perspective on nineteenth-century realism rests on some fundamental misconceptions concerning the historical role and character of the realist movement. For example, realism cannot be considered, in an indiscriminate fashion, as the ideological articulation of nineteenth-century French bourgeois values and, in fact, was often overtly antagonistic to the development of bourgeois power and ideology during the periods of the Restoration, July Monarchy, Second Empire and Third Republic. Whilst it may be the case that realism emerged during a period in which the bourgeoisie wrested political and ideological hegemony from both the conservative aristocracy and the representatives of the radical urban proletariat, this chronological parallelism does not necessarily entail that realism served to articulate and disseminate dominant bourgeois ideology, or serve the interests of the new ruling class.

Another misconception commonly found within the field of film studies is based upon the construction of a distinction between realism and a nineteenth- and twentieth-century modernist movement which appeared to be more overtly aligned against the 'realist' art and ideology of the politically and culturally dominant middle classes. Ironically, this distinction between realism and modernism initially emerged most forcefully in inverted form, within the classical Marxist tradition, when Engels argued that a radical opposition should be made between 'progressive' realism and 'decadent' modernism. Although later writers within media studies were to turn this evaluation on its head, they nevertheless adhered to Engels's belief that a critical distinction must be made between realism and modernism (or, at least, between realism and the modernist avant-garde). However, it will be argued here that no such distinction can be legitimately made, and that advocates of such a distinction have failed to understand the complex intertwined nature of the relationship which existed between realism and modernism during the nineteenth-century. Beyond that, it will be argued that the origins, objectives and central characteristics of nineteenth-century realism have also not been sufficiently understood within the field of film studies, and that this has, in turn, contributed to the institutionalisation of a problematic conception of twentieth-century realist cinema. Before exploring twentieth-century cinematic realism, therefore, it will first be necessary to establish what the origins, objectives and characteristics of nineteenth-century realism were, and how the realist movement was influenced by and interacted with the historical background from which it emerged. These issues will also be addressed through a focus on French nineteenth-century realism, as it is French realism which most keenly encapsulates the key theoretical and historical affinities of the nineteenth-century realist tradition.

Origins, influences and characteristics

The emergence and development of realism must first be understood in relation to both the context of political conflict and turmoil which affected France during the period and the impact which that context had upon the evolution of politically informed artistic culture. By 1789, that culture was dominated by the neo-classical tradition and, to a degree, the aesthetic origins of realism can be located in the transformations which occurred within that tradition from 1799 onwards. The appellation 'neo-classical' was first applied retrospectively, in the mid-nineteenth-century, as a largely pejorative term aimed at work characterised by a normative and uncritical engagement with the classical heritage. However, that which was later to be designated as neo-classicism initially developed towards the end of the eighteenth century as the 'true style': a committed, principled, engaged *risorgimento* in the arts, which rejected both the aesthetic excesses of the Baroque and Rococo and, perhaps less overtly, the political and social inequalities of the *ancien régime*.[4] Far from being a superficial recapitulation of the classical, the 'true style' played an important role in the culminating, revolutionary phase of the Enlightenment, and gave aesthetic expression to some of the rationalist, secular and egalitarian values of contemporary progressive thought.[5] That expression appeared in the field of sculpture, in the work of Antonio Canova, and in architecture, in the work of Claude-Nicolas Ledoux and Benjamin Latrobe. However it appeared most significantly in the tradition of painting which developed within the framework of the true style and, most particularly, within the work of Jacques-Louis David.

The philosophical discourse of the 'true style' was influenced in part by the 'providential' vision of 'man' and reality advanced during the early period of the Enlightenment. Here, it was claimed that man was a creature whose character was shaped by 'natural benevolence', whilst the world and all within it had been brought into being by an act of divine, providential will.[6] This 'providentialist' position was elaborated most distinctively in Pope's influential poem *Essay on Man* (1733), in which it is asserted that the apparent discord and conflict evident in the world disguises an underlying beneficent order, and that, consequently, 'whatever is is right'.[7] This belief in the existence of an underlying providential order is one source of the Enlightenment concept of 'natural law': the doctrine that universal natural and ethical truths exist within the world, and that those truths could be comprehended through the power of reason. Similarly, the belief in a providential order also influenced the emergence of the idea of 'natural religion': the notion that the work of God could be found expressed in an intrinsically benign natural environment which also encompassed the human social order. As Pope put it in the *Essay on Man*: 'The state of Nature was the reign of God'.[8] This belief in a concord between God, society and 'Nature' found expression in numerous Enlightenment texts, including Montesquieu's *Lettres persanes* (1721), in which Montesquieu argued that the 'rules of society and the duties of humanity' were in accord with a divine plan;[9] and Morelly's influential *Code de la nature* (1755), which similarly

endorsed the affinity between God, Nature and the social order. Such sentiments were predicated also upon a belief in historical progress as the outcome
of a greater understanding of the natural order of things and, even as late as
1794, such beliefs in the natural *bienfaisance* of man, and inevitable advance of
progress, could still be found expressed in Condorcet's widely read *Esquisse
d'un tableau historique des progrès de l'esprit humain*, in which the author
asserts that progress is assured by the fact that all men are endowed with 'rigorous and pure principles of justice . . . an active and enlightened benevolence,
[and] a decorous and generous sensibility'.[10] By 1794 these providentialist
views on human nature, reason and progress had, in addition, also become
incorporated into the political programme of the French Revolution, which, in
the eyes of Condorcet and other *philosophes*, stood as the embodiment of the
Enlightenment enthronement of reason and justice.[11]

   The practitioners of the 'true style' were influenced both by providentialist thought and by the millenarian aspirations associated with the French
Revolution and, at one level, those practitioners attempted to create aesthetic
correlatives of a philosophy based on 'unaltering principles', 'classic perfection',
'peaceful universalism' and 'rational humanitarianism'.[12] However, those same
practitioners were influenced also by some of the more disturbing aspects of the
period which they lived through, and this was also to shape the evolution of
the 'true style'. By the time that the 'true style' came to prominence in the 1780s,
for example, the heroic providentialist ideals of the early Enlightenment had
already come under serious critique. The source of that critique was twofold.
Providentialist idealism emerged during a period of relative economic, social
and political stability in Europe, between 1715 and 1740. During this period no
major European war occurred, and social conditions improved generally, if
inequitably, across the continent.[13] However, the overall concord of the period
was eventually shattered, first, by the War of the Austrian Succession of 1740–8,
and then by the Anglo-French Seven Years War of 1756–63. After this a period
of endemic political instability and military conflict ensued, which, in France,
culminated first in the cataclysm of the French Revolution of 1789 and then in
a further period of turmoil which continued relentlessly up to the Bonopartist
coup d'état of 1799. This context of unremitting political and military strife was
interpreted by some as an inevitable consequence of the struggle to bring a new
harmonious society into being, but it did, nevertheless, further undermine the
faith in the future of progress and reason expressed in the works of Pope,
Condorcet, Morelly, Montesquieu and others. At the same time that historical
events began to challenge such faith, the providential belief in the existence of a
changeless inviolate world, brought into being by the hand of divine intercession, was also thrown into doubt by scientific discoveries in the field of geology
which revealed the existence of a far-reaching, and often far from providential
evolutionary history. These discoveries, which entered general intellectual

discourse through the work of writers and philosophers such as Buffon, Diderot, Rousseau, Chastellux and d'Holbach, suggested that nature was grounded in brute materialist factors of 'chance mutation' and 'flux', rather than order and reason; and that the origins of 'man' may have been bestial, rather than divine.[14]

Neo-classicism emerged at a point when criticism of early providentialist Enlightenment theory was circulating widely within liberal intellectual discourse and, whilst adhering to some strains of providentialist idealism, the true style also incorporated the more ambivalent questioning world view of the later Enlightenment into its discursive framework. The aesthetic system which emerged from this confluence of influences was 'classical' in that it was founded on principles of harmony, 'rational humanitarianism' and high-mindedness; but also other than classical in its adoption of a style which could be characterised as grave, mysterious and conceptually diffident. Neo-classicism developed to a considerable extent in repudiation of what was perceived to be the inconsequential concerns and stylistic excesses of the Baroque and Rococo. One consequence of this was that neo-classical painters adopted a severe, spare style of painting, which, far from expressing a rose-tinted providentialist view of the human condition, sought to express universal moral truths in a manner both trenchant and ascetic. Consequently, whilst formal technique in neo-classical painting is used to depict ideal 'classical' form and compositional harmony, the subject matter in many paintings is preoccupied with the representation of such decidedly non-providentialist themes as compromised heroism, fatalistic encounters, tragic circumstance, perverse logic, bad fortune and injustice.

This subject matter was largely derived from the tragedies of Euripides and Sophocles, but was also influenced by certain themes derived from Roman stoicism. During the 1780s stoicism, and the writings of Marcus Aurelius in particular, became an important exemplar for republican reformers, revolutionaries and progressive neo-classical artists, all of whom valued the stress which the stoics had placed on the worth of civic virtue and egalitarian polity.[15] However, although influenced by such themes, neo-classicism was influenced also by less directly political stoic ideas, for example the notion of fatalistic predetermination, and belief in the inevitability of suffering and injustice as a precondition for the ultimate exercise of virtue.[16] Whilst neo-classicism's endorsement of stoic egalitarian values was consonant with the republican/revolutionary sentiment of the 1780s and 1790s therefore, and although neo-classicism itself was adopted as the official art form of the Revolution after 1789, the work of Jacques-Louis David, Philippe-Auguste Hennequin, Fulchran-Jean Harriet, Pierre-Narcisse Guérin and François Gérard also exhibited elements which went beyond a confirming expression of republican sentiment or dominant mores to portray a far more paradoxical vision of the human condition.

Neo-classicism's relationship to the surrounding political context was, therefore, a multifaceted one, and a work such as David's *The Oath of the Tennis Court*

(1791), which depicts the moment at which the representatives of the *tiers état* constituted the National Assembly, is unusual in its explicit endorsement of contemporary governmental ideological imperatives. Neo-classical artists were certainly concerned with the contemporary political context. However, a painting such as Hennequin's *The Remorse of Orestes* (1800) refers to that context metaphorically, rather than directly and, in addition, locates its references within a narrative engaged with issues such as entrapment, predestination and the inescapability of violence and suffering.[17] The same holds true of David's *Marat, at His Death* (1793), which reduces contemporary allusions to a bare minimum, whilst his earlier *Belisarius Receiving Alms* (1780), expresses a 'poignant lament for the transience of human glory, the helplessness of age, combined with a meditation on moral heroism in adversity'.[18] David's most important early work, the *Oath of the Horatii* (1785), the painting which established the dominance of the neo-classical style, is, like his later *Brutus* (1789), also more concerned with universal values of moral heroism, sacrifice and tragic circumstance than with contemporary concerns over nationalism, patriotism or republicanism.[19]

Between the 1780s, and the inauguration of the Napoleonic Empire in 1799, neo-classicism was a relatively autonomous critical aesthetic practice. However, during the Napoleonic period, from 1799 to 1815, and that of the Restoration, from 1815 to 1830, the critical autonomy of neo-classicism depreciated as the movement was commandeered first by the Imperial regime, and then by the restored Bourbon Monarchy, to an extent that had not occurred during the immediate post-Revolutionary period. This decline continued also during the period of the July Monarchy, between 1830 and 1848, when, owing to a combination of increased censorship aimed at curtailing the expression of radical oppositional ideas, the patronage of the Académie, and intervention by the ruling regime, the 'true style' of the late Enlightenment artistic *risorgimento* was transformed into *l'art officiel* of the haut bourgeois Orleanist regime, and into a compromised form of consensual, generic pro-bourgeois historicism.[20]

The fate of neo-classicism is relevant to the study of realism undertaken here because one of the sources of realism – and Romanticism for that matter – can be found in the decline of the neo-classical tradition as a discriminating force from 1799 onwards, and both realism and Romanticism can be understood as critical responses to that decline. Romanticism had initially emerged as early as 1800, in paintings such as Girodet's *Ossian Receiving the Generals of the Republic* (1800–2), as an art-form which emphasised feeling, dynamism, emotion, mysticism and the irrational; and which also discarded both neo-classicism's emphasis on classical pictorial composition and the appropriation, codification and formularisation of the neo-classical tradition which took place after 1799. This resistance to the neo-classical heritage found, perhaps, its most important expression – in the work of painters such as Anne-Louis Girodet, Théodore Géricault and Eugène Delacroix – in a stress on the need for freedom from the provenance of established rule-governed systems; and this emphasis was given added force from the 1820s onwards, when painters such as Géricault moved outside the established beurocratic structures of the Salon, the Académie and the official processes of reward and prize-giving. It should be borne in mind, however, that, although painters such as Géricault and Delacroix may have rejected what they perceived to be both the rule-bound nature of neo-classicism and its appropriation within dominant ideology, the rules of neo-classicism were originally formulated by no means as part of a project to secure official control over cultural production, but as a means through which universal truths could be explored in a rigorous and analytical manner.

As with Romanticism, the origins of nineteenth-century realist painting can be found also in a critical response to the demise of the neo-classical tradition: a response which included an abandonment of the academy, the founding of an art-form which rejected acquiescence to officially sanctioned, formulaic procedures, and an emphasis on qualities of spontaneity and intuitive response. Realism was also influenced by an intellectual renunciation of the ideology of the Orleanist period and, in both the painting and literature of the 1830s and across the political spectrum, realism emerged as a movement which attempted to represent the shortcomings of the new haut bourgeois hegemony.[21] Far from being the 'art-form of bourgeois capitalism', therefore, it could be argued that this form of realism developed as an expression of critical anti-bourgeois sentiment. In the field of literature, for example, a significant form of critical realism emerged in the novels of Honoré de Balzac as a proselytising exploration of the problems arising from the replacement of the traditional culture of the *ancien régime* with one based on bourgeois capitalist values;[22] and, within this, both as a portrayal of the adverse impact of capitalism on a professional petit bourgeois society effectively disenfranchised by the haut bourgeois institutional power structures of Orleanism;[23] and as an attempt to delineate the social institutions and manifestations of lower-middle-class community life which Balzac thought might be doomed to disappear under the rapid pace of capitalist modernisation.[24] However, there are a number of reasons why Balzacian realism cannot be associated too closely with the tradition of critical realism which will be considered within this chapter. In the first place, Balzac's realism expresses the sentiments of the Catholic/monarchist right, rather than the democratic/egalitarian left. Second, Balzac employs stereotypical representations of working-class types, and a substantial degree of conventionalised plot device and rhetoric. Both of these factors place Balzacian realism outside the central tradition of nineteenth-century realism considered here; and locate it more appropriately within a form of social 'Romantic' realism which emerged during the 1830s, and which can be associated with the work of writers such as Eugène Sue, George Sand and Victor Hugo.

One of the key influences on the development of the nineteenth-century French realist tradition can, therefore, be located in the existence within some intellectuals and artists of a prevailing sense of displeasure with, and alienation from, the Orleanist regime and its ideology. At one level, dissatisfaction finds expression in the work of Balzac, and in the emergence of both the *bohème* and *l'art pour l'art* movements. However, and more importantly, it finds expression also amongst groups on the artistic left and, as a consequence, provides a foundation for the later emergence of the radical realist movement of the 1840s. In addition to the need to represent forms of social experience excluded from the ruling culture of Orleanism, however, the emergence of realism was influenced also by the appearance of a network of fast-changing contemporary social and cultural conditions, and by a concomitant public demand for images of, and information about, those conditions. This demand was met, in part, by the development of new processes of representation and mass communication, including lithography, wood engraving, photography and more advanced print publishing, to the extent that, between 1830 and 1850, the period of the emergence of realism, an 'image explosion' took place. [25] These images, appearing in new illustrated periodicals such as *Magaziné Pittoresque*, which was founded in 1833, were often composites of existing generic conventions and, accordingly, displayed a marked tendency to ignore established compositional tenets regarding the pictorial representation of reality in their endeavour to depict the complex and frenzied life of the modern city. One consequence of this was that the 'image explosion' of the 1830s also led to the emergence of an 'aesthetic of disorder' [26] which sprang directly from the social experience of the modern city, and this, in turn, would build upon the stress on spontaneity which realism had inherited from the denial of neo-classicism, to form one of the foundations of the realist tradition.

However, in addition to the influence of this iconoclastic 'aesthetic of disorder', the experience of fast-evolving social conditions also generated another factor which was to become crucially important to the realist movement: a desire to represent and understand the *extensive* social totality of modern life. Of course previous generations of artists and intellectuals had also been motivated by such an imperative, but it has been argued that circumstances positioned early nineteenth-century artists and intellectuals quite differently from their predecessors, to the extent that it was only then that they 'were given the geographical as well as historical perspective' to appreciate the extent of the social change occurring around them. As a consequence, 'no previous generation of writers had felt so conscious of living in a shifting environment', and it was that consciousness which led realists to seek to portray their environment in such a panoramic manner.[27]

In addition to the influence of aesthetic, technological, social and political factors, French nineteenth-century realism was also influenced by a number of philosophical and critical discourses, the most significant of which was a determinist tradition of thought which developed antagonistically in relation to the model of subjectivity and rationality which had emerged from the Enlightenment. As already discussed in relation to the impact of providentialist ideas on neo-classicism, that model was premised on the idea of the rational and morally motivated human agent, and placed the cognitive and morally enlightened subject at the centre of knowledge.[28] However, as we have seen, by the 1740s such providentialist beliefs had come under question and, in France, were increasingly challenged by works such as Buffon's *Histoire naturelle* (1749–89) and Maupertuis's *Vénus physique* (1745), which emphasised the immutability and instability of natural phenomena, and La Mettrie's *L'Homme machine* (1747), which stressed the potential irrationality of the world. Despite their differences of approach, these texts shared a common premise that environmental and other factors, rather than an innate rational benevolence, played a substantial, determining role in shaping human thought and agency. One of the most important precursors to this materialist tradition was Locke's *Essay Concerning Human Understanding* (1690), in which Locke argued that all knowledge was received through the senses, and that none was innate. However, Locke shrank back from the full materialist implications of his theory when he argued that the mind nevertheless retained an autonomous ability to process and reflect upon the raw data acquired by the senses. This notion of an 'autonomous faculty' of mind represented an attempt to marry the empiricist theory of knowledge with Christian conceptions of agency and humanist notions of free will. However, Locke's insistence that all knowledge was acquired through the senses nevertheless opened the way for the emergence of more determinist and relativist theories based on the premise that knowledge was largely determined by the 'milieux' of the senses; [29] and the determinism inherent in Locke's ideas was taken considerably further by later theorists in France, two of whom, Condillac and Helvétius, were to have a direct influence on nineteenth-century French realism.

In his *Traité des sensations* (1754), Abbé Etienne de Condillac, the leading figure in the 'sensualist' school, appropriated Locke's empiricist theory of knowledge, but rejected his notion of an autonomous faculty of reason, arguing instead that all thought was derived from the senses, and that it was the shaping power of environment which determined human agency. However, and despite the clear trajectory of his arguments, Condillac's role as a cleric made him draw back from a completely materialist conception of human nature, and led him to argue that the degree of reflective autonomy which Locke had posited in the mind could also be found in the 'soul'. Condillac's materialist approach was, however, taken further by Claude-Adrien Helvétius, who, in his *De l'esprit* (1758) and *De l'homme de ses facultés intellectuelles et de son éducation* (1773), strongly emphasised the influence of milieu on shaping the mind, arguing in a formulation almost revolutionary for its period – that 'the man of genius is only the product of the circumstances in which he has found himself'.[30] In addition to Helvétius and Condillac, both of whom placed emphasis upon the shaping power of environment, a later group of determinist theorists, the *idéologues*, stressed the importance of heredity and physiological processes in determining human thought and characteristics. Whether premised on notions of environment or of hereditary determination, however, this body of ideas within French thought constituted a fundamental challenge to the conception of human subjectivity which had emerged during the early Enlightenment.

This materialist, determinist tradition had a direct influence on French literary realism during the nineteenth-century. Stendhal drew on the ideas of Helvétius and the ideologues in his *Le Rouge et le noir* (1830), and employed one of Helvétius' key terms when describing his novel as a *chronique* of French society. One of the key ideas which Stendhal and other realists took from the ideologues was the notion that people fell into broad categories of temperament and type, and that this was conditioned by both hereditary and environmental factors. Another key idea, promulgated by the leading *idéologue* theorist Pierre Cabanis, was the notion that subconscious inclinations in the individual, determined by heredity and environment, could overcome rational self-interest. This notion of 'conflicting selves' would have a strong influence on later theories and practices of naturalism, and find expression in works such as Émile Zola's *La Bête humaine* (1890) and, later, Jean Renoir's *La Bête humaine* (1938). Whilst Stendhal was influenced by the ideas of the ideologues, Honoré de Balzac was influenced by the evolutionary zoology of Geoffroy Saint-Hilaire and the theories of physiognomy propounded by Johan Kaspar Lavater.[31] In his *La Comédie humaine*, Balzac attempted to apply the theories of Saint-Hilaire and Lavater to a study of human society and, in particular, sought to develop the literary equivalent of two of Saint-Hilaire's central theoretical principles: the principles of 'unity of composition' and of 'balance'. According to Saint-Hilaire, the principle of 'unity of composition' implied that all vertibrate animals evolved from a common ancestor, but that the different environments within which animals found themselves created different species which nevertheless retained traces of the ancestral original. When applied to an understanding of human society, this principle suggests both that the specific peculiarities of individuals must be related to their particular milieu, and that these different environments had modified, yet also retained, the essential traces of an original 'unitary' human nature. Balzac made his debt to

Saint-Hilaire's 'principle' and zoology explicit in the 1841 Preface to the first volume of *La Comédie humaine*, when he argued that:

> There is but one animal . . . The animal . . . acquires the peculiarities of its form from the environment in which it develops. Zoological species are the outcome of these differences . . . I saw that in this respect, society resembles Nature. Does not society make from Man as many different men as there are zoological species, according to the environment where his activity takes place? [32]

This 'zoological' approach led Balzac to draw close connections between individual and environment in *La Comédie humaine*. However, those connections are conceived not as static but as undergoing a process of constant change, a process which Balzac understood in terms of Saint-Hilaire's other key principle, that of 'balance'. This is based on the notion that, when certain physical features develop within a particular environment, others atrophy, so that an overall, but constantly evolving, 'balance' ensues. This process of atrophy and development is driven by an inner urge within species to seek the most beneficial equilibrium within a changing environmental context, and it is this urge that causes physical characteristics to emerge that are better suited to such changed circumstance. Again following Saint-Hilaire, Balzac conceived this quest for 'balance' as an essentially competitive process, in which, like a human jungle, individuals struggle for dominance and survival. In *La Comédie humaine*, Balzac, attempted to apply this principle in order to show how different facets of society were constantly moving into new relations of equilibrium and disequilibria, towards or away from a state of 'balance'; and this principle, together with that of the 'unity of composition', provided a methodological framework for the *chronique* of evolving French society which Balzac set out in *La Comédie humaine*.

Nevertheless, Balzac's supposedly 'objective' application of a purportedly 'scientific' methodology derived from Saint-Hilaire was also fundamentally steered by his own political convictions, and these convictions ultimately led him to question Saint Hilaire's conception of contemporary society as a biologically precipitated 'human jungle'. Initially, Balzac viewed the culture and society of Orleanism as illustrative of Saint-Hilaire's tenets of 'balance', competitive individualism, and survival of the fittest. However, later, and under the force of his own strongly held Catholic-monarchist political beliefs, Balzac began to conceive Saint-Hilaire's 'impressive law of each for himself', not just as an inevitable evolutionary-biological reality but as one which was also vigorously – and, as far as he was concerned, disastrously – fostered and cultivated by the culture of Orleanism. Consequently, and as a result of his political opposition to Orleanism, Balzac redefined Saint-Hilaire's concept of 'balance', replacing its emphasis on the imperative of continuous adaptation to a shifting competitive environment with the idea that a more 'balanced' society – one which would have the capacity to subdue the *bête humaine* engendered by both republicanism and Orleanism – could eventually be brought into being.

Balzac also believed that such a society could be modelled on the old order of the Catholic, monarchist *ancien régime*, and it was with this in mind that he characterised Catholicism as 'a complete system for repressing the depraved tendencies of Man'.[33] Although Balzac may have genuinely regarded himself as an objective 'chronicler' of society, and a 'simple doctor of social medicine', [34] it is, therefore, also evident that he considered himself a 'judge' of the extent to which society deviated from the monarchist and Catholic ideal.[35] Given this, it also becomes apparent that Balzac's conception of realism combines determinist premises with a particular model of agency: one in which effective agency can be realised within the parameters of the exemplary social environment which he visualises. Although determinism remains an important component of his theory and practice of literary realism, therefore, this deterministic tendency is mediated by the invocation of the 'complete system' that he conjures up: one that 'represses the depraved tendencies of man' and liberates more principled and virtuous tendencies. It is important to grasp this point concerning the presence of a significant conception of agency within Balzac's work, both in order to understand that work the better and, more crucially, because the point illuminates a more general truth concerning the French nineteenth-century realist tradition: that it was by no means unremittingly determinist in character.

Naturalism

During the late nineteenth-century Balzac was to emerge as an important exemplar and model for one branch of realist aesthetics: that elaborated by Engels and others within the Marxist tradition. As we will see in a later chapter, Balzacian realism also had a crucial influence on the most significant twentieth-century theorist of literary realism: Georg Lukács. Nevertheless, Balzacian realism still remains outside the central tradition of realism under investigation in this book: a tradition far more closely associated with Balzac's near contemporary, the 'naturalist' realist Émile Zola. Zola dominated the naturalist movement, and almost the entire body of naturalist theory in France, including the 'Introduction' to *Thérèse Raquin* (1867), *Le Roman expérimental* (1879), *Le Naturalisme au théâtre* (1881) and *Lettre à la jeunesse* (1897), emanated from him. Naturalism was also influenced by different strains of nineteenth-century French determinist thought to those which had influenced earlier, Balzacian realism. Whereas Balzac had been influenced primarily by theories concerned with the determination of the individual by environmental factors, Zola was more influenced by theories which emphasised the determining power of genetics and heredity. In addition to this, Zola, and the naturalist movement in general, were influenced also by contemporary debates over scientific methodology; and by a desire to apply scientific method to the arts. This played a fundamental role in the development of naturalism,[36] and led Zola to define naturalism as 'la méthode scientifique appliquée dans les lettres'.[37]

Zola's theory of naturalist realism was influenced by a number of key works of the period, including Hippolyte Taine's *Histoire de la littérature anglaise* (1863–4), Claude Bernard's *Introduction à l'étude de la médecine expérimental* (1865), Prosper Lucas's *Traité philosophique et physiologique de l'hérédité naturelle dans les états de santé et de maladie du système nerveux* (1847–50), Charles Letourneau's *Physiologie des passions* (1868) and Charles Darwin's *The Origin of Species*, which was translated into French in 1862.[38] Of these, the most important influence on the development of naturalism as a whole was *The Origin of Species*, with its then radical and controversial thesis that man was, like all other animals, the product of an evolutionary process, and that there was, consequently, no fundamental difference between animal and man. The appearance of *The Origin of Species* led to a resurgence of determinist ideas in France after 1862, based on the notion that the activities of man were determined by a 'bestial' past, or 'inner animal'. These ideas were also reinvigorated by then contemporary enthusiasms for theories of heredity which argued both that 'bestial' human behaviour could be explained by assuming some initial transgression in the remote, genetic past, and that such transgression could even be identified through therapeutic process. This idea that all things are the product of a causal chain, that the causal links in the chain could be followed back to their source, and that everything within the chain was determined by that source, was to have a profound impact on the development of naturalism.

Despite their differences of approach, Balzacian realism and Zolaesque naturalism are not fundamentally different from each other, nor mutually incompatible. For example, despite the stress on heredity within naturalism it remains the environment, rather than genetic determination, which actually plays the more prominent role in Zola's novel cycle *Les Rougon-Macquart*; and, although Zola described *Les Rougon-Macquart* as a 'working out of the genetic disorders due to the sins and excesses of the original progenitors',[39] the cycle as a whole does not correspond to this genetically oriented, deterministic programme. Neither does the fact that Zola's twenty-novel series covered a different period of historical time (from the *coup d'état* of 1851 to the liberal victories of 1877) from Balzac's chronicle of the Restoration and July Monarchy periods lead to the conclusion that the two realist *chroniques* should be significantly differentiated from each other.

It has, however, been argued that realism and naturalism *can* be distinguished on the grounds that the two movements mobilised significantly different conceptions of human subjectivity and agency; and that, in particular, naturalism

imposed 'a certain specific view of man on realism's attitude of detached neu-
trality'.[40] According to this argument, the 'view of man' to be associated with
naturalism is more deterministic and extreme than that associated with earlier
realism, and constitutes an 'intensification' of the original realist project. For
example, in his Le Naturalisme (1929), Louis Deffoux asserted that 'Realism is
like the 1789 Revolution in literature while Naturalism corresponds to the 1793
Reign of Terror'.[41] However, the argument that the naturalist view of human
agency is fundamentally more deterministic than the realist view, and that this
is so because of the former's dependence upon theories of genetic dependency,
is problematic in a number of respects. For example, despite its reliance upon
theories of hereditary determination, naturalism also accommodated a conception of agency derived from two convictions: that the process of evolution held
within it the possibility for human betterment; and that science possessed a genuinely emancipatory potential. This more affirmative conception of agency and
reformation exists alongside more pessimistic tropes within naturalist theory,
and means that naturalism cannot be conceived entirely in terms of Deffoux's
metaphorical 'Reign of Terror'.

In fact, a dialectic between freedom and determinism oscillates across the
range and progression of Zola's work. The early novels are the most deterministic, and the first novel of the chronique, La Fortune des Rougon (1871), is predominantly concerned with the underlying prerogative of heredity and
environment. However, in later novels such as Germinal (1885) determinism
and necessity are mediated through the device of empowering fictional characters with both a more insightful recognition and intellectual awareness of circumstance and the facility to respond actively and appropriately in response to
their encounter with oppressive conditions. Furthermore, the idea that exposure to, and immersion in, a traumatic deterministic process can result in the
emergence of a degree of insight and moral idealism which can then be
employed to confront that very process lies at the core of this naturalist conception of agency, and gives that conception a very particular (and not particularly deterministic) figuration.

Indeed, not only was naturalism not completely deterministic in character
but its apparent advocacy of objective and impartial description was also mediated by an emphasis placed on the centrality of aesthetic expression in the
creation of the work of art. Referring to the work of the painter Eduard Manet,
for example, the naturalist critic Castagnary argued that, as with Manet, 'the
naturalist school [also] asserts that art is the expression of life in all its forms
and degrees, and that its sole aim is to reproduce nature at the height and force
of its intensity'.[42] This implies both a mimetic and an expressive intent, which
embraces careful observation, subjective interpretation and aesthetic demon-
stration. This dialectic between objective description and subjective expression
was flamboyantly encapsulated by Zola when he asserted rhetorically that

'I indulge in hypertrophy of the truthful detail. I leap into the stars from the springboard of exact observation. The Truth wings its way to the symbol.'[43] According to Guy de Maupassant, one of Zola's closest disciples, the naturalist movement also sought to distinguish itself from that art which portrayed a 'bland photographic view of life': 'the realist, if he is an artist, will seek not to expand to us a bland photographic view of life, but to provide a vision more complete, more gripping, more searching than reality itself.'[44] It is evident from this quotation that naturalism contains a pronounced symbolic and expressive dimension and, also, that it is substantially concerned with issues of aesthetic form, as well as with mimesis. As Zola's writing developed through the course of his career this symbolic dimension, in particular, also became more pronounced and, in addition to the underlying imperative to achieve verisimilitude, novels such as *L'Assommoir*, *Nana*, *La Terre*, *Germinal* and *L'Argent* are structured around references to abstract concepts such as disintegration, regeneration, innocence and evil.[45]

These concerns with the use of forcefully expressive, symbolic and authored form, set within an overall context of realistic depiction, are particularly evidenced in Zola's critical defence of Manet and the impressionists. Zola regarded impressionism as a branch of the naturalist movement because of its empirical yet formally innovative approach, and influentially argued that Manet was 'above all a naturalist' because his work was the best example of 'nature seen through a temperament'.[46] What was particularly important for Zola was the manner in which Manet's paintings both presented external reality through a socially extensive approach and, via the foregrounding of aesthetic form, also indicated the presence of authorial vision. This endorsement of a particular kind of synthesis between mimesis, manifest form and authorial signature was summed up in a letter written by Zola in 1864, in which he celebrated 'the canvas which, in scrutinizing reality closely, consents to lie just enough to make me sense the human being in an image of creation'.[47] In the same letter, to his friend Antony Valabregue, Zola went on to further define what he meant by the notion of the realistic canvas which 'consents to lie', in arguing that, although, like all writing, realist writing necessarily 'deforms reality', it does so in an apposite and appropriate manner, in that it does not overly disfigure reality. Here, in an argument which will reappear in virtually all the major twentieth-century theories of cinematic realism, Zola asserts that a naturalist portrayal of reality which respects the essential coherence and unity of the visually experienced external world is superior to forms of aesthetic portrayal which do not, or do so to a lesser degree. Still, the question arises as to how naturalist art should retain the experience of the unity of external reality, whilst also transforming that experience aesthetically. What is the precise method, or approach to be adopted, through which the naturalist artist can be sure that he or she is transforming reality in the appropriate manner?

Zola's answer to these questions is a complex one, but one which also rests on the familiar realist notion of the spontaneous and open encounter with reality: an encounter in which aesthetic preconception must always be subordinated to the direct encounter with reality, and to the empirical material emanating from reality. The naturalist artist must be open to the experience of nature in its fullness, must be alert to its varied nuances and must strive to render those nuances both in detail and in full:

> However, I fully accept its [realism's] procedure, which is to place oneself in all openness before nature, to render it in its ensemble, with no exclusions whatsoever. It seems to me the work of art should take in the entire horizon.[48]

What we have here is an emphasis on immediacy and the imprecise. Zola argues that the naturalist is duty bound to abandon 'old routines', and to seek to render the indeterminate character of reality.[49] In this respect naturalism can also be seen to incorporate the central imperative associated with the earlier artistic response to the degeneration of the neo-classical tradition: namely, a tendency to oppose forms of systematic, institutionalised and formulaic art; and to develop a style which captures a more immediate – and therefore less *a priori* regulated – experience of the external world. One consequence of this focus on the empirical and the immediate is that 'naturalist' art often tends to emphasise the transient, the momentary, and the inter connectivity of things, as in Manet's *A Bar at the Folies-Bergère*, which shows its subjects 'as if caught – frozen – in a specific, characteristic instance'.[50] A painting such as *A Bar at the Folies Bergère* can also be related to the interlacing, interconnecting verbal accounts of – working-class life found in a novel such as *L'Assommoir*, with its 'cross-sectional' as opposed to linear plot;[51] and this emphasis on an impressionistic rendition of transient phenomena is also evident in *Les Rougon-Macquart* as a whole, which is more a 'mosaic', than a systematic 'natural and social history'; and only loosely, intermittently connected to historical reference. [52] It is clear, therefore, that the model of naturalist art advanced by Zola fits into the central realist tradition explored within this study. Furthermore, and as will be shown later, Zola's approach to realistic representation is often very close to the theories of cinematic realism advanced by twentieth-century theorists of cinematic realism such as Grierson, Kracauer, Bazin and Lukács.

Conclusions

In this chapter an attempt has been made to identify some of the key factors which influenced the emergence of the nineteenth-century French realist tradition. One of these factors was a critical response to the degeneration of the neo-classical tradition during the Empire, Restoration and July Monarchy periods. Another was a general opposition, from both left and right, to the haute bourgeois values and power structures of Orleanism. Yet another was the emergence of a social imperative, stimulated by the growth of a middle-class reading and visually literate public, to depict the extensive social, economic and political changes that were taking place in France over the period. Realism was also crucially influenced by a desire to apply supposedly 'scientific' method to aesthetic representation, and by critical theories which emphasised the determining (though not completely determining) power of environment and heredity over the individual. Two other important factors, which will be discussed more fully in the final pages of this chapter, were the influence of political radicalism and a desire to represent the underclass. Both of these raise the question of realism's relationship to progressive forces and democracy: a question central to any adequate understanding of the nineteenth-century realist tradition.

It should be clear by now that realism cannot be considered as the 'art-form of the bourgeoisie' in any global sense and, given this, distinctions must be made between the various types of realist art produced in France between the 1830s and 1900, in order to distinguish between art which was essentially normative in character, and art which played a more critical, oppositional role. In his *Mimesis: The Representation of Reality in Western Literature* (1946), Erich Auerbach makes an important differentiation between 'merely comic works which indubitably remained within the realm of the low style', and realistic works which treated their subjects 'seriously, problematically or tragically'.[53] Auerbach's category of 'realistic works of serious style and character' is a helpful conceptualisation because it emphasises the fact that 'serious realism' must be considered as an essentially critical, rather than normative or descriptive, practice. If Auerbach's distinction is adopted it also becomes possible to differentiate this critical realist paradigm from other forms of realistic art of the period and, given that, it can be argued that French nineteenth-century realism can be productively divided into three separate, though interacting groupings of artistic production. The first of these consists of art which was directly oppositional, critical and, in some cases, formally avant-garde. The second consists of art which depicted, rather than critiqued, society. Finally, the third grouping consists of realist work produced during the Second Empire and Third Republic: work which played the same role in celebrating the authority and achievements of the ruling regime as had a compromised neo-classical tradition during the periods of the Restoration and July monarchy.[54]

Of these three categories of realist art, only the second can be relatively easily granted the title of the 'art-form of the bourgeoisie'. This form of realist art developed in order to meet the demands of a growing bourgeois public which required images and stories that matched its own experience of reality. Although this form of cultural production exhibited a social orientation, in that it was made up of accounts of the social environment, that orientation was, for the most part, unanalytical in character. Perhaps the most striking manifestation of this type of descriptive rather than critical realism was the appearance of the 'Panoramas', huge tented enclosures within which panoramic landscapes of the city were painted on circular canvas walls.[55] in addition to the Panoramas, popular periodicals such as *La Caricature* and *Magaziné Pittoresque* also presented numerous tales and illustrations of city life, as did lithographic prints such as L. L. Boilly's *Moving Day* (1826) and daguerreotypes such as Louis Daguerre's *Paris Boulevard* (1838).

In addition to this body of illustrative realist representation, however, a form of officially sanctioned realism also developed from the beginning of the Second Empire, and continued to flourish throughout the period of the Third Republic. Here, realist art was commissioned in order to legitimate ruling bourgeois power structures. For example, realist art sponsored by captains of industry often celebrated the accomplishments of the sponsors, and of industrial capitalism more generally.[56] Under the Second Empire, realist art was also increasingly commissioned by a Napoleonic regime which had turned its back on a neo-classicist tradition which, by then, had become associated with the Catholic/royalist right and Orleanism.[57] Realism also suited the purposes of the Napoleonic system because, unlike neo-classical art, which required a considerable amount of cultural knowledge and education in order to be accurately decoded, realism was distinguished by features such as directness, clarity and accessibility. Realist art was, consequently, able to communicate to an extensive audience, and this suited the purpose of a regime intent on advancing a new set of social, economic and political priorities through the mobilisation of both populist rhetoric and new mass-communications technologies. For example, soon after the coup d'état of 1851, the regime commissioned Salon paintings of the Emperor's civil and military achievements, which were then lithographed and distributed to the provinces as part of a campaign to publicise the achievements of the regime.[58] Between the coup d'état and the Paris *Exposition Universelle* of 1855 the regime also attempted to cultivate its own 'official' realist style, in opposition to both neo-classicism and the critical realism of the left, by influencing art production through forms of patronage and censorship.[59] The style of painting which emerged from this context combined naturalistic reproduction with an affirmative, Romantic idealism, and is apparent in works such as Jules Breton's *Blessing the Wheat in the Artois* (1857), with its evocation of order, hierarchy and tradition; and Wiliam-Adolphe Bouguereau's *Entrance of the Emperor at Tarascon, 14 June 1856* (1856) – a painting which combines a realist approach with undiluted *hommage* to the Emperor.[60]

However, and in contrast to these traditions of illustrative or confirming realism, more progressive forms of artistic realism attempted to represent realities excluded from dominant official art, and in a more critical manner. Although this had been a central characteristic of critical realism since the

1830s, it was given an additional centrality by the overthrow of the Commune in 1848, and the consequent coup d'état. The critical realist/naturalist tradition which developed after 1848 embodied and reflected a sense of pessimism, generated by the belief that democratic progress would always be thwarted, and it was the 'failure' of 1848 which influenced the rise of the naturalist movement, in particular.[61] The events of 1848 also made artists and intellectuals more conscious than ever before of the need to depict a proletarian reality which lay outside the sphere of bourgeois values and representations,[62] and this more profound form of proletarian realism is reflected in paintings such as Courbet's *After Dinner at Ornans* (1849), *Burial at Ornans* (1849), *Peasants of Flagey Returning from the Fair* (1849) and *The Stonebreakers* (1850), as well as in later naturalist novels, such as *Thérèse Raquin* (1867) and *L'Assommoir* (1876). Courbet's quartet of paintings have been described as 'an attack on the technical foundations of bourgeois art', because of their deliberate use of imagery derived from popular working-class lithographs and engravings: forms of communications which were frequently employed as a covert means of communication within the radicalised working class.[63] Linda Nochlin has also argued that *Burial at Ornans*, in particular, embodies:

> a pictorial democracy, a compositional egalitarisme seen as a paradigm for the quarante-huitard ideal itself. As exemplified in such works, both Realism and Democracy were expressions of the same naive and stalwart confrontation of – and challenge to – the status quo.[64]

It is this tradition of critical, rather than illustrative or normative realism which this study is centrally concerned with, a tradition which, far from being an art-form of the bourgeoisie, is often strongly anti-bourgeois in character. This book will now proceed to explore the influence of this tradition on early twentieth-century French film-making, and particularly on Jean Renoir's *La Bête humaine*.

Notes

1 Jameson, Fredric, *Signatures of the Visible* (New York and London: Routledge, 1992), p. 156.

2 Ibid.

3 Winston, Brian, *Claiming the Real: The Documentary Film Revisited* (London: BFI, 1995), p. 26.

4 Honour, Hugh, *Neo-classicism: Style and Civilization* (Harmondsworth: Penguin Books Ltd., 1968), p. 186.

5 Jones, H. M., *American and French Culture 1750–1848* (Chapel Hill: University of North Carolina Press, 1927), p. 120.

6 Hampson, Norman, *The Enlightenment: An Evaluation of its Assumptions, Attitudes and Values* (London: Penguin Books, 1990), p. 99.

7 Ibid., p. 101.
8 Ibid., p. 102.
9 Ibid., p. 105.
10 Ibid., p. 100.
11 Hatton, Ragnhild (ed.), *A History of European Ideas* (London: C. Hurst & Co. (Publishers) Ltd, 1962), p. 134.
12 Honour, p. 13.
13 Hampson, p. 243–4.
14 Ibid., p. 225.
15 Jones, p. 137.
16 Russell, Bertrand, *History of Western Philosophy* (London: Allen & Unwin, 1965), pp. 262–3.
17 Crow, Thomas, 'Patriotism and Virtue: David to the Young Ingres', in Eisenman, Stephen F. (ed.), *Nineteenth-century Art: A Critical History* (London: Thames & Hudson Ltd, 2002), pp. 36–7.
18 Honour, p. 34.
19 Ibid., p. 35.
20 Eisenman, Stephen F., 'The Generation of 1830 and the Crisis in the Public Sphere', in Eisenman, p. 193.
21 Magraw, Roger, *France 1815–1914: The Bourgeois Century* (Oxford: Fontana, 1983), p. 84.
22 Becker, George J., *Master European Realists of the Nineteenth-century* (New York: Frederick Ungar Publishing Co., 1982), p. 8.
23 Magraw, p. 85.
24 Hemmings, F. W. J. (ed.), *The Age of Realism* (Hassocks: Harvester Press, 1978), p. 44.
25 Needham, Gerald, *19th-Century Realist Art* (New York: Harper & Row Publishers, 1988), p. 35.
26 Ibid., p. 42.
27 Larkin, Maurice, *Man and Society in Nineteenth-Century Realism: Determinism and Ideology* (New York: Macmillan, 1977), p. 6.
28 Ibid., p. 17.
29 Ibid., p. 19.
30 Ibid., p. 21.
31 Hemmings, p. 44–7.
32 Balzac, Honoré de, from the foreword (1841) to *La Comédie humaine,* quoted in Larkin, p. 35.
33 Larkin, p. 51.
34 Ibid., p. 40, quoting Balzac, from the 'Introduction' to *La Consine Bette.*
35 Becker, p. 14.
36 Furst, Lilian R., and Skrine, Peter N., *Naturalism: The Critical Idiom* (London: Methuen & Co. Ltd, 1971), p. 22.
37 Larkin, p. 130.
38 Ibid., pp. 128–30.
39 Hemmings, p. 186.

40 Furst and Skrine, p. 8.
41 Ibid.
42 Ibid., p. 4.
43 Hemmings, p. 194.
44 Ibid., p. 210.
45 Becker, p. 119.
46 Lacambre, Genevieve, 'Towards an Emerging Definition of Naturalism in French Nineteenth-century Painting', in Weisberg, Gabriel P. (ed.), *The European Realist Tradition* (Bloomington and Indianapolis: Indiana University press, 1982), p. 235.
47 Ibid.
48 Becker, p. 95.
49 Lacambre, in Weisberg, p. 235.
50 Ibid., p. 239.
51 Becker, p. 109.
52 Ibid., p. 100.
53 Auerbach, Erich, *Mimesis: The Representation of Reality in Western Literature* (Princeton: Princeton University Press, 1953), p. 556.
54 Bezucha, Robert, 'Being Realistic About Realism: Art and the Social History of Nineteenth-Century France', in Weisberg, p. 2.
55 Needham, p. 15.
56 Weisberg, 'The New Maecenas: Regional and Private Patronage of Realism in France 1830–1880', in Weisberg, p. 24.
57 Boime, Albert, 'The Second Empire's Official Realism', in Weisberg, p. 33.
58 Ibid., p. 32.
59 Ibid., p. 31.
60 Ibid., p. 92.
61 Allison, John, 'The Political and Social Background of Naturalism', in Boas, George (ed.), *Courbet and the Naturalistic Movement* (New York: Russell & Russell, 1967), p. 3.
62 Ibid., p. 5.
63 Eisenman, 'The Rhetoric of Realism: Courbet and the Origins of the Avant-Garde', in Eisenman, pp. 212–14.
64 Nochlin, Linda, *Realism* (Harmondsworth: Penguin, 1971), p. 48.

2

La Bête humaine, the evolution of French cinematic realism and naturalism 1902–38, and the influence of the nineteenth-century tradition

The nineteenth-century critical realist/naturalist tradition explored in the previous chapter exerted a considerable influence over the development of an important realist cinema that emerged in France during the silent period; and, within the general parameters of that influence, it was, above all, the ideas and work of Émile Zola that were to have a decisive impact. At one level, it appears anachronistic that a movement such as naturalism, which had lost much of its cultural pre-eminence by the time that the cinema appeared, should have had the influence on the new medium that it did. The naturalist movement began to fragment as early as the 1880s, as members of the original inner circle such as Guy de Maupassant distanced themselves from the movement's core premises. The movement was also surpassed by more subjectivist artistic movements, such as symbolism, as well as by the later, more affirmative, pan-theistic *naturisme* associated with novelists such as Maurice Leblond. This shift from objectivism to subjectivism led to a rejection of the supposedly 'scientific' aspirations which had characterised much naturalist theory and practice and, ultimately, to the decline of literary naturalism as a major force within the cultural landscape. By 1891, another of the original group of writers close to Zola, Huysmans, was even characterising naturalism as *une impasse, un tunnel bouché*.[1]

Nevertheless, despite the general decline of naturalism as an influential movement, Zola himself remained a prominent figure within artistic and public life up until his death in 1902. Zola's increasing involvement in topical public debates, most controversially over the Dreyfus Affair and the publication of *J'accuse* (1898), ensured that both he and naturalism remained within the contemporary spotlight. This degree of public exposure was also bolstered by the extent to which many of Zola's later novels, including *L'Argent* (1891), *La Débâcle* (1892) and *Travail* (1901), and polemical writings, such as *Une campagne* (1882), *Nouvelle campagne* (1897) and *La Vérité* (1901) dealt directly with issues of current topical concern. Finally, Zola's controversial death in

1902, and subsequent official elevation to the ranks of the literary greats in 1908, when his remains were removed to the Panthéon, also sustained a continuing engagement with both his writings, and naturalism in general.

The emergence of the cinema in 1896 also seems to have further revived interest in Zola and naturalism, and provided a new medium of expression for the naturalist vision: one which even offered the possibility of fashioning a more authentic expression of the naturalist ideal than was realisable within the novel. Rather paradoxically, given the general turn to subjectivism which marked the period, it was, precisely, the modern, technological and 'scientific' character of the cinematograph, in conjunction with the inherent potential which the machine possessed for generating photographic accounts of reality, which led some film-makers and critics back to the naturalist premises espoused by Zola in the foreword to *Thérèse Raquin* (1867), with its explicit endorsement of the scientific method. Examples of such a sanction of cinematic naturalism can be found in the writings of a number of critics active during the period. For instance, writing in 1911, Ricciotto Canudo argued that the cinematograph summed up 'the values of a still eminently scientific age'.[2] Similarly, and also writing in 1913, Louis Haugmard focused on the cinema's potential for providing precise information, and Haugmard's assertion that film must turn away from 'trickery', 'artifice' and 'falsification' to 'the reproduction of natural reality' is also analogous to the views expressed by Zola in *Le Naturalisme au théâtre* (1881).[3]

Nevertheless, these 'cinematic' reaffirmations of the positivist tendencies implicit within much naturalist theory were at odds with the general cultural flow of movements and ideas in France, both during the *belle époque* and immediately after. In addition, although such endorsements of the technological positivism made procurable by the appearance of the cinematograph had an impact on the development of early film theory, and formed a meaningful link between one central aspect of nineteenth-century naturalism and early French realist cinema, a more consequential influence on the development of that cinema can be located in another distinctive aspect of Zola's work: the lyrical, pantheistic and idealistic style which was embraced in novels such as *Germinal* (1885) and *La Terre* (1887). This strand of Zolaesque naturalism also influenced an early twentieth-century school of literary naturalistic writing, which included novelists such as Leblond, Charles-Louis Philippe, Henri Bachelin, Pierre Hamp, Octave Mirbeau and René Boylesve.[4] These writers formed a school of regional novelists whose work, in novels such as *Le Village* (Bachelin, 1919) and *L'Enfant à la balustrade* (Boylesve, 1913), combine typically naturalist preoccupations with the exigencies of lower-class experience with an evocative, affirmative treatment of regional subject matter and landscape. In a novel such as *L'Enfant à la balustrade*, for example, Boylesve combines a naturalist thematic perspective with an evocation of the cultural particularity and natural environment of the Touraine region. As with novels such as *La Terre* and *Germinal,* works such as *L'Enfant à la balustrade,* and Mirbeau's better known *Le Journal d'un l femme de chamber* (1900), would provide a narrative model and aesthetic framework for the realist cinema that developed in France between 1902 and 1925.

Although this school of regionalist literary naturalism had a significant influence upon the development of early French realist cinema, the work of Zola itself also provided a persisting theoretical and technical framework for various strands of emerging French film culture during the first three decades of the twentieth century; and also influenced the appearance of a substantial group of films, some of pivotal importance, which were derived from Zola's novels. Between 1902 and 1938 approximately 28 such adaptations were produced. The first film version of Zola's *L'Assommoir* (1877), *Les Victimes de l'alcoolisme* (Ferdinand Zecca, 1902), appeared in the year of Zola's death, and was quickly followed by Zecca and Lucien Nonguet's two versions of *Germinal* (1885) – *La Grève* (1903) and *Au pays noir* (1905). *L'Assommoir* also served as the source for *L'Assommoir* (Albert Capellani, 1909), *Les Victimes de l'alcool* (Gérard bourgeois, 1911), *Le Poison de l'humanité* (Émile Chautard, 1911) and *L'Assommoir* (Charles Maudru and Maurice de Mersan, 1921); whilst *Germinal* provided the basis for *Au pays des ténèbres* (Victorin Jasset, 1912), *Germinal* (Capellani, 1914) and *Germinal* (no known director, 1920).

In addition to *L'Assommoir* and *Germinal,* a number of other novels by Zola also served as the foundation for films made over this period. *L'Argent* (1891) was the basis of *L'Argent* (Marcel L'Herbier, 1928); whilst *Au bonheur des dames* (1883) provided the source for *Au ravissement des dames* (1913) and *Au bonheur des dames* (Julien Duvivier, 1929). *La Bête humaine* (1889) was the source for *La Bête humaine* (Jean Renoir, 1938), whilst *Fécondité* (1899) was adapted as *Fécondité* (N. Evreinoff and Henry Etievant, 1929). Other adaptations included: *Nana* (Renoir, 1926), which was adapted from *Nana* (1880), *Nantas* (Donatien, 1921), adapted from *Nantas* (1879); *Pour une nuit d'amour* (Iakov, Protozanoff, 1921), and *Une page d'amour* (Pina Menichelli, 1924), adapted from *Une page d'amour* (1878), *Le Rêve* (Jacques de Baroncelli, 1920), and *Le Rêve* (Baroncelli, 1931), adapted from *Le Rêve* (1888); *La Terre* (Jasset, 1912), and *La Terre* (André Antoine, 1921), adapted from *La Terre* (1887) *Thérèse Raquin* (Jacques Feyder, 1926), adapted from *Thérèse Raquin* (1887), and *Travail* (Henri Pouctal, 1919), adapted from *Travail* (1901).

Although this body of work is a substantial one, the films which make it up are, in many cases, often very different from each other, and mediated by factors other than their common source in the novels of Zola. For example, a group of generic realist adaptions which appeared after 1920, and which include *Travail, Père Goriot* (Baroncelli, 1921), *La Nuit de 11 septembre* (Bernard Deschamps, 1920) and *L'Assommoir* (Mersan and Maudru, 1920), were produced as part of a commercial production strategy aimed at turning works of nineteenth-century urban fiction into profitable films, and cannot be regarded as carrying on the naturalist vision in an authentic manner.[5] This is also true of many of the earliest film adaptions of Zola, such as *Les Victimes de l'alcoolisme* (Zecca, 1902), *L'Assommoir* (Capellani, 1909), *Le Poison de l'humanité* (Chautard, 1911), *La Grève* (Zecca, 1903), *Au pays noir* (Nonguet, 1905) and *Germinal* (Capellani, 1914), all of which were influenced more by various traditions of popular melodrama and vaudeville than by naturalism *per se*. *Les Victimes de l'alcoolisme* was, for example, directed by Ferdinand Zecca, a director more than prepared to combine elements from almost any filmic genre in order to make a public impact and, according to Sadoul, Zecca's earlier *Histoire d'un crime* (1901) 'est une classique qu'imiteront avec fidélité Gaumont, Méliès et plusieurs autres éditeurs'.[6]

Nevertheless, despite his penchant for 'systematically exploit[ing]' any material that he thought might be commercially effective, Zecca also played a part in the emergence of some of the more notable early realist films.[7] In 1901 Zecca was employed by Pathé to lead the development of the company's film production. As work developed, a number of distinct genres of films emerged, including one given the sobriquet of 'Dramatic and Realist Scenes'. Although many of the films made within this class were relatively inconsequential, others were more important, and films such as Bourgeois's *Les Victimes de l'alcool* (1911) and Capellani's adaption of Victor Hugo's *Les Misérables* (1912) attempted a degree of critical consideration of their source material. Outside Pathé, Victorin Jasset's *Au pays des ténèbres* (1912), part of the *Batailles du la vie* series which he made for Eclair, can also be associated with this group of work.[8] These transitional films, which combine melodramatic forms and moralistic conformism with a degree of verisimilitude and authenticity drawn from location shooting, look forward to the first two important postwar realist films: *Le Coupable* (1917) and *Les Travailleurs de la mer* (1918). Both were directed by André Antoine, who would go on to play a pivotal role in introducing naturalist themes and techniques into the French realist cinema of the 1917–23 period.

Antoine and pictorialist naturalism

Originally a theatre rather than film director, Antoine did not begin his career in film making until 1914, and at the relatively advanced age of sixty. However, his influence on the development of the French cinema can be traced to well before 1914. For example, in promoting Louis Feuillade's series of films *La Vie telle qu'elle est* (1911) as 'slices of life', Gaumont drew on a phrase well known as a slogan describing Antoine's theatrical productions, which were frequently based on naturalist classics by Zola and others.[9] In addition, a number of individuals associated with Antoine's theatre companies, including Henri Pouctal, Maurice Tourneur, Georges Denola and Albert Capellani, all went into film-making during the prewar years. Pouctal was taken on by the Film d'Art company, whilst Capellani became the artistic director and principal film maker of Pathé's Société Cinématographique des Auteurs et Gens de Lettres (SCAGL), the group which was largely responsible, under Zecca, for the production of Pathé's 'Dramatic and Realist Scenes' strand of production. Between its establishment by Charles Pathé in 1908, and the outbreak of war in 1914, the SCAGL was responsible for the development of three major realist productions, all of which reveal the influence of Antoine: *Scènes de la vie cruelle* (Camille de Morlon and René Leprince, 1911) (made in response to the success of Louis Feuillade's *La Vie telle qu'elle est*), *Les Misérables* and *Les Victimes de l'alcool*. Antoine himself had no ambitions to enter the cinema. However, in 1914 his theatre, the Odéon, was forced to close for financial reasons and, shortly afterwards, he accepted an offer of employment by Pathé and Capellani under the umbrella of SCAGL. There he made his first film, *Les Frères corses*, based on the Alexandre Dumas novel, *Père*. *Les Frères corses* was delayed by the outbreak of war, and was eventually released in 1917. This was then followed by *Le Coupable* (1917), *Les Travailleurs de la mer* (1918) (from Victor Hugo), *L'Hirondelle et la mésange* (1920), *La Terre* (1921), based on Zola's novel of 1887, and *L'Arlésienne* (1922).

Antoine can also be associated with the pictorialist naturalist genre of film making that developed in France over the period between 1917 and 1925. As with other films within this genre, Antoine's films combine location shooting of character and environment with dramatic structure, melodrama, naturalist subject matter, a pantheistic treatment of nature and the rural, and considerable attention to the visual and plastic compositional qualities of the image. Antoine's films also depict, and were filmed in, a number of the regions of France most often portrayed within the pictorialist naturalist cinema. For example, *Les Travailleurs de la mer* was shot on location on the Brittany coast, whilst *L'Hirondelle et la mésange* was filmed on the canals of northern France, *La Terre* in the Beuce region near Chartres (where Zola had researched his novel), and *L'Arlésienne* in the Camargue. Little is known of *Le Coupable*, and only a few stills remain of *Les Travailleurs de la mer*. However, they appear to have been transitional films, which combined an impressionist evocation of the sea (in the case of *Les Travailleurs de la mer*) with more standard plot devices. In the case of the latter film, actors from the Comédie Française were also used to depict the Breton fishermen – a technique which apparently placed limitations upon the attempted realism of the film.[10] Despite this, the pictorialist aspect of the film remains impressive, and the same appears to have been the case with *L'Arlésienne*, which combined a melodramatic plot with an impressionistic portrayal of the Camargue landscape, and the recently restored *L'Hirondelle et la mésange*, which is less concerned with its naturalist plot of

jealousy and rivalry amongst bargemen than with depicting the visual experience of life lived on the rivers and canals of France and Belgium. Antoine's son
has described *L'Hirondelle et la mésange* as a 'poem in images',[11] and the extent
to which the film relegates dramatic development in favour of the demonstra-
tion of an extreme visual naturalism even led the film's nervous producers to
bar its release.[12]

The painterly, evocative, yet highly controlled pictorial style of Antoine's
films gives them a somewhat Romantic inflection, which is also often applied
to the treatment of subject matter. This tendency towards the evocative portrayal of lower-class experience and rural experience characterises both
Antoine's films and the pictorialist naturalist school as a whole, and one consequence of this is that, in these films, critical, often bleak (in a naturalist vein)
depictions of the social order are mediated by a tendency to dwell on the beauty
and grandeur of nature and on the inherent natural qualities of long-standing
lower-class and rural cultural practices and mores. In these films, images of
landscape express a constellation of sensibility which both poeticises the
natural environment, and symbolises the psychological-spiritual condition of
the principal characters. Antoine asserted that his films achieved this expressive symbolic effect through the creation of 'impressionistic tableaux' which
encompassed the affiliations which bonded individual to environment.[13] This
reveals a confluence of naturalist and symbolist predispositions, and also suggests how Antoine's films provided one of the foundations for the emergence
of a more directly symbolist inspired 'impressionist' cinema during the mid-
1920s. However, it also reveals the existence of what might be described as a
nostalgic tendency, and one critic has questioned whether these, and similar
films, were primarily 'displayed as so many scenes or documents for the disin-
terested aesthetic pleasure of a spectator, a touring bourgeois spectator.'[14]
Whether this is the case or not, it seems clear that, despite his reliance on the
subject matter of nineteenth-century realism and naturalism – a reliance
which informed his own film-making activity in adapting Dumas, Hugo and
Zola for the screen – it is this fixation with the image and resonance of
landscape which characterises Antoine's film-making most clearly.

The clearest influence of the naturalist tradition on Antoine's films can be
found in his adaptation of Zola's *La Terre*, and a study of this film also serves
to clarify the relationship between naturalism and an evocative impressionism
which characterised both Antoine's own film-making, and the pictorialist naturalist genre in general. *La Terre* commences by making a direct equation
between Zola and Antoine, through showing full-screen portraits of the two
immediately after the opening credits. After this the stylistic focus of the film
is on realism, rather than pictorialism. The hardship of peasant labour in the
fields is emphasised through showing peasants at work, and suffering from
exposure to the elements. At this stage of the film it is the plot rather than visual

pictorialism which is the main focus of attention, as the film follows the main course of the novel. However, as the narrative evolves, the emphasis on plot and characterisation gradually gives way to a growing concern with pictorial qualities. Whilst the opening scenes were rather prosaic in terms of their visual composition, those which follow are now carefully composed, using classical proportions, and a carefully balanced use of black, white and grey. One unexpected feature which also appears at this point is the use of superimposition to portray a dream sequence and, later, a series of flashbacks. This use of formalist devices to depict subjective states of being was uncommon at the time, and more usually associated with the films of the French cinematic impressionist movement.

As *La Terre* proceeds, therefore, the earlier emphases on plot, characterisation and realist verisimilitude gradually gives way to a pictorialist approach which seeks to situate individuals within their rural environment. This becomes the dominant theme in the third reel of the film, which portrays the harvest. An example of this had been apparent earlier, in reel two, when a lone figure is seen to be small indeed in comparison with the vast fields of wheat which surround him. The imagery here is rather diffuse, containing large areas of tonality which interact to evoke the sense of a bountiful and expansive nature. As the third reel continues, a dichotomy seems to appear between the portrayal of life in the village and the depiction of human experience in relation to nature. The scenes shot in the village are Zolaesque in focusing on the curiosities and anomalies of peasant custom. However, scenes shot in the countryside take on a quite different kind of visual realism, which emphasises the vastness and beauty of the land, and the insignificance of individual human destinies.

In many respects, reels three and four of *La Terre* are the most effectual. In this section of the film the pathos and tension of the story gradually mounts, and Antoine adopts a more expressive approach in order to portray this. During the scene where the central character's precious life savings are stolen by his own son, we see the use of evocative, almost expressionistic lighting, as well as some 'deep-focus' photography. Antoine then emphasises the plight of the central character through the use of a motif rendered earlier in the films: shots of a lone, tiny individual lost in a vast landscape of wheatfield. More formalist superimpositions are used at this point to emphasise the metaphor of homelessness, and an expressionistic tone is also employed in order to deepen the sense of tragedy. The land now appears to be a threatening, dangerous place. Yet *La Terre* does not end on this tragic note, which portrays the land as both powerful and destructive. Instead, the final scenes of the film return to the concluding themes of Zola's novel. Here, as in the film, a dialectic is introduced between the land as the bringer of death and as the harbinger of life; and, as the old peasant dies, we see scenes which suggest the augmentation of new life: young farm animals and young women seen engaged in vigorous activity, enjoying life. This final notion of the land as the bringer of both death and life is then summed up in the final title of the film: 'Des morts des semances, et le pain poussait de la terre', which suggests that the land is the womb of both life and death. In its combination of naturalism, realism and impressionism, *La Terre* sums up the general orientation of the pictorialist naturalist genre, and is also one of the two or three most important films to be made within that particular genre.

The pictorialist naturalist cinema of the 1918–25 period is characterised by the same general approach found in Antoine's films, and includes films such as *L'Homme du large* (Marcel L'Herbier, 1920), *L'Appel du sang* (Louis Mercanton, 1920), *Miarka, la fille à l'ourse* (Mercanton, 1920), *Aux jardins de Murcie* (Mercanton, 1923), *Le Roi de Camargue* (André Hugon, 1921), *Diamant noir* (Hugon, 1922), *Notre Dame d'amour* (Hugon, 1922), *Le Retour aux champs* (Jacques de Baroncelli, 1918), *Jocelyn* (Léon Poirier, 1922), *Geneviève* (Poirier, 1923), *La Brière* (Poirier, 1925), *Crainquebille* (Jacques Feyder, 1923), *Visages d'enfants* (Feyder, 1925), *Poil de carotte* (Julien Duvivier, 1926) *L'Ami Fritz* (René Hervil, 1920), *Blanchette* (Hervil, 1921), *Nêne* (Baroncelli, 1924), *L'Atre* (Robert Boudrioz, 1923), *Pêcheur d'islande* Baroncelli, 1924 and *La Belle Nivernaise* (Jean Epstein, 1924). Two later films by Jean Grémillon – *Maldone* (1928) and *Gardiens de phare* (1929) – can also be associated with pictorialist naturalism. After 1925 the pictorialist naturalism tradition gradually declined in importance, and was superseded by both the impressionist movement, and other forms of cinematic modernism. Nevertheless, pictorialist naturalism, and the naturalist tradition more generally, continued to exert an influence on French film production during the remainder of the 1920s.

Of course, after 1930, the French silent realist film tradition was challenged by the emergence of the sound film: a development which posed a potentially decisive peril to an aesthetic and practice of film-making which had been founded upon the primacy of the image. The advent of the sound film, and its attendant transformation of the French film industry, quickly generated an array of critical debates and positions within French film culture over how to respond to a film-making environment which had now been fundamentally altered. Some critics and film-makers, such as René Clair, Marcel L'Herbier, Jean Epstein and Benjamin Fondane, initially reacted with suspicion and apprehension to the emergence of the sound film, whilst surrealists such as Artaud argued uncompromisingly that this unwelcome development consti- tuted a threat to the survival of film as an art-form.[15] However, other French film-makers, theorists and critics also acknowledged, with varying degrees of enthusiasm, that the sound film would soon be a permanent addition to the cultural landscape, and that a new aesthetic language and critical discourse would have to be created in order to accommodate it.[16] These enthusiasms eventually led to the appearance of a number of important films in the 1930–2 period which were substantially concerned with the exploration of innovative sound-image compositional formations, and which also returned to the naturalist heritage for inspiration.[17]

However, the rapid expansion of the commercial cinema between 1930 and 1934 resulted in a situation where attempts to develop a more critical, innovative realist sound cinema were marginalised, as producers tried to cash in on audience demand for more conventional talking pictures. As a consequence, the experimental realist films of the 1930 period were not followed up, and it was not until 1934, and against a context of increasing national and international turmoil, that critical debate returned to the question of realism and the cinema. Within this more politicised context, some critics began to argue for the development of a cinema which could build on the combination of popular appeal, realistic description and depiction of large-scale social and political forces evident in the novels of Zola. Thus, the *Pour Vous* critic, Claude Vermorel, argued for a version of *L'Argent* which would directly refer to the Stavisky scandal, which was then a matter of topical concern; and regretted the untimely death of Jean Vigo, who had been planning a version of *Germinal*.[18] Between 1934 and 1939, the quest to construct an effective cinema of popular realism also became an important political objective for film-makers on the left, and many of the most important films made over this period draw directly upon the realist and naturalist tradition.

Realist cinema, 1930–8

So far, the link between nineteenth-century critical realism/naturalism and twentieth-century French film-making has been followed from Zola to Antoine, then to pictorialist realism and *La Terre*. These connections are strong and unambiguous, although other films and film-makers of the 1902–30 period can also be associated with the central realist trajectory emanating from the nineteenth-century tradition. The period from 1930 to 1938 presents a more complicated picture, however, largely because a more extensive range of realistic films were produced during this period than was the case during the silent period. What is required now is to take the chain emanating from Zola and Antoine up to 1938, and in order to do this it will be necessary to separate that chain from the rest of the realist production of the 1930s. In order to effect this, the films of the period will here be provisionally divided into six distinct categories. This categorical map of the significant realist French film production of the 1930–8 period is meant to be neither exhaustive nor definitive, and the inclusion of this taxonomy here is primarily intended both to focus analysis on those films which appear to articulate the central characteristics of the critical realist tradition explored in this chapter and to bracket out those which do not, or do so to a lesser extent. The six different categories of films which will be postulated here are, therefore (1) 'pioneering/experimental', (2) 'Romantic', (3) 'generic', (4) 'social', (5) 'politically allegorical' and (6) 'poetic' realist.

The first category, that of 'pioneering/experimental realism', encompasses those films made around 1930 that experiment with the use of sound within a realistic vein. These include *David Golder* (Duvivier, 1930) *La Chienne* (Renoir, 1931), *Sous les toits de Paris* (Clare, 1930), *La Petite Lise* (Grémillon, 1930) and, possibly, *A nous la liberté* (Clair, 1931). The second category, that of 'Romantic realism', draws on the nineteenth-century Romantic realist tradition of Victor Hugo, Eugène Sue and others, and includes Bernard's *Les Croix de bois* (1931) and *Les Misérables* (1933). A third category, that of 'generic realism', includes films which, like those associated with Romantic realism, combine realism with more generic features. To varying extents, films such as Pagnol's *Marius* (1931), Duvivier's *Poil de carotte* (1932), Epstein and Benoit-Lévy's *Peau de pêche* (1929) and Feyder's *Le Grand Jeu* 1933 can be associated with this strand of more generic realism. The fourth category, that of 'social realism', includes films made within the realist/naturalist tradition which possess a pronounced social critique. Some films from the pioneering/experimental category may also fit into this grouping, but those which definitely do include *La Maternelle* (Epstein/Benoit-Lévy, 1934), *Boudu sauvé des eaux* (1932), *Madame Bovary* (Renoir, 1934), *Toni* (Renoir, 1935), *Une partie de campagne* (Renoir, 1936), and *La Bête humaine* (Renoir, 1938). The fifth category of realist films include those which, directly, or more allegorically, depict the contemporary political situation. These include *La Vie est à nous* (Renoir, 1936) *Le Crime de monsieur Lange* (Renoir, 1936), *Les Bas-fonds* (Renoir, 1936), *La Grande Illusion* (Renoir, 1937), *La Marseillaise* (Renoir, 1938), *La Règle du jeu* (Renoir, 1939), and *La Belle Equipe* (Duvivier, 1936).

The final category of realist film-making, that of poetic realism, is associated with a group of films made between 1934 and 1939. Films generally taken to fall within this category include the early *La Tête d'un homme* (Duvivier, 1932) *La Rue sans nom* (Chenal, 1933), *Gueule d'amour* (Grémillon, 1937), *L'Etrange M. Victor Remarques* (Grémillon, 1937) *Le Gens du voyage* (Feyder, 1937), *Le Puritain* (Musso, 1937), Marcel Carné's *Jenny* (1936), *Quai des brumes* (1938), *Hôtel du Nord* (1938) and *Le Jour se lève* (1939) and Julien Duvivier's *La Bandera* (1935), *La Belle Equipe* (1936), *Le Paquebot 'Tenacity'* (1934), *Pépé le Moko* (1936), *Un Carnet de bal* (1937) and *Le Fin du jour* (1938). Although *La Bête humaine* (Renoir, 1938) has been frequently identified as an example of *réalisme poétique*, it will be argued here that the film is not a poetic realist film but one more properly associated with the category of social realism.

Given this demarcation, it appears that it is the films within the fourth category posited, that of 'social realism', which correspond most closely to the nineteenth-century model, and that, furthermore, the majority of these films were directed by Jean Renoir. Of all the directors active in the 1930–9 period, Renoir is arguably the one who can be most clearly linked to the naturalist tradition. Renoir was personally connected to Zola through family relations, including those of his father, the impressionist painter Auguste; and also spent his formative years amongst friends and associates who advocated the 'naturalist/impressionist' creed.[19] His first major narrative film, *Nana* (1926), was also an adaptation of Zola. The 'naturalist/impressionist' tradition influences most of the films made by Renoir between 1931 and 1939. *La Chienne* (1931), *La Nuit du carrefour* (1932) and *Toni* (1935) can all be related to this tradition, whilst *Madame Bovary* (1934), *Une partie de campagne* (1936–41) and *La Bête humaine* (1938) are adaptations of Flaubert, de Maupassant and Zola respectively.

Renoir's 'social realist' films – *La Chienne* (1931), *Boudu sauvé des eaux* (1932), *La Nuit du carrefour* (1932), *Madame Bovary* (1934), *Toni* (1935), *Une partie de campagne* (1936–41) and *La Bête humaine* (1938) – incorporate a number of the characteristics of the naturalist and realist traditions identified here. As argued, one of the most important of these characteristics was an aspiration to dispense with institutionalised conventional practices, and to develop more indefinitely composed works which sought a less mediated encounter with the subject matter of the film. This approach runs through most of the films referred to here. For example, *La Chienne* deliberately departs from then conventional practice and procedure in its use of real-time filming, copious location shooting, and creation of a network of equivocal sound-image relationships which express the 'complexity and thickness of the modern world in an audio-visual medium'.[20] However, perhaps the most conspicuous example within this group of films of the aspiration to transcend established, institutional schema is *Toni* – Renoir's most uncompromisingly naturalist film, and one in which he attempted to free himself of both the 'stupid conformism which afflicts so many of the people who run our industry'[21] and the prevailing 'artifices of representation'.[22] To some extent, *Toni* represents a return to the aesthetic concerns of Antoine. However, although *Toni* preserves the preoccupation with actuality footage and location shooting apparent in films such as *Les Travailleurs de la mer* (1918), *L'Hirondelle et lê mésange* (1920) and *La Terre* (1921), it also departs substantially from the more painterly, carefully composed pictorialism of these films.

Renoir has argued that he deliberately set out to model *Toni* on the formal practices of the documentary film.[23] Renoir was familiar with the French poetic documentary tradition of the mid-1920s, and with the 'city symphony' genre of documentaries which appeared between 1926 and 1931. He also shared the widespread enthusiasm in France for films such as Flaherty's *Nanook of the North*, and had worked with the avant-garde documentary filmmaker Alberto Cavalcanti during the late 1920s. However, the influence of the documentary on the realisation of *Toni* should not be overstated. Between

1931 and 1935, the French documentary tradition, like the avant-garde, went into something of a decline and was virtually eliminated from French screens by the rise of the theatrical sound film.[24] It was only after work on *Toni* had begun that a significant tradition of documentary film-making began to re-emerge in France, with films such as Rudolph Bamberger's *La Cathédrale des morts* (1935), Maurice Cloche's *Mont St Michel* (1936), and Jean-Benoit-Lévy's *Un grand verrier* (1937) and *Un grand potier* (1937). Consequently, although Renoir may have been influenced by much earlier silent documentary films, *Toni* cannot be too closely associated with developments within the French documentary during this period. Rather than documentary, it was a naturalist sensibility, already evident in *La Chienne*, *La Nuit du carrefour* and *Boudu sauvé des eaux*, which Renoir took to its furthest limit in *Toni*, and what is particularly important about *Toni* is the way that it deploys documentary naturalism as part of a deliberate rejection of dominant models of film-making. In this respect, *Toni* is best regarded as the most radical example of Renoir's 'social films' of the 1930–8 period because it embodied a 'signifying practice at odds with the dominant cinema of the day'.[25]

In addition to a departure from institutionalised norms of representation, this body of films exhibits another central characteristic of the naturalist tradition: that of a preoccupation with themes of tragedy transgression, retribution, alienation and marginality, set against an oppressive bourgeois culture and society. In *La Chienne*, the amateur painter Maurice Legrand prefers a deluded artistic sensibility to the stifling securities of bourgeois life, before eventually escaping into the realm of the itinerant *clochard*. In *Madame Bovary*, similar sensibilities and drives lead Emma Bovary to suicide. In *Madame Bovary*, *Toni* and *Une partie de campagne*, Emma Bovary, Toni and Henriette find themseves ultimately trapped by the society which they grow up within: that of the marginalised immigrant community and brutalising bourgeoisie in the case of Toni; an insular, suffocating, often imbecilic urban petit bourgeoisie in the case of Henriette Dufour, and an spiritually impoverished provincial rural society in the case of Emma Bovary. In *La Bête humaine*, Jacques Lantier's transgressions and hereditary flaws also lead him to a suicide ultimately caused both by a capitalism which has tainted his very genes, and by a predatory and corrupt bourgeois order which, as in *Toni*, cares little for its victims.

One distinction that can be made within this group of films, however relates to the notion of agency, and the ability of the individual to transcend an oppressive bourgeois order. In both *La Chienne* and *Boudu sauvé des eaux*, the principal characters achieve a kind of emancipation through literal escape into the parallel world of the *clochard*. Nevertheless, although this does signify a kind of liberation, in both films this is ironically stated, as though not to be taken particularly seriously. In contrast, in the other films the principal characters appear inevitably doomed, and their transgressions merely quicken the pace of their eventual fall. This sense of fatalism is reinforced also by the circularity of plot in these films: Henriette and Henri return to the poignant scene of their first encounter in *Une partie de campagne*; whilst *Toni* ends with scenes which place the death of Toni in juxtaposition with the arrival of the next fateful trainload of immigrants.

However, the most striking example of such fatalist circularity is undoubtedly the finale of *La Bête humaine*, in which the train journey from Paris to Le Havre which opens the film is repeated in reverse at the close of the film, thus concluding the narrative with Jacques Lantier's suicide. Nevertheless, and as will be discussed in more detail later, *La Bête humaine* can be distinguished from these other films also in relation to its depictions of agency. It will be recalled that, in Zolaesque naturalism, determinism was mediated by a conception of agency in which enlightenment emerged phoenix-like from the aftermath of tragic events. In the body of films considered here, however, only *La Bête humaine* can be said to correspond to this particular model of agency. It is also only in *La Bête humaine*, with its portrayal of the world of the railway workers, that a genuine alternative to the bourgeois order is established, whilst the accounts of the separate milieux of the *clochard* in *La Chienne* and *Boudu sauvé des eaux* remain unconvincing.

Closely related to the presence of an anti-bourgeois theme within this body of films is an opposition between a fallen, urban society and nature. In many respects, it is the non-bourgeois in these films who are more closely associated with nature. The most extreme example of this is *Boudu sauvé des eaux*, in which the central character, the tramp Boudu, stands almost for the negation of bourgeois values. Boudu's 'natural' environment is the open parks and riverbank of Paris, where he lives his free, anarchic lifestyle. It is only when he loses his dog that he is forced to come into contact with bourgeois society, and the impact of this is such that he also, like Lantier, is driven to attempt suicide. At the beginning of the film, Boudu is also seen through a telescope, almost as though (as Renoir himself has put it) he was a wild animal under observation, prowling the banks of the Seine. Throughout the film, oppositions are set up between Boudu's more natural persona, and bourgeois characters who are seen as constrained and repressed and, at the end of the film, Boudu decides to give up his new bourgeois existence, in order to return to the life of the *clochard*.

One key articulation of the antinomy between nature and culture which appears in these films consists of the depiction of nature as a breached refuge: a place of potential, though ultimately vulnerable and overwhelmed autonomy. This theme is apparent in *Boudu sauvé des eaux*, where the *clochard's* freedom is threatened first by the loss of his dog, and then by the interventions of bourgeois authority and lifestyle into the realm of park and riverside. In *La Bête humaine*, nature is seen as a realm within which a degree of relief and emancipation can be experienced, but also one that is forever threatened by manipulative forces. A key sequence here is the one in which Jacques and Flore meet in the fields near the signal box, and in which their brief moment of Romantic communion is threatened by instinctual drives and entrenched patterns of behaviour which neither can control, and which are ultimately predatory. However, this theme of nature as a realm of potential, but overwhelmed autonomy is perhaps most evident in *Une partie de campagne*. During one scene, in which Henriette and Henri rest upon a small island, some sort of authentic emotion is experienced: an authenticity only available through contact with nature. However, this is quickly dissipated, as the cycle of domination, control and resignation takes over.

La Bête humaine (1938)

The film which has been described as marking the apotheosis of Renoir's engagement with the naturalist tradition, and which is also, arguably, the most important film adaptation of a naturalist novel to have appeared in France during the first half of the twentieth century, is *La Bête humaine* (1938). In this film, Renoir takes pains to situate himself unambiguously within the naturalist canon by explicitly invoking the authority of Zola. After the opening credits, a brief set of captions establishes the central theme, subject and tone of the film to come:

> This is the story of Jacques Lantier, son of Gervaise of the Rougon-Macqart family. At certin times he knew of his hereditary failings, and thought he was paying for the others, his drunken forebears, the generation of drunkards. His mind broke under the effort of being compelled to act against his wishes and for no cause within himself.

This melancholic epigram is then followed by an image of Zola's signature (although the above quotation does not appear to have been taken directly from Zola's novel), followed by a full-screen portrait of Zola, who stares back sagaciously, inviting the spectator to accept the authorial prerogative which the image invokes. These opening shots suggest that the film to follow is resolved to be an authentic expression of the naturalist vision, and that Zola's posthumous authority both endorses and validates the film's interpretation of the earlier novel from beyond the literary sepulchure. The inclusion in the credits, as an adviser on the project, of one of Zola's descendants, Denise Leblond-Zola, whom Renoir had previously worked with on his 1926 film version of *Nana*, also augments these egregiously signalled claims to legitimacy and historical lineage. Renoir's involvement with Leblond-Zola was, moreover, to prove crucial in directing his ambitions away from the adulterated yarn of passion, locomotives and homicide urged by the film's producers, and towards a more trenchant understanding of the original novel. For example, on receiving the commission to direct *La Bête humaine*, Renoir immediately set to work to develop a provisional scenario for the film. However, he quickly grew displeased with this and, thereafter, worked closely with Leblond-Zola in order to bring the film into closer concord with the spirit and character of Zola's vision.[26]

If one of the central objectives behind the development and subsequent promotion of *La Bête humaine*, from the recurrently antagonistic perspectives of both aesthetic realization and commercial return, was that of foregrounding the importance of Zola and naturalism, and of positioning Renoir's film as an important continuation of the naturalist tradition, the invocation of Zola here also marks the forceful adoption of a controversial aesthetic and political position on the part of Renoir. *La Bête humaine* was a contentious film, both at the time of its release and afterwards, because its endorsement of Zolaesque naturalism was regarded as politically regressive, both from right-wing positions, within which the film was regarded as portraying France in an unpatriotic light, and – more significantly for later interpretations of the film – from a Marxist–Stalinist perspective, within which naturalism was viewed as a decadent aesthetic movement which, like its antithetical other, symbolism, had abandoned a progressive nineteenth-century realist project most closely identified with authors such as Balzac and Tolstoy. At the centre of this Marxian account of naturalism is the premise that the movement emerged largely in response to the sense of alienation and political impotency experienced by artists and intellectuals following the political failures of 1848 and 1871, and that it was, as a consequence, permeated by defeatism and pessimism. One corollary of this understanding of naturalism is that, just as a naturalist sensibility was seen as appearing, despairingly and misguidedly, from the overthrow of the Commune, so Renoir's *La Bête humaine* has also been typically perceived as marking a retreat from political engagement into a defeatist pessimism borne of the alienating political context of 1938.[27]

However, in addition to this ostensible historical paralell between the genesis of naturalism and the political context which framed the appearance of Renoir's film, a more specific comparison can also be drawn between Zola's *La Bête humaine* and Renoir's adaptation, in that both appear to stand apart from other works produced by their respective authors. Renoir's return to naturalism in *La Bête humaine* struck some contemporary critics as incongruous in that, between 1936 and 1939, he had directed a series of films – *La Vie est à nous* (1936), *Le Crime de monsieur Lange* (1936), *Les Bas-fonds* (1936), *La Grande Illusion* (1937), *La Marseillaise* (1938) and *La Règle du jeu* (1939) – which conformed to a politically engaged realist rather than a naturalist model. In an analogous way, Zola's *La Bête humaine*, which appeared in 1890, can also be distinguished from many of the novels which he wrote between the mid-1880s and his death in 1902. For example, although *La Bête humaine* was a late work, the seventeenth of the twenty novels in the Rougon-Macquart 'chronique', it remains one of Zola's 'most violent and pessimistic novels',[28] and, as such, appears to adopt the bleak and deterministic stance embraced in the first book of the cycle, *La Fortune des Rougon* (1871). The emphasis on the correlation between sex and death in *La Bête humaine* is also reminiscent of *Thérèse Raquin* (1867), a novel which pre-dates the Rougon-Macquart cycle. In contrast to both of these works, later novels such as *Germinal* (1885), *L'Argent* (1891), *La Débâcle* (1892), *Le Docteur Pascal* (1893) and *Travail* (1901) are more affirmative, and engaged. In the late *oeuvre* of both Zola and Renoir, therefore, *La Bête humaine* appears to stand out as a singular work, and as something of an anachronism.

However, although Zola and Renoir's *La Bête humaine* were both anachronistic in the above sense, they can also be associated with the works which preceded and succeeded them in a number of ways. Although Zola's *La Bête humaine* contains little detailed reference to a larger political context which exists outside of the psychological obsessions of its central protagonists, it does express some, most notably in the form of an *exposé* of incompetence and corruption within the French judiciary and, towards the end of the novel, through reference to the outbreak of the Franco-Prussian War. In addition, the novel was also meant to form part of a loose trilogy, which included *L'Argent* and *La Débâcle*, and which was intended to tie up the social/political themes covered in the Rougon-Macquart cycle against the background of the demise of the Second Empire. *La Bête humaine*, *L'Argent* and *La Débâcle* are, therefore, meant to depict the 'climactic frenzy of the reign',[29] and the 'nightmarish' fatalism of *La Bête humaine* was, in part, supposed to reflect the spirit and temper of the period which oversaw the fall of Bonapartism. However, if *La Bête humaine*, *L'Argent* and *La Débâcle* are linked together in this sense, they can also be differentiated from each other in terms of their respective roles within the trilogy, for, while *La Bête humaine* transposes the peak of the 'climactic frenzy of the reign' into a 'violent and pessimistic' tale of madness, death and murder, *L'Argent* and *La Débâcle* look beyond such nihilism, to depict a wider range of competing social forces and struggles, and to offer a more hopeful vision of the future.

Understood this way, it can be argued that the relationship between Zola's *La Bête humaine*, *L'Argent* and *La Débâcle* is analogous to one which can be postulated as existing between Renoir's *La Bête humaine*, *La Grande Illusion* and *La Règle du jeu*. Most importantly, such an equation allows *La Bête humaine* to be linked meaningfully to the influential *La Règle du jeu*, rather than considered, as it often is, as tangibly distinct from the latter film. Such an argument for coupling the two films is also bolstered by cognizance of the fact that Renoir had initially wanted two of the principal stars of *La Bête humaine* – Simone Simon and Fernand Ledoux – to play the two central characters in *La Règle du jeu*: Robert and Christine de la Chesnaye. Given Simon's display of barely supressed eroticism in *La Bête humaine*, one can only imagine that *La Règle du jeu* would have been quite different, and much closer to the darker spirit of *La Bête humaine*, if she, rather than the cool Germanic Nora Grégor, had played the central role of Christine. Nevertheless, if *La Bête humaine* and *La Règle du jeu* are grouped together in this way, then *La Bête humaine* can be understood as representing the 'nightmarish' atmosphere surrounding the demise of the Popular Front, the rise of fascism, and the triumph of appeasement, whilst *La Règle du jeu* attempts a more broad-based 'realist' analysis of class difference and ruling-class oppression. Within the terms of such an interpretation, it becomes clear that these two films are acutely complementary to each other, for the character, tone and *mise en scène* of *La Règle du jeu* alone would not have allowed a sufficiently intense articulation of Renoir's sense of the nightmarish qualities of the period; whilst *La Bête humaine* could not have incorporated the panoramic analysis of social class encompassed in *La Règle du jeu*.

However, and despite this argument for the complementary character of the two films, further qualification is required in order to achieve a more insightful understanding of the relationship between the 'nightmarish' qualities of *La Bête humaine* and other, less pessimistic features of the film. With this purpose in mind it should, first of all, be made clear that Zola's source novel is a far more fatalistic work than is Renoir's film. During the period in which he was writing *La Bête humaine*, Zola was undergoing an 'emotional and moral crisis' in his private life, and this seems to have played a role in steering him back to the deterministic temper of his first, most uncompromisingly naturalist works.[30] As a consequence, Zola came to conceive of *La Bête humaine* as a 'dramatic tragic novel . . . something nightmarish like *Thérèse Raquin*'.[31] Whilst developing his novel, Zola was also influenced by the ideas of the Italian criminologist Cesare Lombroso, whose *L'Homme criminel* (1887), with its deterministic account of criminal psychology, reinforced Zola's original consideration that one branch of the Rougon-Macquart family (the Macquarts, including Jacques Lantier in *La Bête humaine*) would be represented as genetically flawed and, as a consequence, doomed to experience an existence marked by alcoholism and violence. Yet another contemporary influence on *La Bête humaine* and, in particular, on Zola's portrayal of the murderous Jacques Lantier, may have been reports in the French press concerning the activities of Jack the Ripper, the homicidal killer who was committing his crimes as *La Bête humaine* was being written.[32]

La Bête humaine also incorporates one of the most fundamental tropes of Zola's naturalism: that of the destructive impact of an inhumane industrial capitalist order on the working classes. For example, a novel such as *L'Assommoir* was written by Zola as a critique of the social conditions and culture which created generations of working-class alcoholics, and Zola's naturalist ideology is premised on the conviction that all the genetic flaws experienced by the unfortunate Macquarts were initially caused by the anti-social conditions generated by capitalism and the Industrial Revolution.[33] The presence of this important, and prevailing, naturalist theme, when combined with other determinist tropes, Zola's own personal circumstances, and the pivotal, 'nightmarish' role of *La Bête humaine* within the final 'trilogy' of the Rougon-Macquart cycle, came together to influence the production of a particularly bleak novel.

Nevertheless, within the general magnitude of Zola's writings, *L'Assommoir* and *La Bête humaine* remain exceptionally bleak works, whilst other novels are far more hopeful concerning the possibility of surmounting genetic and environmentally shaped disadvantage. In such novels, this prospect is articulated chiefly through the proposition of two principal strategies of resistance and deliverance. The first of these takes the shape of the purifying restoration referred to in the previous chapter, in which the individual achieves a degree of enlightenment as a consequence of emerging scathed, but renewed, from some tragic, overwhelming circumstance. However, the second is collectively rather than individually figured, and based on the convictions that emancipation can be achieved through the implementation of progressive social, political and democratic reform, and that scientific rationalism is ultimately capable of overcoming entrenched, reactionary dominion. These convictions ultimately stem from the influence on Zola of Enlightenment values and, in addition to the influence of the deterministic ideas already alluded to in this chapter, Zola, and the naturalist movement in general, were also influenced by such values. It was also this influence which led the naturalist movement to adopt both a pro-scientific, positivist stance, and a strategy of political involvement with the policies, aspirations and activities of the reformist and republican left; and this, in turn, entailed that, in addition to portraying the oppressive impact of capitalism on the working class, Zola's novels also contain more hopeful portrayals of proletarian agency and advancement.

This interacting dialectic between determinism and freedom, and between the depiction of both an exploitative social reality, and progressive possibilities, can be found throughout the Rougon-Macquart *chronique*. However, although this dialectic is skewed decisively in one, deterministic, direction in Zola's *La Bête humaine*, it underlines Renoir's *La Bête humaine* far less and, although it is unquestionably the case that the theme of a repressive bourgeois society remains central to the *La Bête humaine* of 1938, Renoir did not conceive of his film as an exercise in pessimistic 'nightmarish' angst to the extent that Zola did in his novel. As a consequence, in addition to the film's evocation of a corrupt, alienated society, *La Bête humaine* also depicts what has been referred to as 'socialist optimism',[34] and Renoir himself has argued that *La Bête humaine* was a 'revolutionary subject' because it implied that 'individuals living in better conditions would act better'. Furthermore, Renoir also argued that *La Bête humaine* amounted to: 'a refutation of the facile reactionary theory which supports the convention that human beings are immutable, destined to act in a certain way, and that it is useless to attempt anything towards their amelioration . . . [and that] . . . equality is a foolish word'.[35] Renoir's assertions concerning the 'socialist optimism' and 'revolutionary' character of *La Bête humaine* will be explored in greater depth later. However, Renoir's claim that his film amounts to a 'refutation' of determinist thought overstates the case, and it is more accurate to argue that, alongside the more affirmative discourses which Renoir alludes to, the theme of determinism still courses potently throughout his *La Bête humaine*.

That theme is, for example, evident from the very beginning of the film, in the celebrated opening sequences which follow the progress of a train from Paris to Le Havre. This sequence has been interpreted as an 'optimistic celebration of technology',[36] and as a 'magnificent overture [to the] awesome power of full throttle technology'.[37] However, the dominant impression here is more one of an overwhelming, menacing depiction of technology. There is little apparent 'optimism' here in relation to the technological potential of modernity, as embodied in the locomotive, but rather a representation which is constructed as spartan and coarse, and as characterised by brute power. There is a severity here, and a lack of discrimination, which is also reflected in the relationship between the two train drivers, Lantier and Pecqueux. Their behaviour is matter of fact, and professionally framed, whilst the din created by the train inhibits their ability to communicate with each other. Depictions of noise, speed, fire, smoke, power and dynamic movement characterise these sequences. However, rather than expressing an optimistic celebration of technology, these sequences convey a more general sensation of alienation, and this more pessimistic ambience is created primarily by the use of editing and camerawork. For example, montage editing establishes contrast, rather than harmonious continuity, and long shots are frequently followed by close ups, resulting in an effect which is, at the same time, both 'full-throttle' and unsettling. The principal formal theme evoked in these opening sequences is that of movement, but it is movement played out at such a pace as to be menacing and inhuman.

In representing the railway as a worryingly powerful and inhuman phenomenon, capable of destroying those who come into contact with it, Renoir remains close to the spirit of Zola's novel. In the novel, the noise and force of the trains shape the destiny of those forced to live with them. Lantier's childhood love, Flore, lives in a desolate level-crossing station, at La Croix-de-Maufras, which is 'cut in two by the railway', and 'shaken by every passing train'.[38] Later, Flore commits suicide by walking into the path of an on-coming train, and is 'hacked to pieces'.[39] At the finale of the novel Jacques and his fireman are also 'hacked to pieces' by their own train:

> The two men, who for so long had lived together like brothers, fell together and were sucked under the wheels by the very speed and hacked to pieces, locked

together in that frightful embrace. They were found headless and without feet, two bloody trunks still crushing each other to death.[40]

In the final paragraph of the novel Zola also conjures up an image of a runaway train as a destructive, uncontrollable entity, speeding troops to the front, and to the awaiting carnage of war:

> What did the victims matter that the machine destroyed on its way? Wasn't it bound for the future, heedless of spilt blood? With no human hand to guide it through the night, it roared on and on, a blind and deaf beast let loose amid death and destruction, laden with canon-fodder, these soldiers already silly with fatigue, drunk and bawling.[41]

It is this more sceptical vision of technological modernity and the destructive machine which is expressed in the novel, and this vision is encapsulated within those passages of text in which characters appear cut off from others who hurtle by them in trains, at break neck speed. The key material metaphor for this sense of the alienation which modernity brings in its wake is the dilapidated, isolated crossing house at La Croix-de-Maufras, where Flore watches Jacques and his lover Séverine flash by on the train, and where the inhabitants of the house appear to have become deranged as a consequence of their unnatural proximity to the speeding trains.

The pervasive atmosphere of physical and psychological estrangement which characterises the opening section of Renoir's film is also continued in adjacent sequences of *La Bête humaine*. The train breaks down in Le Havre, and Lantier and Pecqueux are stranded; Rouboud is unjustly threatened by an haute bourgeois industrialist (the 'sugar king') over a trivial event, and Séverine is, as a consequence, forced to solicit Grandmorin's assistance and, in doing so, to prostitute herself. There is also a hint that Lantier himself will suffer as a consequence of the train breakdown, as an official warns him that he may have 'to pay' for it. The overriding atmosphere expressed by these sequences is that of a harsh social environment, the Zolaesque predatory social jungle, in which working-class and petit bourgeois characters are arbitrarily placed in positions of jeopardy. Throughout, the same style of editing and photography used in the opening sequences is also employed, including extreme camera angles which emphasise the superhuman character of the huge trains, and an alternating use of long shots, moving camerawork and close ups which unsettles pictorial and narrative continuity.

Thus far, Renoir's film remains true to the deterministic vision of the source novel. However, in addition to this portrayal of an alienated, threatened world, in which the lower orders endure alongside menacing technology on the one hand, and a predatory class of proprietors and managers on the other, another important trope within the film begins to emerge, that of proletarian solidarity as a moral response to the distorted exigencies of life. In the novel, Zola moves from the opening chapter, which introduces the Roubauds, to Chapter 2, which elaborates on Lantier's illness, and covers the murder of Grandmorin. Chapters three and four then focus attention back on the Roubauds and the examining detective, Denizet, who is charged with investigating the crime. Plot development in these chapters adheres closely to the developing story of the murder, its witness, and investigation, and centres on a dialectic between the deception perpetrated by the Roubauds, and Denizet's unfortunate misconstrual of the crime.

However, Renoir achieves something quite different at this point. After the opening sequence he establishes a proletarian social space which does not appear in the novel to anything like the same extent. Lantier and Pecqueux are forced to stay overnight in Le Havre whilst their train is repaired. They stay in railwaymen's lodgings, and unlike other sections of the film, which stress the reality of a competetive struggle for survival or dominance, these sequences emphasise the importance of comradeship and solidarity. Furthermore, the key character to emerge here is Pecqueux, played by Julien Carette, the same actor who would play a similar role (that of the poacher, Marceau) in Renoir's next film, *La Règle du jeu* (1939), and who goes on to play a pivotal role in the opposition between proletariat and *bourgeoisie* which forms one of the central concerns of *La Bête humaine*.

Renoir's depiction of Pecqueux is very different from that found in Zola's novel. In the novel, Pecqueux is an inveterate womaniser and drunk, and often too inebriated to do his job properly. More importantly, Pecqueux, like all the other characters in Zola's novel, is trapped within the same deterministic cycle of transgression, violence and revenge. At the end of the novel a drunken Pecqueux fights with the deceitful and murderous Lantier over Lantier's involvement with Pecqueux's mistress, the sluttish Philomène. The fight ends with both their deaths, as they fall under the wheels of the train. In contrast, in Renoir's film, a sober and concerned Pecqueux first struggles with Lantier in order to stop him committing suicide, then grieves over the latter's corpse. This characterisation of Pecqueux contrasts sharply with the more sordid, recidivist figure portrayed in the novel.

To some extent, Pecqueux can also be distinguished from virtually every other character in both film and novel. In the novel, all the principal characters are trapped within a cycle of predestined violence and instinctual drives. However, whilst this also remains largely true of all the figures within the film, the Pecqueux character, in contrast, is defined in terms of self-jurisdiction. This becomes particularly apparent towards the end of the film, in another scene which depicts a proletarian social environment: this time a railwaymen's ball. This scene, which is a complete invention by Renoir, and does not appear in the novel, uses the contrivance of the *bal du nuit* to emphasise Lantier's alienation and Pecqueux's sense of social affiliation and, through this, to demarcate two distinct realities: one positive, the other negative. As the scene develops, the contrast established between the fatalistic, violent world of Lantier, and the open social realm of the other railwaymen is intensified, and reaches a climax as the songs sung at the ball are played over images of both the murderer Lantier, and his victim Séverine.

One unavoidable consequence of this approach to the portrayal of the Pecqueux character is that Renoir's film presents a far more positive representation of the working class than is evident in Zola's novel. In part, this reflects the interpretation of Zola then prevalent in sections of the French communist and non-communist left during the 1930s, within which Zola was regarded not so much as a dubiously fatalistic naturalist but as a crusading writer who 'in situating his heroes in the working class, in allowing them concerns which, in previous literary works, seemed to be the preserve of *bourgeois* and aristocratic characters', acted as a 'great revolutionary'.[42] It was this conception of Zola, one which associated the novelist with one of the core characteristic features of the nineteenth-century realist lineage, that of the committed portrayal of working-class experience, which Renoir embraced in *La Bête humaine*.

In addition to the influence of this interpretation of Zola as a consequential portrayer of working-class experience, the representations of the *cheminots* which appear in *La Bête humaine* were also influenced by the prevailing political discourses of the day, and Renoir's own involvement with the politics of the Popular Front and the anti-fascist alliance. The policy of the Popular Front, based on the strategic establishment of an anti-fascist alliance between the western European progressive bourgeoisie, proletariat and Communist Party, was adopted at the Seventh Congress of the Communist International in August 1935.[43] In France, Frontism led to the election in 1936 of a government of the Popular Front which included members of the Radical, Socialist and Communist Parties.[44] The principles of the Popular Front also led leftist intellectuals such as Renoir to seek closer connection with both the Communist Party and the organised working class. For example, between 1935 and 1936, Renoir travelled to Moscow in order to talk at public events and, during this period he also became closely involved with the French Communist Party (PCF) and a number of political and radical cultural organisations. One of these was the Groupe Octobre, an eclectic congregation of left-wing intellectuals founded in 1932 by the surrealist poet Jacques Prévert and, between 1936 and 1938, Renoir worked on *Le Crime de Monsieur Lange* and *Une partie de campagne* in association with members of the Groupe. In addition, Renoir also directed the collectively produced *La Vie est à nous* and *Les Bas-fonds* (1936) in association with the PCF, whilst the independently produced *La Marseillaise* (1938) attempted to encapsulate the spirit of the Popular Front.

Although, by 1938, and the premiere of *La Bête humaine*, Renoir had ceased his association with the Groupe Octobre, he nevertheless remained politically engaged, and this engagement can be clearly discerned within *La Bête humaine*. The most evident 'Frontist' aspect of Renoir's film can be identified in the invocation of proletarian fellowship found in *La Bête humaine*: an invocation which embodies one of the cardinal principles of Frontism in respect to the role of the intellectual: that is, that the progressive intellectual should seek to familiarise himself or herself with the needs, aspirations and circumstances of *ouvrière* individuals and institutions. Renoir went to considerable lengths to satisfy this prerogative in *La Bête humaine*. In the spirit of Frontism, he, Gabin, Carette and Ledoux fraternised with the *cheminots* of Le Havre during the production of the film, to the extent that Gabin, in particular, 'a véritablement étudié le métier de mécanicien'.[45] Renoir also consulted both the national railway company, the SNCF, and the railwaymen's union for advice; and Frontist convictions persuaded him to fashion *La Bête humaine* as a film which 'pouvoir reconstituer l'atmosphère exacte des chemins de fer . . . un film vrai, un film que les cheminots ne désavoueront pas'.[46] Although this desire to study and portray *les cheminots* accurately also stemmed from naturalist premises, it was primarily influenced by Frontist idealism, as was made evident by Renoir's rhetorical assertion that 'La profession de cheminots n'est pas une rigolade, c'est un métier. Pour certains, c'est presque un sacredoce'.[47]

The affirmative emphasis expressed in the above quotation colours the depiction of proletarian *cheminot* culture in *La Bête humaine* and, most crucially, also determines the characterisation of the pivotal figure, Pecqueux. At the finale of the film, for example, when Lantier dies, Pecqueux takes charge of the train and, it has been argued, thereby becomes conferred with 'social power'.[48] The final scenes of the film also show something amounting to a new social order emerging, as those who have been irreparably brutalised by the existing order fade from the scene, and the train moves off, 'an epic symbol . . . which always has a future', with Pecqueux at the helm.[49] This, of course, is in stark contrast to the scenario which emerges at the conclusion of Zola's novel.

La Bête humaine is arranged around a dialectic between confirming representations, such as those involving Pecqueux and the *cheminots*, and more deterministic ones; and this dialectic shapes the depiction of all the principal characters in the film. It has been argued that *La Bête humaine* is centrally concerned with a trio of central characters: Lantier, Séverine and Roubaud.[50] However, two distinct triangular formations of characterisation can, in fact, be located within the film, each of which is positioned along the axes of positive and deterministic representation. On the one hand, there are Roubaud, Séverine and Jacques, three figures who have been irredeemably damaged by an oppressive bourgeois culture. On the other hand, there are Flore, Pecqueux and Cabuche. The representation of these latter three in Renoir's film differs greatly from their portrayal in Zola's original novel. In the novel, Flore is depicted as an obsessive, homicidal giant of a woman, whilst, in the film, and played by the girlish Blanchette Brunoy, she is depicted as loyal, loving and responsive. Similarly, whereas, in the novel, Cabuche is represented as a simpleton and a 'hulking creature',[51] in the film, he is depicted as free of the duplicity exhibited by others, and as possessing a 'blameless affection for nature'.[52] As we have already seen, Pecqueux is also portrayed very differently in the film, and not at all as the novel's 'lunatic crazy with drink and jealousy'.[53] In addition, however, Pecqueux can also be differentiated from both Flore and Cabuche in that, whilst the latter two remain trapped, and punished, by the alienating world within which they find themselves, Pecqueux is able to transcend such alienation.

Despite these more affirmative representations of Flore, Cabuche and Pecqueux, however and, as has been argued, *La Bête humaine* also contains more pessimistic portrayals, which serve to situate the film within the naturalist canon. The expressionist/realist character of the film also betrays the influence of a German expressionist sensibility. To some extent, this was influenced by the film's chief cinematographer, the German émigré cameraman Kurt Courant. Courant was largely responsible for the chiaroscuro lighting, extreme camera angles and virtuoso camerawork found in *La Bête humaine*: formal techniques which, when combined with an expressionist sensibility, give the depiction of modernity in the film such an equivocal character. The opening section of *La Bête humaine*, in particular, also discloses another feature found in French films of the period photographed by German émigé cinematographers such as Courant, Eugene Shüfftan and Rudolph Maté: a tendency to focus on 'objects and formal patternings', rather than the actor, and to show 'human beings as themselves no more than objects, driven by inexorable forces'.[54] The absorption of Lantier and Pecqueux into the highly composed, expressionistic images of the opening section of *La Bête humaine* is a good illustration of this, but the sense of entrapment, and of individuals 'driven by inexorable forces' is evident elsewhere in the film, and also reinforces Zola's initial, deterministic vision.

One of the reasons often advanced to account for Renoir's deviation from the realism of *La Vie est à nous*, *Le Crime de Monsieur Lange*, *Les Bas-fonds*, *La Grande Illusion*, *La Marseillaise* and *La Règle du jeu* to the naturalism of *La Bête humaine* is that the making of the film coincided with a period of political setbacks for the left in France, and that it was this which led Renoir from progressive optimism to the more pessimistic alignment of *La Bête humaine*. There is some evidence to support this thesis. *La Bête humaine* was shot during August and September 1938, and the government of the Popular Front collapsed in October. This failure, allied to the rise of increasing political confrontation within France, the decline of the left, a deteriorating international situation and the appeasement of fascism by the post-Popular-Front Daladier government, could have provided a context for a turn to the pessimistic vision apparent in *La Bête humaine.*

The argument has also been made that *La Bête humaine* should be distinguished from Renoir's other films of the mid- to late 1930s because its context of production was quite different. Consequently, *La Bête humaine* has been characterised as an untypically 'commercial' venture, influenced by, amongst other factors, the money-making imperatives of the film's producers, Renoir's financial needs, the influence of poetic realism and the established star persona of its leading actor, Jean Gabin. Again, there is some evidence to support this argument. The origins of *La Bête humaine* can be traced back to a proposed film about the drama of the railways developed by the Hakim brothers, commercial producers of the time. Initially, the Hakims had commissioned Jean Grémillon to make the film. However, they were unhappy with the treatment proposed by Grémillon, and turned, instead, to Renoir.[55] It was the Hakim brothers and Gabin (who had been assigned to the shelved Grémillon film), rather than Renoir, who proposed an adaptation of Zola's novel, and this, and the fact that Renoir accepted the commission at the last minute, seems to support the argument that he embarked on the project for largely pragmatic, rather than aesthetic or political reasons.

In addition to the above, the argument has also been put that *La Bête humaine* was substantially developed as it was in order to foreground the figure of Gabin, who then became the 'linchpin of the film'.[56] It is true that, in contrast to Zola's novel, which begins with Rouboud, Renoir's film begins with Lantier and Pecqeaux and, most prominently, with the film's chief star, Gabin. It is also the case that, to some extent, *La Bête humaine* was conceived as a vehicle for Gabin and, to a lesser extent, Simone Simon, Fernand Ledoux and Julien Carette. Gabin's persona of the laconic, terse, proletarian outsider had already been established over a number of films during the 1930s, including Jean Duvivier's *Pépé le moko* (1937), Grémillon's *Gueule d'amour* (1937) and Renoir's *La Grande Illusion* (1937) and, by 1938, he had emerged as one of the leading *monstres sacrés* (leading actors with distinct, generic profiles and formalised characteristics) of the French cinema.[57] To some extent, Gabin's portrayal of Lantier in *La Bête humaine* is influenced by his already established screen persona of the 'archetypal proletarian hero',[58] and this inevitably mediates any attempt on Gabin's part to embody the authentic naturalist vision of either Renoir or Zola. It could be argued, therefore, that, in beginning the film with Gabin–Lantier, rather than with the Roubaud–Séverine drama, Renoir was merely conforming to existing generic expectations about the role and importance of such a prominent *monstre sacré* as Gabin.

There are, therefore, three principal arguments which have been advanced to explain the 'peculiarity' of *La Bête humaine* in relation to Renoir's other films of the period. These are (1) that, unlike Renoir's other films of the period,

La Bête humaine reflects the pervasive pessimism of the period in which it was produced; (2) that it was made for primarily commercial, rather than aesthetic or political reasons; and (3) that it was developed as it was in order to foreground the established star profile of Gabin. However, all three of these conjectures require considerable qualification. For example, Renoir himself strongly denied that *La Bête humaine* was a pessimistic film, and angrily insisted that it should not be grouped alongside the poetic realism of filmmakers such as Marcel Carné.[59] Although *La Bête humaine* appeared in the same year, and just after, Carné's *Quai des brumes*, Renoir believed that the two films were very different from each other, and that, in contradistinction to the Romantic fatalism of *Quai des brumes*, *La Bête humaine* deployed both a thoughtful critique of bourgeois oppression and a portrayal of *les cheminots* which accorded with the ideals of the Popular Front.[60] There is also little evidence to suggest that Renoir's political committment and activity had diminished during the period that he was making *La Bête humaine* and, whilst the film was being edited, he was, for example, writing in the communist journal *Ce Soir*, strongly criticising the Munich agreement, and attacking French complicity with appeasement.[61]

The second surmise concerning the peculiarity of *La Bête humaine* – that the film's atypical adoption of a naturalist style can be traced back to its origins as a 'commercial project' – also requires qualification. It should, for example, be borne in mind that before Renoir became involved with the Groupe Octobre he had made a number of films in a naturalist vein. This strain of naturalist film-making was important to Renoir, and was, in fact, only interrupted during one year, 1937. If the earlier argument that *La Bête humaine* and *La Régle du jeu* form a complementary pair is also borne in mind, then the conjecture that *La Bête humaine* is an untypical, anachronistic, film appears unfounded. In fact, the only respect in which *La Bête humaine* can convincingly be said to differ from Renoir's other films of the period concerns aspects of its visual style and, as has already been made clear, these were influenced by an expressionist sensibility derived primarily from the film's cinematographer, Kurt Courant.

The third contention for the atypicality of *La Bête humaine* to be considered here, one which centres on the salience of Gabin's sway over the film, is as problematic as the previous two, in that Gabin's portrayal of Lantier in *La Bête humaine* does not conform to a by then virtually already established figure of the prototypical Gabin persona, as exemplified in films such as *Le Quai des brumes* and *Hôtel du nord* (1938). For example, in *La Bête humaine*, Gabin's Lantier is far more ambiguously drawn than is the case with the more unequivocally romanticised figure of the deserting soldier, Jean, in *Le Quai des brumes* and, in Renoir's film, Gabin plays a figure who retains the profound inadequacies and lack of insight which characterises Zola's original interpretation. Gabin's performance in *La Bête humaine* is, therefore, out of character with his established star image. Moreover, the evidence makes it clear that Gabin worked extremely hard to achieve an effective realism of performance in *La Bête humaine*, leading François Truffaut, amongst others, to claim that *La Bête humaine* is unquestionably Gabin's best film.[62] All this suggests that *La Bête humaine* cannot be considered as, in any substantive sense, a Gabin 'vehicle'.

The argument that *La Bête humaine* cannot be considered primarily as a star vehicle is also reinforced by the fact that, in addition to Gabin, all the other principal actors in the film play out of character. For example, Ledoux normally played parts associated with a more 'stentorian' tradition of acting, whilst Simone Simon was better known for her roles in farces, and had not played anything like the Séverine character before. Like Ledoux, Simon was played against type as part of a strategy of 'destroying clichés'[63] and enhancing the realism of the film. Julien Carette, who, like Gabin, came from the vaudeville stage, also had his own established profile by 1938 and, like Gabin, normally played working-class characters. However, and in distinction to Gabin's existential loner, Carette tended to play the down-to-earth rogue, a role which he brought to bear on his performances of Pecqueux in *La Bête humaine* and of the poacher, Marcel, in *La Règle du jeu* (1939). However, in *La Bête humaine*, Carette transcends his generic profile even more so than in *La Règle du jeu* and, as a consequence, achieves a performance of far greater realism.

Conclusions

In the previous chapter a number of distinctions were made between different forms of nineteenth-century realism and a specific tradition of critical realism. The origins of that tradition were also identified in a number of historical sources, but, most significantly, in a desire to develop a less formulaic and regulated form of art following the official appropriation of, first, the neoclassical heritage and, then, the emergent realist tradition itself. This imperative led the critical realist tradition to adopt a set of aesthetic conventions which emphasised spontaneity, authenticity, and a more direct and less mediated experience of the subject or object to be represented. Critical realism rejected the overly formulaic or codified, and was characterised by narrative fragmentation, impressionistic depiction and dislocation. In contradistinction to what was referred to as 'photographic realism', critical realism foregrounded the use of form. Critical realism also developed as an oppositional, and explicitly anti-bourgeois movement. However, critical realism was not, typically, an explicitly or overtly political form of art. Instead, critical realism depicted the alienating consequences of a bourgeois-dominated modernity. Critical realism also focused on the portrayal of working-class and lower-class experience, and perhaps the most important feature of the realist pictorial or literary account lay in its ability to transcend and evade ideological positioning through saturating the art work with the rich, raw detail of an alternative reality. This is what links a painting such as *The Stonebreakers*, a novel such as *L'Assommoir* and a twentieth-century film such as *Toni*. These works were also made against the context of great politically tragic events, and this also links a novel such as *La Bête humaine* with films such as *La Bête humaine* and *La Règle du jeu*.

What are the affiliations between *La Bête humaine* and the model of critical realism elaborated previously? There are some obvious parallels which can be briefly accounted for: the focus on proletarian culture, the anti-bourgeois stance, the emphasis on descriptive detail, the reliance on the nineteenth-century realist model, the employment of a form of symbolism which stems from the naturalist tradition, the use of depictions of both determinism and an account of agency which can be associated with naturalism, the foregrounding of aesthetic form, the urge for authenticity of transcription and expression, a certain immediacy of experience and representation, a relationship to an external political context, and a focus on the portrayal of alienation, rather than more openly political forms of depiction. All of these characteristic features link *La Bête humaine* to the critical realist tradition. What differentiates the film from that tradition appears less significant than these associations, and such difference can, perhaps, be located in a visual style which owes more to German expressionism than French realism; and in the presence of an affirmative set of 'Frontist' representations which goes beyond the more typically naturalist concern with the portrayal of a pessimistic context.

In addition to the above, however, there is also a further sense in which *La Bête humaine* can be both differentiated from and related to the realist tradition. There is a respect in which *La Bête humaine* can be associated with the neo-classical culture from which realism originally arose. For example the portrayal of the Lantier figure in Renoir's *La Bête humaine* is very different from that found in Zola's novel, and the source of that distinction is not to be located in either Gabin's 'star profile' or even in Renoir's or Gabin's Frontist enthusiasms. Renoir has suggested that Zola'a *La Bête humaine*: 'reaches back to the great works of Greek tragedy . . . Jacques Lantier interests us as much as Oedipus Rex. This railway mechanic trails behind him an atmosphere as heavy as that of some member of the house of Atreus.'[64] But this characterisation of the novel is highly debatable. For example, in the novel, Lantier is depicted both as a tragic figure 'pursued by destiny'[65] and as a far from praiseworthy individual who, after his killing of Séverine, returns to work as normal, engages in an affair with Pecqueux's mistress, and is content to let Roubaud and the entirely innocent Cabuche go to prison for his crimes. However, in Renoir's film Lantier does become transformed into a genuinely tragic character, indeed pursued by destiny to destroy and be destroyed, but also selfless, honourable and anything but manipulative. At the film's finale, Lantier's suicide also appears to constitute a kind of sacrifice, which leaves the way open for Pecqueux and those he represents to mark the beginning of a new, more hopeful age. This characterisation both couples Renoir's portrayal of Lantier to the thematic preoccupations of the 'true style' and also conforms to one of the founding principles of realism: the raising of lower-class characters up to a sphere of representation previously reserved for the aristocratic and polite strata of society.

In addition to the characterisation of Lantier, *La Bête humaine* can be linked also to the classical and neo-classical traditions through its evocation of the tragic. Renoir has claimed that the theme of 'destiny' in his film plays the same role as in classical Greek drama: it is one of the 'grands sujets' which enables a film to transcend its usual limitations. Here, the dark complex character of destiny allowed Renoir to penetrate what he referred to as the 'contingencies matérieles' of his material, and to express something more profound. Renoir also refers to 'tapping into' some force of tragedy, which then takes on its own momentum, and leads the film-maker to express matters which were initially beyond his intention: 'A mon avis, c'est ce qu'il y a de plus passionnant en litérature et en art, cette force indescriptible qui nous entraine vers des directions, et on ne peut pas lutter. J'aime beaucoup ça.[66] Renoir believes that the dark force of the 'grands sujets' of destiny, linked to the idea of the relationship between sex, love and crime, lies at the heart of *La Bête humaine*. This force creates a 'espèce de délire': a psychological ambience which allows the film to evoke the dark subject matter of the Greek tragedy and, for Renoir, what was particularly important to him about *La Bête humaine* was that it allowed him to tap into this archaic, tragic energy.

La Bête humaine also conforms closely to one of the most important features of the critical realist/naturalist tradition in its employment of an indeterminate aesthetic style. The novel itself was impressionistic in style, 'without sharp outlines and shapes but with wonderful effects of light and shade, beams of light piercing the shadows, flickering lamps, often full of emotional or moral symbolism'. [67] In addition to this descriptive impressionism, Zola's novel also has an episodic structure, and a tendency to cut rapidly from scene to scene. All of these aspects are further accentuated in Renoir's film. In a close analysis of *La Bête humaine*, Michele Lagny has argued that the film contains a number of 'sequences with a weak or indeterminate chronological relationship'[68] and 'internal breaks in the sequential continuities', as well as 'episodic structures' and 'fragmentation effects'.[69] Lagny believes that the indeterminate narrative of *La Bête humaine* functions both to accentuate the tragic dimension of the film and, at the same time, to enable a degree of critical spectatorship to take place:

> The circularity of the film's course, its unwillingness to adopt a coherent, linear chronology, and the play of substitutions produce a condensed narrative which is

riven with cracks, with *fêlures* that let the tragic flood in, but which also maintain possible openings on the realm of the social.[70]

If, whilst providing the spectator with a sumptuous and alluring vision of a dark spirit, the indeterminate structure of *La Bête humaine* also cuts the spectator off from total immersion in that spirit, then the film does, as Lagny suggests, 'offer . . . [its spectators] . . . the shelter which makes a critical position possible'.[71] In this sense, it can also be argued that the levels of incoherence present within *La Bête humaine* work to activate the critical faculties of the spectator, and this, combined with the film's concern with the tragic, allows us to begin to imagine how *La Bête humaine* could be conceived of as a 'weapon against Hitler', as Renoir claimed. Although *La Bête humaine* focuses on a disturbing and morally corrupt social order, that social order could stand as a metaphor, not only for the historical period portrayed by Zola but also for both the spirit of German fascism, and the pro-fascist and pro-appeasement forces which were at large within France whilst Renoir was making *La Bête humaine*. This means that *La Bête humaine* carries out essentially the same kind of intellectual project played out in *La Règle du jeu*, even though the tone of portrayal adopted in *La Bête humaine* is far more intense than the critique of *haute bourgeoisie* triviality and insularity mobilised in *La Règle du Jeu*.

Writing in 1938, Renoir also rejected the charge made by a contemporary interviewer that *La Bête humaine* could be distinguished from *La Marseillaise*, arguing that both these films, and *La Vie est à nous*, were part of one cycle, 'au même cycle'.[72] That cycle, according to Renoir, was primarily motivated by the need to 'combattre' 'l'idée d'Hitler'.[73] Renoir believed that Zola was one of the great combattants de l'idée de liberté' and, so, felt that his novels would furnish an appropriate weapon in the fight against the idea of Hitler. Rather than focusing specifically on the overtly political, therefore, like Renoir's two previous films, *La Bête humaine* should be considered as a naturalist film which focuses on emergent evil and present alienation, and this focus is reinforced by the film's utilisation of both determinist discourses and a fatalism drawn from classical sources. However, this focus is mediated by the inclusion of a concept of tragic agency derived from Zola, the presence of affirmative 'Frontist' elements and, at the level of form, an indeterminate, fractured narrative and visual structure which refuses to allow the spectator to be seduced by the film's arresting stylistic characteristics and thematic motifs.

Notes

1 Furst, Lilian R., and Skrine, Peter N., *Naturalism: The Critical Idiom* (London: Methuen & Co. Ltd, 1971), p. 31.

2 Ricciotto Canudo, 'Naissance d'un sixième art' (1911), in Abel, Richard, *French Film theory and Criticism: A History/Anthology 1907–1939* (vol. 1) (Princeton: Princeton University Press, 1988), p. 60.
3 Louis Haugmard, 'L'Esthetique du cinématographie' (1913), in Abel (1982), p. 82.
4 Green, Fredrick C., *French Novelists From the Revolution to Proust* (New York: Frederick Ungar Publishing Co., 1964), pp. 321–2.
5 Abel, Richard, *French Cinema: The First Wave 1915–1929* (Princeton: Princeton University Press, 1984), p. 123.
6 Sadoul, Georges, *Histoire générale du cinéma II Les Pionniers du cinéma (de Méliès à Pathé) 1879–1909* (Paris: Les éditions Denoël, 1973–7), p. 202.
7 Williams, Alan, *Republic of Images: A History of French Film-making* (Cambridge, MA, and London: Harvard University Press, 1992), p. 45.
8 Abel (1984), p. 95.
9 Williams, p. 114.
10 Abel (1984), p. 98.
11 Ibid., p. 114.
12 Ibid., p. 118.
13 Ibid., p. 96.
14 Ibid., p. 97.
15 Abel, Richard, *French Film Theory and Criticism: A History/Anthology 1907–1939*, vol. 2 (Princeton: Princeton University Press, 1988), p. 124.
16 Martin, John W., *The Golden Age of French Cinema 1929–1939* (Boston: Twayne, 1983), p. 26.
17 Andrew, Dudley J., *Mists of Regret: Culture and Sensibility in Classic French Film* (Princeton: Princeton University Press, 1995), pp. 99–112.
18 Ibid., p. 199.
19 Ibid., p. 301.
20 Ibid., p. 104.
21 Faulkner, Christopher, *The Social Cinema of Jean Renoir* (Princeton: Princeton University Press, 1986), p. 43.
22 Ibid., p. 45.
23 Ibid., p. 46.
24 Crisp, Colin, *The Classic French Cinema, 1930–1960* (Bloomington: Indiana University Press, 1993), p. 17.
25 Faulkner, p. 55.
26 Braudy, Leo, *Jean Renoir, The World of His Films* (New York and Oxford: Columbia University Press, 1989), p. 208.
27 Faulkner, p. 101.
28 Tancock, Leonard, 'Introduction', in Zola, Emile, *La Bête humaine* (Harmondsworth: Penguin Books, 1977), p. 7.
29 Becker, George J., *Master European Realists of the Nineteenth Century* (New York: Frederick Ungar Publishing Co., 1982), p. 98.
30 Hemmings, FWJ., *Emile Zola* (Oxford: Clarendon Press, 1966), p. 248.
31 Becker, p. 101.

32 Pauly, Rebecca M., *The Transparent Illusion: Image and Ideology in French Text and Film* (New York: Peter Lang Publishing, Inc., 1993), p. 184.

33 Magraw, Roger, *France 1815–1914: The Bourgeois Century* (Oxford: Fontana, 1983), p. 204.

34 Lagny, Michele, 'The Fleeting Gaze: Jean Renoir's *La Bête humaine* (1938)', in Hayward, Susan, and Vincendeau, Ginette (eds), *French Film: Texts and Contexts* (London and New York: Routledge, 2000), p. 58, quoting Deleuze, Gilles, 'Zola et la fêlure' in Zola, Emile, *La Bête humaine* (Paris: Gallimard, 1977), p. 23.

35 Faulkner, p. 102 quoting Renoir, Jean, writing in *Les Cahiers de la Jeunesse*, 15 December 1938.

36 O'Shaughnessy, Martin, *Jean Renoir* (Manchester: Manchester University Press, 1988), p. 142.

37 Andrew, p. 307.

38 Zola, Emile, *La Bête humaine* (Harmondsworth: Penguin, 1977), p. 49.

39 Ibid., p. 307.

40 Ibid., p. 365.

41 Ibid., p. 366.

42 Lagny, in Hayward and Vincendeau, p. 46.

43 Nettl, J. P., *The Soviet Achievement* (London: Thames and Hudson, 1967), p. 154.

44 McMillan, James, F., *Twentieth-Century France: Politics and Society 1898–1991* (London and New York: Edward Arnold, 1992), p. 111.

45 *Les Cahiers de la Jeunesse*, no.17, 15 December 1938, reprinted in *La Revue du Cinéma, Image et Son*, no.315 (March 1977), p. 26.

46 Ibid.

47 Ibid., p. 27.

48 Lagny, p. 58.

49 Ibid.

50 Braudy, p. 58.

51 Zola, Emile, *La Bête humaine* (Harmondsworth: Penguin, 1977), p. 318.

52 Andrew, p. 309.

53 Zola, Emile, *La Bête humaine* (Harmondsworth: Penguin, 1977), p. 365.

54 Crisp, p. 172.

55 Faulkner, p. 103.

56 Lagny, in Hayward and Vincendeau, p. 44.

57 Crisp, p. 360.

58 Williams, p. 185.

59 Faulkner, p. 102.

60 Ibid.

61 Faulkner, p. 104.

62 Sesonske, Alexander, *Jean Renoir: The French Films, 1924–1939* (Cambridge, MA: Harvard University Press, 1980), p. 364.

63 Ibid., p. 353.

64 Ibid., p. 356.

65 Tancock, in Zola, Emile, *La Bête humaine* (Harmondsworth: Penguin, 1977), p. 14.

66 Ciment, Michel, 'Entretien avec Jean Renoir, sur *La Bête humaine*', *Positif*, no. 173 (1975), p. 20.
67 Tancock, in Zola, Emile, *La Bête humaine* (Harmondsworth: Penguin, 1977), pp. 15–16.
68 Lagny, in Hayward and Vincendeau, p. 52.
69 Ibid., p. 53.
70 Ibid., p. 55.
71 Ibid., p. 57.
72 Ciment, p. 16.
73 Ibid.

3

'The adequate presentation of the complete human personality', Lukács and the nineteenth-century realist tradition

Generally speaking, the world-wide interest in Marxist literary theory is ultimately an interest in the concept of realism.[1]

Lukács' aesthetic doctrine . . . is a perfect theoretical justification of Stalin's cultural policy. Lukács in fact forged the conceptual instruments of cultural despotism.[2]

This chapter will explore the model of aesthetic realism developed by the Hungarian theorist György (Georg) Lukács (1885–1971), and will then proceed to set out the parameters of a Lukácsian theory of cinematic realism. Lukács' literary and philosophical writings constitute perhaps the most important attempt to establish a comprehensive Marxist theory of aesthetic representation, and his theory of literary realism has influenced a wide range of intellectuals and practitioners. That theory has been particularly consequential within the Soviet Union and eastern Europe where, despite Lukács' often troubled relationship with the communist establishment, it has mentored the development of literary theory and practice, and established a troupe of intellectual disciples such as Agnes Heller, Ferenc Fehér, György Márkus and Mihály Vajda. In addition to this, Lukács' ideas were also influential within the western European Marxist and communist left, from the 1920s onwards, and informed the work of figures such as Antonio Gramsci, Lucian Goldmann, Ernst Bloch, members of the Frankfurt School and many others. Nevertheless, and despite this degree of influence, Lukács' theory of realism has also been the subject of considerable criticism, and this criticism must be fully taken into account before any attempt is made to apply Lukácsian ideas to the formation of a model of cinematic realism.

One of the most trenchant criticisms levelled against Lukács is that his model of realism is umbilically associated with a particular form of literature – the nineteenth century realist novel – and that, as a consequence of this concentrated focus, his work dismisses some of the most vital artistic movements of the nineteenth and twentieth centuries, including naturalism, and most forms of modernism. Lukács' disavowal of Zolaesque naturalism proved relatively uncontroversial, given the extent to which the naturalist tradition had fallen out of favour by the 1930s. However, his unambiguous rejection of modernism brought his theory of realism into considerable disrepute in the west, against a context of the emergence of a critical tradition which embraced modernism as a potentially progressive form of artistic intervention. This disfavour encompassed the accusations of 'formalism' directed against Lukács' by Brecht and Bloch in the 1930s, and the charges of essentialism and authoritarianism levelled against his work from within the post-structuralist, political-modernist and anti-realist tradition which emerged in Europe from the late 1960s. Lukács consistent rejection of modernism also alienated Marxist writers on aesthetics such as Ernst Fischer and Roger Gaurady, and even disciples and students such as Fehér, Heller, Márkus and Vajda eventually felt obliged to distance themselves from a feature of Lukács' thought which 'some of us initially shared and dogmatically defended, whilst others never accepted it, but which all of us have abandoned in the last five years'.[3] The conviction that Lukács' model of critical realism is both organically and inflexibly wedded to the nineteenth-century realist tradition, and incompatible with modernism, has led many to dismiss his thought and contribution, either in part or in whole. However, and as this chapter will attempt to show, an analysis of the core premises which underlie Lukács' theoretical model throws this conviction into some degree of question, and leaves open the possibility that a modernist model of Lukácsian realism can be legitimately theorised.

In addition to the charge of aesthetic essentialism and anti-modernist bias, a second major accusation levelled against Lukács concerns his alleged association with Stalinism and Soviet totalitarianism. This accusation, summed up in Kolakowski's assertion that Lukács helped forge 'the conceptual instruments of cultural despotism', and Isaac Deutscher's claim that Lukács was the 'advocate *sui generis* of the Stalin era', has been reiterated by many commentators, from the 1930s onwards.[4] However, in fact, Lukács' relationship to the Soviet dictatorship was a highly ambivalent and troubled one. Inspired by the October Revolution, Lukács joined the Hungarian Communist Party in 1918, and immediately immersed himself in intense revolutionary activism.[5] In 1919 he was made Minister for Education and Culture during the period of the short-lived Hungarian Soviet Republic (March–August 1919). When the Republic fell to counter-revolution Lukács went into exile, under sentence of death, in Austria, Germany and Russia, and returned to Hungary only after the country had become absorbed into the Soviet orbit following the conclusion of the Second World War. After 1945 he again became actively involved in political and cultural matters within Hungary. However, in 1949 his ideas were severely criticised by communist opponents within Hungary, and he was again forced to depart the political stage. When the Hungarian Revolution broke out on 23 October 1956, Lukács was made Minister of Culture in Imre Nagy's reformist government. However, after the Soviet invasion of 4 November Lukács was deported to Romania, and expelled from the Communist Party. Between 1957, when he was allowed to return to Budapest (at the age of seventy-two), and his death in 1971, Lukács then accommodated himself to the constraints of Soviet orthodoxy and dogma and, thereafter, played only a minor role in national political affairs.

Although Lukács has been criticised for the extent to which he associated himself with official communism, the history outlined above makes it clear that his relationship with the communist establishment was frequently turbulent and disputatious. This was primarily a consequence of the fact that, throughout the bulk of his career, he invariably championed a position on cultural politics which was to the liberal left of official policy. During and shortly after the period of the Hungarian Soviet Republic, Lukács associated himself with 'ultraleft' elements within the Third International and, within the pages of the journal *Communist*, advocated what he later described as a revolutionary 'messianic sectarianism', and a 'total break with every institution and mode of life stemming from the bourgeois world'.[6] However, this position, combined with a left-Trotskyist insistence on fanning the flames of international revolution, contradicted the official policy of consolidating the revolution within the Soviet Union. Lenin's 1920 pamphlet *Left-Wing Communism: An Infantile Disorder* was directed at leftists such as Lukács and, within Hungary, Lukács came under severe pressure also from more conservative elements, including the leader of the Hungarian Communist Party, Béla Kun. In 1928 Lukács published the *Blum Theses*, which, in the internationalist spirit of *Communist*, advocated a popular frontist position of alliance with progressive leftist groups in the west. However, this contradicted the Stalinist policy of consolidating 'socialism within one country', which had first appeared in 1924 as a counterpoint to Trotsky's theory of permanent revolution and which, by 1928, had become unchallengeable official doctrine. As a consequence, the *Blum Theses* were vigorously condemned by the Cominterm – a condemnation which also reinforced the earlier renunciation of Lukács most controversial and important book, *History and Class Consciousness* (1922), which had been denounced as 'revisionist' by the Cominterm in 1924, on account of its indebtedness to Hegel. This context of criticism eventually told on Lukács (or persuaded him), to the point where, in 1933, he himself disowned *History and Class Consciousness* as excessively 'idealist'.[7]

After 1930, following the criticism of the *Blum Theses* and *History and Class Consciousness*, Lukács was forced out of the political arena, and wrote mainly on literary criticism. Between 1930 and 1933 he played an important role in developing an aesthetic literary theory based on Marxist premises, and emerged as one of the most influential Marxist cultural theorists of the period. After 1934, however, Lukács' period of intellectual pre-eminence came to an abrupt end, when his theory of critical realism – the literary expression of the political views expressed in the *Blum Theses* – was displaced by the doctrine of socialist realism advocated by Maxim Gorky, Alexandrovitch Zhdanov and others. Zhdanov's congressional speech to the First Soviet Writers Congress in Moscow, in August 1934, entitled 'Soviet Literature: The Richest in Ideas, the Most Advanced Literature', marked the end of Lukács' ascendancy, and the inauguration of a cultural dictatorship which reflected the 'progressive consolidation of Stalin's powers'. [8]

Rather than a 'Stalinist literary critic', Lukács was always opposed to Stalin's attempt to turn culture into a mere tool of propaganda, and frequently criticised what he referred to as the 'sectarian schematism of the Stalinist period'.[9] Lukács first revealed himself as a critic of Stalinist orthodoxy, and as a liberal socialist reformer, during the 1919–34 period. During this period he aspired to 'humanise Stalinism at the cultural level', and 'build his own personal Weimar – a cultural island among power relations unambiguously hostile to any democratic culture'.[10] During the later period of the anti-fascist popular front, between 1934 and 1939, Lukács' ideas on critical realism and alliance with the progressive bourgeois order again became fashionable, and his influence grew. However, after his return to Hungary in 1945, his position, as expressed in works such as *Literature and Democracy* and *For a New Hungarian Culture*, both of which recalled the perspectives of the *Blum Theses*, came under severe attack from Stalinist ideologues within Hungary whose criticism reflected the new sectarian climate of the Cold War. Following the death of Stalin in 1953, and the rise to power of Nikita Khrushchev, the so-called 'thaw' period of 1953–8 ushered in a period of relative liberalism within the communist world, and Lukács found himself once again able to speak out again about the extent to which – in his view – Stalinist dogma had misrepresented Marxist doctrines.[11] Works such as *The Meaning of Contemporary Realism* (1957), with its criticism of socialist realism, reflect the enhanced liberalism of the times. After the rise to power of Brezhnev in 1964, however, that period of liberalism again came to an end and, following this, and to the chagrin of western and eastern intellectuals who looked to him to provide an opposition to the continued repression of intellectual freedom within the Soviet block, Lukács increasingly accommodated himself to official Party policy. This was the latest, and last, of Lukács' withdrawals from the critical public sphere, and the two most important works which followed – *The Specificity of the Aesthetic* (1963) and *The Ontology of Social Existence* (1970) – complied more fully with orthodox communist tenets.

Early thought: revolution and *Bildungsroman*

Lukács converted to Bolshevism in 1918, at the relatively mature age of thirty-four. This, and the fact that he had published a number of influential works prior to his turn to Bolshevism, has prompted some to suggest that a distinction can be made between Lukács' thought and work prior to 1918, and thereafter.[12] However, as with the speculative distinction which has been drawn between the 'early' and 'late' work of Siegfried Kracauer, this suggestion of a sharp rupture in Lukács' work is significantly overstated. Although it is true that, prior to 1918, it was Hegel, classical Greek philosophy, Kierkegaard and Nietzsche, rather than Marxism, which influenced his ideas the most, Lukács was familiar with Marxist theory, and his *The History of the Development of Modern Drama* (1906) and *Remarks on the Theory of Literary History* (1909) both draw on aspects of Marxist historical materialism. In addition, far from differing substantially from his post-1918 writings, both these works, together with *Soul and Form* (1910), *Theory of the Novel* (1916) and the unpublished 'Heidelberg Manuscripts on Aesthetics' (1912–18), incorporate key themes which Lukács would continue to address throughout the remainder of his career, up to and including the appearance of *The Specificity of the Aesthetic.*

One of these themes centred on the conviction that the possibility of achieving an ethical and harmonious social order had been profoundly undermined by the advance of bourgeois capitalist society. Lukács was particularly influenced in this by Ferdinand Tönnes's topical *Community and Society* (1887), which argued that bourgeois individualist mores had undermined community, and put in place a more impersonal, less fulfilling social order.[13] Prior to 1918 Lukács had been influenced also by a form of romantic anticapitalism then pervasive in eastern European intellectual circles, which sought the inauguration of a new millennium based on non-bourgeois and pre-bourgeois social and cultural values, but which was, at the same time, also deeply pessimistic about the prospects of achieving such a utopian outcome.[14]. This quixotic, pessimistic vision found expression in both *Soul and Form* and *Theory of the Novel*, and Lukács described himself as being in a 'general state of despair' over the state of the world when he wrote the latter work.[15] The contemporary context which induced that sense of despair encompassed the collapse of the Austro-Hungarian Empire, the humanitarian carnage of the First World War, and the potentially bleak prospects confronting a defeated post war central and eastern Europe. As the War drew to a close, Lukács, like others on the Hungarian left, feared that a victory by *either* the *Entente* or the Central Powers would herald the subjugation of progressive forces in central and eastern Europe, and the concomitant collapse of autonomous culture in the region. Far from viewing the cessation of hostilities as offering an opportunity for progressive reform, therefore (as was the case with many western intellectuals), Lukács considered the victorious 'Western civilization'[16] which emerged after 1918 as a potential threat to the attempt to develop a more authentic, progressive Hungarian culture, which, he believed, had been inaugurated around 1900, with the revival of folklorist and other indigenous traditions.[17]

Nevertheless, although *Soul and Form* and *Theory of the Novel* are pervaded by a sense of diffuse metaphysical angst, both works also contain pronounced traces of the aspirations which characterised the utopian anti-capitalist discourses of the period. For Lukács, one source of more positive possibilities lay in the Nietzschean intellectual model of the 'Superman': the extraordinary individual standing outside of pedestrian society, and viewing it from a transcendent position. This iconic model enabled Lukács, at least in part, to transmute his own then deeply perceived sense of intellectual and cultural alienation into a Nietzschean sense of mission to forge a new dispensation, and this possibility finds expression, alongside more pessimistic pronouncements, in his works of the period.[18] Lukács also believed that another source of more positive possibilities for overcoming capitalist alienation was offered by the aesthetic model of the Eighteenth-century *Bildungsroman*, in which a portrayal of the individual literary character as reflexively self-aware, and as encapsulating both concrete particularity and social typicality, allowed a more coherent portrayal of social reality to emerge. So, for example, Lukács described Goethe's *Wilhelm Meister's Apprenticeship* (1775–6) as 'a problematic but partially successful attempt, under *bourgeois* conditions, to represent personal interiority and outer social reality as reconcilable through the intervention of active men'.[19] Although Goethe was unable to portray a fully 'organic world' in *Wilhelm Meister*, because that 'was possible only in the older epics', none the less Lukács believed that Goethe had succeeded in fashioning a novel in which the 'social world is partially open to penetration by living meaning'.[20] The model of the *Bildungsroman*, as an aesthetic form which seeks to counter the impact of alienation through relating individual characterisation to the forms of contemporary society, was also to influence Lukács' endorsement of later German *Bildungsroman*-type novels such as Gottfried Keller's *Green Henry* (1885) and Thomas Mann's *The Magic Mountain* (1924), as well as Russian novels by Tolstoy and Solzhenitsyn.

Lukács also regarded a work such as *Willhelm Meister* as, in many respects, an expression of the positive, progressive goals of the French Revolution, and believed that the novel's importance lay in its articulation of a hopeful vision which emanated from that revolutionary source.[21] However, he also believed that the outbreak of the Russian Revolution in 1917 offered a similar prospect for overcoming alienation, and this also led him to articulate a more hopeful vision of the future:

> The *Theory of the Novel* was written at a time when I was in a general state of despair. It is no wonder, then, that the present appeared in it as a Fichtean condition of total degradation and that any hopes of a way out seemed to be a utopian mirage. Only the Russian Revolution really opened a window to the future; the fall of Czarism brought a glimpse of it, and with the collapse of capitalism it appeared in full view. At the time our knowledge of the facts, and the principles

underlying them was of the slightest and very unreliable. Despite this we saw – at last! at last! a way for mankind to escape from war and capitalism.[22]

In spite of such comments, however, and the ameliorating influences of Nietzsche and Goethe, Lukács' overall world view remained philosophically dependent on the more pessimistic observation of the modern condition expressed in *Theory of the Novel* and, specifically, on the idea that the experience of subjectivity within modernity was marked by a sense of alienation. Furthermore, it is also the influence of the idea of alienation, in conjunction with a conception of the aesthetic derived primarily from Hegel, which forms the foundation of Lukács' mature model of critical realism.

Alienation

Lukács derived his convictions on alienation and modernity from a number of sources. One of these was that of the context of millenarian anti-capitalism already mentioned. However, three others which must be mentioned here, and which exercised a considerable influence on the formation of Lukács' early ideas, were the works of Georg Simmel, Max Weber and Hegel. Simmel's key postulate that, under capitalism, human labour had become 'commodified', and that the worker had, as a consequence, become estranged from his or her life activity, was derived from the theory of commodification initially advanced by Marx in *Capital.* However, Simmel placed even greater emphasis on the alienating consequences of commodification for human subjectivity than had Marx; arguing that commodification turned the products of human labour into autonomous objects and, in doing so, endowed them with a character which was existentially foreign to man. Although not a Marxist, Simmel adopted many of Marx's ideas, and Lukács in turn incorporated Simmel's version of Marxism into *Theory of Novel* and *History and Class Consciousness,* (the fact that that Lukács later repudiated Simmel for 'turning the period's extreme relativism into a philosophy' in his *The Destruction of Reason* (1954) is not significant for present purposes, and largely reflects the predominantly conservative stance which Lukács adopted in the latter book).[23]

In addition to Simmel, Lukács was also influenced by the ideas of Max Weber, who taught Lukács at the University of Heidelberg between 1912 and 1915. Like Simmel, Weber argued that, under capitalism, the quality of individual subjectivity had diminished, and that 'instrumental rationality' and bureaucratisation were typically applied in order to manipulate the individual in the interests of an exploitative system, thus restricting the individual's access to questions of meaning and value. The consequence of this, according to Weber, was that the modern individual experienced a sense of 'disenchantment', and endured an isolated, circumscribed and impaired existence. Lukács was strongly influenced by this dark vision of modernity, and particularly by

Weber's contention that, under capitalism, scientific rationalism was extended to 'the conduct of life itself', to the extent that 'precise calculation' had replaced ethical consideration as the dominant form of organisation of society.[24]

A third, and perhaps most important, influence on Lukács' views on modernity and alienation, was that of Hegel. In works such as *The Phenomenology of Spirit* and the posthumously published *Lectures on the Philosophy of History*, Hegel argued that human history was marked by the evolution of the consciousness of freedom. This consciousness of freedom is not purely individualist in the classical liberal sense, but a 'rational' freedom, based on a union between individual liberty and a community or state which is organised along rational and ethical principles, rather than principles of power and manipulation.[25] In such a union, the individual freely gives allegiance to the state because the state is based on genuine human needs, and on what contributes to genuine human welfare.[26] However, this Hegelian concept of the 'organic community' – of the union of the individual and the social within an organisational imperative based upon the principle of rational freedom – had yet to be achieved in the historical present. On the contrary, far from being structured according to genuine human needs, or the principles of reason, contemporary society and the state were chiefly influenced by the necessities of power and exploitation. As a consequence, 'man' is not free, and does not feel 'at home' in his community, but instead is forced to bow to the established morality; and the effect of this is that the 'evolution of the consciousness of freedom' is diverted along unpropitious directions. This idea of the existence of a sort of existential 'homelessness' within the 'historical here and now' was to influence Lukács' idea that man was 'transcendentally homeless' within modernity, and also guided his general conceptualisation of the experience of alienation.

Whilst, in *Theory of the Novel*, Lukács had combined the ideas of Marx, Hegel, Simmel and Weber in elaborating a conception of alienation which placed emphasis on the existential estrangement of the modern subject, in *History and Class Consciousness* he related this theory more specifically to the Marxist concept of 'reification', which was first advanced by Marx as part of a more general discussion of the phenomenon of 'commodity fetishism'. Here, social relations of production are transformed into relations between things, a transformation which causes objects and their relations to become 'fetishised', whilst their source in human labour is overlooked. The idea of reification, or *Verdinglichung*, first referred to by Marx in volume three of *Das Kapital*, amounts to an extension of the notion of commodity fetishism from commodity production to the generality of capitalist social relations, and suggests a world in which social relations are 'reified' (fragmented and marginalised), and in which commodity relations are 'personified', so that a 'complete mystification of the capitalist mode of production' is effected.[27] However, although the concept of reification played only a relatively minor role in Marx's overall perspective, in

History and Class Consciousness Lukács went beyond this to argue that reification was not only the 'central problem in economics' but the 'central structural problem of capitalist society',[28] and this led him in turn to assert that reification was able to influence 'the total inner and outer life of society'.[29] Drawing on Weber's notion of instrumental rationality, Lukács argued that, within capitalist society, reification increasingly marginalised ethical considerations through emphasising both the autonomy and importance of the commodity, and the 'principle of rationalisation [which is] based on what is and can be calculated'.[30] The subjective impact of reification on human consciousness, and the idea that reification transforms human relations into relations between things, and – crucially – human beings into thing-like entities, was to become central to Lukács' aesthetic of both literature and film.

Although *History and Class Consciousness* was written after Lukács' conversion to Marxism, the concerns with reification and alienation expressed within the book echo parallel preoccupations which can be found in his pre-1917 writings, which are also premised on the conviction that the individual subject exists within an alienating world, hemmed in by inhuman objects and systems, and unable to achieve self-realisation. Following Simmel, Lukács argues that the individual finds himself or herself existentially surrounded by objects, forms and institutions, which merely exist, and which have no intrinsic human relevance. Lukács refers to these phenomena as the 'meaningless necessities' and 'objectivations' which constitute the infrastructure of 'ordinary life', a domain in which the individual is 'trapped and held fast in a web of a thousand threads, a thousand contingent connections and relationships'.[31] Lukács conceives the domain of 'ordinary life' very much in Weberian terms, as a system of rules and conventions which dominate the individual. This system, 'something frozen, alien', exists as a 'spiritually decayed' form of life for the subject. It is a system which operates according to its own imperatives, rather than human values, a 'thing world', which turns human beings into thing-like beings. Lukács argues that 'ordinary life' necessarily fosters a sense of alienation within the subject, because the structure of social life, with its 'tight web of inescapable necessities', inevitably overwhelms the individual's attempts at self-realisation. The consequence of this is that the individual becomes not only alienated from 'ordinary life' but also from other subjects and, above all, from his or her own self.

As interpreted here, Lukács' understanding of existence appears as one in which external reality is defined as fundamentally contingent and meaningless, whilst consciousness is conceived as enduring within a relatively limited sphere, unable to transcend the stifling circumscription to which it is subject. Lukács argues that it is the existential destiny of consciousness that 'objectivations' – objects, institutions, structures – although initially linked to human requirement, eventfully take on an autonomous independence of their own within 'ordinary life', and coalesce into systems and structures which operate according to 'inhuman' imperatives. At one level, this existential tragedy is conceptualised by Lukács in an essentially a historical manner as the prede-termined consequence of the mind's necessary interaction with external reality. However, Lukács' antipathy towards capitalism, one which long pre-dated his 1918 conversion to Bolshevism, also led him to argue that alienation was a central structural feature of capitalist society, because capitalism was founded on laws indifferent to human nature. The existential vicissitudes of 'ordinary life', were, therefore, reinforced by capitalist modernity and Lukács believed that, faced with the alienating reality of 'ordinary life', the individual was faced with two choices: (1) to accept his or her role and position within 'mere existence', and 'inauthentic being'; or (2) to enter the sphere of 'authen-tic being', the domain of what Lukács referred to as the 'soul'. The domain of the soul is conceived of in two respects. In the first instance it represents the necessity to pursue value, rather than merely to exist within the stratified con-ventions of 'ordinary life'. Here, the individual strives to achieve 'the maximum development, the highest possible intensification of the powers of the individual's will'.[32]

Lukács' opposition between 'ordinary life' and 'soul' here amounts to an essentially Romantic polarity between individual freedom and institutional constraint, and can be related to the various strands of *Lebensphilosophie* which were widespread in central Europe at the time. In the second instance, Lukács conceives the domain of the soul as one which strives to transcend ordinary life, not only through forms of individuated resistance but through an attempt to glimpse the totality of things. Because the individual is existentially isolated, the soul seeks to transcend empirical alienation in an attempt to comprehend patterns and relationships within the atomised relations of ordinary life, and to impose a rational unity on the 'multiplicity of facts', so bringing about the 'life-enhancing, life-enriching power of unity'.[33] For Lukács, the vocation of the soul consists in the struggle against alienation and the hegemony of ordi-nary life, through both realising the soul's full potential and transcending the empirical isolation of the subject. Although alienation exists as an omnipresent reality, therefore, the imperative to struggle against alienation, both as a legit-imate existential act of defiance and, more consequentially, through a greater comprehension of social connection, is central to the life-affirming activity of the subject.

Lukács' conception of alienation, and insistence on the need for forms of resistance to historically specific conjunctures of ordinary life, also informed his key concept of 'culture', the 'single thought of Lukács' life'.[34] 'Culture' is the appellation which Lukács gives to the activity which the soul engages in when attempting to achieve self-realisation and transcend empirical isolation. Culture is not necessarily 'high' culture, therefore, but the title given to a more ubiquitous existential and social act of struggle against alienation, which can, but will not necessarily, manifest itself only within the creation of works of art. In fact, at one level, the work of art itself can even be conceived as a form of alienating objectivation (in the sense in which Simmel argues) and, consequently, as possessing the potential, in concert with other objectivised forms, to play a role in reinforcing the suffocating circumscriptions of ordinary life. However, whilst accepting that this can be the case, Lukács also argues that 'great art' possesses another class of potential, and one which significantly differentiates such art from other forms of objectivation. Unlike these other forms, authentic art, like 'authentic being', does not 'merely remain in being through the inertia of mere existence . . . [but remains] . . . valid as a source of meaning and value'. [35] In other words, although the 'meaningful' objectivations of authentic art emerge within historically specific contexts of determination and correlation, and thereby possess the characteristics of the 'thing world', they also possess an enduring merit, because they are objectivised embodiments of 'culture' and, as such, express the existential and social struggle to transcend the 'meaningless, mechanical and isolating empiricism of ordinary life'. [36]

Hegel

Lukács' idea of 'culture', with its advocacy of resistance through overcoming empirical isolation and ideological positioning, is a key element within his general conception of alienation. However, a second major influence on Lukács' theory of aesthetic critical realism was that of Hegel and, in particular, Hegel's conceptions of totality and the 'classical'. The Hegelian concern with totality in art – a concern also central to Lukács' system – is premised on the idea of the 'Absolute'. In Hegel, the Absolute is conceived of as an organic totality which encompasses all the things of which the world is composed, including human consciousness. It is a coherent and dynamic unity, capable of comprehension, in different ways, through the distinct mediums of art, religion and philosophy. [37] For our purposes here, the Absolute can be understood in two linked ways: (1) as a sphere of existence within which all oppositions and contradictions are progressively and concurrently dissolved into tiers of synthesis and, eventually, oneness; and (2) as a phenomenon which embodies and fosters the principle of freedom, because, as we have seen, for Hegel, the course of human history is nothing else but the progress of the consciousness of freedom, and it is this consciousness which strives towards an understanding of unity and the Absolute. Hegel also argues that, in the domain of the aesthetic, the unity and freedom which characterises the Absolute must 'shine forth' through the art work. [38] Art is, accordingly, the 'sensuous parallel' of conceptual comprehension (through philosophy and religion) of the Absolute, [39] and a form of objectivation which unites opposites into a general consonance so that *Schein* (appearance) is recast into *Scheinen* (appearance as revelation of unity and freedom).[40]

This idea of art as the portrayal of *Scheinen* entails two things: first, that 'sensual' aesthetic expression must be based on mimesis; and, second, that such expression must also transform and 'idealise' mimesis. In order to manifest *Scheinen* as revelation of unity, art must conjure up a relationship between the concrete particular and the abstract general, and this, in turn, requires that the sensual form of art must be rooted in the particular, because, whilst the particular can evoke the general, the abstract general cannot figure the particular. Because art is a concrete, sensuous objectivation, an actual, concrete object; it must also, necessarily, be based on particularised figuration. So, in art, and unlike in philosophy, the unity of the particular and the general can only be invoked through the particular. However, mimetic imitation in itself is not the ultimate goal of art because *Schein* is not *Scheinen*, and Hegel argues that art which merely imitates 'provides not the realities of life, but only a pretence of life'.[41] In order to portray *Scheinen*, art must employ its capacity to conjure up the illusion of perceptual empirical reality as a means of disclosing the underlying reality of unity, wholeness and freedom which characterises the Absolute, and that disclosure is effected through an 'idealisation' of the mimetic. Here, aesthetic form and content serve to idealise ordinary reality, and to create an aesthetic 'world of value'.[42] The mimetic image of the world thus becomes imbued with an 'inner luminosity' which idealises that image.[43] Although Hegel believes that there are genres of art (for example social or political art, or satire) which can and do serve functions other than that of the portrayal of *Scheinen*, he describes such genres as *dienende Kunst* (ancillary art), and believes that the highest function of art is to present an aesthetic (nonutilitarian) account of freedom and wholeness. Hegel's idea of art as manifestation of *Scheinen* also leads him to make distinctions between forms of art which portray *Scheinen* in different ways, and he categorises these different forms as the 'symbolic', the 'classical' and the 'Romantic'. In symbolic art, unity and freedom are portrayed in too abstract a manner and, as a consequence, the particular cannot be properly related to the general. The result is that unity, one of the central imperatives of art as sensuous manifestation of the Absolute, cannot be portrayed. Hegel defines this type of art, which he locates historically in the 'primitive artistic pantheon of the East', as excessively and inappropriately symbolic, indeterminate and expressive, as well as often 'bizarre, grotesque and tasteless'.[44] As we will, see, this negative appraisal of indeterminate, excessively symbolic art was also to influence Lukács's repudiation of both naturalism and modernism.

Superior to primitive symbolic art is 'classical' art, whose historical origins Hegel locates in the 'classical' Greek period of Athens in the fifth century BC.

Here, a union of the particular and the general is elaborated which both encompasses the individual, the social and the transcendent and, crucially, locates that union within human, rather than abstract symbolical, terms, so that 'the Gods are understood in human form':[45] a statue of Zeus, for example, represents both the human and the sublime and, in addition, embodies *Scheinen* in a way which illuminates the historically social and cultural. So, the free spirit (nobility) and harmony (balance and proportion) evidenced by Greek sculpture links the concrete image of 'man' to both the social and the divine in a way which echoes the 'organic unity' of classical Greek society, where, as we have seen (according to Hegel), free-thinking individuals grant their allegiance to social institutions which are established on rational and ethical principles, and on assumptions concerning the link between the human and the divine.[46] In the classical, this close bond between the human, the social and the divine is also made manifest in a close relationship between aesthetic form and content. Hegel argues that, in the classical, a 'concrete' relationship exists between idea and form which does not overrun to the extent that a particular plastic realisation of content connotes an indeterminate spectrum of ideas, or a particular content is so abstract that it necessitates a plastic embodiment of equivalently indeterminate abstraction. In the classical, therefore, art emphasises the relationship between the individual, the social and the general in a tightly knit fashion, in which the general is seen through the prism of the individual and the social. In discussing the idea of the classical, Hegel was also at pains to make clear that the inherent realism of the classical mode must not be confused with mere imitation, because, if that were the case, 'every copy of nature . . . would be at once made classical by the agreement which it displays between form and content'. [47] In contrast, true classical art, like great art in general, uses concrete description to evoke unity and freedom. As we will see, Lukács' conception of realism was crucially influenced by Hegel's conception of the 'classical' as the means through which art is best able to portray the relationship between the particular, the social/cultural and the general.

Hegel's thinking on the role of art in portraying unity and freedom had a considerable influence upon Lukács. However, there were also aspects of Hegel's thinking which, under the influence of Marxism, Lukács also came to reject. For example, Hegel had argued that the classical was inferior to what he defined as the 'Romantic' because the classical centred on the world and image of man and, as a consequence of that, was unable to signify that which transcended the world of man. Hegel's elevation of the Romantic over the classical was largely derived from his aspiration to evolve an aesthetic system which would be able to evoke the idea of God. Because he felt that the sensuous realism of the classical would be insufficient for this, he elevated more 'abstract' art-forms, such as music and poetry, above the figurative arts in importance, arguing, as a consequence, that the most important of the arts: poetry, was 'the universal art of the Mind which has become free of its own nature'.[48] Hegel's position on the superiority of Romantic over classical art led him also to argue that art in general was inferior to religion and philosophy, because art, as an object of intuition rather than conceptual analysis, could only manifest the Absolute, rather than represent it, as religious and philosophical thought could.[49] However, Lukács came to reject such assumptions concerning the superiority of 'Romantic' art, and went on instead to develop a model of critical realism based on the Hegelian notion of the classical. Nevertheless, Lukács *was* influenced by the Hegelian notion that some forms of art were superior to others on the basis of their respective abilities to represent conceptual ideas. As we will see, this led Lukács to elevate literature over film in importance (just as he gave greater importance to poetry than to painting), because film was a 'plastic art', and because 'an intellectual problem cannot be expressed by a picture'.[50]

The intensive totality

The influences of Hegel, Weber, Simmel and the concept of alienation are clearly evident in Lukács' key theoretical model of the intensive totality. Before exploring the model itself, however, it will first be necessary to distinguish the notion of the *aesthetic* intensive totality from that of both *der Mensch ganz* (man's totality) and the 'extensive totality'. For Lukács, that which the work of art must attempt to represent is *der Mensch ganz*, 'man's totality'. *Der Mensch ganz* refers to the relationships which exist between the subject and the social environment during a particular historical conjuncture. *Der Mensch ganz* must also be distinguished from the 'extensive totality', which is a more ontological concept referring to all the physical, non-human, aspects of external reality. The raising of this differentiation between *der Mensch ganz* and the extensive totality immediately makes apparent the extent to which Lukács's aesthetic is humanistically oriented. Lukács is far more concerned, for example, with the relations between men and their institutions than with the relationship between man and nature. This is partly because, within Lukács' philosophy, the non-human world is often defined rather negatively, in terms of the notion of 'ordinary life', and the concept of 'objectivation'. The distinction which Lukács makes between 'authentic' and 'inauthentic' being leads him also to focus on the nature of the human condition, and the primacy of this distinction in Lukács' work has led some critics to see a work such as *The Soul and the Forms* as a forerunner of modern existentialism.[51] Lukács' position here is also derived from Hegel's declaration that history is to be primarily understood as the development of *Geist* (mind/spirit), and as the progress of *human* consciousness to an understanding of the Absolute.[52] In the *Introductory Lectures on Aesthetics*, for example, Hegel argues that, rather than portraying nature, the artist must focus on that within nature which allows *Geist* to 'shine through', and that 'we must search out that in Nature which on its own merits belongs to the essence and actuality of the mind'.[53] Following Hegel, Lukács also places the human sphere of *der Mensch ganz*, rather than the extensive totality and nature, at the centre of his aesthetic system.

Like the extensive totality, *der Mensch ganz* constitutes an almost infinite arena of objects, events and relationships, and cannot be captured in its entirety. The role of the aesthetic 'intensive totality', therefore, is not to attempt to represent *der Mensch ganz* in generality but, rather, to portray the crucial factors which figure in any one 'historical here and now'.[54] Lukács does not, therefore, propose, as many mistakenly believe, that the work of art should, or ever could, create a simulacrum of *der Mensch ganz*, let alone the extensive totality. On the contrary, he makes it clear that the verisimilitude and viridicy of the account produced within any work of art must, necessarily, be influenced, and limited, by a number of determining factors.[55] For example, Lukács argues that the internal laws and conventions of a particular aesthetic medium will influence how *der Mensch ganz* and the extensive totality are represented. In addition, the fact that the aesthetic intensive totality cannot encompass the totality of *der Mensch ganz* during any particular 'historical here and now', entails that the work of art must be discriminating in its choice of what to include within the sphere of representation. Finally, a third factor which mediates the ability of the intensive totality to represent reality 'objectively' is that of the subjective vision or ideology of the artist or producer.

All of these factors suggest that the Lukácsian intensive totality does not attempt an 'objective' account of the extensive totality and, in fact, Lukács regards such an ambition as functioning to reinforce the interests of bourgeois ideology, which creates a 'phantom objectivity', in order to naturalise bourgeois capitalist society and culture.[56] Neither does Lukács believe that reality can be represented from some 'Archimedean' point of view and, in contrast, he fully endorses the form of historical conceptual relativism which later theorists have argued is implicit within a Marxism which denies 'the validity of any doctrine that claimed to be able to give an "objective" neutral or static account of the world from an uninvolved position'.[57] This more relativist conception of representation and reality can be found, for example, in Marx and Engels's *Correspondence with Lassalle* (1859), in which the authors berate Ferdinand Lassalle for attempting to write a drama showing *the* history of the revolutions of 1848–49, arguing that 'to write *the* tragedy of *the* revolution is an abstract pursuit and, as such, an undesirable one for literature'.[58]

Nevertheless, neither Marx nor Engels, nor, for that matter, Lukács was a conceptual relativist when it came to the question of the relation between art, and reality and all believed that, whereas no one viridical aesthetic *interpretation* of reality was warranted, one general *approach* to arriving at such an interpretation was preferable to others. The classical Marxist model of aesthetic

representation was formulated in opposition to an empiricist mode of experiencing and representing the world which Marx, and later Lukács, believed
reinforced bourgeois capitalist hegemony through limiting the ability of the
individual to experience totality and the 'historical character' of man's reality.[59]

In contrast, the Marxist model of aesthetic representation aimed to describe
the world in a way which was broader, deeper and more multifarious than an
empiricist mode of understanding which, as Marx put it, 'everywhere sticks to
appearances in opposition to the law which regulates and explains them'.[60]
Lukács' conception of the intensive totality was centrally influenced by this
Marxist critique of empiricism, a critique which also reinforced Lukács' conviction that the experience of the modern subject was one of existential and
socially enforced empirical isolation, and that emancipation could only occur
as a consequence of overcoming such segregation and understanding the connections between things. Lukács believed that 'bourgeois thought' created a
'horizon that delimits the totality' and amounted to a 'refusal to understand
reality as a whole and as existence . . . making the attempt to achieve a unified
mastery of the whole realm of the knowable impossible'.[61] In contrast, Lukács
proposes a model of representation which seeks a more 'unified mastery of the
knowable', and it is this commitment to totality, and opposition to empiricism,
rather than advocacy of an 'objectivist', Archimedean goal, which characterises
his aspirations for critical realism.

But, if the aesthetic intensive totality does not aim at an objectivist rendition
of the extensive totality, but still attempts to 'understand reality as a whole', as
far as this is possible within the constraints imposed by the mediating factors
which influence any aesthetic medium's attempt to do so, how is this to be
achieved? The answer is through the idea of the 'typical', a concept directly
drawn from Hegel's notion of the 'concrete idea',[62] and the chief instrument
through which the particular is joined to the general within the intensive totality. The 'typical', in Lukácsian terms, can be defined as the means through
which universals are 'dissolved' into concrete particulars, so that a unity of the
particular and the general can be achieved.[63] The 'type', which appears in the
intensive totality, therefore, contains the essence of the universal within a
concrete, individuated form. Similarly, the role of the artist is not to present
universals directly but to 'grasp the essence of things', then 'dissolve' this
essence into concrete phenomena in such a manner that the individuality of
the phenomena is retained, and does not become excessively 'abstract'.[64] The
intensive totality, therefore, marks the outcome of a search for totality through
the distillation of the universal into the particular, and it is this distillation
which results in the appearance of the type, the union of particular and
general. Lukács also argues that the most fundamental universal, that which
the artist must seek to explore above all others, is the problematic of 'what
is man' during any particular 'historical here and now'.[65] It is this question

which is given concrete embodiment within the intensive totality through the medium of the typical.

It is also this conception of art as exploration of the problematic of 'what is man' within *der Mensch ganz* which leads Lukács to make a key, and controversial, distinction between 'narration' and 'description'. Within this distinction, narration is regarded as a means of addressing this problematic effectively, whilst description is regarded as inherently inadequate to such a task, owing to its inability to accommodate the typical. However, Lukács does not only establish this distinction in general philosophical terms but also in contingent historical terms, in order to account for the rise and decline of realism, and the appearance of naturalism and symbolism, in nineteenth-century France. Here, Lukács moves away from Hegelianism in discussing aesthetic developments which occurred after Hegel's death. Following Engels, he argues that, in the early to mid nineteenth century, a realist art-form emerged in France which was committed to the depiction of *Der Mensch ganz*, and which utilised narration and the typical to that end. However, according to this Engelsian or Lukácsian account, after the suppression of the Commune in 1848, artists turned away from the realist mission to represent totality and, in despair, began to produce more atomised, fragmented and 'descriptive' accounts of social and historical reality. Description, therefore, emerges as a dominant mode of aesthetic representation after 1848 because the evolution of bourgeois society beyond that point had effectively 'destroyed the subjective conditions which made a great realism possible'.[66] This means that, for Lukács, historical manifestations of narration and description as modes of aesthetic expression are ultimately determined by the circumstances of human experience. It also implies that description emerges as the principal mode of aesthetic representation during periods when life is so alienating that the desire to unite the particular to the general is rescinded. Description, therefore, appears as a sign 'that some vital relationship to action and to the possibility of action has broken down'.[67]

However, despite the omnipresence of alienation and its aesthetic analogues of description and abstraction, Lukács argues that the tendency towards realism can never be completely eliminated, even when that tendency must endure within a bourgeois capitalist society which is inherently inimical to the revelatory aspirations of realism. Lukács believes that the realist tendency is sustained by three principal factors. The first of these is the sense of disillusionment precipitated by the commonplace experience of alienation. Here, a subjective perception of the inauthenticity which prevails within the relationship between consciousness and material reality fuels an interminable struggle against alienation which finds expression in, amongst other things, aesthetic realism. Following Hegel, Lukács argues that man does not feel 'at home' in the modern world, and that, as a consequence, the modern world is an era of 'transcendent homelessness'.[68] One 'objectivised' response to this experience of transcendent homelessness is the appearance of art which seeks totality, and it is this kind of art, one which seeks totality, rather than mimesis *per se*, which Lukács describes as aesthetic realism. However, in addition to this general persisting disposition to seek totality, during the late eighteenth and early nineteenth-centuries a form of aesthetic expression emerged whose very form and structure actually embodied transcendent homelessness. Realist art, in general, is driven by the imperative to search for unity, against a context where unity has been lost, and attempts to draw the fragmented aspects of life into a totality. However the modern realist novel possesses an even greater incentive than earlier forms of aesthetic realism to realise this imperative. Lukács refers to the novel as the 'bourgeois epic', which strives to depict a lost totality.[69] But the form of the novel also 'manifests the fragmentation and dissonance of the world that it represents'.[70] As a consequence, the realist novel is uniquely driven to overcome its emergence as the aesthetic form of transcendent homelessness, through striving particularly hard to achieve totality.[71] It is, therefore, the experience of alienation, and the coterminous existence of an aesthetic form which is impelled to overcome transcendent homelessness, which ensures the persistence of realism against a context in which description and abstraction remain the dominant modes of artistic portrayal.

The second principal factor which sustains realism is fundamental historical change. In addition to the enduring source of realism just discussed which is given fresh impetus by the emergence of the novel, realism also 'flares up' during periods of great historical change, and is influenced by a deeply perceived need to grasp the fullness of a fast-changing sphere of life. It is when history is evidently *occurring*, when the forces of change in a given moment of history become evidently visible, that realism emerges to mount a challenge to the dominant modes of representation.[72] Thus, the realism of Balzac and Stendhal emerges during a period of intense political change between 1816 and 1848, and encompasses the procession of Empire, Restoration, the *haute* bourgeois hegemony of Orleanism, and revolutionary confrontation. In contrast, after 1848, history enters an interlude, and realism falls into decline, to be replaced by naturalism and symbolism as the dominant modes of representation. According to this interpretation, then, realism emerges when 'the possibility of access to the forces of change in a given moment of history' becomes available to the individual subject.[73] Thus, there is a close relationship between realism and revolutionary social historical transformation. Moreover, realism is almost a precondition for such transformation because the realist imperative to understand and portray the total situation provides the overall map which enables action to occur. In this sense, revolution is not possible without realism.

A third source of realism is to be found in the presence of artists who persevere, indefatigably, in attempting to relate the particular to the general, and who attempt to portray the 'inner life of man . . . in organic connection with social and historical factors'.[74] For Lukács, such portrayal is also dependent on active *engagement* with such factors, so that they provide a genuine measure and foundation for the portrayal of historical reality within the intensive totality. Lukács argues that, if such engagement does not occur, and the interpretation of the extensive totality embodied within the work of critical realism does not stem from the direct, lived, material experience of the author, then that interpretation will inevitably become 'superficial and abstract'.[75] Within this conception of authorship, the vision of the author mediates the aesthetic interpretation of the historical here and now, but that mediation is also materially determined by an 'intensive experience of the social process', rather than abstract speculation about it, and this makes it more likely that the author's vision will embody a greater understanding (more organic, more realist) of both the 'essential social factors', the relationships which exist between the 'totality of objects', and the destinies and fates of individual actors.[76]

Besonderheit and the 'poetic' intensive totality

It is clear from what has been discussed up to this point that, although Lukács is considered to be a proponent of a 'realist' aesthetic, it would be more accurate to define his aesthetic system as one based on a synthesis of the classical ideal of mimesis[77], and the Hegelian ideal of organic totality. Lukács refers to this synthesis as 'realist', but it could equally, and perhaps more helpfully, be described as 'mimetic organic'. Following Hegel, Lukács believes that 'when the power of unification disappears from men's lives' art must step in to restore that lost power.[78] This imperative for art to aspire to the portrayal of unity, so that the 'amorphous chaos of life becomes in the work of art, an ordered cosmos', pervades Lukács' thinking, and dominates all other aspects of his work.[79] This emphasis on the ability of the work of art to create order from the empirical atomism of ordinary life also led Lukács to argue that *Besonderheit*, or 'speciality', is the 'central category' of aesthetics. *Besonderheit* refers to the system of mediations and relations which unite particular instances or events to general contexts, and it is *Besonderheit* which, for Lukács, is both the best form and 'true subject' of art.[80] Lukács argued, for example, that, whilst science constantly moves from the particular instance (*Einzelheit*) to the universal (*Allgemeinheit*), art shifts from the particular to the universal, and then back to the intermediate, historically relative domain between: the domain of *Besonderheit*. According to Lukács, this form of reflexive activity both characterises the categories of knowledge produced by art and distinguishes these from those generated by science. True 'realist' art is, therefore, that which specifically aims to portray the relationship between individual, universal and socio-historical intermediate categories, whilst focusing on *Besonderheit* as the area where the general is 'dissolved' into the particular.[81]

In addition to its concern with aesthetic expression, Lukács' theory necessarily encompasses an account of aesthetic reception, because the whole point
of the intensive totality is that it should employ expressive technique in order
to bring the receiver into an enhanced state of both self-knowledge and knowledge of social context. Lukács argues that the organic-realist work of art presents the recipient with a 'new world'. During the encounter between the
recipient and this 'new world', what Lukács calls the 'whole man' – the individual who comes to the encounter with existing assumptions, beliefs and convictions intact is given an augmented 'sense of man's wholeness', an intimation
of the possibilities which could be imagined beyond the already given.[82]
Realism, therefore, presents the recipient with a 'new world' of 'new or freshly
seen contents', and this 'rejuvenates' the senses and thinking of the recipient.[83]
Lukács uses the term 'catharsis' here to describe the process by which art provides the recipient with a greater sense of man's wholeness. However, this
cathartic impact is neither immediate nor direct, but effects 'A shaking of the
recipient's subjectivity, such that the passions that manifest themselves in his
life receive new contents, a new direction'.[84] In repeatedly encountering the
work of art, the recipient observer undergoes a progressive metamorphosis,
and eventually finds a 'new direction', as 'passion' – the emotional energy
which is generated as a consequence of the subject's disquiet with their own
existential condition – is transmuted into a determined endeavour to understand that condition the better. During this process, a chain of 'cathartic
moments' is built up, within which the encounter with art enables the soul to
incrementally overcome the alienating empiricism of 'ordinary life'. The ultimate effect of the art work on the spectator is, then, to 'unsettle' the existing
Zeitgeist of the recipient, and to have a 'moving-shaking effect', rather than
handing out moral codes or prescriptions and, as a consequence, stimulate a
'human readiness' to accept and want change. [85]
    As is clear from the above, Lukács' account of aesthetic reception is gradu-
alist, indeterminate and non-directive in character. Lukács does not believe,
or desire, that the aesthetic encounter will lead to any *direct* changes of outlook
in the recipient, because, on the one hand, any one encounter will be integrated into the recipient's general vision of life, thus dissipating the force of
any direct influence; and, on the other hand, any such direct influence would
be necessarily manipulative. This makes it clear that Lukács' account of the
relationship between aesthetic expression and reception is founded on two
distinct, though related, propositions: (1) that this relationship should be
gradualist in character, and (2) that it should be non-directive. The gradualist element in Lukács' aesthetic is apparent in the contention that realism
works through the provision of a *succession* of cathartic encounters, and that
it is the general, indeterminate impact of this upon the recipient which eventually leads to change, first in consciousness and then in patterns of action.

Like so much else in Lukács' thought, this gradualist approach is derived from Hegel, both in terms of Hegel's contention that a modern, reformed organic community can be built only through a process of progressively searching for what is rational in the existing world, and then giving this fullest expression in social life;[86] and from Hegel's view that art functions in an essentially intuitive manner, so that the encounter between recipient and art object is characterised by 'lack of definition'.[87]

However, this gradualist emphasis in Lukács is also closely linked to an approach which accentuates the importance of indeterminacy and intuitive understanding within the aesthetic encounter. Again the source here is Hegel, and his view that art objects, as sensuous forms, are primarily objects of intuition, rather than of conceptual analysis, in which the revelation of unity and freedom, *Scheinen*, 'shines forth'. This is why Hegel speaks of art as the 'intuitive' mode of the consciousness of *Geist*.[88] In similar vein, Lukács also asserts that the work of literary realism should contain ideas and themes which are 'dissolved' into the art work, so that they are 'experienced' rather than directly known by the subject.[89] The intuitionist aspect of Lukács' system is derived from a number of sources, in addition to that of Hegel, including Kant's notion of art as engendering an intuitive comprehension of the 'harmony of the faculties'; and the discourses of *Lebensphilosophie* which influenced Lukács in his youth. As we will see later, Lukács writings on film (in contrast to his writings on the novel) also appear to suggest that a considerable degree of intuitive activity is generated during the aesthetic experience afforded by the medium.

In addition to its gradualist and intuitionist elements, the third, and perhaps most significant aspect of Lukács' account of aesthetic reception lies in its emphasis on non-directive expression. The notion of art as non-instrumental lies at the heart of the idealist tradition which Lukács inherited from Kant and Hegel. Hegel explicitly argues that the work of art must be neither didactic nor addressed to any particular purpose or outcome.[90] Instead, art should manifest an 'inner freedom made visible outwardly', and this rules out purposive direction.[91] Rather than a means of direction and practical or moral purpose, the function of art is to create a realm of freedom, and art is, thus, a mode of free contemplative activity, rather than of practical engagement with the social and political.[92] The idea of art as non-directive expression which avoids what Hegel refers to as 'contingent instruction'[93] lies at the heart of Lukács's conception of 'critical realism', and is at odds with the more directive 'socialist realism' of communist orthodoxy. This idea is also implicit in Lukács conception of the gradualist and intuitively rendered nature of the aesthetic process, in which the only 'purpose' present is that of unsettling the existing *Zeitgeist* of the recipient in order to establish an aesthetic arena in which free contemplation of complex relationships can occur.

Lukács' adoption of this position on the non-directive nature of critical realism was, initially, congruous with Marxist tenets. For example, in his influential 1888 'Letter to Margaret Harkness', Engels applauds Balzac's *La Comédie humaine* for its 'chronicle'-like, impartial description of French society between 1816 and 1848.[94] Elsewhere in the 'Letter', Engels questions the absence of any account of working-class struggle against capitalist oppression in Harkness's novel *City Girl* (1887), but eventually concedes that Harkness's description of the London working class is, in fact, an accurate one, because 'nowhere in the civilised world are the working people less actively resistant, more passively submitting to fate, more *hebetes* than in the East End of London'.[95] Balzac is also acclaimed for 'describing' the changes taking place within French society and not taken to task for failing to portray more progressive forces; whilst the lack of any portrayal of such forces in *City Girl* is accepted as both accurate and fitting. However, as we have seen, during the 1930s, the doctrine of Soviet socialist realism moved significantly away from the position expressed by Engels in the 1880s, and Lukács' position on critical realism was also increasingly rejected within the official communist world.

A final aspect of Lukács' thought to be considered here, and one which relates closely to the issues of the role of intuition, indeterminacy and non-directive design within the intensive totality, is that of the 'poetic' character of the intensive totality. In his 'Tolstoy and the Development of Realism', which appeared in *Studies in European Realism* in 1950, Lukács insists that the portrayal of the 'totality of objects' within the realist intensive totality should not amount to a 'mechanical or photographic' depiction of the extensive totality.[96] On the contrary, such portrayal should involve an 'epic-poetic transformation of the most important objects making up some sphere of human life',[97] so that the intensive totality becomes the 'poetic reflection of reality', rather than its rationalised, mechanically reproduced *Doppelgänger*.[98] This regard for the poetic also leads Lukács to hold up the 'intense emotional relationships' depicted in the work of Balzac and Stendhal,[99] the 'magnificent poetic vigour' of *La Comédie humaine*[100] and the 'terrible dark poetry' of Tolstoy as emblematic archetypes of an 'epic-poetic' critical realism.[101] Elsewhere, one critic has described the Lukácsian intensive totality as seeking the 'poetically direct portrayal of man's wholeness'.[102]

Lukács' endorsement of an 'epic-poetic', rather than a more rationalised model of literary realism, rests in part on a conviction that the most vital forces of resistance to be found within contemporary bourgeois society contest what Lukács refers to as the 'unpoetic' nature of capitalist society; and are, as a consequence, best represented by such an epic-poetic model. Lukács argues that one of the principal objectives of the realist intensive totality is to 'overcome the unpoetic nature of the world'[103] through portraying the vital elements and forces of genuine experience (i.e., the domain of the soul) which still exist beneath the 'coldness and harshness of bourgeois existence'.[104] At one level, these elements and forces can be recognised in the residual existence of certain pre-capitalist social forms, and Lukács argues that, for example, the contribution and value of a work such as War and Peace rest mainly in its evocation of such vital, pre-capitalist life experience.

In addition to emphasising the 'poetic' dimension of the realist intensive totality, Lukács' delineation of realism's transformation of reality also encompasses an 'epic' magnitude which ensues from the degree of 'intensity' with which the extensive totality is to be rendered. This 'intensive' portrayal of reality is determined by Lukács' belief, following Hegel and Engels, that realism must seek to express typicalities which crystallise and condense everyday phenomena, thereby elevating that which is represented to a more compelling realm of dramatic consideration. However, this characteristic of critical realism was not, according to Lukács, to be expressed through narrative dramatic action and the display of great events but through a sustained process of heightened reflection on ethical and intellectual questions which transcended the more pedestrian requisites of bourgeois society, and which, as a consequence, offered 'a hope of the moral regeneration of mankind'.[105] In Tolstoy's War and Peace and Anna Karenina this possibility of renewal finds expression in the unremitting, challenging discourse proffered by those who question and struggle against their allotted position within the social order, and Lukács believed that it was this form of discourse, rather than the impact of dramatic narrative events, which endowed Tolstoy's work with a 'calm' and 'stable' 'epic dimension'.[106] This notion of the intensive totality as an epic-poetic transformation of 'man's totality', and one which takes the form of free, contemplative theoretical reflection, is clearly indebted to Hegel's notion of art as providing a kind of spiritual refuge, within which consciousness can explore itself.

Lukács' writing on the cinema

Explicit references to cinema in Lukács' writings are relatively scarce, and this is surprising, given that the questions of narration, description, naturalism and realism which he devoted his career to exploring are so central to the film. Lukács' writings on film include a 1913 essay entitled 'Thoughts on an Aesthetic for the Cinema', a series of short articles which appeared in the Italian film journal Cinema Nuovo in the 1950s, and a section in his The Specificity of the Aesthetic (1963). In 1965 he also wrote the 'Introduction' to the Marxist film critic Guido Aristarco's The Dissolution of Reason: Discourses on the Cinema (1965) and, in the final years of his life, gave a series of interviews to the Hungarian film journal Filmkultúra.[107]

Given Lenin's dictum that cinema was the most important of all the arts, this is a relatively slight collection of material from classical Marxism's most

important aesthetician, and this absence of concern with the cinema reinforces the criticism that Lukács was obsessively concerned with a particular
aesthetic tradition – that associated with nineteenth-century literary realism
in the novel – and largely disregarded artistic developments which lay outside
that domain. Such criticisms encompass the accusation of formalism which
was levelled against Lukács by Brecht in the 1930s, the charge of idealism made
by the Italian theorist Umberto Barbaro in 1959 and the indictment over aesthetic conservatism which was levelled at Lukács by Anglo-American and
other film theorists during the 1970s and 1980s.[108] Although Lukács' lack of
apparent interest in the cinema can be attributed in part to the fact that he
rarely wrote on the visual arts,[109] it nevertheless remains surprising that, given
the mimetic qualities and extensive narrative content of film, his writings
neglected the medium to the extent that they did. Lukács' own explanation for
this evident lack of involvement rests on his belief that the cinema lay outside
his own areas of professional expertise, which 'were based primarily on literature . . . my involvement with the cinema was only incidental'.[110] In fact,
Lukács was disinclined to become deeply involved in a study of the cinema
because he believed that such commitment should be the province of experienced specialists in film aesthetics. This stance permitted him involvement at
a certain, relatively amateur level, but placed self-imposed constraints upon
his fuller engagement with the medium. An example of this forbearance can
be found in the *Filmkultúra* interviews, when Lukács is asked for his opinion
concerning the role of language in relation to the other aesthetic attributes of
film. Lukács' response is brusque, disclaiming any authority to pronounce on
the question, and declaring that 'This is a topic I do not discuss . . . I am not
competent to say more about this'.[111] It is important, additionally, not to interpret Lukács' semi-disengagement from film theory as a mere mark of lack of
interest in the subject, or even, for that matter, as stemming from a sense of
his own professional orientation and capability. On the contrary, Lukács' position stems primarily from a philosophical stance, derived first from Hegel's
categorisation of the arts into distinct fields, and then from his own concern
with the specificity of the various arts, which he explored in his *The Specificity
of the Aesthetic.*

Nevertheless Lukács' writings on film embody many of the philosophical
concerns which are central to his overall position on critical realism. In addition, at the outset of his career Lukács also displayed an evident enthusiasm for
serious engagement with the issues raised by the progress of the new medium.
In 1910, for example, he and Ernst Bloch co-founded a film club in Heidelberg
dedicated to exploring the 'latent artistic possibilities of the cinema'.[112] Later,
when Lukács was Minister of Education in the short-lived Hungarian Council
Republic Government, he presented proposals for 'an official institute for the
development of talent for the cinema'.[113] In 1928, Lukács also collaborated

with Béla Balázs in developing proposals for the production of a film about the Council Republic.[114] It should also be borne in mind, in the light of Lukács' later pronouncements on the inherently 'capitalistic' nature of the cinema as an institution, that the government he was a member of was the first in the world to nationalise both film production and distribution.[115] After 1928, however, as Lukács was increasingly forced out of political public life, to take compensating refuge within the field of literary criticism, his engagement with matters relating to the cinema abated. Whether this detachment was associated with his general withdrawal from the political arena, or whether it would have occurred anyway, can only be the subject of speculation, although it is intriguing to consider whether, had he remained in public affairs, his intellectual investment in film theory would have increased.

Lukács' first essay on film 'Thoughts for an Aesthetic for the Cinema', was published in 1913 in the *Frankfurter Zeitung*. Here, in a dialectical formulation which bears close correspondence to the Kracaurian concept of 'distraction', Lukács emphasises both the manipulative and emancipatory potential of film form. Like Kracauer, Lukács believes that the fragmented, ephemeral nature of film rendered the medium radically different from an aesthetic medium such as the drama, which was characterised by a necessarily physical cohesion, and coherent spatio-temporal system of causality. However, and also like Kracauer, Lukács believed that the modern condition itself was marked by the fragmentation and ephemerality which characterised the medium of film. This led Lukács, again, as with Kracauer, to two principal conclusions. First, he argued that, because the film medium exemplified the characteristic *Zeitgeist* of modernity, it was particularly vulnerable to appropriation by the dominant forces of instrumentally rationality. However, and secondly, he also claimed that, precisely because film form was founded in and emerged from the very substance of the modern condition, it possessed the potential to disclose the reality of that condition to the spectator. It will be recalled that Lukács' concepts of 'soul' and 'ordinary life' were grounded in the premise that the individual was adversely affected by a deleterious existential and social condition. Like Kracauer, Lukács believed that the aesthetic formal attributes of film possessed the potential to exhibit and disclose that condition to the spectator and, in so doing, establish a foundation upon which the spectator could acquire a greater sense of 'authentic existence'.

Lukács' position, as set out in 'Thoughts for an Aesthetic for the Cinema' is compatible with the ideas on literature and drama expounded in the contemporaneous *Soul and Form* (1911) and *The Theory of the Novel* (1913). His recourse to the idea of distraction in his 1913 essay also illustrates the extent to which this idea permeated intellectual cultural discourse in central Europe from the end of the First World War to the disintegration of Weimar;[116] and it comes as little surprise to find the concept which Kracauer elaborated so incisively in the slightly later 'Cult of Distraction' (1926) making an early appearance in the 1913 essay. What is surprising, however, is that, in his later writings, Lukács makes no attempt to couple his ideas on the 'distracted' character of film as a medium with the notion of the novel as a similarly 'fragmented' aesthetic vehicle. For, if the condition of 'mankind' within modernity is that of 'transcendent homelessness', and if, as Lukács insists, the novel is the art-form of transcendent homelessness, then so too, surely, is the film. Both appear to share the same fragmented formal condition, and both, within the terms of Lukács's own logic and statements, seek to achieve wholeness and totality in compensation. In fact, the classical Hollywood film, which employs cinematic technique in order to overcome the fragmented character of the edited image and so achieve a state of complete aesthetic coherence, appears more related to Lukács' conception of the unifying imperative which commands the fragmented art of modernity than does the novel.

Lukács' position on the novel as a medium whose formal properties 'manifest the fragmentation and dissonance of the world that it reflects'[117] leads inexorably to a comparison between novel and film, and the fact that Lukács does not make more of this comparison requires some justification. However, none seems possible, and it appears that Lukács' failure to make this correlation rests principally upon his categorisation of the specificity of the arts: a categorisation which also included a hierarchical model within which literature is ceded more importance than a 'plastic art' such as film. This explanation is supported by Lukács' assertion in his 1968 essay for *Cinema Nuovo* that film cannot express the serious intellectual content of literature or drama because 'an intellectual problem cannot be expressed by a picture'.[118] As we have seen, Lukács was also influenced in this view by Hegel's hierarchical categorisation of the arts, in which poetry was seen as superior to the 'plastic' arts. However, Lukács does not go on to adopt the full logic of Hegel's position, which would have led him to argue not only that literature was superior to film but that philosophy was also superior to literature.

Despite these anachronisms, 'Thoughts for an Aesthetic for the Cinema' does provide the starting point for a more fruitful elaboration of a model of Lukácsian cinematic realism. In the essay, Lukács argues that the revelatory and, ultimately, emancipatory aspect of film is derived from the medium's ability to portray the ephemeral and the fragmentary in a 'fantastic' as opposed to a normative manner. Here, the fragmentary and ephemeral establish the *possibility* of difference, liberation and change, instead of purely reinforcing the existing relations of correspondence, influence and control. In his 1913 essay, Lukács regards the portrayal of the 'fantastic' as central to the aesthetic specificity of film, and argues that this aesthetic specificity should be actively foregrounded, so that, by virtue of the medium's capacity to rebut and undermine the logical, perceptual and causal structures of 'ordinary life', alternative modes of experience may be intimated, and the subject become conscious of the fact that the existing forms and structures of everyday life are not the only ones conceivable.

Lukács even goes so far as to assert that film's embodiment of the fantastic constitutes a 'completely different metaphysics', one in which 'Everything is possible – that is the philosophy of the cinema'.[119] What is proposed here is a cinema of 'the possible', dedicated to challenging the existential and social positioning of the subject. This is a conception of film as an inherently liberating aesthetic medium, with an ingrained oppositional sensibility, and intrinsic emphasis on creative freedom and self-expression. In this regard, the fantastic, as the distinctive aesthetic quality and trait of the film medium, can be understood as the specifically filmic equivalent of Lukács' more fundamental philosophical category of 'objectivised culture'. Lukács' conceptualisation of the objectivised cultural fantastic as inherent to the very structure of the film medium also points to a particular *manner* of film-making, which, he believed, could be found in the films of Chaplin. Indeed, Lukács was particularly impressed by Chaplin, claiming him to be 'one of the great figures in the artistic struggle against the alienation of the capitalist epoch'.[120] For Lukács, Chaplin's films not only defied the customary conventions of logic and causality through the use of improbable stunts, illogical plots and fanciful trick effects but also embodied significant forms of resistance to normative ideology. For Lukács, Chaplin was an embodiment of the principle of the possible, which underpinned the 'fantastic', and his persona a figurative incarnation of non-objectivised 'culture'. However, within the terms of Lukács' overall theory of realism it can be argued that, although Chaplin's films illustrate one of the two central principles underlying the concept of 'culture' – that of resistance to oppression they do not exemplify the second: the requirement to transcend empirical isolation in order to grasp the totality. Despite this, however, Lukács' valorisation of Chaplin does echo the essential humanism which underlies Lukács' theory of realism, with its emphasis on the 'adequate representation of the complete human personality'.[121] It could also be argued that the Chaplin character complies with the Lukácsian conception of the 'typical' as that which 'dissolves' universals (in this case the struggle against alienation) into concrete representations in such a way that the individuality of the representations are not destroyed by the force of the universals.[122] However, the Chaplin persona is not paradigmatically typical in the Lukácsian sense because the 'typical' Lukácsian character would be 'ordinary', rather than marginal or fantastic as is the case with Chaplin[123] As Lukács puts it in *The Historical Novel*, when discussing the work of Walter Scott, the 'typical' character in a Scott novel is a 'middle way figure': 'a more or less mediocre, average English gentleman' . . . correct, decent, average representatives[124] The Chaplin persona, in contrast, clearly cannot be accommodated within such a definition of the 'middle way figure'.

As Lukács' thinking on the cinema evolved, his early conception of a cinema of the possible, of the fantastic, was forced to confront two factors which appeared to jar with that conception. The first of these was the overwhelmingly empirical, naturalist basis of the film image which, although capable of articulating difference as a consequence of orchestration via the practices of editing, *mise en scène*, etc., nevertheless remained inherently linked to a more circumscribed and finite sensory experience of external reality. In other words, the cinema of 'the fantastic' and 'the possible' must inevitably be configured and determined by the relationship between the film image and the experience of perceptual reality: a relationship which necessarily imposed limits upon how 'fantastic' and 'possible' the medium could be if it was to operate in a way commensurate with its own aesthetic specificity.[125] The second significant factor which led Lukács to amend the position put forward in 'Thoughts for an Aesthetic for the Cinema' was that, as the case of Chaplin made clear, the idea of a cinema of the fantastic and possible did not sufficiently address the issue of totality, an issue central to Lukács' aesthetic philosophy. What is particularly significant about this is that, in confronting both of these problems, Lukács eventually came – albeit somewhat reluctantly – to develop an implicit model of cinematic realism which departed significantly from his general position on questions of totality, realism and naturalism. Let us take the issue of totality as an example.

In *The Specificity of the Aesthetic*, Lukács argued that, because film was a primarily visual, rather than word-based medium, it was unable to achieve totality through the deployment of conceptual means, as was the case with literature. This meant that, in film, unity should not be attempted primarily at the level of plot and dialogue but at the level of what Lukács refers to as *Stimmung*, or 'atmosphere'. *Stimmung* is the central organising feature of film, and that which ensures that film renders totality in a way commensurate with its aesthetic specificity. *Stimmung*, the 'universal and dominant category of film's effect', is the principle of composition through which individuated diegetic acts of non-objectivised culture (for example, the singular manifestations of resistance apparent within the films of Chaplin) can be linked to other such acts, thus demonstrating that they are more than merely personalised reflexes, and enabling the medium to function as a social exemplar.[126] *Stimmung* is a necessarily expansive concept, which encompasses both connotation, organised across the body of the film, and the formal aesthetic properties used to express such connotation. The central underlying imperative of *Stimmung* is to achieve *Stimmungseinheit*, or 'unity of atmosphere'. Here, in a notion comparable with that of the purpose of pictorial composition within painting, Lukács argues that, in any one scene of a film, all the elements present should work in unison to create *Stimmungseinheit*. It is, therefore, the organising principles of *Stimmung* and *Stimmungseinheit*, in combination with the notion of an oppositional cinema of the fantastic, which enables Lukács to synthesise the two central principles underlying the concept of 'culture': that of resistance to oppression or alienation, and the need to transcend empirical isolation in order to grasp the totality, or *der Mensch ganz.*

Significantly, however, whilst Lukács argues that *Stimmung* and *Stimmungseinheit* are to be organised systematically, leading to the 'ultimate atmospheric unity of the whole', they are, in themselves, characteristically impressionistic models of expression and communication. In this respect, therefore, Lukács' belief that film is a primarily visual, rather than conceptual medium, leads him to develop a theory of film which embraces the sort of impressionism which he, it would appear, rejected in his theory of literary critical realism. At one level, Lukács rejects impressionistic forms of communication and aesthetic expression because such forms replicate the atomised structures of ordinary life, and do not provide a clear sense of perspective. This rejection is also based on Lukács' apparent repudiation of empiricism and naturalism. However, when Lukács comes to discuss the cinema, and applies the concepts of *Stimmung* and *Stimmungseinheit* to film, we are left with a substantially impressionistic model of expression and aesthetic communication. However, in a sense, this should not surprise us. Despite many of Lukács' pronouncements to the contrary, the influence of the Hegelian category of *Scheinen*, in combination with the idea that the universal is 'dissolved' into and 'hidden' within the particular, and then 'experienced' by the spectator or recipient, suggests that Lukács' theory of realism always contained a latent impressionist or intuitionist dimension. What is surprising, however, is that such a dimension should emerge more fully in relation to questions of film, rather than literary form.

If the inherently impressionistic organising principles of *Stimmung* and *Stimmungseinheit* afforded one means of relating the emphasis on individual acts of 'authentic non-conformism' within the cinema of the fantastic to a collective domain, a second was afforded by another aesthetic approach which, like impressionism, Lukács also rejected in his theory of literary realism. In literature, individual gestures are transformed into social exemplars, and the leap from the particular to the general effected through the deployment of conceptual language, which establishes the sphere of *Besonderheit* in considerable detail. One of Lukács' objections to literary naturalism was that the descriptive detail employed within the naturalist approach had the effect of obstructing the delineation of the relationship between the particular and the general by establishing a mass of empirical data which could not refer 'up' to the general in a clearly articulated way. As a consequence, the two core imperatives of 'culture' – the portrayal of authentic nonconformism and the imperative to rise above the concrete empirical in order to apprehend the totality – were frustrated.

Lukács reiterates such views time and again over the course of his writings, making clear distinctions between 'realist' writers such as Balzac, Mann and Scott and 'naturalist' writers such as Zola, Kafka and others. However, when he comes to write about film he turns this distinction upon its head. In effect, Lukács argues that, because film is unable to relate the particular to the general through the conceptual means by which *Besonderheit* is figured in the novel, it must seek to achieve that through other means, and means which must also be based on general aesthetic categories commensurate with the specificity of the medium. One such category, *Stimmungseinheit*, has already been discussed. However, a second bears directly on what Lukács calls the 'truly realistic character of film'.[127] Throughout the section dedicated to film in *The Specificity of the Aesthetic*, Lukács is greatly concerned to identify the categorical aesthetic specificity of the medium, and his final conclusion is that film possesses two specific categorical features which distinguish the medium from other art-forms.

The first of these, as already discussed, is a form which is structurally based on fragmentation and ephemerality (again, Lukács fails to make the connection to his views on the novel in this respect). However, and in a formulation strikingly similar to Kracauer's notion of the 'basic property' of film as a medium[128], Lukács argues that the *essential* aesthetic specificity of film resides in the medium's closeness to perceptual reality, and that 'Film's closeness to life *determines* the essential stylistic questions of the medium'.[129] This closeness to perceptual reality gives film a genuine 'authority', based upon the fact that film 'manifests' *der Mensch ganz*, and bears the image and trace of what Kracauer calls 'physical reality' to an extent that no other medium can. Lukács, in unusual sympathy with many later anti-realist film theorists, is well aware that this inherent 'authority' of the realistic film image can be used for manipulative purposes in reinforcing the structures of ordinary life and institutionalised power. However, he also believes it to be the source of film's emancipatory potential through 'making people reflect seriously about a past or present situation and confront it with their own situation'.[130] Here, Lukács returns to some of his key themes of 'culture' and the reflective nature of the aesthetic experience as consciousness of freedom and unity. However, rather than talking about these themes in terms of plot, dialogue and narrative, as he does when discussing literature, Lukács defines their specific deployment within cinematic aesthetic experience in terms of visual, even documentary realism.

The central point here in relation to Lukács is that, in order for the authority of the medium to be maintained (an authority indispensable if film is to play a role in successfully expressing 'culture'), and for film to represent *Besonderheit* appropriately, as a consequence of conforming to its own specificity as an aesthetic medium, a *modus operandi* must, of necessity, be adopted which can be described only as 'naturalist'. Film's closeness to perceptual experience dictates that *Besonderheit* will be realised through setting depictions of authentic non conformism within a dense empirical network of visual relationships. Whilst naturalism inhibits the establishment of *Besonderheit* in the novel, therefore, because it disrupts the conceptual establishment of the relation between the particular and the general, it *facilitates* the establishment of an aesthetically specific *Besonderheit* in the film, because it enables a primarily visual (aesthetically specific) portrayal of the relation between the particular and the general to be expressed. Lukács' conclusion that naturalism is a categorical aesthetic quality of the medium of film, and one whose authority must be maintained as the 'foundation of filmic construction', clearly has radical implications for the development of a Lukácsian inspired model and theory of filmic realism, and turns previous understandings of Lukács' ideas on filmic realism on their heads.[131]

One can begin to imagine how a 'naturalist' Lukácsian cinematic aesthetic might be conceived through looking more closely at Lukács' assessment of a particular literary work: Alexander Solzhenitsyn's *One Day in the Life of Ivan Denisovitch*.[132] Lukács believed that Solzhenitsyn was a particularly significant author, whose work carried on the great realist project initiated by Balzac and Tolstoy. In his *Solzhenitsyn*, published in 1970, a year before his death, Lukács chose to explore *One Day in the Life of Ivan Denisovitch* in terms of its importance as an example of what he referred to as the *Novelle*. It needs to be clearly understood, however that, although the literal translation of this German word is 'short story', this is not how Lukács interprets the term. By *Novelle* Lukács means a type of art work which, unlike the novel, does not aim to portray totality by depicting all the 'mediations' which comprise that totality but focuses, instead, on a particular concrete exemplar which somehow *evokes* totality. In the *Novelle*, therefore, the realm of *Besonderheit*, of *der Mensch ganz*, is condensed, concentrated and compacted into a portrayal of discrete, finite concrete relationships and subjective experiences.

At face value, this definition of the *Novelle* appears strikingly close to the sort of naturalism practised by Zola in a novel such as *La Bête humaine*, within which the focus on the individual tragedy of the Jacques Lantier figure symbolises the general degeneration of France just before the outbreak of the Franco-Prussian wars. However, Lukács, as would be expected, is at pains to distinguish his conception of the *Novelle* from naturalism, and he does this primarily on the grounds that, although the *Novelle* may dispense with the 'perspectival' framework of the realist novel, it would nevertheless remain anchored in the key Lukácsian category of the 'typical'. So, for example, according to Lukács, every detail within *One Day in the Life of Ivan Denisovitch* is related to the overall project of portraying the general theme of Ivan's imperturbable, heroic struggle against the regime which oppresses him. This distinguishes Solzhenitsyn's work from Zola's novel, because, in the latter, and as in naturalism generally, each detail is not linked to the total project in this way, but often has a relatively autonomous existence. Lukács also distinguishes *One Day in the Life of Ivan Denisovitch* from naturalism on the grounds that the character of Ivan is a positive rather than a nihilistic figure. This position stems from Lukács' definition of 'culture' as positive resistance to social oppression, and certainly marks a distinction between Ivan and, for example, the far more nihilistically drawn Jacques Lantier.

However, if Lukács' attempt to distinguish the *Novelle* from naturalism on the basis of nihilistic content seems warranted (although such a distinction appears to rule out great swathes of human experience from the sphere of representation), his attempt to base that distinction on the issue of typicality seems less so. Lukács argues that *One Day in the Life of Ivan Denisovitch* presents the totality of a 'limited slice of life' through the deployment of 'non-interpretative descriptive methods'.[133] However, this totality is achieved through joining the particular to the general in extremely abstract and, at the same time, very descriptive, terms. Despite Lukács' attempt to distinguish the *Novelle* from naturalism, therefore, *One Day in the Life of Ivan Denisovitch* is indeed, in many respects, a 'non-interpretative descriptive' naturalist novel, and Lukács's overall stance on *Ivan Denisovitch* in particular, and the *Novelle* in general, appears to lead him back to his greatest *bête noire*: naturalism.

Lukács' account of the *Novelle* as a type of realist art which focuses on the concrete particular, rather than on the totality of 'mediations' within a 'historical here and now', corresponds to his equally 'naturalist' account of the aesthetic specificity of film as grounded in 'closeness to life'. In both the *Novelle* and film, a condensed *Besonderheit*, and portrayal of authentic nonconformism, is realised through the establishment of a dense empirical network of relationships, and this almost seems to presuppose a naturalist, rather than 'Balzacian' realist model of cinematic realism. Such a model of naturalist cinematic realism appears to lie at the centre of Lukács' mature thinking on the aesthetic specificity of film, and the argument that this is so seems confirmed when Lukács' assertion that the *Novelle* ought to depict moral-social problematics in a 'sensible perceptible form' is taken into account.[134] The phrase 'sensible perceptible form' is obviously derived from Hegelian distinctions between the arts, within which the 'plastic' arts are distinguished from the more 'intellectual' arts. Within the terms of this distinction, the role of the plastic arts is to evoke freedom and totality through the use of 'sensible perceptible forms' which allow the Absolute to 'shine through'. It follows from this that film, as a plastic art, and one whose aesthetic specificity is rooted in its portrayal of perceptual reality, must be significantly naturalist in character, because the visual sensual depiction of moral-social problematics must, by implication, be rooted in extensive visual description.

However, Lukács position on the *Novelle* not only leads him to a definition of naturalist cinematic realism, it also leads him to another of his *bêtes noires*, symbolism. Lukács actually describes the character of Ivan Denisovitch as a 'symbol' of everyday life in Stalinist Russia.[135] As with naturalism, Lukács also attempts to distinguish this kind of symbolism from 'real' (i.e., bad, or regressive) symbolism, arguing, for example, that a work such as Flaubert's *La Tentation de Saint-Antoine* is excessively symbolic and, thus, too 'abstract'.[136] However, as in the case of the distinction between naturalism and the 'non-interpreted description' found in the *Novelle*, this distinction is also unconvincing and, despite Lukács' manoeuvrings, his account of the *Novelle* does indeed seem to imply the existence in the latter of a significant degree of symbolism, as well as naturalism. In addition, we have already seen that the concepts of *Stimmung* and *Stimmungseinheit*, which Lukács thinks are inherent to the aesthetic specificity of film, are inherently impressionistic and symbolic concepts. This, together with the example provided by the *Novelle*, leads to the conclusion that Lukács' mature conception of cinematic realism must involve a considerable degree of both symbolism and naturalism, and this, in turn, again points to the contrast between his film theory and literary theory.

Finally, Lukács' pronouncements on the *Novelle* also raise the spectre of a third Lukácsian *bête noire* which has yet more implications for his general model of cinematic realism, subjectivism. Despite his praise for *One Day in the Life of Ivan Denisovitch* Lukács was essentially discomforted by the documentary-like orientation of Solzhenitsyn's novel, and criticised it for its 'lack of perspective'.[137] In addition to this, however, he also criticised the lengths to which the book went in order to portray subjective experience. As we have seen, Lukács' conceptualisation of ordinary life as an atomised, fragmented realm of experience, within which an impaired empirical understanding constitutes the only form of comprehension available to the subject, led him to emphasise the importance of the role of totality in the soul's quest to transcend the limitations of the mechanical world, and this necessarily entailed a rejection of subjectivism because this homologically replicated the atomised structural categories of ordinary life. In addition, subjectivism is also rejected by Lukács on the grounds that it involves a degree of abandonment of external reality and posits the subject as the sole source of meaning.[138] This rejection of subjectivism is linked also to the further key distinction which Lukács makes between realism and formalism. For Lukács, 'realism' is a genuinely dialectical art-form, which represents the relationship between subjective consciousness and the 'historical here and now' of a given period of historical time.[139] In this sense, realism can be defined as a 'concrete subjective/objective' form of aesthetic representation. On the other hand, formalism is defined as the 'abstract subjective', because it seeks to represent the self, rather than the self's relation with the extensive totality.[140]

Subjective response is clearly crucial to Lukács' general model of realism, as his insistence that literary characters should be not mere bearers of 'general concepts' but fully fleshed out 'concrete individuals'[141] 'living human beings, with living, changing and developing relationships between them' bears evidence to.[142] There appears, therefore, to be a hiatus between Lukács' more assertive theoretical declarations over the portrayal of subjectivity and a more accommodating attitude which becomes evident when he deals with literary texts, where he actually *emphasises* the importance of rendering subjective experience. One consequence of this discrepancy is that Lukács' key theoretical distinction between realism as dialectical subjective/objectivism and formalism as abstract subjectivism, loses some of its force. As will also become apparent later, the issue of the nature of the relationship between the rendering of subjective experience and the historical here and now becomes even more consequential when discussing the ways in which Lukácsian ideas might be applied to film.

The preceeding discussion appears to suggest that a reconstructed Lukácsian model of cinematic realism may be quite different from the more familiar model of Lukácsian literary realism, and from commonly held understandings of Lukácsian ideas within the field of film studies. This, in turn, suggests that a thorough re-evaluation of the relevance of Lukácsian ideas for film theory needs to be undertaken. What is required is a model of cinematic realism able to accommodate both the central themes of Lukács' general model of the intensive totality and the often quite different themes which he believed to be specifically relevant to, and intrinsic to, film as an aesthetic medium. However, such a project cannot be attempted here, as time and space will not permit. Instead, the following chapter will attempt an exploration of how Lukácsian cinematic realism can be conceptualised in relation to the analysis of particular films.

Notes

1 Bisztray, George, *Marxist Models of Literary Theory* (New York: Columbia University Press, 1978), p. 2.
2 Kolakowski, Leszek, *Main Currents of Marxism, Volume Three: The Breakdown* (Oxford: Clarendon Press, 1978), p. 305.
3 Heller, Agnes, Fehér, Ferenc, Márkus, György, and Vajda, Mihály, 'Notes on Lukács' Ontology', in Heller (ed.), *Lukács Revalued* (Oxford: Basil Blackwell Publishers Ltd, 1983), p. 130.
4 Kolakowski, p. 305, and Heller (ed.), p. 77.
5 Parkinson, G. H. R., *Georg Lukács* (London: Routledge, 1977), p. 7.
6 Lukács, Georg, *History and Class Consciousness: Studies in Marxist Dialectics* (London: Merlin Press, 1990), p. xiv.
7 Parkinson, p. 19.
8 Bisztray, pp. 40–1.
9 Lukács, Georg, *The Meaning of Contemporary Realism* (London: Merlin Press, 1963), p. 135.

10 Livingstone, Rodney (ed.) *Georg Lukács: Essays on Realism* (London: Lawrence and Wishart, 1980), p. 11.
11 Parkinson, p. 28.
12 Márkus, György, 'Life and Soul: The Young Lukács and the Problem of Culture', in Heller (ed.), p. 1.
13 Congdon, Lee, *The Young Lukács* (Chapel Hill: University of North Carolina Press, 1983), p. 10.
14 Löwy, Michael, Georg Lukács: *From Romanticism to Bolshevism* (London, 1979), pp. 30–8.
15 Lukács (1990), p. xi.
16 Lukács, Georg, 'Preface', in his *Theory of the Novel: A Historical-philosophical Essay on the Forms of Great Epic Literature* (Cambridge, MA: MIT Press, 1971), pp. 11–12.
17 Lunn, Eugene, *Marxism and Modernism: An Historical Study of Lukács, Brecht, Benjamin and Adorno* (London: Verso, 1985) p. 96.
18 Kadarkay, Arpad, *Georg Lukács: Life, Thought and Politics* (Oxford: Basil Blackwell, 1991), p. 56.
19 Lunn, p. 95.
20 Ibid.
21 Lukács, Georg, *Goethe and His Age* (London: Merlin Press, 1968), p. 56.
22 Lukács (1990), p. xi.
23 Lukács, Georg, *The Destruction of Reason* (London: Merlin, 1980), p. 451.
24 Held, David, *Introduction to Critical Theory, Horkheimer to Habermas* (Berkeley and Los Angeles: University of California Press, 1980), p. 65.
25 Singer, Peter, *Hegel* (Oxford: Oxford University Press, 1983), p. 35.
26 Ibid., p. 27.
27 Bottomore, Tom (ed.), *A Dictionary of Marxist Thought* (Oxford: Basil Blackwell, 1991), p. 463.
28 Lukács (1990), p. 83.
29 Ibid, p. 84.
30 Ibid., p. 88.
31 Márkus, in Heller (ed.), p. 6.
32 Ibid., p. 8.
33 Ibid., p. 4.
34 Ibid.
35 Ibid., p. 14.
36 Ibid., p. 10.
37 Copleston, Fredrick, *A History of Philosoph, Volume Six: Wolff to Kant* (London: Search Press, 1960), p. 240.
38 Taylor, Charles, *Hegel* (Cambridge: Cambridge University Press, 1975), p. 472.
39 Houlgate, Stephen, *Freedom, Truth and History: An Introduction to Hegel's Philosophy* (London: Routledge, 1991), p. 127.
40 Ibid., p. 130.
41 Ibid.
42 Aitken, Ian, *Film and Reform: John Grierson and the Documentary Film Movement* (London: Routledge, 1992), p. 39.

43 Taylor, p. 472.
44 Hegel, G. W. F., *Introductory Lectures on Aesthetics* (London: Penguin Books, 1993), p. 83.
45 Taylor, p. 476.
46 Singer, p. 35.
47 Hegel, p. 84.
48 Ibid., p. 96.
49 Taylor, p. 467.
50 Levin, Tom, 'From Dialectical to Normative Specificity: Reading Lukács on Film', *New German Critique*, no. 40 (winter 1987), p. 59.
51 Marcus, Judith, and Tarr, Zoltán, 'Introduction', in Marcus and Tarr (eds) *Georg Lukács: Theory, Culture and Politics* (New Brunswick, Transaction, 1989), p. 5.
52 Singer, p. 47.
53 Hegel, p. 84.
54 Királyfalvi, Béla, *The Aesthetics of György Lukács* (Princeton: Princeton University Press, 1975), p. 85.
55 Lukács, Georg, 'Art and Objective Truth', in *Writer and Critic* (London: Merlin Press, 1978), p. 38.
56 Lukács (1990), p. 83.
57 McLennan, Gregor, *Marxism and the Methodologies of History* (London: Verso, 1981), p. 39.
58 Bisztray, p. 25.
59 Lukács (1990), p. 6.
60 Bottomore (ed.), p. 175.
61 Lukács (1990), pp. 120–1.
62 Hegel, p. 84.
63 Királyfalvi, p. 82.
64 Ibid.
65 Ibid., p. 110.
66 Lukács, Georg, 'Tolstoy and the Development of Realism', in *Studies in European Realism*, reprinted in Craig, David (ed.) *Marxists on Literature: An Anthology* (London: Penguin, 1975), p. 282.
67 Jameson, Fredric, *Marxism and Form: Twentieth-Century Dialectical Theories of Literature* (Princeton: Princeton University Press, 1971), p. 201.
68 Lukács (1971), p. 121.
69 Eagleton, Terry, *Marxism and Literary Criticism* (London: Methuen and Co., 1976), p. 27.
70 Jay, Martin, *Marxism and Totality: The Adventures of a Concept, from Lukács to Habermas* (London: Polity, 1984), p. 96.
71 Lukács (1971), p. 121.
72 Jameson, p. 204.
73 Ibid.
74 Lukács, Georg, *Studies in European Realism: A Sociological Study of the Writings of Balzac, Stendhal, Zola, Tolstoy, Gorki and Others* (London: Merlin Press, 1972), p. 8.

75 Lukács in Craig (ed.), p. 291.
76 Ibid.
77 Királyfalvi, p. 55.
78 Zitta, Victor, *Georg Lukács: Marxism, Alienation, Dialectics, Revolution* (The Hague: Martinus Nijhoff, 1964), p. 235.
79 Márkus in Heller (ed.), p. 11.
80 Parkinson, G. H. R., 'Lukács and the Central Category of Aesthetics', in Parkinson (ed.) *Georg Lukács: The Man, His Work and His Ideas* (London: Weidenfeld and Nicolson, 1970), pp. 114–5.
81 Ibid., p. 132.
82 Királyfalvi, p. 118.
83 Ibid., p. 119.
84 Ibid., 118.
85 Ibid., p. 117.
86 Singer, p. 36.
87 Taylor, p. 473.
88 Ibid.
89 Bahr, Ehrhard, and Goldschmidt, Ruth Kunzer, *Georg Lukács* (New York: Ungar, 1979), pp. 1119–20.
90 Hegel, p. 56.
91 Houlgate, p. 132.
92 Ibid., p. 137.
93 Hegel, p. 57.
94 Engels, Friedrich, 'Letter to Margaret Harkness', in Craig (ed.), pp. 270–1.
95 Ibid., p. 270.
96 Lukács, in Craig (ed.), p. 315.
97 Ibid., p. 295.
98 Ibid., p. 315.
99 Ibid., p. 304.
100 Lukács (1972), p. 10.
101 Lukács, in Craig (ed.), p. 303.
102 Királyfalvi, p. 124.
103 Lukács, in Craig (ed.), p. 296.
104 Ibid., p. 300.
105 Ibid., p. 343.
106 Ibid.
107 Levin, in *New German Critique* (1987), p. 36.
108 Lapsley, Robert, and Westlake Michael, *Film Theory: An Introduction* (Manchester: Manchester University Press, 1988), p. 185.
109 Kadarkay, p. 66.
110 Levin, in *New German Critique* (1987), p. 60.
111 Ibid.
112 Ibid., p. 36.
113 Ibid., p. 37.
114 Ibid.

115 Ibid.
116 Rodowick, in *New German Critique* (1991), p. 117.
117 Jay, p. 96.
118 Levin, in *New German Critique* (1987), p. 59.
119 Ibid., p. 41.
120 Ibid., p. 57.
121 Lukács (1972), p. 7.
122 Királyfalvi, p. 82.
123 Jameson, p. 194.
124 Lukács, Georg, *The Historical Novel* (Aylesbury: Peregrine Books, 1976), pp. 32–3.
125 Levin, in *New German Critique* (1987), p. 51.
126 Ibid., p. 50.
127 Ibid., p. 54.
128 Kracauer, Siegfried, *Theory of Film: The Redemption of Physical Reality* (Princeton: Princeton University Press, 1997), p. 28.
129 Levin, in *New German Critique* (1987), p. 54.
130 Lukács, Georg, 'Espressione del pensiero nell'opera cinematografica', in *Cinema Nuova* 18:197 (January–February 1969), p. 8; cited in Levin, *New German Critique* (1987), p. 58.
131 Levin, in *New German Critique* (1987), p. 54 .
132 Lukács, Georg, *Solzhenitsyn* (London: Merlin Press, 1970).
133 Ibid., p. 26.
134 Parkinson, p. 123.
135 Lukács (1970), p. 14.
136 Ibid.
137 Ibid., p. 22.
138 Márkus in Dupré, L., 'Objectivism and the Rise of Cultural Alienation', in Rockmove, Tom (ed.), *Lukács Today: Essays in Marxist Philosophy* (Dordrecht: Reidel, 1988), p. 82.
139 Királyfalvi, p. 86.
140 Eagleton, p. 31.
141 Királyfalvi, p. 69.
142 Lukács, in Livingstone (ed.), pp. 24–5.

4

From the historical cinema of democratic humanism to the film *Novelle*: Lukácsian cinematic realism in *Danton* (1990) and *Senso* (1954)

Although, as we have seen, Lukács' developed standpoint on cinematic realism entails a predominantly naturalist model, his overall stance on aesthetic realism indicates that a number of diverse and conflicting categories of film are potentially equally definable as Lukácsian in some respect. Despite such an apparent compass of interpretation, however, it is possible to argue that a Lukácsian cinema can be divided into two major formal and thematic categories. The formal categories embrace (1) films which employ the focused naturalist orientation of the *Novelle* and (2) films which employ the more 'mediated' framework of the novel. It is, of course, also possible for some films to utilise both of these categories at different points within their overall diegesis. The two central Lukácsian thematic paradigms are (1) films which focus on instances of resistance to ideological positioning and oppression and (2) films which are concerned with totality and/or moments of elemental historical transformation. Again, both of these paradigms may appear within the same film, although, in general, films which depict epochal historical transformation may adopt the form of the novel, whilst those which focus on what Lukács calls 'non-objectivised expressions of culture' will tend to adopt the approach of the *Novelle*.

It is immediately evident that a significant number of films could fall within these parameters. However, that number soon becomes reduced when other Lukácsian concepts are applied to the task of definition. For example, Lukács argues that historical change must be seen through the eyes of ordinary, or 'typical' characters, rather than 'world-historical figures'. This would, to some extent, rule out the 'great man' genre of films, such as, for example, Abel Gance's *Napoléon vu par Abel Gance* (1927). Nevertheless, and as we will see with *Danton*, another film which deals with the French Revolution and which focuses on world historical figures, such films may also possess other Lukácsian characteristics. This issue of a focus on the ordinary, on the *Besonderheit* of the quotidian, is one of many Lukácsian principles which will have to be explored in greater depth in relation to a study of particular films, in order to properly assess the nature and character of Lukácsian cinema. However, one of the most important of these principles, and one which, in conjunction with the two formal and thematic categories mentioned above, defines the core model of the Lukácsian film, is the imperative that cinematic realism must not attempt to manipulate or position the spectator. In contrast, and as already argued, the Lukácsian film must work to present a 'new world' to the spectator, and show the 'whole man of everyday life' the 'sense of man's wholeness'. This particular insistence indicates that the Lukácsian film must possess an unremittingly social critical attitude, which will have a 'moving shaking effect' upon the spectator, and this implies a form of cinema outside the mainstream, and rooted in social orientation. This imperative that the Lukácsian film must address the collective dimension, rather than only individual circumstance, in a critical, liberating manner is also driven by the fundamental Lukácsian principle of the need to connect the particular to the general, in order to express the totality. One film which both does and does not conform to a Lukácsian model is Wajda's *Danton*, and a study of this film reveals the extent to which a Lukácsian model can be profitably applied to film analysis.

Danton (Andrzej Wajda, 1990)

Danton can be first of all considered Lukácsian in the way that it attempts to portray large-scale historical events through the actions of individual agents, thereby uniting the particular and the general. The film is set in Paris, in Year Two of the Revolutionary Republic, in 1794, and focuses on the confrontation between two iconic historical figures, the Revolutionary leaders Georges Jacques Danton and Maximilien Robespierre. In the film, that confrontation is depicted as based primarily around Danton's desire to rein in the Terror which Robespierre unleashed in September 1793 and Robespierre's countervailing conviction that only rigorous and harsh jurisdiction could stave off the threat of counter-revolution. The film follows the course of the encounter between these two, and ends with the execution of Danton, and Robespierre's prescient foreboding of his own imminent doom.

   Although Danton links individual agency to historical events in the manner of the Lukácsian intensive totality, the film's focus on an abstract opposition between liberty and authoritarianism, as personified within the characters of Danton and Robespierre, creates a situation whereby the historical context (after all, a momentous one, which included the abolition of the monarchy, the execution of the king and queen as traitors, the war against the counter-revolutionary coalition, the consequences of the Terror, and political struggles between the Dantonists, the ruling Jacobins and the radical *sans-culottes*) is treated in a vague and inexplicit fashion. Such an approach seems, at first, to be at odds with Lukács' ideal of the mediated, classical intensive totality. However, as will be recalled, Lukács did not argue that the intensive totality should attempt to portray all the intricacies of a particular historical conjuncture. Instead, the intensive totality is expected to employ symbolism, indeed, an 'epic-poetic' orientation, in order to evoke the key, 'nodal points' of that conjuncture. If an opposition between liberty and tyranny can be considered as such a 'nodal point' of discord within the time of the Terror, then *Danton* can, provisionally, be classed as Lukácsian. It should also be remembered that the opposition between liberty and social instrumentality formed the basis of Lukács' key concept of 'culture'. However, and despite these conditional endorsements, the central issue for a Lukácsian-based model of cinematic realism is whether, in evoking such an abstract polarity, *Danton* also depicts social typicality appropriately.

One answer to this problem of how abstraction and typicality should be correlated in a film such as *Danton* can be found in a distinction which Lukács makes between 'classical historical realism' and the realism of 'democratic humanism'. Referring to the conceptions of the 'classical' and the 'concrete individual', both of which are derived from Hegel, Lukács argues that the 'classical' literary historicism of Scott and Balzac is founded on the portrayal of characters who are intimately and concretely linked to their national historical contexts. However, in a chapter in *The Historical Novel* entitled 'The Historical Novel of Democratic Humanism' Lukács argues that, in progressive realist art produced after 1848 (the point in time which marks the demise of bourgeois democracy as an authentically progressive force), such a degree of concrete connection became more difficult to portray and, instead, forms of 'abstract humanism' and 'historical monumentality' were increasingly relied on as a means of depicting both the alienating consequences of capitalism and the modes by which those consequences might be surmounted.

Lukács argued that abstract humanism and historical monumentality played a progressive role in combating capitalist alienation because these features possessed the ability to transform 'the great struggles of history [in]to a contest between reason and unreason, progress and reaction . . . [and in doing so] . . . render them intelligible to themselves and to their readers.[1] Far from regarding humanism as intrinsically reactionary, therefore, Lukács views humanistic art as superior to the initial, despairing aesthetic reaction to the failure of bourgeois democracy, a reaction marked by the rise of naturalism and symbolism. In contrast, Lukács refers to post-1848 'humanist' art as 'the first call to battle in defence of human culture', and argues that the 'historical novel of democratic humanism' presents 'manifestations of a new heroic humanity in a simple and accurate way', through the portrayal of protagonists who 'embody emotionally and intellectually the great humanist ideas and ideals for which they are fighting'.[2] The importance of such protagonists for Lukács lies in 'their ability to generalize, raise to a high intellectual level problems which in life itself are scattered and appear in purely individual forms and purely private fates'.[3] Within the terms of this argument, democratic humanist realism takes on the Lukácsian mantle of 'culture', through expressing, in a charged symbolic manner, abstract oppositions which link the particular to the general through the typical. Given this conceptualisation it seems possible to characterise *Danton* in Lukácsian terms as a work of 'humanist monumentalism' and as a 'historical work of democratic humanism'. *Danton* does, in a sense, transform 'the great struggles of history' into a contest between 'progress and reaction', and the figure of Danton does manifest a 'heroic humanity' which embodies 'emotionally and intellectually the great humanist ideas and ideals'.

Nevertheless, despite his belief that historical democratic humanist realism was superior to symbolism, modernism and naturalism, Lukács believed also that this form of realism was inferior to classical historical realism, and that the critical deficiency within the historical novel of democratic humanism lay within an inherent tendency to reduce concrete historical representation to over-generalised abstraction, so that, as a consequence, 'the immediacy of historical experience disappears, or at least runs this risk'.[4] Here, in a formulation which reflects Lukács's inverted elevation of the Hegelian 'classical' over the 'romantic', and within which democratic humanist realism can be defined as the 'romantic', this form of realism possesses an innate tendency to degenerate into symbolism, causing the 'typical' aesthetic configuration of *Besonderheit* to loose its crucial mediating coherence. Associated with this conversion of *Besonderheit* into *Algemeinheit* is the related problem which Lukács raises of the concentration of historical experience within one dominant 'historical protagonist'. Lukács argues that because, following 1848, such protagonists are compelled to embody 'the great humanist ideas and ideals', their summing up of historical experience must necessarily be a restricted one 'because the whole process takes place *within one person* . . . [and because] . . . the single path leading from experience to generalisation . . . is necessarily too narrow, straight and simple'.[5] In a work of 'classical' historical realism, for example, such as Tolstoy's *War and Peace*, historical experience is, in contrast, disseminated across a range of characters and, in addition, the meaning of such experience is not over-generalised in relation to the psychology of a particular character. Accordingly, characters react to events in ways which are 'intended as a dash of colour to the total canvas, not to carry the meaning of the whole'.[6] The focusing of historical experience 'within one person' also has the effect of reducing the degree of characterisation invested in secondary diegetic figures and, as has been argued, Lukács insists that such diegetic characters should not be mere ciphers for ideas but fully fleshed out representations.

A final, fundamental problem with democratic humanist realism is that, in focusing on Promethean historical protagonists, the role of the 'typical' literary figure in illuminating the sphere of *Besonderheit* becomes inverted, and the social conjuncture is reduced to a background which serves to illuminate the character and vision of the protagonist. So, for example, when discussing Heinrich Mann's *Henry IV*, Lukács argues that the background of a 'definite phase in the life of the French people' is reduced to little more than a sphere in which the 'eternal ideals of the central character may be realised'.[7] It is, therefore, imperative for Lukács that, where the art of realist democratic humanism invests intensive characterisation in a central heroic figure, the art work should also portray such characterisation as an intensification of 'the great social-historical antagonisms' and 'problems of popular life', rather than use such antagonisms and problems as a means of accentuating the idealised psychological traits of a romanticised figure. In addition, although such historical protagonists could, in theory, be 'ordinary' individuals, and therefore 'typical' to an extent, given the innate tendencies of democratic humanist realism they are far more likely to be embodied, as is the case in Mann's *Henry IV*, as 'world-historical figures' and, as has already been argued, within the Lukácsian model it is not permissible for such figures to dominate the aesthetic diegesis, because they lack true typicality. It seems then, that the novel (and, therefore, cinema) of democratic humanism must tread a fine line between employing a romanticised monumentalism as the 'first line of battle in defence of human culture' and depicting historical context in too individuated a manner.

Most of the problems associated with historical humanist democratic realism can be found in *Danton*, where individuation appears to overwhelm the depiction of historical context. *Danton* is a co-production between French and Polish film production companies, and employs a number of important French and Polish actors, most notably Gérard Depardieu as Danton. As in many other similar co-productions, in *Danton* the narrative continuously focuses on the persona of such star actors, and the result is, almost inevitably, a rather schematic treatment of both secondary characters and background context. For example, Danton's wife, Madelin, is pictured, but never utters a word, even when the militia come to her home to arrest her husband; whilst many of Danton's accomplices, such as Camille Desmoulins, are given somewhat stereotyped characterisations. Similarly, the figures of Georges Couthon and Louis Antoine de Saint-Just, the two men closest to Robespierre within the governing Committee, are treated in a very schematic way – the wheelchair-bound Couthon reduced to scrambling around in his perambulator in manic fashion. Such schematism, driven by the imperative of creating easily understood significations, is a common feature of the co-production, and has the effect of marginalising secondary characters and the treatment of historical context in *Danton*. In *Danton*, the figure of Danton also carries all the meaning of the film, whilst those around him mainly function to emphasise the various aspects of his character and spirit. Danton is presented in an almost Nietzschean style, as

a kind of excessive 'superman' figure, who appears to be of a different stature
and energy to all others within the film. Although Danton can be regarded as a
'type', and as a 'concrete individual' in Hegelian and Lukácsian terms, because
he embodies the historical contradictions of the period, the emphasis which the
film places on Danton's persona, as opposed to his typicality, significantly
tempers this diegetic function. This also has the effect that the historical contradictions embodied in the period of the Terror are not brought out in *Danton*,
and the only substantive contradictions established by the film appear to
encompass the dilemmas faced between those who, as in the case of the
Robespierrists, accept terror as a means of carrying out the programme of the
Revolution and those who, as in the case of the Dantonists, reject such tactics.
But this is insufficient, in Lukácsian terms, to address the historical conjuncture
of the period.

If the recourse to mythic stereotype and over-personalisation in *Danton*
makes the film square badly with Lukácsian conceptions of the concrete individual, and the ideal form which the relationship between heroic humanism
and depiction of historical conjuncture should take within the realist art form
of democratic humanism, the Lukácsian distinction between 'ordinary life'
and 'soul' appears to fit *Danton* more closely. Robespierre, for example, is presented as an individual whose initial moral imperatives have become absorbed
into, and tainted by, the administrative 'thing world'. Unlike Danton, whose
discourse always centres on issues of value, Robespierre's concerns are fundamentally to do with the calculated, pragmatic exercise of power, and with the
submission of ethical questions to that imperative. Robespierre is also characterised physically as a representative of the 'thing world', in that he is depicted
as emasculated, authoritarian, pompous, cold and over-refined. Throughout
the film he is variously shown as sick, lying in bed, covering his face with his
hands and admitting to feeling 'fatigue'. In contrast, the figure of Danton
(drawing on the established persona of the actor Gérard Depardieu, as well as
familiar historical understandings of Danton) presents a character full of the
appetites and energies of life. At one point, in a private meeting between
Danton and Robespierre, Danton accuses Robespierre of not being 'a real
man', never having 'been with a woman', and of being 'powdered'. During this
scene Danton eats and drinks with relish, but Robespierre eats nothing. We also
learn that Robespierre does not drink alcohol, an attribute which seems to
suggest a certain lack of humanity.

The Lukácsian concept of 'culture' is also evident here in the motivated
idealism expressed by the Dantonists. For example, both Danton and
Desmoulins are offered the opportunity to save their lives at different points in
the film. However, both refuse because that would mean resigning themselves
to accept their place within a system which they regard as alienating and
inhuman. In this sense, the Dantonists can be associated with other figures in

realist literature, such as Anna Karenina, who refuse to accept their place within the system, and can also be linked directly to Lukács's concept of non-objectified culture. There is one crucial difference, however, between Wajda's *Danton* and Tolstoy's *Anna Karenina* which suggests that, if the Lukácsian concept of culture is to be deemed applicable to these works, it is far more germane to the latter than the former. In both *Anna Karenina* and *War and Peace*, non-objectified acts of culture find expression as mediated personal reactions to larger historical events. Anna Karenina's actions are a response to the way in which her everyday experience is affected by social historical structures which she has no directly conscious engagement with. Similarly, according to Lukács, in *War and Peace* the conversation between Bolkonsky and Bezukhov on the eve of the battle of Borodino, whilst covering the subject of the forthcoming battle, is more concerned with assessing its impact on their overall psychological dispositions. What is happening here, as in *Anna Karenina*, is that portentous historical events are shown distilled through the personal lifeworld of the individuals concerned. It is that refracted lifeworld, rather than the events themselves, which is the real focus of attention, and personal experience is not, as Lukács would put it, 'over-generalised', in order to directly address the overarching historical context. In contrast, in Wajda's *Danton* the everyday lifeworld hardly exists at all, and individual experience is, at all times, directly linked to what Lukács has described as the 'nodal points' of the historical conjuncture. The consequence of this, in terms of Lukácsian analysis, is that the characters in *Danton* cannot be sufficiently fleshed out so that 'war is felt directly in their private lives, both in the outwards transformation of life and in the inner change of social-moral behaviour'.[8]

Danton can also be regarded as Lukácsian in its portrayal of an alienated environment. The Lukácsian idea of modern experience as marked by alienation is evidently present in the film. For example, the opening shots of the film show a succession of scenes which are marked by their harsh visual and thematic tonality: clandestine coach journeys by night, insistent surveillance activity, people waiting in the rain to receive scarce supplies of bread, shots of the guillotine, and of prisoners being taken to execution, etc. Later scenes also portray street mobs, inhumane prison conditions, rigged court trials, scenes of accusation, betrayal, plots, anger and despair. The trial of Danton itself is seen to be intrinsically corrupt, the lack of justice evident, and the punishment rudimentary and primitive. This appears to be a world which is suffused with alienation, and in which the individual can only either struggle hopelessly against the rising tide of violence and oppression, as in the case of Danton, or embrace it fully, as in the case of Robespierre. The domestic and professional world of Robespierre, for example, appears suffused with a climate of severe instrumentality, within which there is no place for sentiment or human contact. This is illustrated, for example, in the scene where Robespierre's female partner punishes her young son for making mistakes in reciting Revolutionary speeches. To some extent, this aspect of *Danton* is influenced by Büchner's play, which is permeated by an existential despair about the nature of an immoral world and the pointlessness of action.[9] However, and as will be argued, it is also influenced by Wajda's own ideological perspective on the authoritarian nature of the 'revolutionary' communist system which held power in Poland up to 1986. Whatever the influence, it is clear that, If the Lukácsian concept of the individual act of non-objectified culture as creating a social exemplar is evident in *Danton*, it is substantially overdetermined by the air of fatalism which pervades the entire film. Wajda believed that, in making *Danton*, he had created a film of 'tragic inevitability',[10] suffused with a fatalism reminiscent of the neo-classical style, and visually inspired by the paintings of Jacques Louis David. It is in this sense that, as Wajda put it, *Danton* should be considered a 'very classical film', rather than in any Lukácsian sense of the term.[11]

Nevertheless, despite these correspondences between *Danton* and the Lukácsian model of democratic humanist realism, it is also clear that, in a number of other significant respects already addressed here, *Danton* falls crucially short of that model. However, there is, in addition to this, a paradoxical sense in which *Danton* can also be considered as an *antithetical* work of democratic humanist realism in Lukácsian terms, because the true source of alienation in the film is not capitalism but, directly, authoritarian revolutionary dogma; and, indirectly, Polish communism. The manifest subject of *Danton* is the French Revolution and, more specifically, the Terror. However, the underlying fixation of the film is not so much with events in 1794 as with the contemporary political, social and cultural situation in Poland during the 1980s, and this underlying fixation effectively determines the rhetorical perspective through which *Danton* portrays the French Revolution. Both Wajda and *Danton* can be related to a school of Polish film-making which emerged during the 1970s and which was committed to a critique of the dominant communist culture. During the early 1970s changes in government led to an easing of official censorship, and this stimulated the growth of a more critical cinema, which, although still unable to voice political criticism directly, was, nevertheless, able to express such criticism indirectly through a focus on the quest for individual, ethical fulfilment, within authoritarian conditions. Thus, films such as Wajda's *Man of Marble* (1976), Zanussi's *Camouflague* (1976) and Kieslowski's *The Scar* (1976) can be related to this innovative critical moment of Polish film-making. In addition to this political context, these films can also be related to a more enduring 'romantic' tradition within which Polish artists felt under obligation to use their work in order to shape historical and political events.[12] One prominent theme within this tradition, and one particularly relevant to *Danton*, is also that of the 'saviour', the driven figure who fights for the rights of the ordinary man.[13]

All of these influences are evident in the three 'political' films which Wajda made between 1976 and 1990: *Man of Marble* (1976), *Man of Iron* (1980) and *Danton*. For example, in *Man of Marble* the central character, played by a student film-maker, attempts to review the life and fate of a 'Stakhanovite' worker hero who, despite his elevation to hero status during the 1950s, had since been erased from public and official memory. The film implicitly criticises the authoritarian and instrumental nature of the Polish communist regime, focusing on the way in which individual destinies are determined by the imperatives of the system. The figure of the student film-maker also draws on the idea of the 'saviour', although, in this case, her efforts at illuminating the past are shown to make little difference to the overall system. Both these themes of criticism of the regime, based around an opposition between individual freedom and social oppression, and the idea of the saviour, are even more evident in, *Man of Iron*, a film made at the height of the counterrevolution, and at a time when Wajda was now free to make direct political criticisms of the regime. In *Man of Iron*, Wajda sides unambiguously with the anti-communist opposition, and the figure of the saviour takes on epic, almost religious proportions, in the real-life figure of the head of the Solidarity movement, Lech Walesa. These twin themes of an opposition between freedom and oppression, and of the role of the saviour, are also evident in *Danton*, and it is this perspective, derived from his own experience of living and working in Poland, which leads Wajda to portray the French Revolution as a kind of replay of the anti-communist Polish revolt of the 1980s. The inevitable consequence was that the Revolution and its servants were depicted negatively, whilst the Dantonist 'rebels' were fitted with the guise of aspiring 'saviours'.

In addition to the influence of a critical Polish film culture, the anti-communist revolt and the tradition of 'Polish romanticism', the ideological orientation of *Danton* was also influenced by the two main literary sources from which the film's screenplay was derived: the German playwright Georg Büchner's 1837 play *Danton's Death*; and the Polish dramatist Stanislawa Przybyszewska's 1937 play *The Danton Affair*. Of these two works, which are separated by exactly one hundred years, it is the more recent and indigenous Polish play which furnished the direct narrative source for Wajda's *Danton*. However, and despite this, the thematic orientation of *Danton* is considerably closer to the earlier Büchner play. The author of *The Danton Affair*, Przybyszewska, was a committed communist and, as a consequence of this, *The Danton Affair* emphasises the progressive, revolutionary attributes of the French Revolution. However, whereas *The Danton Affair* focuses on the Revolution, rather than the Terror, the Büchner play is 'deeply anti-revolutionary' in spirit,[14] and, far from portraying the Revolution in a positive light, shows it as led by political fanatics who would 'smother the Republic in blood'.[15]

In 1975 Wajda directed his own version of the Przybyszewska play for the stage. However, in doing so, he infused it with the spirit of *Danton's Death*, rather than *The Danton Affair*. Whilst *The Danton Affair* focuses on the figure of the 'incorruptible' Robespierre, for example, and on the progressive attributes of the Revolution, *Danton's Death* images the Revolution through the perspective of the Terror, and turns much more on the personal conflict between Danton and Robespierre. As in *Danton's Death*, Wajda's 1975 adaptation of *The Danton Affair* focuses on the personal conflict between Danton and Robespierre and, as in the Büchner, centres positive representation on the figure of Danton, establishing a clear opposition between the dogmatic authoritarianism of Robespierre and the more benevolent, humanist liberalism of Danton. Both Wajda's 1975 play and 1990 film also echo well established, pre-existing understandings of Danton and Robespierre. For example, both draw on the sensualist, passionate character described in Carlyle's *The French Revolution: A History* (1837), where Danton is revealed as 'a Man, fiery real, from the great fire-bosom of Nature herself'; and both also draw on Büchner's play, in which Danton is depicted in heroic terms, as a lively, volatile defender of the republic against the architects of the Terror. Wajda draws on this pre-existing mythic formulation of Danton as 'a hearty fellow . . . inclined to indulge his taste for pleasure . . . [who] . . . knew little of jealousy or bitterness and declared himself willing to join with others for action' as the basis of his representation of Danton in 1990.[16] Similarly, Wajda's Robespierre also draws on pre-existing conceptions of this historical figure. However, and in contrast to the positive mythologisation of Danton, these are almost entirely negative characterisations of an individual considered as a 'petty tyrant' and 'man of blood'.[17]

As has already been made clear, Lukács's conception of aesthetic realism allows a significant role for the creative vision and subjective values of the author in shaping the artistic intensive totality, when that vision and those values stem from authentic engagement in the important events and relations of the day. Clearly, Wajda was heavily involved in the events and relations of his day, and that involvement is manifested in the recapitulation of the 1794 period which is portrayed in *Danton*. Like Marx, Lukács accepts that any work of historical recapitulation will view the past through the prism of the present, and that the trace of the present will influence the interpretation of the past. However, the problem with *Danton* lies in the extent to which the prism of the present determines the portrayal of the past, and the extent to which a discourse concerning Polish resistance to communist authoritarianism is superimposed over a discourse concerning the political complexities of one of the defining moments of European history, to the extent that the Revolution itself is seen as a reactionary event. If there is one overall message emanating from *Danton* it is a conservative one: that when powerful men attempt to impose a system, however rational, upon the course of events, those events will run out of control, and ordinary men and women will be the ones to suffer.

Given such a message, it is hardly surprising that *Danton* was subject to considerable criticism, particularly in France, when it appeared in 1990. Although at one level the film's general ideological perspective seemed justified by the events of 1989, and the slow collapse of the Soviet empire, its conservative recapitulation of the Revolution was not appreciated. Wajda's portrayal of Robespierre, in particular, was strongly criticised, against a context in which a significant reassessment of Robespierre's role as the leading public figure of the Revolution, and its most consistent democrat, was taking place.[18] At the same time, Wajda's portrayal of Danton and the Dantonists was also criticised for its historical inexactitude. For example, the fact that the Dantonists reflected the interests of sectors of the haute bourgeoise and property owning classes who had suffered from the economic controls which the Convention had placed on business during the war[19] is ignored in the film, apart from one singular line, in which Robespierre remarks that Danton 'has the support of the bankers'.

Such a degree of historical inexactitude is, perhaps, inevitable in a film in which Robespierre is not Robespierre but the Communist leader of Poland, General Jaruzelski; and Danton is not Danton but Lech Walesa, the leader of the Solidarity movement.[20] However, it means that *Danton* fails to fit the Lukácsian model of realist democratic humanism on two main counts: (1) that it over-personalises social context, and reduces that context to a background; and (2) that it is, in Lukácsian terms, an 'eccentric' account of historical conjuncture, because, although Wajda is an engaged artist, his engagement is not principally with the historical conjuncture which his film depicts. *Danton* is not, therefore, in the end, an antithetical work of Lukácsian historical democratic humanist realism because it posits the source of alienation in socialism or revolution, rather than capitalism. After all, Lukács was to argue that the contribution of Solzhenitsyn lay in achieving such a portrayal. Lukács himself was also to argue that communist society was frequently oppressive. What makes *Danton* problematic in terms of Lukácsian theory is not this, but the way in which the portrayal of the historical conjuncture is personalised and distorted. As a work of cinematic realism, *Danton* emerged at a moment of intense historical change, and also portrayed another moment of intense historical change. In both cases, 1794 and 1989–90, history was clearly 'occurring', in the evident Lukácsian sense. However, the problem with *Danton* lies in its confused conflation of these two, profoundly different moments of historical transformation – from feudalism to the democratic bourgeois state, and from state socialism to market capitalism.

At the visual level, it is possible to argue that the Lukácsian categories of *Stimmung* and *Stimmungseinheit* can be applied to *Danton*. The film is carefully

shot to evoke the visual style of David, and this creates the kind of visual cohesion which Lukács indicated was required. For example, different colour
schemes are used to connote the different worlds of Danton and Robespierre,
with strong yellows, greens and reds for Danton, and cool whites and blues for
Robespierre. However, the effect of *Stimmung* as an organising principle is, to
some extent, undercut by the narrative operation of *Danton*, which tends to fragment, rather than unify, the film. Although Wajda has argued that he had
intended to make 'a very calm film in its form, a very classical film',[21] *Danton* is
not a 'calm' film, nor is it calm and reflective in the sense in which Lukács uses
these terms when considering works of classical historical realism such as *War
and Peace*. On the contrary, *Danton* often gives the impression of consisting of
a series of fleeting encounters, as individual characters appear, deliver their
speeches and then disappear peremptorily. This may have been influenced by
Büchner's play, which has been described as a 'series of snapshots, with the
background constantly changing'.[22] So, also, in *Danton* there are few large-
scale scenes and, instead, innumerable close ups and shot-reverse shots. The
result is one of fragmentation and, in this sense, the structure of *Danton* matches
Lukács' view of film as replicating the fragmented condition of modernity.
However, in *Danton*, in the dialectic between fragmentation and totality, it
is fragmentation which triumphs over *Stimmung*, and the end result is a film
which does not succeed in drawing its various aspects into a wholly meaningful
totality.

There is one final respect in which *Danton* fails conclusively to match the
demands of the Lukácsian intensive totality. As previously argued, a central
imperative of the Lukácsian film is that cinematic realism must not attempt to
manipulate or position the spectator. In contrast, the Lukácsian film must have
a 'moving, shaking effect' upon the spectator, presenting him or her with a 'new
world'. In this sense, the most Lukácsian of Wajda's three 'political' films is
undoubtedly *Man of Marble*. Although this film remains dominated by an
overall ideological position concerning the authoritarian nature of the ruling
regime, it leaves many positions open and ambiguous. Those within the film
are generally shown as lacking full understanding, and this includes the central
figure. Her quest is to achieve enlightenment, but, at the end, her role is essentially one of illuminating paradoxes, deceptions and simplistic understandings
of reality. *Man of Iron*, on the other hand presents a clear picture of the world,
in which the various participants are not fully fleshed out, but represent clear-
cut historical forces. *Man of Iron* is far more normative than *Man of Marble*,
and the same is true of *Danton*. Both *Man of Iron* and *Danton* marginalise
private life, and focus on world-historical figures, whilst *Man of Marble* is
concerned with the ordinary victims of authoritarianism. The path from *Man
of Marble* to *Danton* then, is one from ambivalence to normative positioning,
and *Danton* can be seen as the embodiment of a lucid vision, based on Wajda's

convictions. On this final hurdle, then, *Danton* fails the Lukácsian test. However, one film that does not fail such a test is Visconti's *Senso*.

Senso (Luchino Visconti, 1954)

There are a number of reasons why any consideration of Lukácsian film theory must address Visconti's *Senso*. Firstly, both Visconti and his film were directly influenced by a knowledge of Marxist, and Lukácsian aesthetic theory. As a member of the Italian Communist Party, Visconti was familiar with such theory, and participated in a number of debates at this time over Marxist theory and the cinema. In this respect, *Senso* can be connected more directly to Lukács than can the later *Danton*. Whilst, during the 1970s and 1980s, Wajda was influenced by the Marxist-based model of socialist realism, Lukács was no longer a major figure of substance, and Wajda's film does not embody any direct and concrete Lukácsian influence. This was not the case, however, with *Senso*, which was made just after the death of Stalin, and during a period when Lukácsian ideas were once again on the agenda. Furthermore, *Senso* occupies a pivotal position within leftist Italian film culture of the period in that it was regarded as a film which marked the transition from the naturalist style of neo-realism to a more 'realist' style consonant with Marxist aesthetic theory.

Although Italian neo-realism emerged as the most important movement in world cinema in the immediate aftermath of the Second World War, it was always problematic in terms of official Marxist theory, and the dominant Soviet model of socialist realism. One of the origins of neorealism lay in the French poetic-realist cinema of the 1930s. For example, Visconti's *Ossessione* (1942), which is considered to have inaugurated neo-realism, was influenced by Marcel Carné's *Quai des brumes* (1938). However, 1930s French poetic realism was considered to be a decadent movement in the eyes of the proponents of socialist realism, because of its intrinsic thematic fatalism, and because it was seen as turning its back on the fight against fascism. As we have seen, this line was adopted on the communist left even in France, during the late 1930s, and was responsible for the critical attacks made against Renoir's *La Bête humaine*. After the war, the relationship between poetic realism and neo-realism continued to be a problem for some Marxist film theorists in Italy, and this influenced the critical reception of *Senso* in that country.

However, for many Marxists the most problematic aspect of neo-realism was the movement's relationship to naturalism. Italian cinematic neo-realism was influenced by a school of realist literature which emerged in Italy during the 1930s, which included prominent writers such as Alberto Moravia, Elio Vittorini, Cesare Pavese and Vasco Pratolini. These writers rejected the 'positive' portrayals of cultural life required by fascist ideology, and focused, instead, on the experiences of the poor and socially marginal. Realist novels such as Vittorini's *Conversazione in Sicilia* (1941) had a particularly strong influence on directors such as Visconti and De Santis, becoming a 'bible to the neorealists'.[23]

Another important influence on neo-realism was that of the nineteenth-century Sicilian *verist* novelist Giovanni Verga. Verga's ideas shaped the approach to cinematic realism adopted by the journal *Cinema* and Visconti's *La terra trema* (1947) was also based on Verga's best known novel, *The House by the Medlar Tree*. Visconti, De Santis and others were particularly impressed by the way in which Verga combined a poetic, humanist sensibility with the detailed, concrete depiction of Sicilian landscape and society, and De Santis argued that, besides being a 'great poet', Verga had also created a body of work which

> seems to offer the strongest and most human, the most marvellously virgin and authentic ambience that can inspire the imagination of a cinema seeking things and facts in a time and space dominated by reality so as to detach itself from facile suggestions and decadent *bourgeois* taste.[24]

The emphasis which De Santis places on 'things', 'facts' and 'reality' here also echoes one of the first formulations of the neo-realist aesthetic, as elaborated by Arnaldo Bocelli in 1930, where Bocelli argues that neo-realism was 'sunk as deeply as possible into "things", adhering to the "object" '.[25] This emphasis on the concrete, when combined with opposition to both fascist ideology and a literary culture grounded in 'autobiographical lyricism' and 'elegiac introversion', was to have a profound influence on later neo-realist film-making.[26] However, Verga's affirmative humanism was also to prove as influential as his penchant for detailed observation. For example, Vittorio De Sica's claim that Verga's work amounted to 'a revolutionary art inspired by, and acting, in turn, as inspiration to a humanity which hopes and suffers', reflects the affirmative humanism found within many neo-realist films.[27]

De Santis's designation of Verga's work as 'humanist' also indicates an important distinction which must be drawn between French nineteenth-century naturalism and its Italian counterpart, *verismo*. During the nineteenth century, Italian critics such as Francesco de Sanctis, Luigi Capuana and Verga criticised French naturalism for its pessimism, scientism and emphasis on the genetically flawed, Darwinian *bête humaine*. Whilst adopting the factual, observational style of French naturalism, these critics insisted on the infusion of a more hopeful dimension into the naturalist vision, and Verga's insistence that, in addition to showing things as they are, *verismo* should also indicate how they could, ideally, be, was later to influence the engaged, humanist orientation adopted by neo-realism.[28]

These various influences led neo-realist cinema to focus on the relationship between individual and environment, and on the suffering of 'the poor, the underprivileged, the ordinary'.[29] Consequently, films such as *La terra trema* (Visconti, 1947) and *Ladri di biciclette* (De Sica, 1948) situate working-class characters within social and cultural environments marked by poverty, social hardship and injustice, and also depict the relationship between character and environment in considerable empirical detail, furnishing that 'concrete homage to other people, that is, to all who exist', which the critic and scenarist Cesare Zavattini called for in his influential 'A Thesis on Neorealism'.[30]

In addition to this concern with the concrete and the ordinary, neo-realist films such as *Ladri di biciclette, Germania anno zero* (Rossellini, 1947) and *Umberto D* (De Sica, 1951) also emphasise the ambivalent character of everyday experience. This concern to depict the ambiguous nature of existence was partly influenced by the unresolved conclusions of French films such as *La Bête humaine, Quai des brumes* and *Pépé le Moko* (Carné, 1937). However, it was also influenced by a rejection of the tendency towards superficial, and often highly normative, narrative resolution which typified the cinema of the fascist period. It was in reaction to what Luigi Chiarini called the 'web of censorship' which surrounded the fascist cinema that the neo-realist films which appeared after the liberation deliberately attempted to depict postwar Italian society in all its unsettling complexities.[31] Consequently, even though neo-realists such as Chiarini emerged from the liberation committed to a form of film-making which would make a positive contribution towards social reform, they also insisted on the right to depict the Italian social formation as, in Chiarini's words, 'a world in ruins'.[32]

However, after 1948, neo-realist film-makers came under criticism, as Italian politics moved further to both left and right. Following election victories by the conservative Christian Democratic party in 1948, neo-realist films were increasingly criticised for their 'negative' depiction of Italian society, and neo-realism also received a further blow in 1949, when the so-called 'Andreotti Law' came into force. The Andreotti Law established a series of quotas and subsidies designed to raise the level of home film production. However, subsidies and export licences could also be denied to films which, in the government's view, 'slandered Italy'.[33] As it turned out, many of the exclusion orders made under the Law tended to target neo-realist films, and Andreotti even intervened directly to condemn De Sica's *Umberto D* as a 'wretched service to his fatherland, which is also the fatherland of . . . progressive social legislation'.[34] Such criticism mirrors the assault made on *Ossessione* by Vittorio Mussolini in 1942, when he asserted that 'This [*Ossessione*] is not Italy',[35] and also reflects the fact that, from 1942 until at least the early 1950s, neo-realism retained its oppositional character in relation to the government of the day.

In addition to criticism from the centre-right, neo-realism also came under censure from the communist left during the late 1940s. In 1948 the Soviet Union's attempt to incorporate the western sectors of Berlin into the eastern bloc led to a marked intensification of the Cold War. The official Soviet policy of the Popular Front had been abandoned in 1946–7 and replaced by one which revisited the 'class against class' politics of the early 1930s.[36] This also coincided with the reaffirmation of Zhadanovist Soviet socialist realism as the official aesthetic doctrine of the Communist Party. However, neo-realism had evolved within the ideological configurations of popular frontism, and the humanist, social-democratic tendencies which characterised many neo-realist films could not be squared with the new political context. In 1948, De Santis's *Riso amaro* was also castigated by the communist daily *L'Unita* for its lack of 'positive heroes' and 'decadent' displays of female flesh, whilst Visconti received the ultimate rebuke of having his films compared to what, in Stalinist eyes, represented one of the worst excesses of 'decadent', European bourgeois cinema, the *réalisme poétique* of Renoir, Carné and others. Just as Renoir's *La Bête humaine* had been condemned by the French Communist Party during the 1930s, *Ossessione* was also accused of taking up the 'worst and most condemnable aspects' of the prewar French cinema, including 'the erotic ambience of Renoir's films'.[37] Over the period from 1948 to the mid-1950s virtually every neo-realist film-maker came under critical assault from the communist left. This criticism reinforced that emerging from the Christian Democratic right, and yet further censure arrived from the Catholic Church, which classified neo-realism in general, and *Riso amaro* in particular, as 'forbidden for believers'.[38]

As neo-realism declined as an identifiably coherent aesthetic position during the early 1950s, the films of the major neo-realist directors also evolved stylistically. Luchino Visconti drew on Marxist theory in making films such as *Ossessione* and *La terra trema*, both of which, and particularly *La terra trema*, were made within the neo-realist style. However, with *Senso* (1954), Visconti departed radically from the documentary style of *La terra trema* (which he had made in close association with the Italian Communist Party). *Senso* was acclaimed by the communist left in Italy because of the extent to which it abandoned the 'negative naturalism' of neo-realism, and because it appeared to adopt a model of realism more in accord with the prescriptions of Soviet socialist realism. For example, whilst criticising both Roberto Rossellini's *Viaggio in Italia* (1953) and Federico Fellini's *La strada* (1954) as 'regressive', Guido Aristarco, the editor in chief of *Cinema Nuovo*, described *Senso* as 'a great historical film, a revolutionary film which brought our cinematic history to a new peak'.[39] Aristarco's admiration for *Senso* reflected his own understanding of Marxist and Lukácsian theory, and his criticism of *Viaggio in Italia* and *La strada* also reflected the condemnation of neo-realism which the communist left had put forward from 1948 onwards. Nevertheless, although it was admired by Aristarco and other communist film theorists, *Senso* was also criticised by the leading lights of neo-realism. For example, Chiarini and Zavattini strongly criticised *Senso* for abandoning 'The most substantial merit of neo-realism . . . to propose only subjects which were near in time and space'.[40] For Chiarini and Zavattini, the historical melodramatic approach of *Senso* stood in opposition to the entire aesthetic system of neo-realism. Nevertheless, the purist neo-realist position advocated by Chiarini and Zavattini in 1954 was already being discarded by many Italian film-makers, and the historical importance of *Senso* resides in the fact that it was made at a time when, following the death of Stalin and consequent liberalisation, Marxist film theorists and film-makers were turning again from a dogmatic socialist realism, to the models of critical realism elaborated by Lukács.

Like *Danton*, *Senso* can be considered Lukácsian in the way that it attempts to portray a historical conjuncture through the prism of individual characters, thereby fusing the particular and the general. Both films are also concerned with moments of revolutionary change. Whilst *Danton* is set in 1793, during the transition from radical Jacobin governance to bourgeois control and the eventual establishment of the Napoleonic empire in 1799, *Senso* is set some seventy years later, in 1866, during the final stages of the Italian *Risorgimento*. However, there is an important sense in which *Senso* differs from *Danton* in its portrayal of historical context, and this also has implications for the extent to which either film can be considered as more, or less, Lukácsian. Whilst *Danton* portrays a pivotal juncture of revolutionary import and transition, *Senso* is set well after, and is, consequently, rhetorically and affectively distanced from, the key events and substance of the *Risorgimento*, which are addressed more directly in the later *Il gattopardo* (1963). The political objective of the *Risorgimento* was the unification of Italy from foreign rule, and under national haute bourgeois control. However, that had been largely achieved by 1861–2, apart from the recovery of Venice from Austria, and Rome from France. *Senso* is set in 1866, during the final months of the Austrian occupation of Venice, and in the final phase of Italian unification.

This historical and discursive distance from the central core events of the *Risorgimento* also grants *Senso* a diegetic detachment from its explicit subject matter, and this degree of reserve is further augmented by the historically contentious and controversial character of the Italian war to liberate Venice. By 1953, the campaign for Venice was still largely feted within the Italian establishment as a celebrated military triumph. However, the recovery of Venice by Italy came about largely through Austria's defeat at the hands of Prussia in the battle of Sadowa and, in fact, the Italian attack on the occupying Austrian forces began with a shambolic defeat at the battle of Custoza, in 1866.[41] After the Austrian defeat at Sadowa, which occurred one month after Custoza, Venice was ceded to France, and then given back, through France, to Italy as part of a larger European territorial settlement, rather than as a consequence of Italian military prowess. In addition, neither Custoza nor the Italian military campaign against Austria in general need ever have taken place, as it was already clear to the Italian authorities that Austria was prepared to give up Venice peacefully. Rather than accept the return of Venice through such means, however, nationalist sentiment insisted on military engagement in order to achieve the same end. Yet another factor which added to the controversial nature of the campaign was that, during the clash at Custoza, the irregular republican militias of Garibaldi were deliberately barred from fighting alongside the royalist Italian troops. The exclusion of the *Garibaldini*, which some commentators have argued played a role in bringing about the eventual defeat of the Italian forces, was not merely based on insular military sensitivities, however, but also reflected a more general political marginalisation of popular republicanism and, in particular, of Garibaldi's radical Partito D'Azione, by the emerging ruling elite based around the constitutional monarchy of the Savoy dynasty. It appears, then, that Custoza was a battle which need never have been fought in the first place, and one which was lost on the anvil of political expediency, just as the campaign for Venice was fought on sectional political grounds rather than on the basis of national military necessity.

In focusing on this decidedly problematic episode within the 'Third War of Independence' of the *Risorgimento*, rather than, for example, on the more successfully prosecuted military operations at Gaeta and Calatafimi, Visconti provided himself with the facility to elaborate a particularly critical and complicated account of historical context within *Senso*. Visconti had initially wanted to call his film 'Custoza', after the Italian defeat, because, as he put it: 'What interested me was to tell a story about a mismanaged war, fought by a single class and ending in disaster'.[42] Visconti's intentions in this respect were informed in part by Antonio Gramsci's demand that the *Risorgimento* should be portrayed not in hagiographic terms, and through the prism of nationalist mythology, but rather as a struggle fought on the grounds of class interest and privilege.[43] However, Visconti's aspirations to base *Senso* on such a Gramscian perspective were, ultimately, mediated by a number of external interventions aimed at reducing the degree of class criticism contained within the film. For example, the idea of naming the film after a military defeat was opposed by the military, and eventually dropped as a consequence. Two key sequences were also removed from the film by the official censors. In the first of these, Ussoni, the leader of the republican irregulars, is denied a part in the battle for Custoza by the spokesman for the royal army on the grounds that the revolutionaries must be excluded from the expected royalist victory. The cutting of this scene significantly weakens the Gramscian interpretation of the *Risorgimento* as 'conquista regia', rather than 'movimento popolare', which Visconti had intended to deploy in *Senso*.[44] The second scene occurs at the finale of *Senso*, where Visconti has a young drunken Austrian soldier celebrating the victory at Custoza, in ignorance of the fact that, barely a month later, the Austrian Empire would be fatally defeated. Again, the excision of this scene, which invokes the demise of an Austrian military caste which had ruled Venice with the complicity of the Veneto aristocracy, removes some of the political energy from *Senso*, and channels the film's final scenes back into a politically less dangerous depiction of the individual destinies of its chief protagonists.[45]

Despite these external interventions, however, *Senso* was, nevertheless, able to deliver an influential evaluation, both of the *Risorgimento* and of contemporary conceptions of national identity. This evaluation generated substantial critical attention when the film was premiered. For example, the young Vittorio Taviani recalls that *Senso* was immediately regarded as occupying a central position in an ongoing debate about the future of a committed, progressive Italian cinema.[46] Although criticised by neo-realists such as Chiarini and Zavattini,[47], writing in *Cinema Nuovo* in 1955 Guido Aristarco argued that *Senso* was 'a great historical film, a revolutionary film that brought our cinematic history to a new peak'.[48] Later critics have also argued that *Senso* 'was the most relevant film of the decade',[49] that it 'dragged the previously untouchable Risorgimento through the mud'[50] and 'struck at' conceptions of Italian nationalism.[51]

The critical, 'moving-shaking' approach adopted within *Senso* fulfils the crucial Lukácsian imperative that the work of critical realism should present an indeterminate account of historical reality and, within the terms of such a Lukácsian categorisation, it can also be argued that the portrayal of historical context within *Senso* is considerably more Lukácsian than that portrayed within *Danton*. Whilst, in *Danton*, Wajda disengages with the historical specificity of the events of the French Revolution in order to *validate* metaphorically a, by then, conventionally held conception of Polish national identity, in *Senso* Visconti portrays the *Risorgimento* through a more critical and deconstructive perspective in order to *contest* established conceptions of Italian national identity. Of course, *Danton* does challenge some conceptions of the French Revolution (for example, the idea that the Revolution should be regarded as constituting the triumph of reason and democracy over religious mysticism and privileged oligarchy), but this 'challenge' occurs unintentionally and inadvertently, rather than critically, and is also subsumed beneath the film's more normative predispositions. In contrast, in *Senso*, a normative discourse concerning the reality of *transformismo* is clearly subject to the force of more critical dispositions which 'underline the ambiguities and the equivocal motives of the events of 1866'.[52]

However, although this aspect of *Senso* may conform to one Lukácsian principle, it is more difficult to place the film squarely within the parameters of two other Lukácsian categories: those of classical and 'social critical' realism. It will be recalled that, according to Lukács, after 1848 the production of classical literary realism, in which individual characters were concretely linked to their historical contexts, became more difficult to achieve, and symbolism, modernism, naturalism and democratic humanist realism then emerged from the downfall of classical realism. As with the post-1848 *Danton*, Visconti's similarly historically challenged work cannot be classed as a work of classical critical realism, both *de facto* and (as will be described later) because, like *Danton*, *Senso* employs a range of symbolic affective measures, rather than a tight web of narrative 'mediations', in order to link the particular to the general. Visconti had, apparently intended to model *Senso* on one archetypal 'classical' realist source, Tolstoy's *War and Peace*. However, the final film differs markedly from the approach adopted in Tolstoy's novel.[53] Rather than *War and Peace* it was another canonic realist work, although not a 'classical' one – Stendhal's *La Chartreuse de Parme* – which was to have the greatest influence on Visconti's aspirations for *Senso*:

> I should have liked to make *La Chartreuse de Parme* – that was my ideal. If my film had not been cut, and if it had been edited as I wanted, it would have really been Fabrice at the Battle of Waterloo . . . My ideal I confess, would be a film on one of Stendhal's great novels'.[54]

There are many similarities between *Senso* and Stendhal's novel which can be used to relate both film and novel to each other, and to a Lukácsian framework. For example, Lukács argues that *La Chartreuse de Parme* presents a 'magnificent picture of court life within the framework of an Italian petty state' through portraying 'the outwardly insignificant events' which 'manifest' the 'big political problems'.[55] This is very much the approach adopted within *Senso*. Similarly, Lukács' argument that the basis of Stendhal's realist achievement lay in transforming the romantic, Byronic, 'demonic hero' type in a 'social-historical, objective-epic manner' could equally be applied to the portrayal of the Franz Mahler character in *Senso*.[56] Lukács apart, there are also a number of correspondences between *Senso* and novels such as *La Chartreuse de Parme* and *Le Rouge et le noir* (1830). For example, Stendhal employs an ironic style which often establishes an empathetic distance between narration and characters described, and this is also the approach adopted in *Senso*. An anti-bourgeois stance and concern with the need to explore the values of the outcast is also shared by both *Senso* and *La Chartreuse de Parme*, whilst both works portray the deployment of sexuality as a dominating force. One Stendhalian theme which could be related to Lukács's ideas of 'soul' and 'culture', and which, though absent in *Senso*, is present in *Il gattopardo*, however, is the focus on the person of integrity, who seeks to transcend the empty materialism of bourgeois life. Despite these similarities, however, *Senso* must also be distinguished from a novel such as *La Chartreuse de Parme* on the grounds that the film lacks the 'simultaneous presence of the antithetical elements of baseness and sublimity' found in the novel.[57] There is, in fact, little 'sublimity' in *Senso*, although plenty of 'baseness'.

The absence of 'sublimity' in *Senso* also means that Visconti's film cannot be entirely identified with a Stendhalian realism which Lukács places within the more general category of 'social critical' realism. Lukács accounts for the *presence* of 'sublimity' within the work of Stendhal through a distinction which he makes between classical realism, democratic humanist realism and 'social critical' realism. Lukács argues that Stendhalian realism cannot equal the 'extraordinary realism'[58] of classical Balzacian realism because Stendhal remains linked to a form of pre-1848 idealism which has its roots in eighteenth-century Enlightenment progressiveness and absolutist conceptions of reason. Lukács argues that the 'social critical' realism of Stendhal is an earlier precursor to post-1848 idealist democratic humanist realism, rather than a form of classical realism, because Stendhal 'universalises' his material exceptionally[59], instead of relating it more closely to the mediating domain of *Besonderheit* – which Lukács regards as the true focal point of the classical realist approach – and because the idealism associated with the Stendhalian method is neither necessary nor sufficient to the classical style (Lukács argues, for example, that the classical can legitimately be very dark in 'emotional accent', and talks about Balzac's 'sense of universal doom').[60] However, even if this distinction is accepted, it would appear that, despite the presence of a dark 'emotional accent' in *Senso*, Visconti's film must be distinguished from classical Balzacian realism, on grounds already discussed. Similarly, the presence of such an accent also means that *Senso* cannot be related to the more aspirational 'social critical' approach of Stendhal, which Lukács also associates in spirit and inclination with post-1848 democratic humanist realism (indeed, Lukács appears largely to distinguish the two forms on historical grounds alone, rather than on the basis of stylistic difference).[61] But if this is the case, if *Senso* is neither an example of 'classical', 'social critical' or 'democratic humanist realism', the question remains as to precisely how to categorise *Senso* in Lukácsian terms.

A number of previous attempts made at applying a Lukácsian perspective to an understanding of *Senso* have tended to use Lukácsian ideas in a general and sometimes indiscriminate manner, often eliding the important distinctions which Lukács himself drew between the various forms of realism, some of which are referred to above. In these attempts, passages from Lukács's writings are sometimes taken out of context in order to define *Senso* as Lukácsian in a self-legitimating manner, and the subsequent conclusions drawn are often unclear and wide-ranging. This sort of selective treatment of Lukács leads to significant misinterpretations of what Lukács actually meant, and to an inappropriate application of Lukácsian ideas to films such as *Senso* and *Il gattopardo*. For example, a passage from 'Balzac und der franzöische Realismus' celebrating Balzac as bringing 'out the specifically individual and the class-bound typical features of every single character' is applied directly to Visconti and *Senso*, even though *Senso* cannot be classed as an example of classical

Balzacian realism.[62] Similarly, *Senso* is described as 'living up to Lukács' definition of the historical novel wherein the "personal destinies of a number of human beings coincide and interweave within the determining context of an historical crisis " '.[63] Again, here, the actual passage quoted does not, in fact, refer to either early works of 'social critical' realism, or later works of 'democratic humanist' realism but to the classical realism of Sir Walter Scott's *Waverley* (1814), which cannot be identified with a film such as *Senso*.

At one level, both of these applications of Lukács to *Senso* do make some sense. However, at other levels they are misleading: *Senso* does not, for example, unite the individual and typical features of 'every single character' in the film, and nor, in Lukácsian terms, could it ever do so. The problem is that such blanket applications of Lukács do not aid in the task of understanding precisely how *Senso* can and cannot be best explored from a Lukácsian perspective. Many other examples of such selective quotations from Lukács could be given here, but these should suffice to make it clear that it is not enough to impose an all-embracing notion of Lukácsian realism on films such as *Senso*, particularly given that the notion of aesthetic *specificity* lies at the heart of the Lukácsian system. So, to return to the question posed in the previous paragraph, precisely how can *Senso* be defined in specific terms as a form of Lukácsian realism? As argued above, *Senso* cannot be characterised as a work of either 'social critical' realism or 'democratic humanist' realism, because of the markedly ironic and paradoxical stance which the film adopts. When it first appeared, *Senso* was criticised for its apparent lack of 'positive' attributes, and for its generally fatalistic attitude,[64] whilst later critics have described the film as a 'degenerate'[65] and 'degraded' melodrama[66] which appears to possess none of the latent idealism associated with the Lukácsian categories referred to previously. However, it may, at this stage, be possible to advance a provisional characterisation of *Senso* as a work of 'negative' democratic humanist realism, and as an ironic form of critical realism bent on the deconstruction of humanist-nationalist discourses. In addition, this categorisation of *Senso* as 'reversing' one of the key Lukácsian categories also needs to be considered in conjunction with another Lukácsian category which will be considered later, that of the modern work of critical realism which, in departing from the paradigm of idealist democratic humanism, is forced to adopt a form of 'lowered vitality' and attenuation of positive representation.[67] This provisional Lukácsian categorisation of *Senso* will be returned to and developed further in this chapter, as other aspects of *Senso* are considered.

If *Senso* is regarded as deploying a reverse or converse model of democratic humanist realism, one of the key means through which the film achieves this is through its portrayal of the Verdian 'operatic'. Visconti retained an interest in opera, and Verdi in particular, throughout his career, as is evidenced by the productions which he staged of *La traviata* (1955*)*, *Macbeth* (1958), *Don Carlos*

(1958) *La traviata* (1963), *Il trovatore* (1964), *Don Carlos* (1965), *Falstaff* (1966), *La traviata* (1967) and *Simon Boccanegra* (1969). In some respects the idealistic Verdian operatic melodrama can be compared to Lukács' idea of democratic humanist realism. In the Verdian world, for example, emotionally charged characters strive nobly to fulfil their individual destinies, although those same individuals may be ultimately ground down by the overbearing material forces surrounding them. The forms of 'abstract humanism' and 'historical monumentality' (Lukács' phrases) found in Verdi's *I due Foscari*, *Simon Boccanegra*, *Don Carlos* and *Aida* also embody what Lukács refers to as 'the great humanist ideas and ideals'. However, although the influence of Verdi is clearly apparent in *Senso*, the Verdian world depicted in the film is also portrayed as beyond contemporary possibility, as though, in a fallen post-*Risorgimento* world, it cannot be attained and can only be parodied.[68] In fact, *Senso* discards this Verdian aesthetic model, just as it rejects the spirit of the democratic humanist ideal, because Visconti does not believe that the idealist temper of the Verdian horizon, and the humanist, nationalist discourse which it accommodates, is any longer appropriate to the portrayal of an Italian history which must now be rendered primarily in terms of a critique of class privilege and licence.

Senso has been described as a 'degraded melodrama in its violation of the moral laws which govern the Verdian world'.[69] However, at the beginning of *Senso* the Verdian world still seems intact, as a discourse of honourable intent, budding romantic liaisons and effusive patriotism unfolds against the background of the Fenice Opera, and a performance of *Il trovatore*. However, this romantic milieu soon begins to fissure, as it becomes clear that the two central characters, Franz Mahler and Countess Livia Serpieri, fall far short of the Verdian ideal. For example, Livia appears to be torn between patriotic idealism and a preoccupation with romantic liaisons which threaten to marginalise that idealism. Similarly, although Franz looks the part of the romantic hero, he is also shown to be a cynic and, possibly, also a coward. This distance from the Verdian ideal is also emphasised by contrasting the behaviour of Franz and Livia fairly directly with the performance of the central characters of *Il trovatore*, Manrico and Leonora, both of whom exhibit qualities of high duty and noble virtue.[70] This 'ironic' approach, where one set of connotations undercuts or refutes another, is typical of *Senso* as a whole and, after this opening section, *Senso* continues its work of undermining the Verdian *Zeitgeist*, as the 'degraded' melodrama of Livia and Franz evolves into a personalised allegory for the 'degradation of the *Risorgimento* ideal' itself.[71]

Senso also embodies the Lukácsian idea of 'culture' as accommodating both the notion of individual resistance to instrumental manipulation and the imperative to grasp totality. However, the manner in which this idea is articulated within *Senso* results in a situation whereby the possibility of grasping totality in any fruitful way is completely denied, and whereby individual resistance is, as a consequence, transformed into romanticised delusion. For example, if the emotionally 'operatic' in *Senso* stands for the opposite of the rationalised prosaic life which Franz and Livia seek to transcend – 'soul' rather than the 'thing world', in Lukácsian terms – it is also an inherently inadequate expression of soul. Far from seeking to realise her own inner qualities, Livia is fatally undermined by a conception of self which is class-specifically determined, rather than authentic, and this leaves her unable to discern the difference between her real needs and an artificial discourse of personal subjectivism. In this respect Livia stands as an example of Lukács' conception of regressive subjectivism as that which turns inwards, and away from, external reality.

At the finale of *Senso*, for example, Livia finds herself completely isolated, having voluntarily cut herself off from her previous existence, only to confront the reality of her alienated predicament in the darkened streets of Austrian-occupied Verona. Livia's journey into oblivion appears to stem from a repudiation of the public in favour of the personal. At the beginning of the film Livia is a public figure, conscious of her social responsibilities. As the film progresses she gradually loses this consciousness of social and public responsibility. The outcome is a loss of psychological 'balanced composure' and equilibrium, as the public sphere is overwhelmed by irresistible subjective imperatives.[72] It is as though the world of private, subjective emotion is a dangerous place which, when entered, can destroy those who do so. In this respect, Livia embodies the Lukácsian perspective of regressive subjectivism as destructive, because such subjectivism denies any possibility of grasping the totality of things. In Lukácsian terms, Livia is doomed because her behaviour stands in opposition to both requisites of the foundational idea of 'culture'. Her individual struggle against the thing world is not driven by an authentic urge to self-realisation, and she makes no attempt to understand the sum of her situation. However, Livia is also a 'typical' character in the Lukácsian sense, because she is a representative of a decadent social class which has abdicated its own sense of social responsibility in favour of private pursuits, and has, consequently, abrogated responsibility for bringing manifestations of objectivised and non-objectivised culture into existence.

However, Livia is not the only character within *Senso* whose psychological and affective preoccupations cause them to misunderstand external reality, and the same is true of her cousin, the nationalist patriot, the Marquisse Ussoni. Whilst Livia's immersion within an upper-class-based ideal of 'courtly love'[73] leads her into a particular form of subjective delusion, Ussoni's allegiance to an ideological discourse of patriotic nationalism also leads him into another. Like the nationalist discourse which he espouses, Ussoni is a peripheral figure in *Senso* and, compared to Livia and Franz, is portrayed in schematic terms, in a way which emphasises the inadequate character of his essentially class-based, rather than genuinely populist, motives and ideology. Like Livia, Ussoni is impulsive, rather than reflective. For example, he risks the success of his political cause by initiating a needless confrontation with Mahler at the beginning of the film, and endangering his life pointlessly during the ill-fated battle of Custoza. Despite the fact that he is her devoted cousin, Ussoni also completely misreads Livia's motives throughout the course of the film. Ussoni's world view is a simplistic one, and as such, stands as a metaphor for the official conception of the *Risorgimento* which *Senso* critiques, just as the film's portrayal of Custoza mocks conservative estimations of the battle.

However, although an apparently peripheral figure within *Senso*, Ussoni was also Visconti's own creation, and does not exist at all in the source novel. He must, therefore, serve some sort of important function within the film. In fact, in addition to representing the *Risorgimento* as a '*bourgeois* revolution and therefore as an incomplete revolution', Ussoni also appears to have a number of other functions within *Senso*.[74] First, he stands for the alternative to the parodied Verdian world of *Senso* in that, if it were he, rather than Mahler, who was to embark on an affair with Livia, the couple would become a filmic equivalent of Manrico and Leonora in *Il trovatore*. The possibility that Ussoni might romance Livia is raised a number of times during the course of the film, and this has the effect of acting as a metaphorical counterpoint to the more perverse relationship which exists between Franz and Livia, as well as pointing to the more positive form of representation which *Senso*, as a whole, denies. In Lukácsian terms, however, a relationship between Livia and Ussoni would still not conform fully to the ideal of culture, because their understanding of the world would be constrained within the circumscribed configuration of a bourgeois nationalist conception of reality: their individual struggle would be misconceived and they would, consequently, fail to grasp totality.

The second narrative purpose which Ussoni appears to serve in *Senso* is that of invoking a form of characterisation which could be described as socialist realist. As Ussoni strides across the battlefield of Custoza, for example, he resembles those heroic figures found in the Soviet cinema of socialist realism. At one level, Ussoni could be read as a metaphor for the Italian partisan resistance fighters of the Second World War and, if this were so, his inclusion within the film would mark the presence of at least one overtly 'positive' tone. However, Ussoni is not convincing as a fictional character, and this raises the possibility that Visconti may actually be parodying this form of socialist realist characterisation in *Senso*. Given his contact with the Italian Communist Party, and his knowledge of the socialist realist style, Visconti must have expected that *Senso* would attract criticism from some on the left who believed that the film did not possess sufficient 'positive' elements, or departed too radically from the socialist realist (and neo-realist) model. Visconti may have responded to such criticism in advance, through portraying the character of Ussoni in a one-dimensional way, thus demonstrating the kind of simplifications which would be forced upon *Senso* were he to submit to the requirement that the film must accommodate positive role models within its predominantly dark perspective. As with so much in *Senso*, the figure of Ussoni is to be read at a number of different, and sometimes dissonant levels, and his portrayal as a committed revolutionary figure is interwoven with this more negative depiction. This approach clearly conforms to the Lukácsian demand for critical representation, but it also conforms to Lukács' support for the notion that works of bourgeois art such as *Senso* should adopt a critical, rather than socialist realist, aesthetic style.

The most important character in *Senso* is undoubtedly Franz Mahler. Unfortunately, however, Visconti was unable to realise his full vision of the Mahler character in his film. Initially, Visconti had wanted Marlon Brando to play the part. However, the Hollywood studio which was bankrolling the production, 20th Century Fox, insisted upon Farley Grainger, and he proved so inadequate that Visconti was forced to change his initial intentions. This is why, in the finished film, it is Livia, rather than Franz, who is portrayed the most, even though, as will be argued, Franz is the more important character.[75] Just as Livia represents a Venetian aristocracy which has forsaken its ability to grasp totality, and turned to regressive subjectivism, Franz is the representative of an imperial Austrian military caste which is facing eradication.[76] Franz can also be understood in terms of Lukács' definition of post-Byronic 'demonic heroes' as 'eccentric', but as nevertheless 'portray[ing] the struggles and antagonisms of history', and 'who, in their psychology and destiny, always represent social trends and historical forces'.[77] Franz's psychology is essentially nihilistic in outlook, and is characterised by forms of cynicism and hedonism which are adjuncts to his role as an agent of imperial repression.[78] His destiny is to expire, just as it is the providence of the Austro-Hungarian Empire to descend into decay. The 'struggles and antagonisms' which Franz embodies also reflect the clash between a declining, imperialist aristocratic-militarist class, and an emerging bourgeois nationalist one; and between the age of imperialism and the era of nationalism. Franz is thus, in Lukács' terminology a romantic anti-hero who embodies the spirit of an imperialist regime in terminal decline. Consequently, Franz must be portrayed as a 'decadent' character, manipulative, exploitative, cowardly and narcissistically self-absorbed.

However, in addition to his role as representative of a decadent and doomed social order, Franz is also the most insightful person in *Senso*, and from the outset he is conscious of his inescapable destiny.[79] He is, for example, able to comprehend the inadequate character of the world views of Livia and Ussoni. Franz knows that Livia's faith in the romantic discourse of courtly love is at odds with the material reality of her social position. Unlike Ussoni, Franz is also well aware that Livia's professed love of her country ('like my cousin, I am a true Italian') is only a compensating appearance disguising her affective fixation with a realm of the private which her social position as a member of a dissolute and dissipated collaborating aristocracy leads her to embrace. Franz's situation as an occupying soldier, and agent of imperialism, also allows him an insight into the limitations of the nationalist rhetoric which Ussoni espouses. However, in addition to this degree of privileged portrayal in relation to Livia and Ussoni, Franz is also able to grasp the reality of the general social-historical situation more clearly than they. For example, in the key confrontation between Franz and Livia which occurs towards the end of the film Franz delivers Visconti's message concerning the *Risorgimento*: that there is nothing to celebrate here, only the decline of an older more aristocratic culture, and its replacement with a less vital bourgeois order: 'In a few years Austria will be finished. A whole world will disappear. A world to which you and I belong. I'm not interested in your cousin's new world. I'd rather stay out of the whole business.' Unlike Livia and Ussoni, therefore, Franz understands that the *Risorgimento* is not a national popular movement but an essentially bourgeois revolution, and that Ussoni's 'new world' will embody a form of *transformismo* to be led by a new middle-class or aristocratic establishment.

There is also a sense in which Franz can be regarded as corresponding to the Lukácsian idea of culture. For example, Franz attempts to carry through his own form of resistance to the estranged social-historical 'thing world' which he finds himself part of. As argued, Franz is also able to comprehend totality with an insight not granted to any other character within the film. However, Franz's fate is guaranteed by his decision to turn from resistance and comprehension to subjectivism and, according to Lukács, such a turn can only lead to nihilism and self-destruction. It is also the *extent* to which Franz has succumbed to the allure of subjectivism which leads to the downfall of Livia. Although Livia is initially shown as inhabiting a public world, the social class of which she is a member has turned its back on totality, and Franz proves to be the catalyst, igniting latent regressive behavioural patterns within her, as a representative of the Italian ruling class, which leads to her increasing self-absorption, and to a gradual withdrawal from the public sphere into a private world where she will be masochistically 'subject to domination by her lover'.[80] Just as *Senso* inverts both the Verdian milieu and conservative conceptions of the *Risorgimento*, therefore, Franz is also an 'inverted' representation of the Lukácsian idea of culture, and this inversion has its source in the subjectivist turn which Franz is compelled to take. If, as already argued, Ussoni is the rhetorical embodiment of the official, conservative view of the *Risorgimento* in *Senso* and of the class alliance which came to power in 1866, and Livia a metaphor for the misguided and deluded disposition of that view, then Franz can be regarded as one of the principal means through which Visconti mounts his 'inverted' and ironic critique of both conservative understandings of 1866 and more contemporary conceptions of Italian national identity.

Nevertheless, there remains one area where Franz and Livia do embody the Lukácsian ideal of culture in a more straightforward way, and that is in the emotional intensity of their relationship. Here, Visconti invests the pre-bourgeois world with genuine sensuality, and contrasts that 'operatic' world with the more rationalised, pragmatic 'new world', which is represented, in particular, by the collaborator Count Serpieri. It has been argued that *Senso* is a film in which feelings are shown to be dangerous, and the contrary of reason.[81] However, it is not feelings and emotions as such which are dangerous (Ussoni is similarly motivated by 'feelings', but is, nevertheless, part of the 'new world') but sensuality. Visconti's films often link sensuality to defeat and pessimism[82] and, in *Senso*, sensuality is clearly associated with the 'old world' of the more vital pre-bourgeois; a world which is also, however, fated to disappear. As the title of the film suggests (the English translation would be 'sensuality'), *Senso* is an excessively sumptuous film, particularly in its use of aural and visual expression. For example, the music of Verdi is used to enhance or counterpoint moments of dramatic tension, whilst Bruckner's Seventh Symphony is used to express the sense of alienation which suffuses certain sections of the film, and particularly the final scenes of Livia's abandonment and Franz's execution.[83] The scene of the execution also draws heavily on the pictorial style of Goya's painting *El 5 de Mayo*,[84] whilst, elsewhere in the film, colour schemes derived from Titian and Tintoretto are employed[85] in order to give the *mise en scène* an 'excessive' character.[86]

In almost all these cases the sensual is expressed through pictorialism and musical composition, rather than dialogue, which is often 'insipid and banal' in contrast, and habitually performs an ironic function, in order to build a distance between the spectator and the central characters of the film.[87] This in turn implies that, whilst the aesthetic style of *Senso* works to disrupt spectatorial identification with the discourse and motives of the central characters in the film, it also works to encourage spectatorial identification with the visual and aural sphere of the 'old world' which the film invokes with such intensity. It is this use of excessive *mise en scène*, in conjunction with ironically diminished forms of character identification, which is largely responsible for providing *Senso* with its particularly fatalistic ambience; and it is now to this question of fatalism, and alienation, that this analysis of *Senso* must turn, in order to situate the film more clearly within a Lukácsian model of the intensive totality. In carrying through such a return, we also return to a question posed earlier, in relation to the influence of Stendhal on *Senso*: if *Senso* is not a true work of 'classical' realism, because it is insufficiently 'mediated', nor a work of 'social critical/democratic humanist' realism, because it is insufficiently idealistic, how can the film be classified more precisely as Lukácsian? As will be argued in the forthcoming pages, the answer to this question turns largely on the *extent* of the presence of themes of alienation within *Senso*.

Like *Danton*, *Senso* is suffused with themes of alienation. All the characters in *Senso* appear to be either trapped in an inescapable cycle of destruction or delusion, or willing to compromise their principles in order to advance their interests. However, there is a crucial difference between the ways in which alienation is portrayed in *Danton* and in *Senso*. In *Danton*, as in the work of social critical/historical democratic humanism generally, idealist discourses are set against the background of the oppressive 'thing world'. So, in *Danton*, the idealism of the Dantonists is placed in opposition to the instrumentality of the Robespierre regime. However, in *Senso*, oppositions between idealism and regressive instrumentality cannot be effectively established because romantic idealism is treated in such a circumscribed manner. Where *Senso* may be said to be at variance both with *Danton*, and with the Lukácsian models of aesthetic realism elaborated so far within this study, therefore, is in the measure and extent to which the film portrays alienation. Lukács' general stance on this issue is ambiguous. In late works, such as *The Destruction of Reason*, he adopts a dogmatic position in associating all forms of nihilistic expression with irrationalism. This same posture can be observed in a less militant manifestation in his *Solzhenitsyn*, where, despite his praise for Solzhenitsyn's novella, he is, as was argued in the previous chapter, clearly troubled by the lack of 'positive perspective' in *One Day in the Life of Ivan Denisovitch*.[88] On the other hand, in earlier writings such as *Theory of the Novel* and *Soul and Form* Lukács appears to adopt a quite different position in relation to the question of nihilistic expression, seeing it as a viable form of portrayal of a world which is *objectively* alienating.

The most insightful guide to an understanding of Lukács' underlying stance on this issue of the relationship between the representation of positive and negative elements within the intensive totality can be found in yet another late work, but one which, unlike *The Destruction of Reason*, was written during a period of relative liberalism within the Soviet era. In *The Meaning of Contemporary Realism*, Lukács argues that works of critical realism produced during the post-classical phase experience inherent difficulties in attempting to portray 'positive' exemplars of 'culture' because of their location within a fallen post-1848 bourgeois society. As we have seen, one way of surmounting such a difficult location is to adopt the form of what Lukács calls idealistic 'democratic humanism'. However, if this path (which contains a number of drawbacks) is not followed, Lukács believes that important works of critical realism produced within bourgeois society may suffer a 'lowered vitality' and, consequently, an attenuation of positive representation.[89] This conceptualisation provides the foundation for Lukács' defence of Thomas Mann, whom Lukács regards as the 'great exponent' of a form of critical realism which is 'confined' within the framework of a bourgeois sensibility, and which defines the world from an apprehensively circumscribed '*bourgeois* point of view'.[90] More importantly, however, Lukács's model also provides a theoretical justification for the work of critical realism which may be predominantly fatalistic. Lukács' earlier insistence in *Theory of the Novel* on the inherently existentially alienating character of the objectivised 'thing world' may be missing here, but Lukács still nevertheless insists that works of critical realism produced within bourgeois society must inevitably be marked by a substantive portrayal of the estrangement which delineates the modern condition; and he also defends this as an aesthetic strategy. In this sense, *Senso* can be defined, in Lukácsian terms, and in opposition to the humanist *Danton*, as a work of critical realism of 'lowered vitality' and attenuated representation of the positive, which describes the world from an anxious and apprehensive aristocratic, and also self-deluded bourgeois point of view.

However, this raises yet another question. In *The Historical Novel* Lukács appears to make a distinction between the more idealistic social critical realism of Stendhal and others, and the classical realism of Balzac. Classical realism is constrained within a framework of bourgeois humanism which did not consider the necessity for future post-bourgeois social revolutions in order to ensure progress. Future development is merely assumed on the basis of these past revolutionary achievements. Classical realism thus focuses on the good that comes from the French revolution, whilst critically highlighting the presence of various 'contradictions of progress'.[91] Classical realism, founded within the circumscribed remit of a bourgeois point of view, does not look beyond the bourgeois revolution to a future popular revolution of the proletariat, and so does 'not consider any new revolution to be necessary for the final realisation of these positive things'.[92] However, within this bourgeois perspective and, unlike the social critical realism of Stendhal, classical realism is capable of a 'ruthlessly truthful investigation and disclosure of all the contradictions of progress':[93]

> There is no criticism of the present from which it will shrink. And even if it cannot consciously transcend the spiritual horizons of its time, yet the constantly oppressive sense of the contradictions of its own historical situation casts a profound shadow over the whole historical conception . . . Think of the old Goethe's theory of 'abnegation', of Hegel's 'Owl of Minerva' which takes flight only at dusk, of Balzac's sense of universal doom.[94]

It seems, therefore, that, although classical realism was constrained within a bourgeois ideological framework, unlike both social critical realism and later democratic humanist realism, classical realism could walk an extremely dark path, exposing the 'oppressive contradictions' of its historical situation, and casting a 'profound shadow'. Works of critical realism which appear in the post-classical era can then revive the spirit of the classical, whilst being able to look beyond a bourgeois framework, and this suggests that, within Lukácsian terms, the work of critical realism of 'lowered vitality' and attenuated representation of the positive, like the Owl of Minerva, can legitimately expose the 'profound shadow' of alienation. Such a formulation suits *Senso*, and also rescues the Lukácsian system from a necessity of optimistic representation, precisely the thing that Visconti so wanted to resist when making his film.

Such a formulation also fits other attempts to argue that a Marxist aesthetics influenced by (modified) Lukácsian thought could also focus substantially and legitimately upon the portrayal of alienation. For example, both Roger Gaurady, in his *D'un realisme sans rivages* (1963), and Ernst Fischer, in his *The Necessity of Art* (1963) and *Art and Co-existence* (1966), argue that the use of distorted stylisation in works of art does not amount to a disintegration, or corruption, of realism, as Lukács had argued; but a valid attempt to modify existing realist conventions in order to represent a changing reality of alienation more appropriately. For both Fischer and Gaurady, this means that the stylised, symbolic representation of an alienated atomistic world constitutes a valid form of aesthetic realism.[95] This position on 'modernist realism' was, as has been argued, also eventually adopted by Lukács' immediate historical disciples in Hungary; and the significance of such a position for this present project is that it allows us to define *Senso* in Lukácsian terms as a work which (1) inherits the 'ruthless' approach of the classical tradition, (2) seeks to focus on the 'contradictions of progress' and (3) casts a 'profound shadow over the whole historical conception' through the employment of an estranged style aimed at the portrayal of alienation, but a style which, nevertheless, still interprets the historical context in a 'social-historical, objective-epic way'.[96]

Senso can also be regarded as closer to the Lukácsian model than *Danton* in that, in *Senso*, 'the great social-historical antagonisms' are embodied within the guise of relatively commonplace or 'maintaining' individuals, as opposed to the 'world-historical' figures of *Danton*. One of the main drawbacks of democratic humanist realism – that the historical context often becomes reduced to a backdrop for the portrayal of the 'eternal ideas' of the central character is, therefore, avoided in *Senso*, because none of the central characters in the film is capable of entertaining such ideas.[97] Livia and Franz are also more 'typical' in the Lukácsian sense than Danton and Robespierre. As we have seen, Lukács' idea of typicality is based on the idea that general concepts are 'dissolved' into concrete characterisations, which are then 'experienced' by the spectator as representative of wider forces.[98] In *Senso* general concepts are never directly given, or, where they are, are given ironically, or are meant to be read indirectly. The 'universal' general concept in *Senso* concerns the idea of a ruling social class fallen into a valueless, superficial self-obsession, and about to remake itself in an inferior mould. However, this universal is never given rhetorically, but is 'dissolved' into the individual personas and actions of Livia, Franz and Ussoni. The only point within *Senso* at which this universal *is* directly touched upon is during Franz's key speech towards the end of the film. Even here, however, the universal is delivered obliquely, not in terms of the inevitable termination and remaking of a dissolute ruling group but as the decline of a quixotically striking manner of existence. This contrasts significantly with *Danton*, where a 'universal' opposition between humanitarianism and dictatorship is insistently articulated. This use of typicality in *Senso* also conforms to Lukács' insistence that the intensive totality should enable the spectator to 'experience' the dissolution of the universal within the particular, rather than be guided towards it. However, Jameson's conceptualisation of the Lukácsian typical as 'an analogy between the entire plot, as a conflict of forces, and the total moment of history itself considered as process', seems to fit *Danton* better than *Senso*, because, in *Senso*, there is no real 'conflict of forces' (one cannot take the film's 'opposition' between romantic love and public duty seriously, as it is presented ironically), but rather a historical process which proceeds relentlessly, though analogously, to its denouement.[99]

Like *Danton*, *Senso* views the historical past through the prism of the present. In the case of *Danton*, that prism was the collapse of communism in Poland during the late 1970s and 1980s, whereas, in the case of *Senso*, it was the decline of the left and resurgence of the conservative establishment in Italy during the early 1950s. One film celebrates the demise of communism, whilst the other is an advocate for the further development of socialism, and communism. Both films emerged at moments of pivotal historical change when history was clearly 'occurring' in the Lukácsian sense, further reinforcing the argument that realism tends to emerge during significant moments of crucial historical transition. However, in *Senso*, the contemporary prism through which the past is portrayed seems to be less manifestly *imposed* upon the past than is the case with *Danton*. According to the Lukácsian model, although any work of historical realism views the past through the concerns of the present, the principal objective of the intensive totality remains that of presenting an account of the historical past. Whilst Lukácsian realism accepts the role of authorial and cultural determinations in any attempt to portray reality, and also rejects naive objectivism, it is not a relativistic philosophy, and continues to insist that the past can, and should, be significantly accounted for. In *Danton*, in contrast, it is far more the case that the present is imposed upon the past.

Finally, a number of correspondences between *Danton* and *Senso* can be posited in relation to the Lukácsian concept of *Stimmung*. Just as *Danton* employed the pictorial style of Jacques Louis David to evoke the period, *Senso* also draws on visual Verdian operatic melodramatic forms in order to evoke the spirit of the period.[100] Similarly, just as a dialectic between unity and fragmentation is turned in the direction of fragmentation in *Danton*, through that film's use of narrative discontinuity and close-ups, so *Senso* often uses visual and aural style to fracture the thematic and diegetic unity of scenes in order to provoke, if not narrative fragmentation, then ironic deconstruction. In *Senso*, music is often used in a way which creates a 'subtle interplay of irony and melodrama', which breaks up overall diegetic unity;[101] whereas, in *Danton*, music also plays a deconstructive role, adding to the disruptive, alienating impact of the narrative style. However, the fact that neither *Senso* nor *Danton* can be very closely equated with the idea of *Stimmung* – the main aesthetic means of achieving totality for Lukács – seems to bring this aspect of the Lukácsian system into some question. What is at issue here, therefore, is the extent to which the idea of *Stimmung* as totality can be effectively rendered within a film.

Made nine years after *Senso*, *Il gattopardo* (1963) is conceived on a much larger scale, and budget. Like *Senso*, *Il gattopardo* also suffered from the intervention of American distribution companies, in this case 20th Century Fox, who edited the film against Visconti's wishes, and who insisted that major stars such as Burt Lancaster, Alain Delon and Claudia Cardinale should be involved. The resulting film exists in two versions. The dubbed English copy, which Fox reduced from an original length of 205 to 161 minutes in length, was disowned by Visconti, who complained about the way the film had been edited and processed, and about the fact that it had been dubbed into English.[102] The superior Italian version was not released until twenty years after the premiere of the English-language version.

Whilst *Senso* is set towards the end of the *Risorgimento*, *Il gattopardo* is set during the pivotal years of 1860–2, during which Garibaldi's redshirts landed in Sicily, bringing to an end the French occupation of the Island and setting the scene for the emergence of a unified Italian kingdom under the leadership of a ruling-class alliance of old aristocracy and haute bourgeoisie. One distinction which can be drawn between *Senso* and *Il gattopardo*, therefore, is that the latter film is much closer to the key historical events of the *Risorgimento* than the former, and this proximity precludes (to an extent) the type of ironic approach adopted in *Senso*. Instead, the dominant tone of *Il gattopardo* is one of sober nostalgia, as Visconti focuses on a world which is about to disappear under the extension of bourgeois hegemony. In contrast to the almost pathological 'courtly' world view of Livia and Franz in *Senso*, therefore, *Il gattopardo* presents a sympathetic portrait of the fading aristocratic world of its central character, Count Salina, comparing that world favourably in contrast to an emergent bourgeois order which lacks both inner vitality and outer nobility. If *Senso* conforms to the Lukácsian model in conferring an (admittedly troubled) emotional vitality on the pre-bourgeois then, *Il gattopardo* goes further, in portraying the aristocratic pre-bourgeois as an important arena of 'cultural' resistance to the pragmatic instrumentality of the bourgeois era, and as ethically and spiritually superior to that era. So, for example, Count Salina declares that his class consists of 'leopards and lions', whilst 'those who will follow us [the bourgeoisie] will be 'jackals and sheep'.[103] This opposition between bourgeoisie and aristocracy is articulated throughout the course of *Il gattopardo*, both thematically and through the use of *mise en scène* which emphasises the grandeur and nobility of the Salina household.

If *Il gattopardo*, *Danton* and *Senso* are considered together, it is clear that *Il gattopardo* also fits the Lukácsian model of 'democratic humanist realism' more closely than do the other two films. Much of that model is embodied in the figure of Count Salina, who encapsulates the Lukácsian 'call to battle in defence of human culture', and who embodies 'emotionally and intellectually the great humanist ideas and ideals'.[104] However, the epic sweep of *Il gattopardo* also corresponds to the 'epic-poetic' and 'historical monumental' approach which Lukács associates with the historical work of democratic humanist realism. Count Salina can also be distinguished from the 'world historical figures' of *Danton*, and can be more closely related to the class-typical 'maintaining' characters who inhabit the diegetic world of *Senso*. In one respect, however, Salina may be less 'typical' in the Lukácsian sense than Livia and Franz. As has been argued, in the Lukácsian notion of the typical, general concepts are dissolved into concrete characterisations, which are then 'experienced' by the spectator or reader. However, this does not really occur in *Il gattopardo* and, in fact, can occur only when, as in *Senso*, the central characters are primarily 'ordinary' or 'maintaining' figures. However, Salina is just too much of a *gattopardo*, too much of a 'hero of history', as Lukács puts it, to function as a genuinely 'typical' character.[105]

The form of spectatorial experience elicited by *Il gattopardo* also conforms to the key Lukácsian principle that the realist work must stimulate the critical faculties of the spectator, rather than impose upon the spectator. However, this works quite differently than in *Senso*. In *Senso*, irony is used to counterpoint and critique the thematic content, so that the spectator is faced with an inability to identify with the central characters, and is forced into a more critical position. In *Il gattopardo*, this also occurs to a certain extent, as visual spectacle and aural texture are used as a counterpoint to the sordid political events taking place. However, there is a greater role for identification in *Il gattopardo*, because it is a more conventional work of historical democratic humanism in the Lukácsian sense than is *Senso*. In *Il gattopardo*, therefore, spectatorial experience consists of a combination of pleasure in viewing sensuous forms, and a more critical reflection on these forms as the traces of a disappearing world.

However, although *Il gattopardo* can be associated with the 'mediated' model of Lukácsian epic democratic humanism, the film can also be associated with the third major Lukácsian category of realism, and one which, as we have seen, Lukács specifically associated with the cinema – that of the *Novelle*. *Il gattopardo* can be regarded as a divided film, in which the least successful parts are those which are most 'mediated': the widespread narrative structure of the film is often too sketchy, and characterisation too schematic (this is most notable in the heavily edited English version of the film). However, the 'ballroom scene' in *Il gattopardo*, which actually takes up a quarter of the entire film, is quite different from these more mediated sections. In this extended sequence, a primarily visual portrayal of the relation between the particular and the general is attempted, in which totality is *evoked*. Here, the realm of *Besonderheit* is condensed, and compacted into a portrayal of discrete, finite concrete relationships and subjective experiences, and a dense network of relationships which depicts 'moral-social problematics' in a 'sensible perceptible form' is generated. The preceding chapter in this book suggested that a reconstructed Lukácsian model of cinematic realism might be imagined quite different from the more familiar model of Lukácsian literary realism, and from commonly held understandings of Lukácsian ideas within the field of film studies. In the ball scene in *Il gattopardo* we can see the material evidence for the possibility of such an imagined reconstruction.

Notes

1 Lukács, Georg, *The Historical Novel* (Aylesbury: Peregrine Books, 1976), p. 335.
2 Ibid., p. 345.
3 Ibid.
4 Ibid.
5 Ibid.
6 Ibid., p. 346.
7 Ibid., p. 337.
8 Ibid., p. 344.
9 Price, Victor, 'Introduction', in *The Plays of Georg Büchner* (Oxford and New York: Oxford University Press, 1971), p. xiii.
10 Falkowska, Janina, *The Political Films of Andrzej Wajda: Dialogism in Man of Marble, Man of Iron, and Danton* (Oxford: Berghahn Books, 1996), p. 147.
11 Ibid.
12 Ibid., p. 149.
13 Ibid., p. 152.
14 Price, p. xv.
15 Ibid., p. 58.
16 Lefebvre, Georges, *The French Revolution: From Its Origins to 1793* (London: Routledge & Kegan Paul, 1971), p. 239.
17 Rudé, George, *Revolutionary Europe 1783–1815* (London: Fontana, 1965), p. 143.
18 Falkowska, p. 109.
19 Rudé, p. 109.
20 Falkowska, p. 103.
21 Ibid., p. 47.
22 Price, p. xii.

23 Liehm, Mira, *Passion and Defiance: Film in Italy from 1942 to the Present* (Berkeley and London: University of California Press, 1984), p. 37.
24 Armes, Roy, *Patterns of Realism* (London: Tantivy Press, 1971), p. 52.
25 Marcus, Millicent, *Italian Film in the Light of Neo-realism* (Princeton: Princeton University Press, 1986), p. 18.
26 Ibid.
27 Deveny, Thomas G., *Cain on Screen: Contemporary Spanish Cinema* (London: Scarecrow Press, 1993), p. 135.
28 Marcus, p. 14.
29 Armes, p. 185.
30 Deveney, p. 69.
31 Ibid., p. 149.
32 Ibid.
33 Bordwell, David, and Thompson, Kristin, *Film History: An Introduction* (New York: McGraw Hill, 1994), p. 417.
34 Ibid., p. 418.
35 Liehm, p. 57.
36 Nettl, J. P., *The Soviet Achievement* (London: Thames and Hudson, 1976), p. 154.
37 Liehm, p. 93.
38 Ibid., p. 94.
39 Ibid., p. 148.
40 Marcus, p. 173.
41 Bacon, Henry, *Visconti: Explorations of Beauty and Decay* (Cambridge: Cambridge University Press, 1998), p. 68.
42 Ibid., p. 69.
43 Gramsci, Antonio, *Il risorgimento* (Turin: Einaudi, 1952), p. 44, quoted in Marcus, p. 166.
44 Marcus, p. 168.
45 Servadio, Gaia, *Luchino Visconti: A Biography* (London: Weidenfeld and Nicolson, 1982), p. 137.
46 Bondanella, Peter, *Italian Cinema from Neorealism to the Present* (Northampton: Roundhouse, 1983), pp. 98–9.
47 Marcus, p. 173.
48 Liehm, p. 148.
49 Ibid.
50 Schifano, Laurence, *Luchino Visconti: The Flames of Passion* (London: Collins, 1990), p. 276.
51 Servadio, p. 136.
52 Bondanella, p. 99.
53 Ibid., p. 98.
54 Armes, p. 120.
55 Lukács (1976), p. 44.
56 Ibid., p. 33.
57 Becker, George J., *Master European Realists of the Nineteenth Century* (New York: Frederick Ungar Publishing Co., 1982), p. 18.

58 Lukács (1976), p. 93.
59 Becker, p. 17.
60 Lukács (1976), p. 28.
61 Ibid., p. 92.
62 Bacon, p. 191.
63 Lukács, quoted in Marcus, p. 178.
64 Liehm, p. 148.
65 Nowell-Smith, Geoffrey, *Luchino Visconti* (New York: Viking, 1973), p. 83.
66 Marcus, p. 182.
67 Lukács, Georg, *The Meaning of Contemporary Realism* (London: Merlin Press, 1963), p. 99.
68 Marcus, p. 185.
69 Ibid., p. 182.
70 Nowell-Smith, p. 83.
71 Marcus, p. 185.
72 Partridge, Colin, *Senso: Visconti's Film and Bioto's Novella, a Case Study in the Relation between Literature and Film* (Lampeter: The Edwin Mellen Press, 1992), p. 84.
73 Marcus, p. 175.
74 Bondanella, p. 98.
75 Partridge, p. 105.
76 Leprohon, Pierre, *The Italian Cinema* (London: Secker & Warburg, 1972), p. 148.
77 Lukács (1976), p. 33.
78 Partridge, p. 92.
79 Liehm, p. 148.
80 Partridge, p. 84.
81 Ibid., p. 85.
82 Tonetti, Claretta, *Luchino Visconti* (Boston: Twayne, 1983), p. 65.
83 Schifano, p. 277.
84 Partridge, p. 103.
85 Leprohon, p. 150.
86 Tonetti, p. 66.
87 Ibid.
88 Lukács, Georg, *Solzhenitsyn* (London: Merlin Press, 1970), p. 22.
89 Lukács (1963), p. 99.
90 Ibid., p. 107.
91 Lukács (1976), p. 28.
92 Ibid.
93 Ibid.
94 Ibid.
95 Bisztray, George, *Marxist Models of Literary Theory* (New York: Columbia University Press, 1978), p. 168.
96 Lukács (1976), p. 33.
97 Ibid., p. 337.

98 Királyfalvi, Béla, *The Aesthetics of György Lukács* (Princeton: Princeton University Press, 1975), p. 87.

99 Jameson, Fredric, *Marxism and Form: Twentieth Century Dialectical Theories of Literature* (Princeton: Princeton University Press, 1971), p. 195.

100 Liehm, p. 149.

101 Bacon, p. 72.

102 Ibid., p. 86.

103 Liehm, p. 232.

104 Lukács (1976), p. 335.

105 Ibid.

5

'And what about the spiritual life itself?', distraction, transcendence and redemption: the intuitionist realist tradition in the work of John Grierson, André Bazin and Siegfried Kracauer

The work of Grierson, Bazin and Kracauer makes up the core of what is here referred to as the intuitionist realist tradition in film theory. Most of this work has, generally, been classified as falling into the frame of' 'classical' film theory, although this is an all-embracing term, often used to consign most film theory appearing before the rise of the Saussurian paradigm within one general 'early' explanatory model. The insistent inclusion of the work of Grierson, Bazin and Kracauer within this category also reflects the fact that this body of work was regarded as relatively passé until quite recently, and the object of little critical analysis. This situation is now changing, as it should, because the models of cinematic realism developed by Grierson, Bazin and Kracauer make up one of the most sophisticated bodies of theory to emerge within film studies, and this is so partly because that body of theory is linked to substantive intellectual traditions. Nevertheless, this chapter will not attempt to embark on a comprehensive intellectual reconstruction of the work of these three writers, as such a reconstruction has already been carried out in the partner volume to this book, *European Film Theory and Cinema*, as well as elsewhere.[1] Instead, an attempt will be made here to define three of the central components of the intuitionist realist tradition: first, that tradition's conceptualisation of the 'problem' of modernity; second, the proposed 'solution' to that problem; and, third, the elaboration of an aesthetic vehicle through which such a solution can be realised.

The problem of modernity: Grierson

Like Lukácsian realism, cinematic intuitionist realism is premised upon a profoundly sceptical attitude towards the modern condition and its impact upon the subject. Influenced by philosophical idealism, and by the Romantic critique of post-Enlightenment modernity, Grierson, Bazin and Kracauer see the advance of capitalism, industrialism and materialism as posing a threat to both

the autonomy of the individual and the quality of social relationships. A dis-
trust of capitalism was particularly prominent in the case of Grierson. Grierson
spent his formative years in central Scotland, and experienced the impact of a
period 'in which unbridled capitalism grossly misused resources . . . A period
of intensive exploitation of working people.'[2] The economic problems that
affected Britain as a whole following the First World War appeared in Scotland
in their starkest form,[3] with unemployment in the region close to Grierson's
family home reaching levels of over seventy per cent. Nearby Glasgow had
some of the worst housing conditions in western Europe, and the highest
infant mortality rates in Britain.[4] This context, when combined with a progressive political attitude which he inherited from his parents, left Grierson
with a decidedly antagonistic attitude towards laissez-faire capitalism, and one
which he retained throughout his life. Having said this, however, Grierson was
not anti-capitalist as such and certainly not a socialist. As has been, argued elsewhere, he is best defined as a progressive corporatist, who believed in the
importance of state and cultural regulation of capitalism.[5]

Grierson's sceptical attitude towards capitalism and the impact of industri-
alisation upon society was also reinforced by some of his earliest serious
reading, of Carlyle, Coleridge and Ruskin – all critics of the impact of industrialism on modern society. Later, at university, he immersed himself in a
philosophical idealist tradition which incorporated the work of Kant, Hegel
and, in particular, the English philosopher W. H. Bradley. Idealism had initially
emerged in Germany in the eighteenth and nineteenth centuries as the intellectual armature of feudalism, but also as a critical response to the way that
capitalism and classical liberalism had distorted the humanist values of the
Enlightenment. As such, idealism could be said to possess both a progressive
and a conservative dimension in relation to the bourgeois capitalist order: conservative, in that it functioned in part as the representative ideology of a highly
elitist feudal order, and progressive in that it highlighted the problems posed
by the onward destructive charge of capitalism. Towards the end of the nineteenth century philosophical idealism was introduced into Britain, where it
quickly developed into an ideology which was strongly critical of laissez-faire
capitalism. Again, though, few British idealists were completely anti-capitalist,
and most favoured the continuation of a reformed capitalist system which
would also strengthen traditional and long-standing social relationships
deemed to be under risk.[6] During the early twentieth century, idealism also
became established as a prominent philosophical discipline in two major
centres, Oxford and Glasgow Universities; and it was at Glasgow that Grierson
first encountered this school of thought, and where he took honours in moral
philosophy, logic and metaphysics.[7]

British idealism reached the zenith of its influence as an intellectual force
between 1880 and 1914. After 1914 that influence began to decline. It was at

this point that idealist thought began to join together with other strands of thinking which emphasized the need to use new mass-communications media in order to both enhance community cohesion and advance the cause of progressive social reform. For example, many from an idealist background in Oxford, Glasgow and elsewhere took up positions in the newly created BBC in the 1920s, and used radio to consolidate new, and more socially inclusive conceptions of national identity. Grierson (and the documentary film movement which he inaugurated) also has to be regarded as part of this more general context of the movement of an idealist sensibility into post-1918 British discourses concerning social unity, mass communications and the aspiration to attain a progressive transformation of society.[8]

In addition to idealism, a significant influence upon Grierson's attitude to capitalism, industrialism and modernity as such was American scientific naturalist theory, and its attendant anxieties concerning the unmanageable nature of modern society. In 1924 Grierson travelled to America in order to carry through a funded social science research project on the impact of recent mass immigration, mainly from Ireland and southern Europe, upon American society.[9] The remit of the project had not, initially, covered the role of the mass media. However, and under the influence of Hollywood and the 'yellow press', Grierson tailored the project to accommodate aspects of public opinion and the mass media; and, between 1924 and 1927, he investigated both the editorial and the reporting practices of local and national newspapers, and the social impact of the cinema. It was at this point that Grierson also came into contact with scientific naturalism.

Like philosophical idealism, scientific naturalism had its questionable, conservative, even reactionary, dimension – a dimension which left a definite imprint upon Grierson's thought. Influenced by forms of positivist, social Darwinist thought, much scientific naturalist discourse focused on group conflict and the 'survival of the fittest' as the generative motors of social change. One, perhaps unavoidable, consequence of such an orientation was an emphasis on the inevitability and indeed affirmative worth of social inequality; and it has been argued that scientific naturalism levied a radical and sceptical critique against traditional conceptions of egalitarianism and democratic governance.[10] In addition, and associated with this position, scientific naturalist discourses also evidenced both a pronounced scepticism concerning the ability of the ordinary citizen to act in a fully 'rational' manner and a concomitant conviction that 'scientific tests' should be applied in order to distinguish between 'capable' and 'less capable' citizens so that 'The ignorant, the uninformed and the antisocial . . . should be excluded from the franchise, and government controlled by . . . an aristocracy of intellect and character'.[11] However, despite the intrinsically discriminatory character of such proclamations, scientific naturalism was by no means an unremittingly conservative body of thought, and also encompassed a more liberal dimension, as, for example, in the writing of John Dewey, William James and C. A. Ellwood – writing which defended the authority of democratic institutions, and was more perceptive of the social harm caused by the uninhibited development of capitalism.[12]

Although Grierson was influenced by both the liberal and the conservative strands of scientific naturalist thought, he was influenced less by the latter. This is apparent, for example, in the position which he adopted in relation to Walter Lippmann, an influential public figure during the period who popularized the more conservative strands of the scientific naturalist agenda, and who, in his *The Phantom Public* (1924), argued that democracy should be abandoned. [13] Grierson met Lippmann in 1925, at a time when Lippmann was editor of the *New York World* and Grierson was carrying out research into newspaper reporting practices. However, given Grierson's personal experience of the havoc wrought by unfettered capitalism in his native Scotland, and given also the influence on him of philosophical idealism, he could hardly have identified with Lippmann's belief that democratic control over capitalist power elites should be entirely discarded. As a consequence, Grierson came to reject the majority of Lippmann's views, declaiming that he had 'met Lippmann, who is the high priest in public opinion hereabouts, we disagreed a whole lot about it. And I never thought much of Lippmann to begin with.'[14] Grierson's repudiation of Lippmann was symptomatic of his attitude towards the conservative phase of scientific naturalism in general, and he rejected what he referred to as 'the intellectual's case against the people'.[15] In contrast, he was far more sympathetic to a thinker like Ellwood who, although concerned (as Lippmann was) about the impact of 'mass society' upon traditional values, also believed that modern socio-cultural institutions could evolve and improve within a democratic framework informed by ethical and religious imperatives.[16]

Nevertheless, Grierson *was* influenced by some aspects of the conservative strand of scientific naturalism, and those aspects entered into a dialectic within his general outlook alongside other more progressive features which he derived from Ellwood and Dewey. For example, he appears to have accepted Lippmann's contention that the average person was incapable of comprehending a complex variety of social data, indeed that the ordinary citizen was not entirely 'rational' in action and judgment. This led him to adopt a sceptical position regarding the practical possibilities of entirely popular-based democratic government, and a belief that modern society must be managed and regulated to a considerable extent (even if not entirely) by elite groups. Accordingly, he came to argue that the classical doctrine of democratic equality was 'Romantic and impracticable', and egalitarianism 'an anarchic and dangerous doctrine [which] threatens the disciplines of a community'.[17] 'Universal suffrage' and 'Absolute freedom of speech' are also defined as 'extreme things'.[18] If, therefore, within the terms of Grierson's thought, the problems of modernity can be laid

at the door of *laissez-faire* capitalism, they are also at the same time the consequence of an attachment to what Grierson regards as a deluded idealistic form
of egalitarianism incongruent with modern social reality. Although he accepted
the centrality of democracy within modern mass society as a means of precisely
countering the influence of the power groups which many scientific naturalist
theorists saw as constituting the very quintessence of capitalist modernity, he
was also sufficiently swayed by the arguments of those theorists that he came to
regard such centrality itself as constituting a potential hazard. As a consequence
of this, Grierson's overall theoretical position on the question of democracy and
elitism could be regarded as approaching paradox, though, as will be argued
shortly, he attempted to circumvent such paradox through recourse to a key
idealist notion – that of the 'elect'.

However, it was neither democracy, elitism nor capitalism *per se* which
Grierson supposed to constitute the greatest danger posed by modernity, but
the inclination towards the endorsement of individualism which was fostered
by all three, and which also (Grierson believed) had its source in disquieting
aspects of the human condition. At the root of Grierson's conception of
modernity, therefore, is a troubled evaluation of the social hazards posed by
individualism. Grierson believed that, in the modern period, an emphasis on
the centrality of individual satisfaction and fulfilment had gravely undermined
the commitment to collective duty, ethical value and social conscientiousness
which had characterized the premodern theist era; and one ruinous consequence of this had been the emergence of a dangerously self-seeking system of
industrial capitalist modernity. Grierson also believed that these developments
stood in opposition to the advocacy of totality which lay at the heart of the
idealist philosophies he had inherited from Hegel and Bradley and, in this
sense, an idea such as Bradley's 'concrete universal' – where the Absolute is
regarded as a totality which contains all 'concrete' content within itself – stands
as the ethical and intellectual converse of the egocentric 'pursuit of happiness
[which was never, as far as Grierson was concerned] anything other than an
aberration of the human spirit'.[19]

Grierson contrasted this 'aberration' with what he referred to as a 'school of
philosophy', within which 'some of us learned', and which 'taught that all was for
the common good and nothing for oneself'.[20] At one level, what Grierson means
by a 'school of philosophy' here is merely a universal predisposition which
reflexively elevates the social above the individual in a qualitative sense. At
another level, Grierson's words can be associated more closely with strands of
philosophical or cultural disposition, encompassing Spartan communalism,
Greek and Roman Stoicism, Augustinian Catholicism, Calvinist Presbyterianism,
and various ideologies (including Marxism, which impressed Grierson in this
particular respect) which preached forms of subornment of the self to the general
cause, whatever that cause might be. However, the 'school of philosophy' within

which Grierson actually learnt was idealism, and his overall position is most clearly associated with a neo-Hegelian belief in the importance of totality and, within this, of the superiority of the state (as a mediated category of 'concrete universal') over the individual citizen and the intricate, disordered (and therefore worrying) flux of civil society. The key influence on Grierson here are Bradley's conceptions of the state, the Absolute and historical development, where the institutions of the state are regarded as the product of a historical evolution in which social structures move ever closer to the ideal model of the concrete universal and totality.[21] Given such a premise, it is possible to regard Individualism as that aspect of modernity which possesses the potential to frustrate such a movement, and foil the realization of the Absolute within the social relationships of the modern world.

However, and as suggested earlier, the 'aberration of the human spirit' which led to an excessive focus upon individualism was not only brought about by fashionable philosophical discourses (the utilitarianism of Bentham, rather than Mill, being the prime *bête noire* for Grierson in this respect) or modernity but by human nature itself. The chief influence on Grierson in this respect was not idealism but forms of religious thought. Grierson's father had been a lay preacher, and he himself had delivered some sermons in his youth, in which he pontificated on such portentous issues as the obligation to 'live and live strongly for the community of men'.[22] But Grierson also argued that the largest part of humankind would probably 'take no part' in such an enterprise of obligation, and this sombre conviction led him to adopt a conception of human nature based on the idea of the individual as fallen, and therefore as flawed, and – significantly for his later writings – as requiring to be *led* on to the true course by those whose charge it was to do so. This conception of fallen man was also derived indirectly from an Augustinian vision of man as a corrupted and fallen sinner and, in particular, from the distinction which St Augustine drew between the 'elect' and the 'reprobate', where the elect were those who understood and communicated the word of God, and where the reprobates were the remainder of an unfortunate and somewhat bestial mankind.[23] These Augustinian precepts had been taken up by Calvin during the Reformation, then by the established Calvinism of the Church of Scotland during the nineteenth and twentieth centuries, and issued on to those such as Grierson, who were brought up within a family background influenced by debate over religion.

However, Grierson's general vision of human nature cannot be equated too closely with that endorsed by the contemporary Scottish Calvinism which he was familiar with during the 1914–24 period, and which he strikingly referred to as amounting to the 'conservatism of death'.[24] Instead, these Augustinian themes became linked to a more liberal form of Presbyterianism in his outlook, so that the idea of man as fallen and flawed entered into a dialectic within his thinking with more positive accounts of human agency. At the same time, the

Augustinian/Calvinist distinction between the elect and the reprobate became somewhat diluted in his thought, and was given a far more secular orientation under the influence of the British nineteenth-century idealist distinction between the 'clerisy' and the mass. This distinction was drawn from Carlyle, Coleridge, Byron and Ruskin, but was given its most articulate expression in Matthew Arnold's *Culture and Anarchy* (1869). Here, Arnold argued that, in each social class, a 'remnant' existed who were capable of placing 'the love of human perfection above their class spirit', and Arnold went on to argue that these remnants should form a cultural clerisy which would act as the guardian of national values.[25] Grierson's notion of the 'agents of the state' – those who would lead society back from the abyss of rampant individualism into closer accord with the Absolute – was essentially a combination of the existential Augustinian distinction between elect and reprobate, and this later, more socially oriented distinction between the clericy and the mass.[26]

However, here again we also see the same dialectic, or paradox, within Grierson's thought which was remarked on earlier, in relation to his position concerning questions of elitism and democracy. Just as that position held back from a full endorsement of elitism, whilst nevertheless preserving its spirit, so the same stance is evident in relation to Grierson's conception of human nature, where he holds back from accepting the full-blooded Augustinian demarcation between elect and reprobate, whilst retaining its essence in a sec- ularised form. Grierson may be exhibiting a characteristically Hegelian *modus operandi* here, which manoeuvres by design between thesis and antithesis to arrive at a mediated 'middle way' synthesis. But such a *modus operandi* is never convincingly theorised in Grierson's writings, leaving a lasting sense of gaps and unresolved issues, which later critics would fasten on to with some vigour. In addition, in both cases it can be argued that the basis of the synthesis arrived at is a conservative one, and one premised upon the sanction of exclusivity.[27]

Grierson's belief that, within modernity, an existential proclivity towards self-centred individualism was exacerbated by a misfiring social order driven by capitalism, individualism and industrialism also led him to argue that modern culture and, in particular, the cinema, was similarly suffused with 'reprobate' individualism. This conviction was also informed by a distinction which Grierson drew between the 'phenomenal' and the 'real', where the 'real' refers to an underlying reality of important generative and structural features, and the 'phenomenal' points to the forms of everyday life which these features bring into being.[28] Here, the idea of individualism as a sub-standard form of category becomes associated with the 'phenomenal', and both are contrasted qualitatively with a more 'realist' strategy which seeks to recognise underlying generative mechanisms and totalities which extend beyond particular demon- stration. However, the 'phenomenal' is not and cannot be 'reprobate' in the sense that individualism is. It simply is, and exists as the atomised manifestation of an underlying generative apparatus. Nevertheless, this also means that the phenomenal is unable to play a sizeable role in the acquisition of knowledge, and may even play a misleading or illusory role, when driven by individualist affinities and predispositions. Grierson's view that the contemporary cinema was suffused with a reprobate individualism eventually directed him towards the realm of the documentary film, a territory which he felt to be relatively free of such corruption. However, the distinction which he drew between the real and the phenomenal also makes it evident that Grierson's theoretical position here cannot be classed as empiricist, and that, in fact, his position falls in line with more recent scientific models of explanatory realism.[29]

Grierson's idea of 'the real' was never clearly articulated, and so remains a rather nebulous formulation, derived from three principal sources. These are Kant's distinction between 'noumena' and 'phenomena', Bradley's distinction between the Absolute and the phenomenal world, and Hegel's idea of *Zeitgeist*, or 'spirit of the age'.[30] However, of these, it appears to have been the third which influenced Grierson the most, and which he equates most closely with his idea of the 'real'. Even so, Grierson's definition of the modern *Zeitgeist* was imprecise and general, and consisted of such abstract formulations as 'the feeling for movement and change which is the only verifiable distinction which our twentieth century possesses'.[31] This is clearly inadequate as a general theorisation of *Zeitgeist*, but also effectively verges on the meaningless, as a 'feeling for movement and change' cannot possibly be the *only* verifiable distinction which the twentieth century possesses. It could be argued here that the intuitionist approach which Grierson derived from Bradley and Lippmann actually inhibited him from conceptualising the modern *Zeitgeist* in a more meticulously evaluated Hegelian manner and, furthermore, to the disadvantage of his overall ideological position. Intuitionist approaches may have their merits, but they also clearly have their demerits.[32]

What can be said of Grierson's position here is that, despite the failure to theorise *Zeitgeist* in an even tenuously adequate manner, Grierson believed that art and culture should strive to represent the 'real', and the 'essence and spirit of things', rather than the phenomenal.[33] However, whatever that 'essence' and 'spirit' may have consisted of, Grierson believed that modern culture largely failed to portray it and, consequently, failed to penetrate below the level of what he called the 'bank holiday of frenzied events' which characterised particularised, inchoate everyday existence.[34] This failure to portray *Zeitgeist* amounted to a failure to connect the particular to the general in order to arrive at more totalising forms of representation; and this also led to the appearance of a particularly negative and associated correlation within the arts – that of an over-preoccupation with aesthetic experimentation. Within the terms of this argument, aesthetic experiment – and over-preoccupation with the aesthetic at the expense of the contextual life-world – is bracketed alongside individualism and empiricism as yet another consequence of the fracturing of totality within modernity.

Grierson was not against formalism or modernism *per se*, as is evident both from his own film *Drifters* and from his admiration for formative films such as *Battleship Potemkin* (Sergei Eisenstein, 1925) and *Turksib* (Victor Turin, 1929). However, he believed that the principal objective of formal exploration was to disclose what he called the 'significant form' of a work: that which encapsulated the 'mental feeling of the time'.[35] When aesthetic experimentation went beyond the realisation of 'significant form' it amounted to little more than 'self-indulgent license', and Grierson argued that the 'more obstreperous friends of modern art have never made it quite clear where this flip flap of morning papers and pajama patches ended and where art began'.[36] Ultimately, for Grierson, a fixation with purely aesthetic matters represented a failure of realism and a failure to connect the particular to the general through disclosing the trace of the general within formal method or technique. Such a breakdown also lies behind Grierson's criticism of modernist film movements such as, for example, German expressionism, as indulging in inward-looking 'studio-mania',[37] and his criticism of commercial Hollywood cinema for subordinating the 'background' (i.e., the general social or historical context) of films to a tale of a banal love affair, so that 'The story . . . becomes like any other story of gentle gentle heroines, and nasty, nasty villains'.[38] Here then, both aesthetic exclusivity and psychologically oriented subject matter reinforce the preoccupation with individualism and the particular within modernity, and obstruct the rendering of totality. It seems apparent, here as elsewhere, that Grierson's criticism of both modernism and mass popular cinema stem from his overriding concern for totality, or 'the real'. But what precisely is Grierson's conception of totality, and how does he imagine that totality can be realised within modernity?

Totality: Grierson.

Grierson's model of totality and his view of how the difficulties posed by modernity could be transcended, can be divided into two separate though linked dimensions: the social or political and the metaphysical, though it is the metaphysical which ultimately determines the general pattern of his thought. As we have seen, Grierson derived his philosophical orientation from a synthesis of Kantian and Hegelian ideas and, in particular, from Bradley's ideas on the Absolute and aesthetic experience. Like Hegel, Bradley argued that there was a universal order: the Absolute, which both encompassed and transcended the world of phenomenal appearance and was a 'seamless whole, comprehensive and harmonious, in which all contradictions and antinomies are overcome'.[39] According to Bradley, the infant subject was able to experience this transcendent reality. However, this 'immediate experience' of the Absolute was undermined by the growth of self-consciousness, which caused the 'world of the manifold' to appear as exterior to the subject.[40] This experience of externality was then reinforced by the development of thought, language and reason, all of which further articulated and fragmented the organic totality. Nevertheless, Bradley argued also that, in spite of this irreversible dissection of the Absolute, immediate experience of the manifold could still recur, during moments when the externality of thought to being was overcome. However, because thought was part of the 'relational' world of appearance and contradiction, it could not be the means through which such externality could be overcome. [41] Instead, Bradley argued that forms of religious and aesthetic experience were better able to comprehend ultimate reality because such forms of experience were essentially intuitive and as such, capable of penetrating the veil of appearance and contradiction in order to grasp the organic totality. [42].

Bradley's ideas on the role of intuition in comprehending the Absolute were to have a considerable impact upon Grierson's developing thoughts on how the problems inherent within modernity might be overcome. For example, Grierson adopted Bradley's contention that the 'ultimate harmonies' could be comprehended only intuitively, through forms of religious and aesthetic experience, in arguing that 'The artistic faculty means above all the power to see, the power to grasp from among the dross of time and place, the hidden harmonies of man and nature'. [43] The contrast between the two phrases 'hidden harmonies' and 'dross of time and place' is particularly revealing here, in that it suggests a desire to make contact with some more meaningful reality, but and significantly, also a surprisingly low regard for the consequence of the everyday reality of immediate experience. It does not even appear that, in employing the latter phrase, Grierson believes such 'dross of time and place' to be a condition brought into being by modernity. On the contrary, he seems rather to conceive it in a more general, existential manner, as a fateful and ongoing fact of human existence that 'man' is destined to be for ever enclosed within a phenomenal quagmire. It is, ultimately, rather startling that Grierson should choose to define immediate experience of reality in such negative terms and, in so doing, he also sets himself apart from the other two theorists to be discussed later in this chapter, both of whom regard familiarity with the world of immediate experience as a requirement of the highest importance.

For Grierson, therefore, art possesses a clear potential and ability to transcend the fragmented condition of modernity and portray totality. However and, in addition, such an ability to portray 'continuing reality' and the 'hidden harmonies' also has important social consequences, in that such a portrayal would play a role in reinforcing and unifying social relationships and in fostering a deeper sense of identity between the individual and society. However, it was not only to be artists who would be involved in this process of inspiring accelerating social cohesion, but also those whom Grierson referred to as the 'educators'. The 'educators' were those who understood the truth that all individuals within society were involved in what Grierson called a 'matrix of interdependence' and their role was to communicate that knowledge to the general public. The educators would work within the state apparatus to publicise the reality of the 'matrix of interdependence' and, as a consequence, the state itself would necessarily have a crucial role to play in ensuring social concord. Grierson believed that the state represented the means 'by which the best interests of the people are secured [and this implied that] Since the needs of the state come first, understanding of those needs comes first in education'.[44] Here, artists, educators and the state are conceived of as working in unison within a process of 'education' whose objective was to consolidate social accord around the institutional structures, priorities and needs of the state.

In Grierson's vision of a modernity refashioned in the image of the Absolute, therefore, considerable importance is vested in the role to be played by the state and its servants. However, Grierson is by no means a campaigner for the creation of an authoritarian, autocratic state. Grierson conceived of the state in neo-Hegelian terms as an amalgamation of relatively autonomous corporate entities, staffed by intellectuals, artists, educators, politicians and administrators, all working in unanimity both to foil the disruptive impact of capitalism, individualism and industrialism and to bring the various sectors of society into ever closer concurrence.[45] This conception of the state cannot be associated with either a classical libertarian or totalitarian model, but can be related more palpably to an idealised 'corporatist social responsibility' model of the relations between state and civil society. However, Grierson's idealised image of a reform-minded, co-operating, socially ameliorating state was far removed from the brute reality of the state monopoly-capitalist apparatus which he encountered in the 1930s; and this degree of severance from political actuality made it impossible for him to turn the neo-Hegelian conception of civic education which he promoted so vigorously into a reality.

Despite such direct experience of disillusionment, however, and regardless of the enormous difficulties and setbacks which Grierson felt had been, and would always be, created by modernity, he is, in the end, actually, perhaps defiantly, more confident than either Bazin or Kracauer that modernity can, yet, still be rehabilitated. This is because he believes that, although underlying reality had become obscured within modernity by forces and ideologies which were, ultimately, working for the interest of sectarian groups, rather than the good of society as a whole, an understanding of the 'real' could, in principle, still be inculcated in the modern subject if the right form of intervention and regulation was effected. This degree of conviction lends aspects of Grierson's theory of cinematic realism a degree of assurance and self-belief which is markedly lacking in the ideas of Bazin and Kracauer. Grierson is confident that his mission must eventually succeed in the long (perhaps very long) term, and that totality will be grasped. Nevertheless, Grierson's conception of both the problem of modernity and its solution is drawn from a set of models which problematically endorse both consensus and hierarchy, without seriously questioning the negative facets of such endorsement; and as will be argued, this has implications for the inherent value of Grierson's general model of cinematic realism.

Griersonian cinematic realism

The idea of totality was central to Grierson's thoughts on cinematic realism and, because of this, he believed that the principal function of the realistic film should be to represent the interdependence of things in both a descriptive and a symbolic manner, using imaginative and affective means to that end.[46] He also believed that the documentary film was ideally suited to represent the interconnected nature of things because it was 'the medium of all media born to express the living nature of inter-dependency . . . it . . . outlined the patterns of interdependency more distinctly and more deliberately than any other medium whatsoever'.[47] At the core of Grierson's model of cinematic realism, therefore, is the idea that the realistic film should portray totality through linking particular forms of representation with more general symbolic parameters. Examples of such parameters and 'patterns of interdependency' can be found in most of the major early films associated with Grierson. For example, in *Drifters* (Grierson, 1929), montage is used to illustrate the way that the practices, labour, culture and economic institutions of the fishing industry combine to form a holistic whole. Similarly, in *The Song of Ceylon* (Basil Wright, 1934), the links between the traditional and the modern, the religious and the secular are emphasised; whilst, in *Night Mail* (Harry Watt, Basil Wright and others, 1936), the country and the city are shown as bound together through nationwide communication processes. In all these films, descriptive information is combined with techniques whose primary function is to express a poetic sense of concord and fusion, thus realising Grierson's aspirations for the development of a new type of 'totalising' and purposive documentary film.

However, although Grierson is best known for his contribution to the documentary film, his initial concerns for cinematic realism focused on the fiction film and, in America in the mid-1920s, he elaborated a model of 'epic cinema' in which individual characterisation within the feature film was to be set alongside representations of social and national institutions, in order to direct the spectator's understanding into a recognition of the underlying unity of social and interpersonal relationships.[48] But Grierson soon came to the conclusion that Hollywood would never be willing to produce such films in either appreciable number or quality, and so he turned his attention to the documentary film. It is important to understand, therefore, that Grierson was concerned not with documentary *per se*, but with the more fundamental question of cinematic realism, and that it was purely pragmatic consideration which led him to develop a theory of documentary realism, rather than a more general theory of cinematic realism.

In 1927 these pragmatic considerations led Grierson back to Britain, where he obtained employment as a public relations officer in the Empire Marketing Board, an institution of government charged with improving market conditions for Empire goods within the British Empire. There, in an unpublished paper entitled 'Notes for English Producers', he first elaborated his theory of documentary or realist film. In the second part of this paper, entitled 'English Cinema Production and the Naturalistic Tradition', Grierson postulated two different categories of realistic film, one consisting of films between seven and nine reels in length, the other of films of around four reels. The first of these categories had its origins in the theory of 'epic cinema' which he had elaborated in America. However, Grierson's model of epic cinema bore little relation to the limited resources available when he joined the Empire Marketing Board in 1927 and, in the second section of his 1927 paper he defined a form of cinema more appropriate to those circumstances. This second category of film production would consist of shorter films whose objective would be to represent 'social interconnection in both primitive cultures and modern industrial society'. Grierson believed that these films would mark a 'new phase in cinema production', and that they would be superior to, and different from, existing actuality film genres[49] in that, within them, visual material 'could be orchestrated into cinematic sequences of enormous vitality' through a sophisticated use of montage editing and visual composition.[50]

A number of points can be made about this first tentative model of Griersonian cinematic realism. First, although one can certainly argue that the portrayal of 'primitive cultures' was prominent in some of the earliest films made by the documentary films movement, Grierson's primary concern was for 'modern industrial society'. So, even in two key early films – *Drifters* and *Industrial Britain* (Flaherty and others, 1931) – the focus of attention is on the deployment of working-class craft skills within an industrial (*Industrial Britain*) or commercial market-oriented (*Drifters*) environment. Like the other theorists within the intuitionist realist camp, Grierson's concern for modernity led him inexorably back to a fascination for the life-world of the city and its border areas. However, that concern was also fuelled by the philosophical distinction which Grierson drew between the 'real' and the 'actual' (or 'phenomenal') discussed earlier. Writing about *Drifters*, shortly after its premiere, Grierson argued that the empirical content (the actual) of its documentary images was organised so as to express general truths (the real), which existed at a level of abstraction beyond the empirical, and which could not be directly represented.[51]

As we have seen, Grierson's conception of 'the real' was primarily derived from the Hegelian notion of *Zeitgeist*, or 'spirit of the age', and referrs to the general determining factors and predispositions specific to a particular historical time and place. Grierson argued that documentary films should be organised so as to express *Zeitgeist*, and his first definition of documentary was based on the revelation of the real through the use of documentary footage and formative editing technique. However, in *Drifters*, the 'real' is most apparently evident as an imprecisely articulated symbol of social interdependency, as opposed to any more general emotional or connotative atmosphere, or 'spirit', laid across the texture of the film; and this is because the positioning of much of the film within a 'primitive community' of working-class craft workers largely rules out the possibility of portraying the *Zeitgeist* of modern cosmopolitan life. In this sense, the ability of *Drifters* to portray the Griersonian 'real' – one which is umbilically linked to a portrayal of modernity – is undercut by the social setting of the film itself. However, as has been argued, Grierson's conception of the 'real' was always an ambiguous and sweeping formulation to begin with and, when, such an elusive formulation is combined with the 'intuitive' approach to aesthetic representation and spectatorship adopted in *Drifters*, the possibility of a more targeted articulation of a portrayal of the real recedes into the distance. Even if Grierson's first film had been set in a modern urban milieu, therefore, it would still not have been able to render the *Zeitgeist* of that background in an incisive or involved manner. One concludes from this, therefore, that one of Grierson's key concepts – that of 'the real' – may contain inherent weaknesses, and this may pose problems for his overall theory of cinematic realism.

It is also evident that, although Grierson's initial definition of cinematic realism explicitly emphasised modernist, formative editing technique, the actuality content of film remained an important factor for him. Grierson believed that the documentary image was better able to signify the real than the image produced within the more 'artificial' environment of the film studio, because it registered and transcribed the 'phenomenological surface of reality'.[52] One of the major influences on Grierson in this respect was the Hungarian theorist Béla Balázs, who argued that film was able to express a poetic reality which existed beyond, but could only be comprehended through, the empirical. This emphasis on the importance of the empirical reinforced Grierson's conception of the relationship between the phenomenal and the real (one in which the real is approached *through* the empirical); and there is a considerable resemblance between Balázs' assertion that film 'could represent . . . the soul's bodily incarnation in terms of gesture or feature' and Grierson's claim that the documentary film could represent 'the characteristic gestures and features which time has worn smooth'.[53] Both formulations are concerned with the way in which the naturalistic image is able to signify more abstract and underlying realities (such as the 'soul'); and it is this which links the ideas of these two theorists during the 1920s and 1930s to a more general context of interest in gesture and the visual, where the concrete, the visual and immediate experience were seen as embodying a more 'primal' mode of communication, and a means of 'seeing' the world through the veil of ideology.[54] Beyond this, it is clear that the idea that empirical material possessed a tremendous intrinsic value is also central to the intuitionist realist tradition in general. Along with intuition, the empirical provides the means by which the distorting ideologies which circulate freely within the modern *Lebenswelt* can be surmounted through a return to the very essence of the *Lebenswelt*. It seems then that, despite Grierson's general theoretical position (discussed earlier) on the superiority of the noumenal 'real' over the socially experienced 'phenomenal', he is prepared to grant the cinematic 'actual' a relatively high degree of importance, based on the ability of the documentary image to slice through the phenomenal, and signify *Zeitgeist*.

Grierson's early theory of cinematic realism can be said to consist of three principal parts: (1) a concern with the importance of the actuality image, (2) an emphasis on the interpretative potential of modernist film technique and (3) the need to represent social and other forms of inter relationship. All these aspects can be found both in (some of) the films produced by the documentary film movement between 1929 and 1935 and in Grierson's early writings on the cinema. After that, the poetic montage style of films such as *Drifters* and *The Song of Ceylon* gave way to a more didactic, journalistic style, whilst the earlier concern with philosophical aesthetics was replaced by a more functionalist discourse, which Grierson expressed in essays such as 'The Documentary Idea' (1942), in which he argued that his documentary film movement was really an 'anti-aesthetic movement'.[55] It is also here that Grierson startlingly applauds Goering's infamous saying 'when anyone mentions the word culture, I reach for my gun', as a 'successful recognition' of the need, in a new 'era of action', to give 'law' to the 'wilderness' of inaction which contemporary culture had become.[56]

At the level of theory, this shift of emphasis was to have crucial implications for the role which the foundational concept of totality was to have in Grierson's later thought. That concept was, as has been argued, initially derived from philosophical idealism, and was inherently concerned with metaphysical and abstract formulations. However, from as early as the 1910s Grierson had also linked this metaphysical conception of totality with Bradley's conceptualisations of the 'concrete universal' and the 'state', in order to define a more mediated, or intermediate form of totality existing at the social level – one which, as we have seen, he variously referred to as the 'informational state', or the 'continuing reality'. As Grierson's career progressed, it was this more socially mediated, and also more limited, concept of totality, rather than any esoteric link to the Absolute, which assumed the greater importance in his thought, and this eventually had a number of significant implications for his general theory of cinematic realism.

At one level, such a transition in levels of thought could be seen to mark the evolution of both a theory and its instigator from youthful idealism to more pragmatic and useful considerations. However, there is also a problem here, and a crucial contradiction, in that, whilst Grierson may have moved on consciously from such youthful romanticism, fundamental and elementary aspects of idealist thought continued to unconsciously influence the basic patterns and substance of his thought throughout the rest of his career. In effect, Grierson abrogated a critical awareness of the theoretical concepts which, in fact, determined and shaped what he otherwise increasingly took to be a 'common sense', pragmatic theory of 'civic' education.[57] At one level, such philosophical amnesia led to a situation where his later ideas lost much of their initial theoretical complexity and philosophical ambition. That is a pity in itself for a thinker associated with the tradition of Kant, Hegel and Bradley. More importantly, however, it also appears that, within this general vector of the insensible yet pervasive influence of idealism, it was the more conservative, intransigent aspects of the idealist tradition which ultimately exercised the longer-term hold on Grierson's thought. Thus, a concern for the management of the public sphere began to hold greater sway in his thoughts than the inherently more progressive idealist concerns for reform, intellectual reflection, spirituality, anti-capitalism and the importance of the aesthetic. Grierson's later position also appears to possess limited scope in terms of amounting to any sort of genuine *theory* of cinematic realism, because any such theory must, by implication, possess substantive abstract theoretical categories as part of its core model, and Grierson's later model of 'civic education' film-making does not appear to possess such categories.

The particular rhetoric of presentation and explication adopted by Grierson in his later writings also brings another problem to light, in that, in these writings, a relatively normative consensual trajectory of legitimation is adopted and, as a consequence, the potentially rich critical dimension of cinematic realism articulated in the earlier work becomes reduced in magnitude. Yet another fateful consequence of Grierson's later position on cinematic realism is that the revelatory utopian aspect of realism, which, it will be argued, is so crucial to the theories of Bazin and Kracauer, does not enter into Grierson's mature intellectual concerns. Finally, although, like Kracauer and Bazin, Grierson wished to use cinematic realism in order to reveal a world – 'the ordinary world, the world on your doorstep'[58] – Grierson's 'world', the one illuminated by his discourses of 'civic education', is caught up in the kinds of persuasive and 'purposive projects' that the cinematic realism of Kracauer and Bazin was always keen to transcend.

Like Kracauer, Grierson's writings on the cinema are often rather piecemeal and fragmentary. However, a number of common themes can be discerned within them. The kind of films which he admired all attempted to combine innovative technique with a degree of social realism. Like Bazin and Kracauer he insisted that realist films should place the portrayal of social reality over formal or overly rhetorical experimentation. In this latter respect he spoke approvingly of American films such as The Big Parade (King Vidor, 1925), The Iron Horse (John Ford, 1924) and The Covered Wagon (James Cruze, 1923). Three films which corresponded even more closely than these to his early theory of cinematic realism, however, were Storm Over Asia (Vsevolod Pudovkin, 1928), Turksib (Viktor Turin, 1929) and Earth (Alexander Dovzhenko, 1930). Of these three it was probably Turksib which had the greatest influence upon Grierson. Turksib depicts the construction of the Turkistan to Siberia railway, and represents each stage of that process from beginning to final completion. Grierson admired the fact that, although Turksib was replete with naturalist detail, it was still able to represent the interrelation of individuals with an important contemporary social institution. In addition, according to Grierson, Turksib also handled its themes with 'astonishingly skilful editing' and 'sheer brilliance of technique'.[59] Grierson's preferred model of cinematic realism can, in fact, be closely associated with Turksib, and less so with two other important influences upon him at the time: Robert Flaherty's Nanook of the North (1922) and Moana (1926) and Eisenstein's Battleship Potemkin (1925). Grierson regarded Moana as too concerned with 'natural beauty', too 'poetic'. Similarly, Nanook dwelt on issues which confronted primitive rather than modern man, and Grierson believed that it was more important to investigate the 'jungles of Middlesbrough and the Clyde, than the native customs of Tanganyika or Timbuctoo'.[60] Battleship Potemkin, on the other hand, whilst set within contemporary society, dwelt on 'the mass in war, not the mass in peace'.[61] None of these films provided the model for the social realist imagist film, whereas that model was provided by both Drifters and Turksib.

It seems apparent from what has been argued so far that any convincing rearticulation of Griersonian cinematic realism must return to Grierson's early position on realist film theory, as set out in his writings of the 1918–36 period, and as embodied in Drifters. Such a return allows us to imagine a more valuable Griersonian theory of cinematic realism, one which reunites a concern with mediated intervention within the public sphere with more abstract theoretical categories, and more complex critical and aesthetic positions. Such a synthesis, in which a 'visual art' could convey 'something magical', and 'a sense of beauty about the ordinary world',[62] did, after all, find expression in Drifters (1929), surely an important film within the history of the cinema. However, this is not the place to carry out such a rearticulation of early Griersonian cinematic realism. What is required here is the integration of Grierson's key themes within a more general model of intuitionist cinematic realism, and this will be attempted both towards the end of this chapter, and in the following chapter.

The problem of modernity: Kracauer

Although, like Grierson's, Kracauer's conception of modernity was also shaped by the idealist tradition, his conception differed from that of Grierson's in the extent to which it viewed modernity through a particularly dark perspective. That perception was influenced by a number of factors, one of which was the influence of Max Weber. Weber had argued that contemporary society was controlled by bureaucratic systems of 'instrumental rationality' which dominated the modern subject. According to Weber, the individual experienced a sense of 'disenchantment' as a consequence of this, in which the sense of value which accompanies metaphysical or utopian convictions had been replaced by a more instrumental and functional set of concerns, which ultimately served the interests of the ruling scheme.[63] This view of the modern subject as disenchanted, and controlled by prevailing organisations of authority, was to have a crucial influence upon Kracauer's developing understanding of both modernity, and the way in which cinematic realism might counter the force of modernity.

The Weberian notion of disenchantment also provided the specific basis for Kracauer's two key conceptions of 'abstraction' and 'distraction'. The idea of 'abstraction' is premised upon the conviction that modernity is so dominated by systems of technical and conceptual rationality that immediate experience of the physical environment as a possible object of contemplation for the modern subject has become sharply abridged, and therefore more 'abstract'.[64] However, Kracauer also argued that the modern subject's relationship to the world was, in addition, a 'distracted' one, because the cultural products available to the subject within a disenchanted world lacked any genuine substance, and this, in turn, led to the appearance of a 'distracted' form of cultural spectatorship and consumption which reflected that lack of import. Kracauer endowed these novel cultural products with the appellation of 'mass ornament', and argued that such 'ornamental' forms of mass culture had become 'desubstantiated' and replaced by shallow spectacle, the 'functional but empty form of ritual' and the 'aesthetic reflex' of the dominant social rationality.[65] The concept of distraction employed by Kracauer amounted to the theorisation of a form of cognitive and sensory experience of the modern environment in which an unfocused, disjointed mode of being prevailed; and the idea of distraction, combined with that of abstraction, provided the basis for Kracauer's pessimistic, neo-Weberian account of the modern condition.

In addition to the influence of Weber's conception of disenchantment, Kracauer's notion of modernity was also informed by the emphasis on the idea of a vanished sense of totality found in the early work of Georg Lukács, and particularly in *Theory of the Novel*. Following Lukács' contention that the experience of totality had diminished within modernity, Kracauer also argued that the unity of the modern life-world had been 'shattered', and that, as a consequence, the world no longer offered itself as meaningful to the modern subject.[66] As also with *Theory of the Novel*, Kracauer's early conceptualisation of modernity as having been 'emptied of meaning'[67] was, in addition, also suffused with the apocalyptic presentiment that the gathering forces of modernity were in some sense fast approaching the verge of a catastrophic impasse.[68] This premonition was based upon a conviction, one shared by both Kracauer and Lukács, that the innermost and most negative tendencies of modernity – those of fragmentation, disenchantment and alienation, would, if left to course freely, eventually reach such an intolerable measure, or point of critical mass, that some cataclysmic implosion was bound to occur. During the 1910s Kracauer fully embraced this portentous Lukácsian vision of a modernity destined soon to self-destruct. However, during the 1920s he adopted a more sanguine orientation, and began to imagine what he saw as the forthcoming 'crisis' of modernity as more pivotally balanced between either a plunge forward into the dead zone of abstraction and disenchantment which lay at the heart of modernity, or a turn backwards, towards meaning, value and immediate experience of the life-world.[69]

Kracauer referred to this point of profound historical option as the '*go-for-broke game* of history',[70] and, as he was writing in the 1920s and 1930s, that game appeared to be approaching its conclusion in speedy and concrete fashion, with the growth of Nazism in Weimar Germany, and the inevitable slide into worldwide conflagration. Kracauer seems to have been in little doubt that, during the 1930s, the entire history of modernity was approaching some sort of climactic point at which thesis and antithesis would confront each other dramatically until a new postmodern synthesis emerged phoenix-like from the debris. For him, the events of the late 1930s and early 1940s always amounted to much more than a struggle between right-wing totalitarianism and democracy; they were, on the contrary, associated with an even more historically important struggle for the existential condition of humanity, within a modernity which would become comprehensively inscribed either with the demented spirit of instrumental rationality or, more optimistically, with the liberating energy of the *Lebenswelt*.[71]

In addition to these, perhaps more abstract theoretical concerns, the prescient historical developments of the period also affected Kracauer directly and personally; and, in addition to his writings of the 1920s, both of his two major books were marked by this traumatic context. *From Caligari to Hitler* was written between 1937 and 1946, whilst Kracauer was in exile – first in France, Spain and Portugal during a period of great personal danger – and then in

America. *Theory of Film* was also conceived and begun during the most per-ilous period for Kracauer: one of 'anguish and misery', during 1940–1, when he and his wife were stranded in Marseilles awaiting extradition to America – or possible repatriation back to Nazi Germany.[72] Although the actual text of *Theory of Film* was written between 1948 and 1959, after the apocalypse had occurred, and during a time in which capitalist modernity had embarked upon a period of relatively stable globalisation, Kracauer's book nevertheless remains deeply marked by the decisive historical moment within which it was conceived.[73]

However, it nevertheless remains the case that both *Theory of Film* and Kracauer's final important work, the posthumously published *History: The Last Things Before the Last,* were both completed long after the great 'go-for-broke' confrontation of the 1930s and 1940s had occurred and, moreover, as far as Kracauer was concerned, had occurred without bringing either pre-dominantly benign or adverse consequence in its wake. The apocalypse of the 1930–45 period did not usher in pandemonium, as Kracauer had feared, or a new utopia of human consciousness, as he had hoped; but instead only rein-forced the wellsprings of capitalist modernity. The clash between thesis and antithesis did not lead to the birth of a new, providential synthesis, but one still embedded within the old, instrumental order. Despite this, Kracauer remains constructively hopeful in both *Theory of Film* and *History: The Last Things Before the Last,* and this optimism is grounded in a conviction that the inher-ently unsafe milieu of the modern situation might, still yet, be conquered, and that auxiliary crossroads of opportunity – a series of potentially providential (though of lesser order, compared to that of the 1930–45 period) 'go-for-broke' moments – could gradually heave into sight. For example, in the 'Epilogue' to *Theory of Film* Kracauer reflects upon the idea of humankind as approaching yet another impending point in time where humanity can either head further into the 'prevailing abstraction' or bring into play the new and historically significant medium of film in order to 'look for, something tremendously important in its own right – the world that is ours'.[74] Similarly, in *History: The Last Things Before the Last,* when discussing questions of historical methodol-ogy, Kracauer also draws an analogous distinction between 'universal' (i.e., abstract) historiography and a form of 'anteroom' historiography which is able to recover the historical 'Utopia of the in-between – a terra incognita in the hollows between the lands we know'.[75] Here, the possibility of an escape from abstraction is established within the, albeit more circumscribed area of academic history writing, just as the prospect of a more universal flight from abstraction is established by the appearance of a medium such as film.

It is apparent from the above that, throughout the course of his writing, Kracauer did not loose sight of the possibility that the problems of modernity could yet be overcome, and this possibility is summed up in his central idea of 'redemption', an idea that will be discussed more fully later in this chapter, in relation to Kracauer's related conception of 'totality'. Before that, however, three further major influences upon Kracauer's conception of modernity – those of Kant, Freud and Husserl – will first have to be considered.

One of the most important influences upon Kracauer's conception of modernity was that of Kantian aesthetics and, in particular, the Kantian notion of the 'harmony of the faculties'. Kant had argued that aesthetic judgment should, ideally, arise from a propitious interaction between the faculties of 'understanding' and 'imagination', in which the role of rational critical 'understanding' within aesthetic experience is to cause the imagination to seek order within the object of aesthetic perception – rather than allow the imagination to otherwise engage in a form of freewheeling activity governed by the rule of 'lawless freedom'.[76] However, and following Kant, Kracauer believed that, in modernity, the ideal form of interaction between the faculties of understanding and imagination which should occur had, in fact, become debased; and one consequence of this was that a form of 'lawless freedom' had in fact come to permeate the modern imagination. This debasement of the imaginary and the understanding has, Kracauer believes, considerable consequence, because it leads to a situation where human consciousness is increasingly led away from reality, totality and immediate experience, and towards the pseudo-reality of a form of distracted mass culture.[77] This idea that, within the modern condition, an existential harmony of the faculties has been thrown into dissonance also reinforces the models of disenchantment which Kracauer inherited from Weber and Lukács, and further consolidates Kracauer's conception of the modern subject as both socially and existentially alienated.

In addition to the influence of Weber, Lukács and Kant, Kracauer's pessimistic conception of modernity was also deeply influenced by his interpretation of both Husserl's conception of the *Lebenswelt* and Freud's theory of the unconscious and the psychological symptom; and, of these two theories, it was undoubtedly that of the *Lebenswelt* which had the greatest impact upon him. Following Husserl, Kracauer conceived of the *Lebenswelt* – the world of immediate subjective experience – as an essentially experiential and psychological domain, made up of (Kracauer is quoting Lewis Mumford here) a 'world of interpenetrating and counterinfluencing organisms', and a complexity of satisfactions, discords, wants and pursuits which often lie below the conceptual and the conscious.[78] Husserl had argued that, in order to achieve true fulfilment, the modern subject should remain aware of, and become immersed in, this realm of existence. However, Husserl also believed that the objectifying abstract discourses of modernity obscured the more transient and subjective meanings generated within the *Lebenswelt*, which, as a consequence, became something of a lost and repressed realm of experience.[79] As we have seen, and as will also be argued further later, Kracauer adopted all of these views, to the extent that the Husserlian conception of the modern *Lebenswelt* underlies all his thinking concerning the problems of modernity.

A final influence on Kracauer's conception of modernity to be considered here is that of Freud and, in the especially shadowy vision expressed in *From Caligari to Hitler*, Kracauer's conception of the *Lebenswelt* comes strongly under the sway of Freudian thought, as he conceives of the then contemporary *Lebenswelt* of 1920s Weimar as so warped that it can only be glimpsed as the 'symptom' of psycho-social disturbance.[80] In a healthier situation (in the premodern, for example, or even in a less disjointed period or site of modernity), the subject would generally have an intuitive understanding of the unconscious psychological dimension of the *Lebenswelt*. Such an understanding meant that the subject was able to apprehend intuitively his or her own unconscious desires and needs without being unduly discomfited by this. However, when the prevailing social abstraction reaches such a peak that it actually invades the subject's understanding of his or her own unconscious desires, such beneficial apprehension becomes impossible, and the psychological unconscious of the *Lebenswelt* then only becomes apparent as the disturbing symptoms of that more general abstraction.[81] Such symptoms also appear in films such as Murnau's *Nosferatu* (1922) as 'visual hieroglyphs' of these 'unseen dynamics of human relations',[82] and find expression when 'inner life' is thrown into turmoil by disruptive events. Kracauer argues that, in such periods of radical disruption, these 'core underlying motifs' rise to the surface and become embedded in films such as *Nosferatu*[83] and, in particular, *The Cabinet of Dr Caligari* (Wiene, 1920), which

> exposes the soul wavering between tyranny and chaos, facing a desperate situation . . . Like the Nazi world, that of CALIGARI overflows with sinister portents, acts of terror and outbursts of panic . . . The appearance of these traits on the screen once more testifies to their prominence in the German collective soul.[84]

However, Kracauer was not disposed to regard the *Lebenswelt*, even the psychological unconscious of the *Lebenswelt*, as so existentially disengaged from human consciousness and, in *Theory of Film*, he clearly implies that Freud's conception of the unconscious must be inferior to Husserl's conception of the *Lebenswelt* (though he does not specifically refer to Husserl here) because the latter conception was able to embrace both conscious and unconscious aspects of experience.[85] *From Caligari to Hitler* may have been influenced by Freud's *The Interpretation of Dreams* and *The Psychopathology of Everyday Life*. However, in *Theory of Film*, Kracauer went on to reject an essentialist approach, which he found expressed in Freud's *Civilization and its Discontents*, and which argued that the more general crisis in society was the product of man's 'innate tendency towards aggression' and 'the death instinct'.[86] Kracauer argues that this is merely a 'religious definition of evil thrown out by the front door . . . [and slipping in] . . . again in the guise of a psychological concept';[87] and, in contrast, grounds his own concept of crisis within the *Lebenswelt* squarely within the historically determined and disruptive parameters of modernity.

Totality: Kracauer

Kracauer's alternative to a disenchanted modernity is summed up in the subtitle of his *Theory of Film*. Kracauer's objective is 'The Redemption of Physical Reality', and his approach is premised upon bringing the individual into a closer proximity with a physical reality currently obscured by the forces of modernity. Before coming into meaningful contact with that reality, however, Kracauer believes that the individual must first become responsive to its current 'damaged condition', and that the key to achieving this lies dormant within the latent potential of 'distraction'.[88] As has been argued, the concept of 'distraction' describes the sterile nature of the encounter between self and world within modernity, as well as a form of culture which attempts to remake reality in the image of the mass ornament.[89] Such a form of culture also aims at the '*mechanization*' of life, and a 'rationalisation of life that would accommodate it to technology', so that

> such a radical flattening out of everything living can be achieved only by
> sacrificing man's intellectual [*geistigen*] constitution, and since it must repress
> man's intermediate spiritual [*seelisch*] layers in order to make him as smooth and
> shiny as an automobile, one cannot easily ascribe any real meaning to the bustle
> of machines and people that it has created.[90]

However, in addition to such '*mechanization*' of the psyche, distraction contains the embryonic potential to make the true and ill-fated character of modernity as 'the world of the dead' known to the modern subject, who can then become a '*real*' person: one 'who has not capitulated to being a tool of mechanized industry'.[91] First, distraction suggests its opposite, in that the presence of distraction suggests an alternative *absence*, and the possibility that something other than the current 'dead' and 'empty' state of things might be imagined. It is this perception that something other than the damaged condition of modernity might exist which makes it possible for the modern subject to begin to view modernity itself as inadequate, and the mass ornament as desiring 'nothing other than the greatest possible technologizing of all activities'.[92] Second, Kracauer argues that what he calls 'higher meaning' also leads a secreted existence within the culture of distraction. Employing a distinction (drawn from religious thought) between the 'sacred' and the 'profane', Kracauer argues that the culture of distraction, the 'profane', has become invested with the 'sacred', that is, with 'higher meaning', so that 'ideal categories are now located in the superficial'. So, for example, such ideal categories as the 'infinite' and the 'eternal' re-emerge in secreted and bounded form in popular genres such as dance and travel.[93]

Kracauer insists that, although the dominant culture has tried painstakingly to completely eradicate such unsettlingly meaningful ideal categories from the sphere of public discourse, they have not been nor can they be totally eliminated; and have, instead, found a fresh and sheltered domicile deep within the garish configurations of the mass ornament. As with the related argument concerning the absent 'other' of the mass ornament, Kracauer also argues here that an intuitive grasp of the reality of something profoundly dissimilar to the spirit of the dominant culture – in this case an insight that weighty conceptual forms may lay buried deep within the topography of the mass ornament, shimmering like mislaid philosophers' stones – leads to an enhanced appreciation of the more wide-ranging shortfalls of both instrumental rationality and the mass ornament. In other words, and as Kracauer puts it, nowadays 'only from its extremes can reality be grasped'.[94] Kracauer bases his position here on the importance of 'insight' into the fact that, within the mass ornament, 'nature is deprived of its substance',[95] as the force of instrumental rationality attempts to 'destroy the natural organisms that it regards either as means or as resistance'; and 'Community and personality perish when what is demanded is calculability'.[96] But this also means that it is precisely this diminution of 'substance' and imperative towards calculability that points to a situation in which something like the 'mass ornament' – a form of culture whose 'conformity to reason' is 'an illusion', and whose 'rationality' is also characterised by 'impenetrability' – can resist such mechanisation. The mass ornament may amount to a 'relapse into a mythology of an order so great that one can hardly imagine it being exceeded', but that 'relapse' also opens up a gap between the mass ornament and instrumental rationality, and enables the mass ornament, 'devoid of explicit meaning' as it is, to suggest more 'ideal' and less 'abstract' or 'mechanized' categories of meaning.[97]

All this strongly suggests that Kracauer does not regard the culture of distraction as an exclusively unconstructive phenomenon, but as one which contains both negative and positive attributes. Two of those positive attributes have already been discussed in the previous paragraphs. However, in addition to these qualities, Kracauer also contends that the culture of distraction is, additionally, characterised by an inherent vigour, which can be legitimately regarded as a form of persistent remonstration against the barrenness of modern life – as a 'flashing protest against the darkness of our existence, a protest of the thirst for life' – and as antidote to the 'nervousness in the everyday world', a nervousness which is generated through living within the bounds of an alienated condition.[98] The importance of distraction, therefore, lies not only in the way that its lack of substance indicates alternative veiled depths but also in the way that its animated character, which amounts to a form of resilient if self-oblivious protest, provides a means of coping with the unsatisfactory nature of modern life. This is true also of the way, for example, that mass ornamental forms such as travel and dance constitute 'essential possibilities' through which those in the grip of mechanisation can still 'live', albeit inauthentically.[99]

Nevertheless, and despite these beliefs in the potential value of certain aspects of the culture of distraction, Kracauer does not believe that the 'flashing protest' which can be associated with that culture can ever fully redeem what has been lost within modernity, and stand up against the dominant forces of instrumental rationality. This is largely because what Kracauer calls 'pasttimes', such as 'travel' – which may indeed be characterised by a certain inherent vigour, and also contain 'ideal categories' such as the 'infinite' – remain overdetermined by their overall character as 'mundane spheres' whose *raison d'être* is, ultimately, to reinforce instrumental rationality. In addition, distraction cannot, at the end of the day, achieve the 'redemption of physical reality' which Kracauer desires, because it always looks away from, and beyond, the physical, empirical *Lebenswelt* of immediate experience, and towards the simulated features of the mass ornament. So, even at its most accommodating, the culture of distraction is still unable to disclose fully or seriously the ideal categories which have taken up an expatriate-like status within its strange heartland. In addition, the culture of distraction is also indissolubly linked to the presentation of pseudo-realities, rather than 'physical reality', and partakes of the 'abstractness' which 'is the current site of capitalist thinking', and so 'is incapable of grasping the actual substance of life'.[100]

Whatever significance may reside within the culture of distraction, therefore, the primary objective, as far as Kracauer is concerned, is to return to 'the world which is ours'. That world is the *Lebenswelt*, as defined by Husserl, and it will now be useful to explore that definition in greater depth, in order to better understand how Kracauer has appropriated it. As already discussed, the *Lebenswelt* is the world of direct, immediate perceptual experience. As such the *Lebenswelt* encompasses all that the individual encounters within the sphere of immediate experience, and Husserl defined the *Lebenswelt* as the 'the world of the presently actual [aktuel] life in which the world-experiencing and world-theorising life is enclosed' which is experienced by the subject.[101] This means that the *Lebenswelt* encompasses not only individual perceptual experience but also interpersonal interaction, encounters with thoughts and ideas and the products of human activity and the natural. The *Lebenswelt* is a place of active inter-engagement by individuals, and all aspects of human experience have their basis in the *Lebenswelt*, the 'actually concrete surrounding world' which is encountered by the individual as his or her most tangible mode of being during the process of perception.[102]

In addition to his insistence on both the subjective relativity and the communality of the *Lebenswelt*, Husserl also argued that the *Lebenswelt* was always experienced as a totality. This predisposition to regard the *Lebenswelt* as unified stems from our earliest perceptual experiences, in which no conceptual distinctions between subject and object exist. Husserl calls this the 'primordial world', or 'sphere of ownness', in which a 'thoroughly uniform, continuous internally coherent world is experienced prior to all thinking about it or theorising'.[103] This predisposes the individual to assume and believe that all his or her perceptions, gathered as he or she moves through the *Lebenswelt*, are connected to each other in ways which are accommodating and confirming; and, before we encounter some specific instances of the *Lebenswelt*, we already believe that such encounters and instances will be linked in ways which make sense for us, because we count them as belonging to a world whose reality and coherence we are committed to prior to such encounters. This is what Husserl refers to as the *Vorgegebenheit*, or 'pregivenness', of the *Lebenswelt*.[104] In addition to this model of a unified *Lebenswelt*, however, Husserl also argued that the *Lebenswelt* was more 'objectively' unified because it possessed a universal general structure of experience for the individual, consisting of a constant temporality, spatiality, causality and mode of 'subjective relativity and intersubjective praxis', which transcended all individual subjective encounters with the *Lebenswelt*.[105]

In addition to these conceptions of the *Lebenswelt* as subjectively experienced, communal and unified, Husserl also argued that the Lebenswelt is largely perceived through intuition. Because the *Lebenswelt* embraces all aspects of lived experience it contains both intuitive and conceptual or rational modes of being and activity. However, the general character and mode of experience of the *Lebenswelt* is non-conceptual and non-cognitive: it is an 'unhistorical "world of intuition".[106] However, even though the *Lebenswelt* is a sort of indeterminate experiential flux which we traverse in a predominantly intuitive manner, and even though such an intuitive mode of being must, therefore, be central to the human condition because it is characteristic of our most concrete mode of being, the hegemony of the cognitive and conceptual within modernity threatens to undermine that centrality and thereby diminish the quality of human experience, despite the fact that conceptual reasoning, particularly as exemplified in the methodology of the natural sciences, is only one of many possible forms of human activity carried out within the *Lebenswelt*.[107] This is why Husserl argues for the elaboration of a new balance between the existence of 'purposeful projects', and modes of being which are more in tune with the true spirit of the *Lebenswelt*.[108]

But, in addition to this, Husserl also argues for a return to the intuitive character of the *Lebenswelt*, as a means of nourishing the human condition.[109] Associated with this emphasis on intuition is an attention to the role of aesthetic experience in understanding the *Lebenswelt*. For example, Husserl argues that, in order for the individual to immerse him or herself genuinely within the intuitive indeterminate spirit of the *Lebenswelt* an '*epoché*' (abstention) must be practised. Here Husserl asserts that an intentional decision must be taken to abstain from the mounting of, or acceptance of, or interpellation within, aims, objectives and 'purposeful projects' which enclose us within restricted horizons. Such an *epoché*, the phenomenological equivalent of a religious fast, provides the foundation which makes a more genuine encounter with immediate experience possible.[110]

All of these themes from Husserl influenced Kracauer's thinking in both *Theory of Film* and *History: The Last Things Before the Last*. Kracauer is very clear that our contact with the *Lebenswelt* is of an inherently intuitive quality and, therefore, *ought* to lack systematic orientation if it is to approximate to the true spirit of the *Lebenswelt*. Such an imperative even applies to forms of academic study of the *Lebenswelt*, as, for example, when Kracauer, quoting from a letter written by Jacobs Burckhardt to Nietzsche, argues that the application of a 'philosophy of history' to a study of the historical *Lebenswelt* should be undertaken in the manner of 'a sort of pastime', rather than methodically.[111] Similarly, *Theory of Film*, in particular, is founded on the idea that, in modernity, the dominance of conceptual reason threatens the true indeterminate and intuitive spirit of the *Lebenswelt*; and both *Theory of Film* and *History: The Last Things Before The Last* call for a new balance to be struck between systematic rational thought and intuitive understanding.[112] Like Husserl, Kracauer does not call for a Romantic abandonment of scientific rationalism, but only for its scope within modernity to be reduced. Like Husserl, Kracauer also believes that the 'evidences' derived from the *Lebenswelt* carry more weight than the products of more 'abstract' forms of conceptual enquiry. Such evidences are intimately linked to our actual experience of living, and have a powerful impact upon the individual because, when they are encountered, they allow us 'for the first time, to take away with us the objects and occurrences that comprise the flow of material life'. Such evidences, then, are 'literally redeeming'.[113] Finally, like Husserl, Kracauer is also centrally concerned with the role of totality, and the communal, public material nature of the *Lebenswelt*, and both of these concerns course broadly through *Theory of Film*.[114]

How, then, does Kracauer utilise the various influences upon him and particularly Husserl's concept of the *Lebenswelt*, in order to advance a coherent position on how the problems of modernity can be overcome? In the 'Epilogue' of *Theory of Film*, in a section entitled 'Vistas', Kracauer speculates upon the relative worth of the various contemporary answers then being proposed to this question.[115] Kracauer initially addresses the question by rejecting two possible scenarios of solution. First, he addresses the 'liberal progressive' contention that continued scientific advance will eventually lead to the emergence of a more enlightened society because scientific rationality is, ultimately, more progressive than the mythological discursive systems which it replaced. There is one respect – one again based upon his understanding of the idea of the *Lebenswelt* – in which Kracauer agrees with this contention concerning the relatively progressive character of science in relation to pre-scientific thought. Kracauer believes that the decline of 'master ideological discourses', such as religious, mythological or metaphysical systems, is a progressive development in that the physical world has, as a consequence of such decline, become more 'visible' to us in its concrete particularity, because 'material objects' have now become divested of their ideologically totalising 'wraps and veils'.[116] Whereas, in the premodern era, all items of experience were understood within such totalising frameworks, in modernity the diminution in the authority of such frameworks has led to the conferment of more autonomy upon our objects of experience and, this, in turn, means that there is greater potential for us to become reacquainted with physical reality in a more immediate manner.

However, although Kracauer accepts this argument because he is opposed to ideology *per se*, and therefore to doctrinal systems of belief such as those advanced by organised religion, he goes on to argue that scientific modernity has nevertheless made the objects of our experience even more intangible to us by subsuming them within a discourse of technical knowledge, control and use-value which, perhaps even more than before, divests them of their autonomy.[117] This idea is summed up in Kracauer's formulation of the 'abstractness' of modern life, an abstractness which 'is not regulated according to man's needs', and so '*does not encompass man*'.[118] This notion implies that science, as it has developed since the Enlightenment, can never satisfactorily resolve the problems of modernity, or lead to the establishment of a more enlightened social or existential order of things, because it has become too enmeshed in a process of the 'rationalisation of life that would accommodate it to technology'.[119] In addition to this rejection of the liberal progressive idea that scientific rationalism possesses the potential to emancipate the modern subject, however, Kracauer also rejects the contrary option, that such an emancipation may be brought about through a return of the religious world view, and prescientific modes of thought.[120] Kracauer regards such a return as unrealisable and unfeasible, because the master ideologies of myth and religion would never be able regain their old power in the face of a hegemonic scientific world view and an overwhelmingly secular society. Consequently, Kracauer concludes that there is no possibility of any meaningful return to 'ancient beliefs'.[121]

In contradistinction to these two scenarios, which mark the polar extremes of any attempt to resolve the question of the problem of modernity, Kracauer actually sees the 'process of history' in largely pessimistic terms, as a 'battle between a weak and distant reason and the *forces of nature* that ruled over heaven and earth in the myths'.[122] On the one hand, the progressive reason of the Enlightenment has been transformed into instrumental rationality, and

thus made 'weak', so that the 'thinking promoted by capitalism resists culminating in that reason which arises from the basis of man';[123] whilst, on the
other, ideologically saturated 'ancient beliefs' continue to hold sway. In both
cases, additionally, instrumental rationality and the modern myths of the mass
ornament are 'a consequence of the unhampered expansion of capitalism's
power . . . preventing the advent of the man of reason'; and are 'sponsored by
those in power'.[124]

Kracauer argues that the way to escape from the 'spiritual nakedness' of this
debilitating modern condition is through transcending our abstract relation to
our own experience of the world, and experiencing the world in its phenomenological richness. Employing terminology derived from Alfred North
Whitehead's *Science and the Modern World* (1925), which Kracauer discusses
briefly in *Theory of Film*, Kracauer argues that the solution to the problem of
modernity lies in a return to the concrete labyrinth of the *Lebenswelt*, in order
to experience things in all their 'poignancy', 'preciousness' and 'concreteness'.[125] Later in *Theory of Film* Kracauer also quotes Whitehead more fully, in
order to expand on what the latter might mean by such a return to the
'poignancy preciousness and concreteness' of immediate experience:

> When you understand all about the sun and all about the atmosphere and all
> about the rotation of the earth, you may still miss the radiance of the sunset.
> There is no substitute for the direct perception of the concrete achievement of a
> thing in its actuality. We want concrete fact with a high light thrown on what is
> relevant to its preciousness.[126]

Whitehead is referring to the limitations placed upon knowledge by conceptual reason here, and to the need to transcend such limitations through immediate experience of the phenomenal world. Like Whitehead, Kracauer argues
that the concrete detail of reality must become the object of focus, and that
such a focus should involve both 'intense' and 'detached' scrutiny: intense,
because of the close observation of the world required; and detached, because
aesthetic experience can occur only in the absence of all instrumental means,
ends and 'purposive projects'. In focussing on 'the radiance of the sunset',
therefore, we gain access to what Kracauer calls the 'lower depths' of reality,[127]
the world of 'interpenetrating' 'counterinfluencing' organisms and the world
in its 'concreteness'.[128]

However, although it is to a certain extent possible to appreciate the claim
that close scrutiny of the *Lebenswelt* will 'reveal' something if that something is
being observed very carefully, it is less clear how such scrutiny can have 'spiritual', or 'redemptive' or 'utopian' consequences for the individual observer. In
what way can the experience of 'the radiance of the sunset' be defined as a 'spiritual' one? Towards the end of *Theory of Film*, in a section entitled 'The Family
of Man', Kracauer addresses this issue by posing the question, 'And what about

the spiritual life itself?' [129] His answer to this question takes him fully into a phenomenological perspective, as he argues for an equation to be made between the experience of a large number and multiplicity of sense perceptions, and some kind of *qualitative* transformation which occurs within the individual observer as a consequence of undergoing such an experience. The transformation which Kracauer signals here occurs when immersion within physical reality reaches such a stage that an intuition is reached concerning the connectedness of all things within reality. A sense of totality is, therefore, attained, and it is this intuitive revelation of totality which emerges from the 'direct perception of the concrete achievement of a thing in its actuality'. The 'high light' thrown on the concrete here is one which is able to generate an intuition of totality.

The 'spiritual life itself', is, therefore, a mode of being characterised by revelatory insight, of a secular rather than religious tenor, in which a sense of the unity of the general, intermediate and particular is intuitively experienced. However, this sense of unity is rooted in the *particularity* of concrete immediate experience – and, crucially, also in the surrogate medium of film – a medium which possesses the ability to re-present such existential particularity to us and, consequently, to provide us with renewed access to both phenomenal reality and the 'spiritual life itself'.

Kracauerian cinematic realism

One of the cornerstones of Kracauer's theory of realism is his argument that both film form and the specific types of spectatorship adopted within the film-viewing experience correspond to the 'damaged condition of modernity'. It is in this sense, and not in any naive realist sense, that Kracauer understands film to be 'realistic'. This, in turn, means that Kracaurian cinematic realism must be so constructed as to replicate the damaged condition of the *Lebenswelt* within modernity, and this leads Kracauer to endorse a type of cinema which is indeterminate in character, and which possesses 'affinities' with such aspects of the *Lebenswelt* as 'unstaged reality', 'chance', 'the fortuitous', 'the indeterminate', the 'flow of life' and 'endlessness'.[130] Because our experience of modernity is disjointed, consisting of 'bits of chance events whose flow substitutes for meaningful continuity', Kracauer asks for a cinema characterised by 'vague indefinability of meaning' and 'uninterpretable symbolism'.[131] Natural objects and events represented in films must, therefore, generate a significant number of 'psychological correspondences' and be bounded by a 'fringe of meaning'.[132]

Such a model of cinematic realism led Kracauer to support forms of avant-garde film-making which deploy an impressionistic style, and to praise films such as Alberto Cavalcanti's *Rien que les heures* (1926), Joris Ivens's *Regan*

(1929), and Jean Vigo's *A propos de Nice* (1930). These films conform to Kracauer's requirement to depict physical existence through types of representation which are undefined, imprecise and, therefore, 'cinematic'. However, in addition to the avant-garde, Kracauer also looks back in this respect to the earlier, more commercial films of Louis Lumière, highlighting the way that such films portrayed 'a jumble of transient, forever dissolving patterns accessible only to the camera', and (quoting from she Parisian journalist Henri de Parville) the ripple of leaves stirred by the wind.[133] Kracauer argues that these are subjects which film appears 'pre-destined (and eager) to exhibit'.[134]

In addition to such films, Kracauer also includes Italian neo-realist films such as *Paisà* (Roberto Rossellini, 1946), *La strada* (Federico Fellini, 1954) and *Ladri de biciclette* (Vittorio De Sica, 1948) within this category of films which are indeterminate. An example of the latter is Fellini's *I Vitelloni* (1953), which Kracauer (quoting Henri Agel) argues is 'composed of instants whose only *raison d'être* is their instantaneousness . . . [and which] . . . appear to be interlinked at random, without any logic, any necessity'.[135] Nevertheless, despite such endorsement of an apparently 'artless' cinema, Kracauer does not call for a form of cinematic realism which would merely 'record' physical reality in some *cinéma-vérité*-like fashion. On the contrary, he argues that film technique should be intentionally deployed in order to portray both perceptual physical reality *and* the underlying characteristics of the *Lebenswelt*. One consequence of the need to portray the latter of these two aspects of the *Lebenswelt* is that film form may be used in a formative and modernist manner, in order to portray something which exists beyond the immediately empirical.

If the kind of cinema referred to above is to be considered 'realistic' in a Kracaurian sense, then it follows logically that the type of cinema which would be considered 'non-realistic' (or 'un-cinematic') in Kracaurian terms would be one in which film technique was used to create a narrative and visual style which was purposive, instrumental, directive and highly composed – in other words, a visual style (and content) which *did* operate primarily 'through logic or necessity'. Kracauer's objection to such a style of film-making is based on four related grounds. First, he believes that such a style would be incompatible with the aesthetic specificity of film as an artistic medium. Second, he believes that such a style shares similar structural characteristics with instrumental rationality. Third, he associates such a style with what he regards as conventional, or traditional, 'art', and is at pains to dissociate cinematic realism from such forms of art, because such art-forms transform the world through the use of aesthetic conventions, and 'sustain the prevailing abstractness'.[136] Fourth, such art-forms seek to establish an 'autonomous' aesthetic reality, which, again, sustains prevailing abstraction. All of these varied grounds are evident in the criticism which Kracauer brings to bear against a film such as *The Cabinet of Dr Caligari*, a representative of the expressionist movement, the *bête noire* of all the realist theorists, including Lukács. According to Kracauer, this film is incompatible with the aesthetic specificity of the film medium because it transforms the normal physical world excessively, through the use of aesthetic conventions. *Caligari* is also 'intended as [an] autonomous whole', a 'self-sufficient composition' which 'organises the raw material' and 'frequently ignore[s] physical reality or exploit[s] it for purposes alien to photographic veracity'.[137]

In addition to such uncinematic, formal compositional tendencies, Kracauer also defines certain kinds of thematic content as 'uncinematic'. These include 'conceptual reasoning', and 'the tragic'; and, as with the case of autonomous aesthetic form, he argues that these are also to be avoided.[138] Kracauer actually sees the presence of language in a film as a potential problem in itself, though he argues that this 'liability' can be 'surmounted' by ensuring that the film 'divest[s] the spoken word of its leading role'.[139] Beyond this, Kracauer argues that conceptual reasoning is 'an alien element on the screen', and incompatible with the medium.[140] In addition to conceptual reason, Kracauer also regards 'the tragic' as incompatible with the medium, arguing that it is more suited to literature or the theatre. This is partly because tragic subject matter necessarily concerns *human* affairs: in fact, it 'is exclusively a human affair',[141] and this means that a film which accentuates the tragic must necessarily underscore the importance of the relations between human beings and 'inanimate objects', or nature. As with Kracauer's criticism of Luis Buñuel's *Un chien andalou* (1928), this means that the portrayal of physical reality in such films must be subordinated to the depiction of characterisation and conceptual theme, as the tragic 'covers' reality and, once more, sustains prevailing abstraction.

At the heart of Kracauer's conception of cinematic realism is the conviction that, at the level of form, film should allow images of the world a degree of autonomous existence from the controlling drive of narrative, action and plot; and, at the level of content, should mobilise truly 'cinematic' subject matter such as 'the flow of life' and the 'indeterminate'.[142] In *Theory of Film* Kracauer expands on these convictions concerning authentic 'cinematic' realism through an analysis of a key scene in *Un chien andalou*, in which, he argues, the opportunity to achieve such autonomous imagery and authentic cinematic thematic material is almost grasped, but ultimately forsaken. The scene, near the beginning of the film, shows a young man and a woman, who are seen looking down through the window of an apartment at a small crowd which has gathered around another young woman, who is prodding a severed hand lying on the road. A policeman arrives and places the hand in a box, then gives it to the woman. We then see a shot, taken from above, of the woman in question surrounded by the crowd, then a further shot of the couple looking down from the window of their apartment. As the two continue to gaze in fascination at the woman in the street, she is run down by a passing car.

Kracauer does not comment on the more obviously surrealist or Freudian aspects of this scene, but instead focuses on the way that the plot and narrative is related to the background environment of street, buildings and urban iconography which appear in this sequence:

> One familiar example [of such a failure to capture autonomous imagery] is the fascinating and truly realistic shot of a small street crowd seen from far above in *Un Chien andalou*. If this shot were integrated into contexts suggestive of camera-reality and the flow of life it would invite us dreamily to probe into its indeterminate meanings'.[143]

Kracauer goes on to argue that, because *Un chien andalou* is a surrealist, rather than realist film, such a potential for indeterminate signification cannot be realised, because 'the symbolic function assigned to surrealism automatically prevents them [signifiers] unfolding their inherent potentialities'.[144] If this scene in *Un chien andalou* were to be genuinely 'suggestive of camera reality and the flow of life', the camera would cut from the activities and desires of the characters portrayed to show substantive, concrete and relatively autonomous images of the environment around them. The characters in the film would thus be shown as more incorporated into their immediate physical environment, instead of dominating that environment, and forcing reality to the periphery of the diegesis. Both character and environment would, therefore, be 'equal partners' in such an exemplar of cinematic realism.[145] At the same time such cutting would also create 'autonomous' areas within the narrative, in which the spectator would be able to engage in a greater degree of free, self-directed interpretative activity.[146]

However, according to Kracauer, *Un chien andalou* does not function in this way. Instead of being integrated at an equal level with their environment, the characters in the film appear to exist within a hermetically sealed subjective world and, consequently, *Un chien andalou* does not, according to Kracauer, portray 'camera reality', or 'the flow of life'. In addition to such criticisms, Kracauer also contends that the continuity editing employed in the scene under question here is shot from one, organising point of view, and Kracauer goes on to argue that this exercises influence over the awareness of the spectator, and inhibits the emergence of free spectatorship. In contrast, a film such as *Regan* dispenses with such an organising viewpoint, and employs editing to build up an assemblage of impressions seen from a variety of viewpoints, thus maximising the potential for free spectatorship to take place.[147]

Kracauer's analysis of *Un chien andalou* and *Regan* also makes it clear that his conception of cinematic realism embodies a very particular conception of totality, and one quite different from those found in the thought of Grierson, Bazin and Lukács. For example, Kracauer criticises films, and other works of art, which seek to attain an autonomous aesthetic wholeness, because this would make such films and works of art 'self-contained' entities and, therefore, necessarily disconnected from much of their surrounding *Lebenswelt*. In this sense, Kracauer equates the autonomous work of art with the Husserlian 'purposive project', one whose internalising and inclusive imperatives create a limit boundary between itself and the surrounding *Lebenswelt*, thus causing that project to become alienated from the authentic interpenetrating, indeterminate spirit of the *Lebenswelt*. In order to achieve the representation of a form of cinematic totality more in tune with, rather than cut off from, the spirit of the *Lebenswelt*, film must constantly refer to a larger totality existing outside of its own diegetic world. In this way cinematic totality would be inclusive of both the film as a fictional 'intensive totality' (to use Lukács' phrase) and the 'extensive totality' of the 'historical here and now' (again, Lukács' terminology seems particularly helpful in allowing us to grasp Kracauer's meaning). This is why Kracauer constantly demands that films should contain diegetic 'gaps' within them – areas of compositional incompleteness, or incongruity, which set limits upon the film's latent drive to become 'autonomous'.

The images of 'physical reality' which *might* have appeared in a film such as *Un chien andalou,* and which *would* have been internally 'autonomous' from the plot of the film (thus denying autonomy and unity to the film as a whole) would of course remain part of the diegetic world of the film, because a film is a finite autonomous entity, like any work of art. Kracauer is fully aware of this, but nevertheless believes that cinematic realism should struggle against such a reality. A film which depicts the flow of life is, therefore, a form of intensive totality which struggles against its own character as intensive totality, as well as the object-character of all art. Such a struggle is of course doomed to failure, but that does not particularly matter, because art and, therefore, cinematic realism, is not an insular end in itself; and a film which contains 'camera reality', but is none the less circumscribed by its own objectness, still provides inspiration for the spectator to draw on in order to transcend his or her own circumscribed, rationalised existence within the 'damaged' modern *Lebenswelt*. In replicating the indeterminate character of the *Lebenswelt* such forms of cinematic realism also force us to become more conscious of the indeterminate nature of our own experience within the *Lebenswelt*. In addition, such images also enable us to imagine a totality which lies beyond both the fictional world of the film and our own circumscribed daily world of pragmatic purposive concerns, fears and desires: a totality which offers the prospect of freedom, self-determination and opportunity. This is because films which depict the flow of life *both* imply the possibility of transformation, which is a quality at odds with the forces of instrumental rationality and determination, and link the idea of transformation to the perception of a greater totality. It seems, then, that the experience of transformation and totality which we obtain through looking into the indeterminate gaps and ellipses offered up to us in realist films is an essentially liberating one.

In addition to arguing that film should be 'realist', of course, Kracauer also argued that film should be 'redemptive'. However, and as the passages above suggest, realism and redemption are in fact closely related to each other, in the sense that realism is the precondition for redemption. Nevertheless, although realism may be a precondition for redemption it does not necessarily *entail* redemption. This is because realism, as Kracauer conceives it, is engaged in an ongoing struggle – one which could go either way – with the prevailing forces of modernity. In other words, realism is conceived of as a form of struggle against limitation which takes place within the film text, and also as a more extensive form of resistance to the forces of abstraction within modernity (the similarities here with Lukács's notions of 'culture' and 'soul' are very clear). Because this dual struggle is a continuous and uncertain one, what Kracauer referred to as the '*go-for-broke*' game of history carries on, and we can either return to the 'Utopia of the in-between'[148] or head further into the 'dead world of things' which lies at the heart of modernity.[149] In the course of this process, realism will endure both successes and failures, but will always subsist as the standard bearer for an important conception of human agency and freedom, and experience of reality.

Cinematic realism, must, therefore develop as part of a committed campaign to bring the real character of the *Lebenswelt* back into view, and counter the 'dead face of things' generated by a soulless modernity. At the same time however, realism also appears to be something of a David fighting Goliath, with the odds similarly stacked solidly against it. This is also why, in spite of his evident enthusiasm for his work on film theory (Walter Benjamin argued that Kracauer would require a 'long life' in order to finish writing his 'encyclopedia of film'),[150] an air of resigned fatalism is often evident in Kracauer's work. Such fatalism persists at two distinct levels. At the level of the film text, the struggle against the object-character of the film clearly cannot succeed, because film *is* a finite object. Similarly, at the social or historical level the struggle against modernity also appears doomed, because modernity and instrumental rationality are so prevailing, and so acutely entrenched within the power structures of contemporary culture and society.

Although Kracauer's general theory of cinematic realism was based on the strong intellectual foundations provided by Kant, Husserl, Lukács and Weber, it could be (and has been) argued that he did not use that foundation in order to develop a particularly rigorous theory of cinematic realism.[151] His writings, taken as a whole, do not in themselves amount to a strong, coherent position, but are rather impressionistic, like the model of 'anteroom' historiography which he advocated in *History: The Last Things Before the Last*, or the model of film-making which he celebrated in *Theory of Film*. However, this lack of systematicity in Kracauer's theory is not as forbidding a problem as some have argued, as it it remains perfectly possible to reconstruct a coherent intellectual position from Kracauer's various writings. After all, Kracauer did not himself actually *want* to be 'systematic', and it is, therefore, the task of later commentators to reconstruct a coherent systematic position from his various writings. What may be more of a problem, however, is that the 'impressionistic' style of analysis adopted by Kracauer meant that he did not engage in any substantial analysis of any particular films. Instead, the examples which he quotes, particularly in *Theory of Film*, are brief, sketchy and unrewarding. One objective of a rearticulated form of Kracaurian analysis would, therefore, appear to be the more substantial application of Kracauer's ideas to particular cases of film analysis. However, that is a task to be undertaken as part of another project, and one which cannot be adequately addressed within the space available here. Instead, the task here will be to incorporate Kracauer's key themes and premises into a more general model of intuitionist cinematic realism.

The problem of modernity: Bazin

As mentioned at the beginning of this chapter, Bazin will not be considered here as fully as Grierson and Kracauer, because his thought is influenced by an intellectual tradition which is somewhat tangential to the main concerns of this study. Instead, this more targeted scrutiny of Bazin's thought will focus on three areas of his thinking which are of particular relevance to this study of intuitionist cinematic realism: those concerning 'alienation', 'totality' and 'agency'. In, addition, this analysis will focus also on one of Bazin's most relevant essays, 'The Ontology of the Photographic Image'.[152] To some extent, and as has been implied, Bazin's conception of modernity can be distinguished from those held by Kracauer and Grierson. Whilst Grierson was influenced by Hegel and British idealism, and Kracauer by Kant, Weber, Husserl and Freud, Bazin was influenced by forms of French Catholic existentialism more or less unknown to the other two intuitionist realist theorists. The origins of Bazin's encounter with this division of existentialist thought can be traced back to 1938. That year, whilst studying to be a teacher at the Ecole Normale Supérieure at Fontaney Saint-Cloud (a predominantly secular teacher training institution), Bazin joined a study group inspired by the ideas of the Christian intellectual Marcel Legaut. The Legaut group were Christian activists, committed to the reintroduction of religious values and debate into the secular French educational system, and Bazin was particularly influenced by the call, expressed in Legaut's *La Condition Chrétienne* (1937), for a revolution in consciousness, premised on the need to build a new spiritual community inspired by Christian moral and social values. *La Condition Chrétienne* was, somewhat anachronistically, dedicated to Karl Marx, although Legaut was opposed to the focus upon materialism (and, obviously, atheism) within the Marxist tradition.[153]

Alongside Legaut, another associated influence on Bazin at this time was that of the French Jesuit Emmanuel Mounier, who in 1932 helped found the radical Catholic journal *Esprit* – a journal which Bazin would also became associated with in the late 1930s. Mounier was a leading figure within the 'personalist' movement, a Christian association opposed to what its affiliates considered to be the widespread 'depersonalisation' of existence and lack of spirituality within contemporary secular society. As with Legaut, Mounier propounded a doctrine which attempted to bridge the gulf between the accent on individualism within the existentialist tradition and the focus upon the social and political domain found within Marxism.[154] Although he described personalism as 'a branch of the existentialist tree',[155] Mounier nevertheless also rejected what he regarded to be the more nihilistic aspects of the existentialist philosophies of Kierkegaard, Nietzsche and Heidegger, and adopted a more hopeful position regarding the possibilities of human emancipation.[156] Mounier can also be related to the rise of a postwar humanist – individualist movement in France, exemplified by Sartrean existentialism and the journal *Les Temps Modernes*, both of which emphasised the importance of human freedom and individual autonomy. Bazin was deeply influenced by Mounier, and by the existentialist tradition more generally. In terms of that latter tradition, he was particularly influenced by Sartre's *Psychology of the Imagination* (1940), from which he adopted the idea that 'man' feels himself to be existentially alienated from the material world of objects which surrounds him. [157] Such a view was compatible with Mounier's conception of a 'depersonalised' reality, and can also be associated with the thinking of another early influence upon Bazin, the protestant literary and film critic Roger Leenhardt, who began to write about film in *Esprit* from 1934 onwards. Adopting the Christian view of man as fallen, and as seeking redemption and atonement, Leenhardt argued that man was destined to embark upon a quest for insight and wisdom, against the background of an ambiguous and uncertain world.[158]

These concerns with the depersonalisation of experience were also reinforced by another influence upon Bazin's conception of the problem of modernity and, perhaps, the most important influence on him overall: that of Henri Bergson's conception of 'duration'. Bergson considered the experience of temporality to be an essential aspect of the human condition, and the most important kind of such experience to be 'duration'.[159] In his *Time and Free Will* (1889) Bergson argued that 'duration', or *durée*, is of such importance because it is 'the form which our conscious states assume when our ego lets itself *live*, when it refrains from separating its present state from its former states'.[160] In the experience of *durée*, past and present are fused into a totality, so that we experience 'succession without distinction'.[161] However, Bergson's conception of duration as succession without distinction was also derived from a more fundamental ontological and epistemological position on the nature of mind and reality. Bergson regarded life as a kind of vital 'force', which he called the *élan vital* – a force which permeates the evolutionary process, causing life to evolve and transform itself in an 'endless stream of becoming'.[162] The *élan vital*, as an evolving flux, constantly changing, and never 'fixed', characterises all of life, including human consciousness; and this conception of life as a fluctuating current of force led Bergson to make a key distinction between three different modalities of comprehending that force: the modes of 'intellect', 'instinct' and 'perception'.

For Bergson, the most basic mode of experiencing reality is perception. However, Bergson – the phenomenologist – also differs markedly from Husserlian phenomenology in the weighting that he bestows upon the importance of perception. For Husserl, as we have seen, immediate experience of the *Lebenswelt* is an important prerequisite for human emancipation. Although the *Lebenswelt* also consists of 'purposive projects' and, therefore, intentionality, it is in essence an experiential web which enfolds the subject, and invites the subject to immerse himself or herself intuitively within it at the level of immediate, empirical experience. For Bergson, on the other hand, perception is the 'lowest degree of mind – mind without memory',[163] because submersion of the self in the immediate object of perception rules out a fundamental aspect of the human condition – the ability to engage in reflective activity. Although, like Husserl, Bergson argued that, in order to truly experience reality, we must 'dive back into the flux itself', the Bergsonian 'flux' is marked by a far higher degree of intentionally reflective activity than is the case with the Husserlian *Lebenswelt*.[164] However, if perception is problematic because it lacks reflective intentionality, then reason, or 'intellect', is also equally problematic because of its tendency to transform the *élan vital* into a series of artificially 'fixed' states. Bergson believed that the proper role of intellect was to conceptualise the connections between things, and thus reproduce the spirit of the *élan vital* through conceptual analogy and symbol. However, he also believed that, in modernity, intellect tended to emphasise the distinctiveness of things and, because of this, was unable to grasp the interconnected disposition of the *élan vital*.[165]

Bergson believed the third of his three categories, that of 'instinct', to be by far the most important. However, instinct, like perception, is not of any weighty consequence when it is merely the upshot of an 'automatic' response to the world based on ingrained association and repetition. Instinct is, on the contrary, of significance when it attains the level of 'intuition', or 'self-conscious instinct'.[166] Intuition does not operate in the way that intellect does, through dividing up the fluctuating *élan vital* into a series of artificially fixed states, but, instead, transcends both perception and reason by comprehending the *élan vital* as flux. In intuition, we 'return to the flux through suprarational reflection . . . . we "grasp" meanings in flux as a global experience closed to analysis'.[167] However, such a 'return' is not just a reactive impulse. For Bergson, the bringing to bear of 'self-conscious instinct', and – in the form of memory – 'independent recollection', upon the world of experience is also an *act*; and it is through the exercise of such actions that the individual finds his or her true being.[168] Unlike the Husserlian assimilation within the *Lebenswelt*, therefore, Bergson defines the exercise of self-conscious instinct in terms of a self-motivated quest to achieve an intuitive understanding of reality and global experience. Of course, the exercise of such 'self-conscious instinct' concerning the true nature of *durée*, like the experience of 'succession without distinction', is made difficult by the dominant character of modernity, and by the hegemony of a scientific approach which 'consists essentially in the elimination of duration'.[169] The contemporary world is dominated by an 'intellect' which attempts to divide up and fix meaning and, in so doing, discourage the exercise of 'independent recollection' and, even, the understanding of reality as 'inwardly apprehended flux'.[170] One consequence of this is that we lose the ability to intuitively 'grasp' higher meaning through 'suprarational reflection', and this contributes to what Kracauer also calls the increasingly 'abstract' nature of experience, and what Lukács, after Weber, refers to as 'disenchantment'.

Bergson's conceptions of 'self-conscious instinct', the *élan vital* and *durée*, together with ideas taken from Mounier, Legaut and Leenhardt, led Bazin to adopt a particular conception of human nature within modernity. In his essay 'The Ontology of the Photographic Image', Bazin drew specifically upon the Bergsonian conception of *durée* to argue that mankind was troubled by the inevitable corruption and decay associated with existence within temporality.[171] Here, Bazin is referring to three related aspects of what he takes to be the human condition: (1) the physical decline of the subject within time; (2) the manner in which the tapered driving force of temporality progressively prevents the subject from experiencing the world in its sum; and (3) the Bergsonian distinction between *durée* as the essence of temporality and 'distinction without succession' as the more typical experience of time as something 'divided up' into separate states.

In 'The Ontology of the Photographic Image' Bazin, albeit unsystematically, explores all three of these aspects of our experience of psychological time. However, he also draws upon yet another conception of temporal experience, this time derived from existentialism, concerning the 'imbalanced' nature of our experience of temporality. Here, an ideal model of 'successiveness' is drawn upon in order to stress the fact that the linear nature of our actual experience of time implies the existence of an almost unbridgeable chasm between the separated conditions of past, present and future – a severance which suggests that reality as interconnected flux can never be truly experienced.[172] This, more overcast conceptualisation of successiveness, is also compounded by the submission, again drawn from existentialism, that our experience of temporality is inherently 'imbalanced', because the temporal maze within which we are caught up is not only fragmented into three domains of conscious experience but is also commonly in a state of imbalance, with one domain or the other normally prevailing.[173] It is this conception of a flawed existential experience of temporality characterised by succession with distinction, together with the idea of an imbalance within the three domains of temporal experience, which Bazin draws on in 'The Ontology of the Photographic Image', and other essays.

For example, in 'The Ontology of the Photographic Image', Bazin argues that human perception and consciousness is necessarily partial and, consequently, fragments the 'complex fabric of the objective world';[174] whilst man is also imprisoned within 'the flow of time', and unable to step outside that current in order to grasp phenomenological reality as a whole.[175] Bazin believes that 'man' longs to transcend temporal distinction, and experience genuine successiveness. However he also believes that such transcendence is made difficult because we can never be 'freed from [our] destiny', a destiny marked by the 'proper corruption' of time.[176] Bazin's concern with the fragmentary character of temporal experience leads him also to assert that one of the primary functions of art is that of offering enduring objects and images which will stand against the 'corruption' and 'distinction' which characterise 'ordinary' temporality. However, he also views such a function as, ultimately, misleading. In 'The Ontology of the Photographic Image', Bazin refers to this misleading imperative as the 'mummy complex' – the aesthetic predisposition to imitate nature and life in order to provide 'a defence against the passage of time'.[177] However, such attempts to stand outside the flow of time and halt the corruption of temporality are merely 'artificial', and cannot constitute a genuine experience of standing outside our destiny. What Bazin calls 'the primordial function of statuary, namely the preservation of life by a preservation of life', cannot 'entirely cast out the bogey of time. It can only sublimate our concern with it to the level of rational thinking.'[178]

Bazin is critical of the mummy complex also because, within modernity, it has manifested itself most strongly in what he calls the 'resemblance complex' – the 'original sin' of western art.[179] Here, the 'psychological' desire to 'have the last word in the argument with death' leads to the production of art which attempts to achieve 'as complete an imitation as possible of the outside world', in a nevertheless hopeless quest to 'cast out the bogey of time'.[180] Bazin believes that, just as a statue (or mummy) cannot have any bearing upon the reality of human finitude and endurance of temporality, so such a 'complete' imitation can also never be achieved because there can be no 'ontological identity of model and image'.[181] Bazin's position on the nature of human finitude and the fragmenting experience of temporality appears to imply that totality can never be meaningfully experienced, and this, in turn, places him within the more pessimistic constituencies of the existentialist tradition. However, and as with the Catholic existentialists in general, such pessimism is qualified and, as we will see, Bazin also argues that the individual possesses the potential to transcend such alienation, and experience 'successiveness without distinction'.

Totality: Bazin

According to existentialism, it is the imbalance in our temporal consciousness and experience of reality, in conjunction with the transient successivity of our existence, which stimulates a desire for the kind of unified experience which will gather together past and present into a more consequential whole, and transcend the limitations of a fractured human condition.[182] Although, as we have seen, Bazin rejected the ideas of the 'mummy' and 'resemblance' complexes, in which art attempted to attain such a unified experience through mimetic representation, he did believe that photography and film could realise such an objective through other modalities, and particularly because both media performed in a manner similar to that of the act of memory in the way that they brought the past into conjunction with the present. The ability of photography to reproduce external reality is not, consequently, as important for Bazin as this ability to portray 'successiveness without distinction' and 'independent recollection; a portrayal which transforms these mediums into objectified incidents of *durée* – the experience of which is, according to Bergson, so necessary for the advancement of the human ego.[183]

However, whilst Bazin believes that photography can reveal *durée* through 'embalming' the momentary, he also believes that film can reveal *durée* in an even more consequential sense, through the ability which the medium possesses to embalm a *continuous span* of past and present. Bazin refers to this process whereby a 'span' of duration is captured as 'change mummified', a process of embalmment in which 'The image of things is likewise the image of their duration'; and where such imagery links past and present into an evolving dynamic unity of succession without distinction.[184] Whereas Bazin rejects the 'mummy complex', because it advances an *illusion* of unity, he believes that film's ability to portray the unified experience of *durée* renders totality in a psychologically and phenomenologically authentic manner.

In addition to Bergsonian conceptions of duration, this idea of a 'span' of duration is also drawn from the existentialist idea that the individual is able to transcend the experience of successive, fragmented instants of time through creating coherent and meaningful 'spans' of meaning through active intentionality, thus bringing a degree of unity to his or her own experience of the world.[185] Whilst a 'thing' merely 'endures through a succession of instants', therefore, the 'existent' brings the memory of his past with him into the present, anticipates the future, and also projects both memory and anticipation across

'spans' of linear time in a quest for 'a wholeness quite different from the unend-
ing succession of the 'everlasting'.[186] This idea that man lives through a series
of existential 'spans' of duration, and that, when this is occuring, we truly
possess ourselves,[187] led Bazin to conceive of film as a medium able to replicate
such spans, and so create coherent and meaningful accounts of contiguous
experience. Such accounts are not only structured into the film text, however,
but are also created by the spectator, because their presence within the text
encourages the spectator, as agent rather than subject, to engage in an active
quest to lay down his or her own construals of wholeness across the linear body
of the film narrative.

Bazinian cinematic realism

The model of cinematic realism developed by Bazin can be differentiated from
that advanced by Kracauer in the sense that Bazin was more antipathetic to
modernist or formalist art – or at least more directly committed to 'realistic'
art – than was the case with Kracauer. As we have seen, Kracauer argued that
some avant-garde and formalist films were able to exhibit cinematic realism
through effective and aesthetically specific modalities. In addition, there is also
a sense in which Kracauer's model of indeterminate cinematic realism conforms more closely to a film such as *Regan* than to a more conventionally 'realistic' film, such as *La strada*. In contrast, Bazinian cinematic realism is more
substantially grounded in the conviction that films should be comparable to,
and also attempt to render, our perceptual experience of reality.

Bazin appears to believe that there are two main reasons why such realistic
films are more effective in portraying reality. First, he believes that forms of
cinematic realism which remain close to perceptual experience possess the
capacity to present the world to the spectator in considerable empirical detail,
as a world that is existentially close to the spectator's own life-experience. As
previously argued, Bazin is not principally concerned with the depiction of
empirical reality, but with that of more existential aspects of the human condition, which he sometimes refers to as the 'symbolic'.[188] However, not only are
such aspects encountered *through* the empirical but the empirical image also
forms a *familiar* image of the world; and it is this feeling of acquaintance which
overcomes the intrinsic sense of alienation which the individual characteristically feels when confronting a reality which is, after all, largely non-human,
inanimate and – above all – external to his or her subjective consciousness. In
other words, the recognisably familiar character of the empirical image also
works to combat the tendency for the spectator to regard the image on the
screen as radically separate from him or her (separate because it is part of a
world which exists outside of his or her own subjective consciousness); and
enables conditions to arise whereby a bond of identity can be established

between the mind of the spectator and the image of the world on the screen. The recognisable image of the world – one which appears to be analogous and comparable to our own experience of reality – provides the grounding for spectators to feel more secure in placing themselves in what is an inherently perilous position, one in which they offer up their most genuine feelings and beliefs concerning themselves and their understanding of reality to the test of identity, as the image of a world which may confirm such feelings and beliefs, but which may also throw them into question, materialises before them on the screen.

The second reason why Bazin believes that the film image should be similar to our experience of perceptual reality is that such an image is assumed (by Bazin and, according to him, by us) to constitute a form of totality. Of course, there are many aspects of reality which the empirical image cannot embody, and this would seem to suggest that such an image cannot, in fact, be regarded as constituting a form of totality. Nevertheless it remains the case that such film images do embody a certain *kind* of wholeness, based on the concordant fit between their internal spatial and temporal relations, and the logical inter-action between objects which are portrayed within a scene, all of which leads to that scene making sense to a spectator *as a whole*. Such a rendering of this limited totality, what Lukács referred to as 'the totality of a limited slice of life', is important for Bazin, because, like all the theorists within the intuitionist realist school, he believes that the summoning up of such micro-totalities is important in a world in which modernity has chipped away at our experience, desire and need for totalising modes of experience. In addition to the ability to instil a sense of identity and familiarity within the mind of the spectator (a sense which Bazin sometimes refers to as a sensation of 'love', or 'grace'),[189] therefore, the realistic film image is also capable of rendering this other, essential aspect of the intuitionist realist credo – an experience of a totality, the experience of which is capable of countering the prevailing forces of instru-mental rationality. Finally, the portrayal of such 'micro-totalities' is also con-sonant with the notions of successivity and *durée*, in that what film does is enable the spectator to create 'spans of meaning'.

What we find in this respect also is that Bazin appears to offer up a different notion of cinematic totality to that advanced by Kracauer. It will be recalled that, for Kracauer, authentic cinematic totality consists of a succession of inter-sections between the filmic diegesis and references to aspects of the world exist-ing beyond that diegesis.[190] This is what Kracauer calls 'camera life', a form of cinematic realism which not only seeks to represent reality, but also allows images of reality to disrupt the aesthetic unity of the film.[191] However, for Bazin, cinematic totality (at least within the area of Bazin's thought considered here) consists more of an interaction between the content of the film image in terms of the focus of characterisation, action and visual data and, crucially, the more peripheral visual data which are also at hand within the image and scene. At one level, Bazin's account, appears to be less indeterminate than Kracauer's, and more concerned with stability and wholeness than with the Kracaurian fleeting glance into the ever-fluctuating *Lebenswelt*. However the key difference between these two accounts lies in the fact that whereas, for Kracauer, flashes of reality are inserted into the film text through an interventionist (and therefore instrumental) editing process, for Bazin, they are already present in a latent form within the boundaries and subterranean structures of the image itself, waiting to be set in motion by the self-directed activity of the spectator as he or she creates 'spans' of meaning. So, Bazin's model of cinematic realism evokes reality as a simulacrum and a continuum, but does not seek to go beyond the mainstay diegetic world of the film in the way that Kracauer's model of totality does.

In addition to its concern for the totality and familiarity of the realistic image, Bazin's theory of cinematic realism is also premised upon the central intuitionist realist concern with indeterminacy. Although the Bazinian film image evokes both familiarity and totality it is also rich in complex detail and, consequently, in potential signification; and it is this combination of familiarity, totality and complex potential connotation which generates the Bazinian 'long hard gaze'. In the experience of cinematic realism a 'flood of correspondences' are revealed 'under the pressure of the long hard gaze';[192] and it is the realistic film which enables the 'long hard gaze' to emerge, as the spectator sees, and makes connections between, the complex, structurally dense content of the film's images. So, although the type of cinema which Bazin advocates contains substantial empirical information about the world set within 'the totality of a limited slice of life', the idea of the '*flood* of correspondences' suggests also that the experience of watching the realistic film should also be a discursively indeterminate and empirically engulfing one. To put it another way, the totality of a limited slice of life situated within the film will contain material which, though organised and ordered, also displays a tendency, by virtue of its volume and density, to resist such organisation and ordering, in order to promote discursive indeterminacy and spectatorial autonomy. In this sense, Bazin and Kracauer are as one in endorsing cinematic styles founded on indeterminacy. However, and as already argued, for Kracauer, indeterminacy (and therefore equivalence to the spirit of the *Lebenswelt*) is achieved through a form of realism which launches shafts of reality into the general logic of the filmic diegesis through a constructed editing process; whereas for Bazin it is achieved through submerging that logic in a surfeit of empirical signifiers. However, in both cases, the same outcome is achieved, as the spectator is encouraged to engage in free explorative activity, and construct 'spans' of coherence from an array of atomised signifiers.

In conclusion, it can be argued that Bazin's theory of cinematic realism contains five principal aspects: (1) a concern for the recognisable familiarity of the image, (2) a focus on totality, (3) an emphasis on indeterminacy, (4) a support for active spectatorship, and (5) an empiricist theory of knowledge. These five aspects also determine the general visual style of Bazinian cinematic realism. For example, Bazinian realistic cinema would be incompatible with an over-expressive or over-ornamental style, as well as with the over use of formalist montage, because such an approach and usage would diverge too much from our everyday perception of reality, and therefore make it more difficult for the spectator to observe the 'flood of correspondences' which might be set against his or her own life-experience. In other words, such a style would not be capable of establishing a *familiar* image of *durée*, or successiveness – one of the key requirements of Bazinian realism. Consequently, whilst Bazin praises an 'expressive' film such as *Citizen Kane* (1941), he directs his eulogies at the way technique in the film is used to create integrated spatio-temporal totalities, and not at the highly stylised applications of such technique in the film. So, for example, Bazin argues that '*Citizen Kane* can never be too highly praised. Thanks to the depth of field, whole scenes are covered in one take'.[193] It is also for this reason that the American deep-focus photography school of the 1940s is less distinctive of Bazin's theory of cinematic realism than a movement such as Italian neo-realism, or realistic European films such as Bresson's *Le Journal d'un curé de campagne* (1951), which, he contends, is concerned with the 'phys-iology of existence'[194] rather than 'expressionism'.[195] Although films such as *Citizen Kane* or *The Magnificent Ambersons* (1942) are certainly 'dense' in their degree of pictorial detail, it is the wrong kind of density – one which is too aesthetically structured and, therefore, more likely to direct rather than eman-cipate spectatorship.

Bazin's theory of cinematic realism led him to address the work of a number of film-makers who, he believed, had made films in accord with the model of film-making which he advocated. This canon, which spanned both the silent and sound eras, includes figures such as Robert Flaherty, F. W. Murnau, Erich von Stroheim, Carl Theodor Dreyer, Roberto Rossellini, Vittorio De Sica, Robert Bresson, Jean Renoir, Orson Welles and William Wyler. Bazin argued that these directors were important because they had 'put their faith in reality',[196] and, in writing about films such as *Greed* (Von Stroheim, 1924), *Le Journal d'un curé de campagne, La terra trema* (Visconti, 1948), *Umberto D* (De Sica, 1952), *Limelight* (Charlie Chaplin, 1952), *The Best Years of our Lives* (Wyler, 1946) and *Ladri di biciclette* (De Sica, 1948), Bazin attempted to describe how such films stripped away cinematic artifice and the object-character of the cinema, in order to trans-fer 'the *continuum* of reality' to the screen.[197]

At the heart of Bazin's theory of cinematic realism is the idea that the film image should present a kind of simulacrum of our perceptual experience of reality to the spectator. The principal function of such a simulacrum is to re-present reality to us as a field which is at the same time familiar, unified and indeterminate. The advocacy of such a form of portrayal is based on Bazin's conviction that instrumental manipulation permeates the modern human condition. Such instrumentalism functions to limit our ability to experience the concrete texture of the world, because it covers the phenomenal world with ideological screens. In addition, such manipulation also works to 'shatter' (to use Kracauer's term) our vision of the phenomenal world as a potential totality. Both of these factors doubly limit our ability to understand our true relationship to reality. The importance of the portrayal of familiarity, unity and indeterminacy in the realistic film image, therefore, lies in the fact that such a portrayal makes it possible for the 'long hard gaze' to pierce the veils of ideology; and, as a consequence, enable us to gain a better understanding of our own human nature, and of our relationship to reality. All of this suggests that Bazin's ideas are substantially premised upon phenomenological ideas concerning the need to transcend the limitations placed upon human experience by both the human condition and modernity.

However, and as argued previously, in addition to this concern with phenomenological subjectivity and modernity, Bazin's thinking also includes a pronounced metaphysical dimension derived from forms of Christian existentialism, and this aspect of his thought becomes particularly evident when he writes on the subject of religion. For example, in writing on *Le Journal d'un curé de campagne*, Bazin declares that

> probably for the first time, the cinema gives us a film in which the only genuine incidents, the only perceptible movements are those of the life of the spirit. Not only that, it also offers us a new dramatic form, that is specifically religious – or better still, specifically theological; a phenomenology of salvation and grace.[198]

Many aspects of Bazin's general model of cinematic realism are evident in this quotation. These include the endorsement of a form of cinema which contains no dramatic 'incidents', only non-material 'perceptible movements'; the conjuring up of insight which arises from cinematic sequences grounded in the familiarity of the image; the ability of the film to engender a sense of identity between the spectator and his or her lifeworld; and the idea of a 'dramatic form' which is based on ideas rather than on action or 'purpose'. What the quotation also makes clear, however, is the extent to which Bazin's model of cinematic realism combines a secular phenomenology of the empirically familiar, unified and indeterminate with an existentialist ethics based on the quest for meaning and revelation, and a more theological set of concerns, which he identifies here as a 'phenomenology of salvation and grace'. This also marks a difference in the ideas of transcendence held by Bazin and Kracauer. For Bazin, such transcendence implies a religious dimension, whereas, for Kracauer, transcendence is firmly grounded in identity with the *Lebenswelt*. For both, however, the object of transcendence is totality.

Notes

1 Aitken, Ian, *European Film Theory and Cinema: A Critical Introduction* (Edinburgh: Edinburgh University Press, 2001).
2 Glover, Janet, *The Story of Scotland* (London: Faber & Faber, 1960), p. 364.
3 Ferguson, W., 'Scotland, 1689 to the Present', in *The Edinburgh History of Scotland, Vol. 4* (Edinburgh: Oliver & Boyd, 1968), p. 364.
4 Glover, p. 362.
5 Aitken, Ian, *Film and Reform: John Grierson and the Documentary Film Movement* (London: Routledge, 1990), p. 195.
6 Williams, Raymond, *Culture and Society 1780–1950* (London: Chatto & Windus, 1958), pp. 123–8.
7 Aitken (1990), p. 38.
8 Ibid., pp. 186–7.
9 Ibid., p. 48.
10 Purcell, Edward A., *The Crisis of Democratic Theory: Scientific Naturalism and the Problem of Value* (Lexington : University Press of Kentucky, 1973), p. 10.
11 Aitken (1990), p. 53.
12 Novack, George, *Pragmatism Versus Marxism: An Appraisal of John Dewey's Philosophy* (New York: Pathfinder, 1975), p. 40.
13 Lippmann, Walter, *Public Opinion* (New York; London: Allen & Unwin, 1922), p. 106.
14 Aitken (1990), p. 53.
15 Ibid., p. 57.
16 Ellwood, C. A., *Cultural Evolution: A Study of Social Origins and Development* (New York and London: The Century Co. Social Science Series, 1927), p. 258.
17 Aitken (1990), p. 57.
18 Ibid.
19 Ibid., p. 45.
20 Ibid.
21 Ibid., pp. 42–3.
22 Ibid., p. 25.
23 Russell, Bertrand, *History of Western Philosophy* (London: Allen & Unwin, 1965), p. 362.
24 Aitken (1990), p. 27.
25 Arnold, Matthew, *Culture and Anarchy* (London: Murray, 1869), p. 70.
26 Aitken (1990), p. 45.
27 Ibid., p. 194.
28 Ibid., pp. 109–10.
29 See Chapter 6 below on the work of Rom Harré and the principal of 'ontological depth'.
30 The three studies which Grierson drew on most for this are: Kant, Immanuel, *Critique of Pure Reason* (Oxford: Clarendon Press, 1978); Bradley, F. H., *Essays on Truth and Reality* (Oxford: Clarendon Press, 1914); and Hegel, G. W. F., *Philosophy of History* (New York: The Colonial Press, 1900).
31 Aitken (1990), p. 60.

32 For a more extended discussion on this subject see Chapter 6.

33 Aitken (1990), p. 60.

34 Ibid.

35 Ibid., p. 63.

36 Ibid., p. 27.

37 Ibid., p. 70.

38 Ibid., p. 84.

39 Bradley, F. H., *Essays on Truth and Reality* (Oxford: Clarendon Press, 1914), p. 188.

40 Mukerji, A. C., 'British Idealism', in *A Dictionary of Eastern and Western Philosophy* (London: Allen & Unwin, 1953), p. 308.

41 Passmore, John, *A Hundred Years of Philosophy* (London: Duckworth, 1957), pp. 62–5.

42 Bradley (1914), p. 175.

43 Aitken (1990), p. 44.

44 Ibid., p. 189.

45 Aitken, Ian, 'John Grierson, Idealism and the Inter-war Period', *Historical Journal of Film, Radio and Television*, vol. 9, no. 3 (1989), p. 254.

46 Grierson, John, 'Answers to a Cambridge Questionnaire', *Granta* (Cambridge: Cambridge University Press, 1967), p. 10.

47 Grierson, John, 'The Challenge to Peace', in Hardy, Forsyth (ed.), *Grierson on Documentary* (London and Boston: Faber & Faber, 1979), p. 178.

48 Grierson, John, 'Preface', in Rotha, Paul, *Documentary Film* (London: Faber & Faber, 1952), p. 16.

49 Aitken (2001), p. 166.

50 Ibid.

51 Ibid.

52 Ibid., p. 167.

53 Grierson, John, 'Flaherty, Naturalism and the Problem of the English Cinema', *Artwork* (autumn 1931), p. 124.

54 Aitken, Ian, 'Distraction and Redemption: Kracauer, Surrealism and Phenomenology', *Screen*, vol. 39, no. 2 (summer 1998), pp. 124–5. (Henceforth 1998a).

55 Grierson, John, 'The Documentary Idea', in Hardy (1979) p. 112; reprinted in Aitken, Ian (ed.) *The Documentary Film: An Anthology* (Edinburgh: Edinburgh University Press, 1998), pp. 103–115. (Henceforth 1998b).

56 Ibid., p. 121.

57 See, in particular, the essays 'Education and the New Order' (1941), 'Education and Total Effort' (1941) and 'Propaganda and Education' (1943), reprinted in Hardy (1979).

58 Aitken (1990), p. 11.

59 Ibid., p. 87.

60 Grierson (1931), p. 124.

61 Grierson, John, 'The Russian Example', in *The Clarion* (November 1930); quoted in Aitken (1990), p. 81.

62 Aitken (1990), p. 11.

63 Held, David, *Introduction to Critical Theory, Horkheimer to Habermas* (Berkeley

and Los Angeles: University of California Press, 1980), pp. 65–6.

64 Kracauer, Siegfried, *Theory of Film: The Redemption of Physical Reality* (Princeton: Princeton University Press, 1997), pp. 291–7.

65 Elsaesser, Thomas, 'Cinema – The Irresponsible Signifier or, "The Gamble with History": Film Theory or Cinema Theory', *New German Critique*, no. 40 (winter 1987), pp. 78–9.

66 Frisby, David, *Fragments of Modernity in the Work of Simmel, Kracauer and Benjamin* (Cambridge, MA: MIT Press, 1986), p. 183.

67 Ibid., p. 127.

68 Bratu Hansen, Miriam, 'Introduction', in Kracauer (1997), p. xi.

69 Frisby, p. 121.

70 Bratu Hansen, in Kracauer (1997), p. xii.

71 Ibid., p. xiii.

72 Ibid., p. xiv.

73 I part company with Bratu Hansen (in Kracauer, 1997) here, when she argues that *Theory of Film* does not express, or suggest, the idea of modernity in crisis. This does not seem to interpret the tone of the book accurately.

74 Kracauer (1997), p. 296.

75 Kracauer, Siegfried, *History: The Last Things Before the Last* (Princeton: Markus Wiener Publishers, 1995), p. 217. (Henceforth designated as 1995a.)

76 Aitken (2001), pp. 171–2.

77 Aitken (1998a), p. 126.

78 Kracauer (1997), p. 299, and quoting from Mumford, Lewis, *Technics and Civilisation* (New York: 1934), p. 340.

79 Husserl, Edmund, *The Crisis of European Science and Transcendental Phenomenology* (Evanston: Northwestern University Press, 1970), p. 139.

80 Kracauer, Seigfried, *From Caligari to Hitler: A Psychological History of the German Film* (Princeton: Princeton University Press, 1974), pp. 5–7.

81 Aitken (2001), p. 174.

82 Kracauer, (1974), p. 7, quoting Kallen, Horace M., *Art and Freedom* (New York, 1942), vol. 2, p. 809.

83 Ibid., p. 10.

84 Ibid., p. 74.

85 Kracauer (1997), pp. 190–1.

86 Ibid., pp. 289–90.

87 Ibid., p. 290.

88 Frisby, p. 155.

89 Frisby, p. 148.

90 Kracauer, Siegfried, *The Mass Ornament, Weimar Essays* (Cambridge, MA, and London: Harvard University Press, 1995), p. 69. (Henceforth designated as 1995b.)

91 Ibid., p. 68.

92 Ibid., p. 69.

93 Frisby, p. 184.

94 Ibid., p. 133.

95 Kracauer (1995b), p. 83.
96 Ibid., p. 78.
97 Ibid., pp. 84–5.
98 Frisby, p. 142.
99 Kracauer (1995b), p. 71.
100 Ibid., p. 81.
101 Bernet, Rudolph, Kern, Iso, and Marbach, Eduard, *An Introduction to Husserlian Phenomenology* (Evanston, IL: Northwestern University Press, 1993), p. 221.
102 Ibid., p. 224.
103 Ibid., p. 227.
104 Carr, David, *Interpreting Husserl: Critical and Comparative Studies* (Dordrecht, Boston and Lancaster: Martinus Nijhoff Publishers, 1987), p. 232.
105 Bernet, Kern and Marbach, p. 221.
106 Ibid.
107 Ibid., pp. 221–2.
108 Ibid., pp. 219–26.
109 Natanson, Maurice, *Edmund Husserl, Philosopher of Infinite Tasks* (Evanston, IL: Northwestern University Press, 1973), pp. 14–16.
110 Carr, p. 8.
111 Kracauer (1995a), p. 217.
112 Ibid.
113 Kracauer (1997), p. 304.
114 Ibid., p. 300.
115 Ibid., p. 291.
116 Ibid., p. 299.
117 Ibid.
118 Kracauer (1995b), p. 81.
119 Ibid., p. 69.
120 Kracauer (1997), p. 287–91.
121 Ibid., p. 291.
122 Kracauer (1995b), p. 79.
123 Ibid., p. 81.
124 Ibid., pp. 82–3.
125 Kracauer (1997), p. 296. This citation is derived from John Dewey, although Kracauer does not provide a precise reference.
126 Ibid.
127 Ibid., p. 298.
128 Ibid.
129 Ibid., p. 309.
130 These aspects are mainly discussed in Chapter 4 of *Theory of Film*, pp. 60–76.
131 Ibid., p. 298. Kracauer is quoting here from Auerbach's *Mimesis*, where Auerbach writes about Virginia Woolf's *To the Lighthouse*.
132 Ibid., pp. 68–9.
133 Ibid., p. 31.
134 Ibid., p. 41.

135 Ibid., p. 256.
136 Ibid., p. 301.
137 Ibid., p. 39.
138 Ibid., pp. 263–5.
139 Ibid., p. 264.
140 Ibid.
141 Ibid., p. 265.
142 Ibid., p. 273.
143 Ibid., p. 190.
144 Ibid.
145 Ibid., p. 265.
146 Aitken (1998a), pp. 135–6.
147 Ibid., p. 135.
148 Kracauer (1995a), p. 217.
149 Koch, Gertrud, *Siegfried Kracauer* (Princeton: Princeton University Press, 2000), p. 101.
150 Bratu Hansen, in Kracauer (1997), p. xiv.
151 Koch, p. viii.
152 Bazin, André, 'The Ontology of the Photographic Image', in *What Is Cinema? Volume I* (Berkeley, Los Angeles and London: University of California Press, 1967), pp. 9–16.
153 Andrew, Dudley, *André Bazin* (New York: Columbia University Press, 1978), pp. 25–9.
154 Gray, Hugh, 'Translator's Introduction', in Bazin, André, *What Is Cinema? Volume II* (Berkeley, Los Angeles and London: University of California Press, 1972), pp. 2–4.
155 Mounier, Emmanuel, quoted by Gray, p. 4.
156 Andrew, p. 34.
157 Ibid., p. 70.
158 Ibid., p. 33.
159 Russell, Bertrand, *History of Western Philosophy* (London: George Allen & Unwin, 1965), p. 759.
160 Ibid. Russell does not cite his precise source in Bergson here, but does refer to *Time and Free Will*, the first English edition of which appeared in 1910.
161 Ibid.
162 Ibid., p. 758. Again, Russell does not give a precise reference, but refers to *Matter and Memory*, the first English edition of which appeared in 1911.
163 Ibid., p. 761.
164 Ibid., p. 760.
165 Ibid., p. 758.
166 Ibid.
167 Andrew, p. 19.
168 Russell, p. 763.
169 Larrabee, Harold, A., 'Introduction', in Larrabee (ed.) *Selections from Bergson* (New York: Appleton-Century-Crofts, 1949), p. xiii. Quoting Bergson writing to

William James. Initially cited in Perry, Ralph Burton, *The Thought and Character of William James: Volume Two* (Boston: Little Brown, 1935), p. 623.

170 Ibid., p. xv.
171 Bazin, 'The Ontology of the Photographic Image', pp. 9–10.
172 Macquarrie, John, *Existentialism* (Harmondsworth: Pelican, 1973), pp. 155–6.
173 Ibid., p. 157.
174 Bazin, 'The Ontology of the Photographic Image', p. 15.
175 Ibid., p. 9.
176 Ibid., p. 14.
177 Ibid., pp. 9–10.
178 Ibid.
179 Ibid., pp. 12–13.
180 Ibid., pp. 10.
181 Ibid.
182 Macquarrie, p. 157.
183 Bazin, 'The Ontology of the Photographic Image', p. 10, and Russell, p. 759.
184 Bazin, 'The Ontology of the Photographic Image', p. 15.
185 Macquarrie, p. 156.
186 Ibid., pp. 156–7.
187 Russell, p. 760.
188 Bazin, 'The Ontology of the Photographic Image', p. 11.
189 Ibid., p. 15.
190 Aitken (1998a), pp. 134–6.
191 Kracauer (1997), p. 267.
192 Andrew, p. 122.
193 Bazin, André, 'The Evolution of the Language of Cinema', in Bazin (1967), p. 33.
194 Bazin, André, '*Le Journal d'un curé de campagne* and the Stylistics of Robert Bresson', in Bazin (1967), p. 133.
195 Ibid., p. 132.
196 Bazin, André, 'The Evolution of the Language of Cinema', in Bazin (1967), p. 24.
197 Ibid., p. 37.
198 Bazin, André, '*Le Journal d'un curé de campagne* and the Stylistics of Robert Bresson', in Bazin (1967), p. 136.

6

Transcendental illusion and the scope for realism: cinematic realism, philosophical realism and film theory

In the previous chapter the principal concerns and characteristics of the intuitionist realist cinematic tradition were discussed. This chapter will commence with a recapitulation of those concerns and characteristics, and those of the nineteenth century or Lukácsian tradition. The chapter will seek to evaluate the importance of these traditions, and the various problems inherent in the positions which they adopt. Following this, the chapter will relate these realist traditions to two different theoretical contexts. First, cinematic realism will be placed within the context of philosophical realism, and an attempt will be made to establish the extent to which the realist film theories explored here can be defined in philosophical terms, and what the value of such an enterprise might be. Second, cinematic realism will be compared to a tradition of film theory which will be referred to here as 'pragmatist cognitivist'. The chapter will conclude with an assessment of the importance of realism in general, and cinematic realism in particular.

It has been argued here (see Chapter 1) that no consequential division can be drawn between the abstract idea of a nineteenth-century modernist avant-garde and the realist movement which emerged in France during the early nineteenth century. This is because that realist movement, and particularly the form of 'serious' realism (to use Auerbach's term) which Chapter 1 of this book is concerned with, was both modernist and avant-garde from its inception.[1] The terms 'modernism' and 'avant-garde' have, of course, always been highly contested ones, defined through an assortment of perspectives and an industry of critical literature on the subject. However, this is not the place to return to an examination of such definitions and perspectives. Instead, for purposes of efficacy, one designation of each will be used in order to advance the central concerns of this book. Nevertheless, what follows next will, to an unavoidable extent, still represent something of a conceptual detour around the topography of such definitions. However, it is important, at this stage, to make more closely subject-defined – and also historically grounded – demarcations between the terms of modernism, realism and the avant-garde, not as an enterprise in itself but in order to better appreciate the specific character of nineteenth-century realism. This is what will be attempted next.

The term modernism will be engaged with here in the sense that Clement Greenberg (sometimes, see below) employed it, to refer to a form of art which both represents reality in a more or less figurative manner and, in doing so, also explores its own means of representation in a reflexive manner. According to Greenberg, some modernist works of art are first and foremost preoccupied with a reflexive study of their own means of representation, and can be labelled 'abstract', 'non-figurative', 'non-representational' or 'non-objective' as a consequence. An example might be an early twentieth-century painting such as Kasimir Malevich's *Black Square* (1915). However, the term 'non-representational' can be misleading because, even though *Black Square* is clearly 'non-figurative' and, as Malevich admits, 'suprematism' was also openly engaged with 'the inter-relation of colours';[2] this historically important painting remains more than solely reflexive in intent, and is still about reality in some respect. So, for example, Malevich argues that *Black Square* seeks to achieve 'philosophical penetration'[3] and can also be regarded as the aesthetic analogue of the historical changes then sweeping the Soviet Union: 'The economic life of the new world has produced the Commune. The creative construction of the new art has produced the Suprematism of the square.'[4] So, modernist work of this type remains representational in a sense, even though what is represented is both intangible and rendered through the deployment of non-figurative portrayal.

Black Square may be both representational and non-figurative in the above sense but other modernist works of art have been concerned with both representation and the realisation of a reflexive imperative, but have yet remained predominantly figurative in tendency. An example here might be *Berthe Morisot with a Fan* (1872), a late nineteenth-century work by Eduard Manet which uses brushwork in an evident, reflexive manner, whilst still equally evidently representing a subject. Greenberg has argued that 'Manet's paintings became the first Modernist ones by virtue of the frankness with which they declared the surfaces on which they were painted'.[5] However, both *Black Square* and *Berthe Morisot with a Fan* can equally be declared 'modernist' in this Greenbergian sense, because representation and abstraction exist as a relation of degree on a shifting scale within modern art, with one polarity dominating the other to a lesser or greater extent in any particular work.

As is well known, in the latter part of his career Greenberg increasingly emphasised the importance of aesthetic specificity and medium-awareness, arguing that what was specific to painting as an art-form was its 'flatness' and two-dimensionality.[6] This account also led him to conflate the terms 'modernism' and 'avant-garde', as he increasingly defined the avant-garde in terms of 'advanced' 'modernist' paintings which were principally concerned to explore their own means of representation. So, for example, in 'Towards a New Laocoon' (1940), Greenberg argues that the historical evolution of painting can be seen as a 'progressive surrender to the resistance of the medium; which resistance consists chiefly in the flat picture plane's denial of efforts to "hole through" it for realistic perspectival space'.[7] Yet, in 'Avant-garde and Kitsch', an essay written only a year earlier, Greenberg had defined the avant-garde in another sense, when he insisted that such a detachment from representation is also the consequence of a commitment to keep culture alive in the face of a deadening capitalist hegemony. As Greenberg put it, 'Hence it was developed that the true and most important function of the avant-garde was to keep culture moving in the midst of ideological confusion and violence'.[8] Here, modernist form has an oppositional avant-garde role to play, as a constituent component within a residual movement of anti-capitalist resistance. Such a view is, of course also similar to Theodor Adorno's position on 'autonomous art', as is evident in the essay 'Commitment' (1962), in which Adorno argues that, in autonomous art, modernist artistic form 'becomes an analogy of that other condition that should be . . . politics has migrated into autonomous art, and nowhere more so than where it seems to be politically dead'.[9]

Two decades after writing 'Towards a New Laocoon', however, Greenberg reinstated his 1940, as opposed to 1939 position, in an influential essay entitled 'Modernist Painting', in which he abandoned the term avant-garde completely, and defined 'modernism' in terms of 'a self-critical tendency', and as 'the use of the characteristic methods of a discipline to criticise the discipline itself'.[10] Now it is not Courbet who is regarded as the first modernist, but a philosopher: 'I conceive of Kant as the first modernist'.[11] Here, in 1965, the terms modernism and avant-garde come to mean more or less the same thing, but the sense of an oppositional political role for art, which was implied in 'Avant-garde and Kitsch', and is exemplified in Adorno's notion of autonomous art, has been replaced with a view of 'advanced' art as that which is 'self-critical' of 'all that was unique to the nature of its medium'.[12]

So, here we have two distinct conceptions of modernism and the avant-garde: (1) (Greenberg circa 1940, 1965) that modernism is concerned principally with the means of representation and aesthetic specificity, and *it is this which also makes it* avant-garde; and (2) (Greenberg 1939 and Adorno 1962) that *both* modernism and the avant-garde are concerned with the means of representation, *and* significant, oppositional representation and expression. However, these are not the only two conceptions available and, within later film theory, these terms have been interpreted in yet another way, in relation to notions of a 'reactionary' aesthetic modernism and a politically 'progressive' avant-garde. An example might be Peter Wollen's essay 'The Two Avant-gardes' (1975), in which Wollen puts forward a conception of modernism in which French cinematic impressionism, *cinéma pur* and various forms of structural and abstract cinema are strung together; whilst a conception of the avant-garde, in which the more politically important work of Dziga Vertov, Dada, surrealism and Jean-Luc Godard is held up for the greater praise.[13] This tendency, one which is at odds with the positions of Greenberg and Adorno, has also been reinforced in more recent critical writing, as, for example, in Peter Bürger's highly influential *Theory of the Avant-Garde* (1984), and elsewhere within the field of film studies.[14]

However, it will be argued here that such a notional severance of modernism and the avant-garde from each other will not allow a full understanding of the development of a realist tradition in the nineteenth century to be reached, and that, in contrast, such an understanding will be made more possible by adhering to the Greenberg (1939) and Adorno (1962) position. It also now becomes clearer why this detour around definitions of the terms modernism and the avant-garde proved to be necessary, for, in order to understand nineteenth-century realism in a more appropriate way, the definitions of these terms which have taken root within some critical writings in film studies (or at least anglophone film studies) must be amended, or replaced by a more inclusive conception of the historically based relationship between realism, modernism and the avant-garde.

Let us carry on this process of amendment first, with an account of the relationship between nineteenth-century realism and modernism. As argued, the tradition of critical or 'serious realism' explored here was concerned with *both* representation *per se* and the foregrounding of the means of representation, and can, therefore, be defined as a form of modernism in terms of Greenberg's 1940 and 1965 formulations. In attempting to define some of the core characteristics of this 'modernist' aspect of the critical realist tradition Raymond Williams also adopts a similar stance to Greenberg in arguing that realism was (1) 'distinct from surface appearances' and (2) 'represented reality in different mediums which produced different "objects" to that which was represented'.[15] Similarly, Gerald Needham has also argued for a distinction to be made between the more mimetic academic painting of Jean-Léon Gérôme, Ernest Meissonier, Alexandre Cabanel and others and contemporaneous 'realist' painting which 'does not create a smooth, invisible surface which is a window into the scene beyond'.[16] As we have seen, the naturalists also made a clear distinction between what they thought of as 'genuine' realism and the art work which puts forward 'a bland photographic view of life'.[17] This means that nineteenth-century critical realism must be distinguished from art which is principally concerned with the faithful mimetic reproduction of perceptual reality – a concern which leads such art into the dubious embrace of what has been labelled the 'reproductive fallacy' – the misplaced confidence that art can ever, or should ever, attempt to render reality transparently, rather than through the prism of a means of representation.[18]

However, the question then arises that, if this realist tradition cannot be associated with work principally concerned with the representation of perceptual reality, should it also be distinguished from forms of modernism in which the means of representation are employed in an entirely non-figurative manner? Nineteenth-century realism was closer in spirit and technique, as well as (to state the obvious) in chronology, to *Berthe Morisot with a Fan* than to *Black Square*. But does this mean that these two paintings are *basically* different from each other *vis-á-vis* realism? Jürgen Habermas believes that a distinction should be drawn between these two paintings. Following Kant, Habermas has, according to Holub, argued that the 'project of modernity' within the field of art consists of the growth of the autonomy of the aesthetic sphere, that and a chief aspect of this drive towards autonomy consists in a 'turning away from representation', until an increasingly 'elitist' art becomes progressively separated from the remainder of the public sphere:

> Eventually the type of formal experimentation and elitism we associate with twentieth century art becomes the norm: in literature and the pictorial arts representation gradually relinquishes its sway and is replaced by the foregrounding of the media themselves. Lines, colours, shapes, sounds, words or even letters themselves become aesthetic objects. Art appeals to experts, not to a larger community.[19]

Taking his argument from Kant's three critiques (of 'science', 'morality' and 'art'), and Weber's notion of the formation of the 'three spheres' (the 'technical', 'aesthetic' and 'ethical'),[20] Habermas argues that the rise of such 'autonomous', modernist abstract art can be associated with the inexorable abandonment of a unified life-world under the fragmenting impact of modernity, and the consequent transformation of the 'aesthetic sphere' into an area of increasing specialisation, and remoteness from the needs of the 'larger community'. One consequence of this is the decline of 'representationalism' and, therefore, realism. However, the characterisation of *all* foregrounded art as constitutive of an entirely negative historical development is surely questionable, and also opposed to all the positions (Greenberg 1939, 1940, 1965; Adorno 1962; Wollen 1975; and Bürger 1984) previously discussed. It may be, in contrast, that the tradition of modernist 'abstract' art which developed in the twentieth century can be set more valuably against the instrumentally barren materialism of modern capitalist culture than can some forms of fully 'representational' art. In this respect, Adorno's position on modernism, with its endorsement of formalism as a protest against instrumentalism, appears more compelling than Habermas's blanket negation, which appears reminiscent of the classical Marxist dismissal of modernism.

It can also be argued that, in the case of critical nineteenth-century realism, it was not paintings 'which declared the surfaces upon which they were painted' which constituted an abandonment of the everyday life-world, and led to the enhanced autonomy of the aesthetic sphere, but, rather, the highly mimetic academic paintings of official art. The paintings of Gérôme had little indeed to do with the *Lebenswelt* of his day, even though they were very 'representational'. Given this, the critical nineteenth-century realist tradition is better considered as a form of reflexive practice which arose in order to resist an aestheticisation of art, and intensifying specialisation of the aesthetic sphere, which was *based* on the hegemony of figurative representation. In a painting such as *Berthe Morisot with a Fan*, therefore, the subject is represented in a reflexive manner which 'declares' a concern for aesthetic specificity and, also, endorses forms of spontaneous response to immediate experience which, historically, developed in painting as a protest to the growing autonomy of art. Nineteenth-century realism was, therefore, in Greenberg and Adorno's sense, *both* modernist and oppositional.

If realism can be considered as 'oppositional' in this modernist sense, and as an aesthetic response to an officially sanctioned diminution of the *Lebenswelt* within the sphere of art, it can also be considered as oppositional in a more customarily understood avant-garde sense, in that it was characterised by a tendency to be *politically* oppositional, rather than legitimatory, in relation to hegemonic bourgeois society. This oppositional tendency characterises the nineteenth-century realist tradition from painters such as Gustave Courbet to writers such as Emile Zola. While not all realists were directly politically engaged, all were engaged with the impact of bourgeois capitalist culture upon the arts and society, in one way or another, and to one extent or another. This means that the tradition of serious realism discussed here cannot be described as, in any direct way, the art-form of capitalism, or the bourgeoisie.[21] Of course, realism can, has been and will continue to be used for reactionary purposes, including that of naturalising dominant ideology. Perhaps realism even has an inbuilt affinity for such iniquitous deployment. But, even if this is so, it was not the case within the tradition of realism under discussion here.

If serious realism can be defined as both modernist and avant-garde in the terms previously discussed, then it was also historically characterised by a particular tendency – the rejection of the provenance of rule-governed systems and the *a priori* formulaic. In contrast to such provenance, realism sought a more immediate, and intuitively responsive, encounter with reality. Such an encounter with immediate experience, also based on the desire to portray the fast-changing, spirallingly extensive society of the period, led to the appearance of what has been described as a realistic 'aesthetic of disorder', in which pre-existing generic conventions were torn asunder, and then recombined without much respect for precedent.[22] Yet, despite this emphasis upon the intuitive, lawless and spontaneous portrayal of disarray, realism was by no means an unremittingly anti-rationalist form of art, but one which sought to combine reason, impartial observation and even the scientific method, with an intuitive approach. Realism inherits the legacy of the rationalist Enlightenment, as well as the Romantic critique of rationality, and it is this combination of rationality and intuitive spontaneity which provides realism with its critical, imaginative force.

If nineteenth-century realism was a form of aesthetic which engaged rationality in a qualified though committed manner in order to centre on the open and spontaneous encounter with reality, it was also centrally concerned with the ideas of totality and evolution. Zola argued that 'it seems to me the work of art must take in the entire horizon',[23] and this concern with totality was based upon the need to understand the new capitalist bourgeois social order as a whole and as it evolved: to understand what was really happening at the individual, intermediate and general levels, in order to describe, contest and challenge the course of events. It is not particularly surprising either that realism should emerge so robustly in France, given the unremitting context of political unrest in that country from 1789 onwards; and also given the influence of a French intellectual tradition of determinist thought which accented the role of environment and evolution in moulding individual subjectivity and social institutions.

However, true to the overriding intuitionist imperative of realism, totality was mainly to be grasped through insight and suggestion, rather than rational explication. This focus on suggestive intuitive experience meant that totality was also conceived of as essentially indeterminate in character, and to be understood through exploring the fluid interpenetration of nuance. This led realism to focus upon the more asymmetrical aspects of experience. As Charles Baudelaire put it, this new type of art was concerned with 'the ephemeral, the fugitive, the contingent, the half of art whose other half is the eternal and the immutable'.[24] It was through a portrayal of such contingency that the larger picture, 'the entire horizon', was to be grasped; and realism enthusiastically sought to distance itself from that which was eternal and immutable, preferring the vagaries of shifting immediate experience. As the naturalist critic Jules-Antoine Castagnary, writing in 1867, expressed it:

> Nature and man, the countryside and the city; – the countryside with the depth of its sky, the green of its trees, its transparent horizons and waters dimly perceived through the mist, all the attractions of vegetative life under the changing light of the seasons and days . . . all the recurring surprises of individual or collective life . . . is the domain set out before the eye of the painter.[25]

If realism is considered as a form of intuitionist representational modernism, inspired by an aspiration towards the evocative comprehension of an indeterminate and evolving totality, and grasped through the immediate experience of a particular subject, it can also be said to possess a distinct point of reference: the lower depths of experience. Totality is to be encountered from the bottom up, through a resurgence and revitalisation of the everyday and the ordinary, because, in previous art-forms, this base of society had been so disqualified from representation, in order to sustain hierarchical aesthetic or social structures. Just as the realist encounters reality at the basis of experience, i.e., immediate experience, he or she also must encounter reality at its social foundation. This is why Williams argues that what characterises realism most is 'social extension',[26] why Auerbach argues that realism arose in opposition to the classical doctrine of distinct levels of literary representation, in which the representation of 'everyday practical reality' had a 'low status';[27] and why Nochlin argues that the most important feature of realism was its portrayal of 'the commonplace':

> The realists placed a positive value on the depiction of the low, the humble and the commonplace, the socially dispossessed or marginal as well as the more prosperous sections of contemporary life. They turned for inspiration to the worker, the peasant, the laundress, the prostitute, to the middle-class or working class café or 'bal', to the prosaic realm of the cotton worker or the modiste . . . viewing them all frankly and candidly in all their misery, familiarity or banality.[28]

In discussing Courbet's *Stonebreakers* (1850), Courbet's associate, Max Buchon, puts this realist imperative to portray the lower *quotidien* even more starkly:

> The painting of the *Stonebreakers* represents two life-size figures, a child and an old man, the alpha and omega, the sunrise and the sunset of that life of drudgery. A poor young lad, between twelve and fifteen years old, his head shaven, scurvy and stupid in the way misery too often shapes the heads of the children of the poor . . . a ragged shirt; pants held in place by a breech made of a rope, patched on the knees, torn at the bottom, and tattered all over, lamentable, down-at-heel shoes, turned red by too much wear, like the shoes of that poor worker you know. That sums up the child.[29]

A desire to portray 'prosaic realms', in order to evoke the shifting totality of the social formation within modernity was, therefore, a characteristic of realism; and, because such realms were also often, not just prosaic, but also debased, and 'base', the 'alpha and omega of drudgery' by virtue of their position at the underside of the social hierarchy, the lower depths of a human condition brutalised by a repressive social order; realism is also concerned with the role of mundane determining fate, as both an aspect of the human condition and one also precipitated by the forces of modernity. But, and as argued in Chapter 1, realism was also frequently close to the political. Courbet's *A Burial at Ornans* (1850) deliberately employed pictorial and symbolic forms taken from radicalised popular culture, and the same allegiance to radical politics is detectable in the *Stonebreakers*. As Buchon puts it, discussing the elderly figure in the painting, 'Just as you see him there, this man, with his years, with his misery . . . Just think what would happen if he would take it into his head to side with the Reds'.[30] To return to the definitions of avant-garde and modernism provided by Greenberg and Adorno, we can conclude by arguing that *Stonebreakers*, like many other examples of nineteenth-century realism, is both modernist and avant-garde, in terms of both a rejection of the institutionalised aestheticisation of art and a rejection of dominant bourgeois capitalist mores.

The nineteenth-century Luckácsian and intuitionist realist traditions

These characteristics of the nineteenth-century tradition influenced the realist cinema which emerged in France from 1902 to 1938. Cinema appeared to be the natural medium of expression for this critical realist tradition, because of film's ability to capture such a quantity of nuanced detail. This predisposition, together with the dark thematic orientation of nineteenth-century realism, finds embodiment within the cinema of pictorialist naturalism, and in some of the more important adaptations of Zola to be produced between 1902 and 1938, particularly *La Bête humaine*. Such an orientation can also be found in what have been referred to here as the 'social realist' films of Jean Renoir: films which endeavour to dispense with existing institutional practices in order to gain more immediate experience of reality, and saturate the image with the rich, raw detail of an alternative reality. This is true of *La Chienne* (1931), with its attempt to render the 'complexity and thickness of the modern world'[31], *La Règle du jeu* (1939), with its highly symbolic 'hunt scene', and *Toni* (1935), a film described as a 'signifying practice which was at odds with the dominant cinema of the day'.[32]

Before Renoir turned to the nineteenth-century realist tradition, however, it was reinterpreted by Georg Lukács and, in this process, a deformation occurred. Lukács adopted the distinction between realism and modernism put forward initially by Engels, then enshrined within official Marxist doctrine, in which modernism was posited as necessarily regressive. It is a pity that Lukács did not look to Marx himself, rather than Engels for the lead here. If he had done so he would have discovered that Marx never used the term 'realism' in the way that Engels did in the 1880s. Marx's own aesthetic position was largely derived from eighteenth-century German aesthetic traditions which emphasised the idea of *praxis,* and Marx did not refer to later traditions of Balzacian realism in the canonising way that Engels did. So, for example, in the *Grundrisse* (1857), Marx refers to art as 'having still the aim in itself' and, in *Capital* (1867), as a form of play of mental and physical powers, and an area of relative freedom, where human beings are able to exercise both free will and creative activity.[33] Neither of these formulations implies a rejection of modernism, or the canonisation of a particular form of realistic art.

However, the influence of Engelsian distinctions between realism and modernism is not, in the end, particularly significant for the intellectual reconstruction of a Lukácsian theory of cinematic realism, and this is because, despite his apparent endorsement of such distinctions, almost all of Lukács's foundational intellectual and aesthetic concepts emphasise the indeterminate nature of the aesthetic in a way which resonates with the core characteristics of the nineteenth-century critical realist position. Such concepts include those of *Scheinen*, art as 'revelation' of unity and freedom'; and the idea that art should possess an 'inner luminosity'.[34] The idea of art as 'sensuous manifestation' of the Absolute is also an essentially impressionistic and intuitionist model of aesthetic experience; as is Lukács' formulation of the 'typical' as the 'distillation' of the universal into the concrete particular[35] and his conviction that true realism 'flares up' during certain prescient historical conjunctures. This indeterminate, impressionistic, intuitive aesthetic is also encapsulated in what Lukács refers to as the 'central category of the aesthetic', *Besonderheit* and, within the area of film aesthetics, in the highly evocative concepts of *Stimmung* and *Stimmungseinheit*. These are all impressionistic concepts, designed to configure a 'poetic intensive totality' which will have a 'moving shaking effect',[36] and which will combat the 'unpoetic' character of ordinary life. Such a 'poetic intensive totality' will be characterised by a 'lack of definition'[37], as art manifests an inner freedom made visible outwardly.[38] In addition to such key concepts, all of the key Lukácsian categorisations of historical realism also conform to this evocative intuitionist approach. Even 'classical historical realism', the most 'rationalistic' of Lukács' categories, can still reflect the 'helplessness and desolation of the subject',[39] whilst 'democratic humanist realism' can be highly symbolic, and 'social critical realism' marked by a nihilistic 'lowered vitality'. These concepts and distinctions dominate Lukács' aesthetic system, and suggest that his aesthetic theory, particularly of film, should be classed as gradualist, indeterminate and non-directive, rather than 'classical realist' in the Engelsian sense.

Like the nineteenth-century and Lukácsian tradition, intuitionist cinematic realism is based upon a primarily intuitionist, as opposed to a rationalist or empiricist approach to cinematic signification and spectatorship. Despite the emphasis upon the empirical which underlies both sets of traditions, neither can be said to rely upon an empiricist theory of knowledge, in that, neither Lukács, Grierson, Bazin nor Kracauer adopts the view that all knowledge stems from experience, and can only be understood through a process of rational generalisation from perceived instances. Similarly, none of the above fully accepts the alternative rationalist proposition that real knowledge may be given completely independently of experience, and may also subsist within some ideal realm separate from the world of nature, accessible through reason. Instead, the

Lukácsian, and particularly intuitionist realist, traditions, picture the possibilities and limitations of human knowledge in terms of intuitive insight. For
example, Lukács' concepts of 'culture' and 'soul', Grierson's notion of the 'real',
Kracauer's concept of 'redemption' and Bazin's models of 'grace' and 'love' all
imply that knowledge (both of experience and of ideal categories) is to be
reached through some intuitive flash of insight.

However, these theorists also assert strongly that such a flash of insight has
foundations mainly in experience, rather than abstract thought; and, in addition to an intuitionist theory of knowledge, these traditions are grounded in
the conviction that insight can only be achieved through a focus on the empirical, because it is the empirical, rather than reason, which is the guarantor of
enlightened insight. This clearly suggests that these traditions cannot be
defined as primarily 'rationalist' in disposition either. In fact, the work of
Lukács, Bazin, Kracauer and Grierson emerged in response to what was perceived to be the overarching hegemony of instrumental rationality and, as a
consequence, this body of work looks to intuition and the empirical, as
opposed to a rationality which had become 'abstract' and dehumanising, as the
preferred catalyst for effecting emancipation and insight. In addition, Kracauer
and Bazin are also influenced by the idea that the true character of the
Lebenswelt, or *durée,* is essentially non-conceptual and indeterminate, and
therefore distinct from rational 'purposive' analytical thought. Nevertheless,
and to repeat, this does not mean that intuitionist cinematic realism can be
classed as anti-rationalist, or irrationalist. The intuitionist realist theorists do
not reject rationality *per se,* but rather wish it to be re-sited within its proper
place, as a *part* of the *Lebenswelt,* rather than as a force which *governs* the
Lebenswelt. Kracauer makes this point very clear in both *Theory of Film* and
History: The Last Things Before the Last; but Grierson also emphasises the
importance of rational communication (as well as symbolic expression); whilst
Bazin stresses the consequence of rational reflection and meditation as a
necessary preface to volition and associated action.

A further defining principle of cinematic intuitionist realism, therefore, is
that neither an empiricist nor a rationalist approach should play a leading role
in cinematic representation and spectatorship. Instead, that role should be
exercised by non-cognitive and sensory processes which seek to generate emotional states, and an ineffable sense of association with what is portrayed.
Above all, such processes should seek to generate insight, a sense of totality and
a feeling for the 'flow of life'.[40] In addition to such insight, though, reason also
has its role to play, just as it is a crucial part of the *Lebenswelt;* and the empirical underpins both intuitive insight *and* enlightened reason.

These realist traditions also possess a latent utopian dimension, premised
upon the ability of film to transform human consciousness and circumstance.
The source of this utopian trope can, once again, be located in the intuitionist

character of this type of cinema and theory, because intuitive hopes and prospects are generally more able to imagine the possibility of transcending existing reality than more rationally conceived sets of expectations. Historically, in relatively recent times, intuitionist aesthetic movements such as romanticism have also embodied ideas concerning the revolutionary transformation of modernity; and intuitionist cinematic realism in particular can be associated with such movements. However, this utopian modality also frames realism in general, and realism is associated with 'epochal' levels of change and transformation – with 'grand narratives' of historical evolution and transformation – as well as with more circumscribed everyday concerns.

It also follows from the imperative to depict the underlying character of reality that intuitionist realist cinema will not necessarily be predominantly 'realistic' in terms of its accommodation to our sensory awareness of reality; and, consequently, it can be argued that such realism is capable of accommodating both a 'realistic' and a formative approach to aesthetic representation. Of the three theorists considered here, only Bazin insists on the 'common-sense' visually realistic paradigm as exemplified in a film such as *Ladri di biciclette*.[41] However, Bazin also asserts that the primary function of cinema is to represent the 'symbolic', rather than 'embalm' reality in a naive-realist sense.[42] This implies that a more 'formalist' Bazinian cinema is potentially imaginable. However, it is possible to argue that, although intuitionist cinematic realism is capable of embracing both the visual realism of *Ladri di biciclette* and, at the same time, a more formalist approach, summed up in Kracauer's praise for *Regan*, and Grierson's praise for a montage film such as Alexander Dovzhenko's *Earth*; it cannot accommodate films in which aesthetic formalist experimentation overly dominates the portrayal of perceptual reality. Thus, a film such as *Ballet mécanique* (Fernand Léger and Dudley Murphy, 1924) is criticised by Kracauer because, in it, the 'flow of rhythms' dominates the 'flow of life'.[43] Such a film 'covers' reality, and disrupts the balance between representation and reality which intuitionist realism ideally seeks. This also suggests that intuitionist realist cinema will not be in the main a cinema of event, action or compulsive 'expressive' drama. Such drama is necessarily substantially *structured*, whereas what is required is a relatively unstructured configuration, one more conducive to a more free form of spectatorship, and portrayal of the 'flow of life'. Intuitionist realist cinema would, therefore, use symbolism and connotation to evoke powerful meaning, rather than figure a controlling diegesis.

Intuitionist realism, in particular, also insists that genuine cinematic realism should be distinguished from more 'traditional' forms of art. Here, 'traditional' art (for example, *Ballet mécanique*) is conceived like ideology, as a type of intentional construct whose degree and depth of intentionality must of necessity impose itself upon the spectator through a process of management and manipulation. Like instrumental rationality, such 'art' also 'adds' to reality, or the 'world of objects', instead of 'revealing' reality. At the reverse extreme to such traditional art is a film such as F. W. Murnau's *Nosferatu* (1922) which, according to Bazin, adds 'nothing to the reality, it does not deform it, it forces it to reveal its structural depth to bring out the pre-existing relations which become constitutive of the drama'.[44] A film such as *Nosferatu* is genuinely 'cinematic' because it is *not* 'independent of nature' in the way that a 'traditional' art film would be. Unlike such 'independent' art films, 'cinematic' films 'incorporate aspects of physical reality with a view to making us experience them'.[45] Here, the idea of the 'independent' or 'free' film is applied negatively, to denote a form of 'abstract' human praxis torn from its roots in 'material phenomena', whilst cinematic realism remains part of the world of nature, as opposed to being 'independent' of that world and, as would be the consequence, part of the world of objects.[46] As we have seen, intuitionist realism accepts that a film such as *Nosferatu* is, inevitably, part of the world of objects. However, because it incorporates 'aspects of nature' into its 'objectness' it can be classed as a type of object which struggles against such objectness. So, intuitionist cinematic realism can be regarded as a type of art object which resists its own objectness in order to incorporate into itself that which is not 'objectified', that is, the *Lebenswelt*, human freedom and totality. One evident paradox here, therefore, is that the rejection of 'independent' art goes hand in hand with a desire to cultivate self-determining 'independent' knowledge of reality within a free spectator.

Cinematic realism, philosophical realism and film theory

After identifying the distinctive features of the nineteenth-century Lukácsian and intuitionist realist traditions it will now be necessary to inquire into how these cinematic realist traditions can be related both to more general philosophical conceptions of realism and to other forms of contemporary film theory which bear on the question of realism. Such an inquiry is necessary both in itself, and because of the fact that these realist traditions have, in the past, often been intellectually isolated. If they are not related to other important contemporary voices, such isolation may continue. However, it is beyond the scope of this book to conduct such an inquiry into the entire field of either of these two extensive areas, and so the more constrained, but also more workable, approach adopted here will rather be one of focusing on a particular tendency within relatively recent philosophy, that of philosophical realism; and on a tradition of film theory which will be referred to here as 'pragmatist'. In adopting this approach, some important areas of both philosophical enquiry and film theory will necessarily be excluded from the course of investigation. However, the objective of this book is not to provide a comprehensive overview

of such areas but, instead, to advance a coherent realist position, which encompasses only germane sectors of theory relevant to that position. Additionally,
another objective to be pursued here will be to explore the question of to what
extent it is actually or fruitfully *possible* to relate cinematic realism to more
general philosophical definitions of realism. Let us, therefore, commence with
an assessment of the affiliations which can be discerned between Lukácsian
intuitionist realism, and philosophical conceptions of realism. As suggested
above, it will not be possible to track such affiliations in great detail here, as the
area in question is an extremely opaque, perhaps inherently impenetrable one,
and is also not the central concern of this study of cinematic realism. What
follows, therefore, will attempt to outline a number of philosophical distinctions which have a bearing on the study of cinematic realism, particularly those
concerning 'direct realism', 'representational realism', 'metaphysical realism',
'ontological idealism' and 'conceptual idealism'.

Realism and philosophy

The first point to make is that the nineteenth-century Lukácsian and intuitionist realist traditions must be distinguished from 'direct' realism, which contends
that representation can correspond *directly* to reality. Such theories of representation as a 'mirror' of reality have long historical traditions, and also underlie many empiricist epistemologies, which generally restrict 'the real' to that
which can be observed through sense experience.[47] Because of this, and other
factors, such 'direct' or 'naive' realist epistemologies are difficult to support at a
theoretical level, and few contemporary theorists subscribe to them.

If the realist film traditions discussed here cannot be associated with direct
or naive realism, they can be associated with what will be referred to here as
'representational realism'. In contrast to direct realism, representational
realism is premised on the conviction that, although external reality may exist
independently of our representations of it, it cannot be known independently
of such representations. According to this premise, representations are largely
our own constructions, but also have some sort of substantive and authentic
relationship to reality; and it is this relationship which allows our conceptual
schemes to track an oblique, imperfect, but nevertheless homologous path,
flanking events in external reality.[48] As will be argued in more detail later, representational realism shares the twofold conviction with 'metaphysical' realism
that reality exists independently of representation, and that representation can
also 'converge' with reality.[49]

However, representational realism carries within it the potential for a certain
scepticism and relativism, based on the idea that we might have only knowledge
of our own representations, rather than any substantial knowledge of the external world, and this can lead to a belief that, because we cannot stand outside

our own representations, we cannot even prove the existence of a world which exists outside consciousness. Such a position on mind and reality entails a commitment to forms of 'ontological idealism' and solipsism, and is implicit in, for example, Bishop Berkeley's postulate that the world may be considered as an 'emanation of the ego';[50] and in a sceptical Cartesian tradition which argues that, for all we know, all our thoughts about reality may be false, and could have been implanted in us by – for example – some mischievous 'demon'.[51] A more modern version of this possibility is the droll notion of a 'brain in a vat', in which, it is imagined, a human brain is placed in a 'vat of nutrients', and linked to a 'super-scientific computer'. Here, not a 'demon' (Descartes) or 'God' (Berkeley) but an 'evil scientist' feeds misleading information to the brain, systematically building up a 'false' conception of reality in the 'mind' of the brain.[52] A solipsist would argue that it would be impossible to know whether or not we were actually in such an inopportune situation, whereas the realist can only respond that is unlikely that we are.

Like direct realism, such ontological idealism is, however, difficult to maintain because it leads to the evident proposition that mind is the only reality, and that reality is the creation of mind, or, at least, 'conceptual schemes'. Few idealist philosophers have been prepared to go as far as this, though and, although the spirit of such subjectivism may have been revived within recent traditions of post-structuralism, postmodernism and relativism, it remains the case that, since Berkeley and Descartes, 'most philosophy' has attempted to distance itself from a position 'inimical to social sanity';[53] and has sought, instead, to argue that, although experienced reality is, to a considerable extent, the creation of subjective consciousness, consciousness is also part of a phenomenal and underlying reality which exists independently beyond it.

The species of ontological idealism associated with Berkeley and Descartes can also be distinguished from 'conceptual idealism', a more common form of idealism, and perhaps the dominant epistemological stance today. Conceptual idealism picks up on the palpable weakness in any realist position, and asserts that, although 'reality' may exist in some sense, we can have little or no knowledge of reality, only of our concepts, consciousness and representations of reality. There is no '*reality itself*' (whatever *that* might be) but reality-as-we-picture-it . . . reality-as-we-think-it = our reality, is the only reality we can deal with'.[54] Conceptual idealists do not adopt the ontological idealist position that reality is *entirely* the product of mind, but do argue that the main task of the philosopher is to understand how our conceptual schemes construct meaning for us, and how that meaning then becomes developed into socialised forms of inter subjective understanding which have little relationship to a '*reality itself*' about which virtually nothing can be said.

This 'conventionalist' account of representation and reality[55] is also summed up in the idea that a representation is 'true' not by virtue of its *correspondence* to reality but by virtue of its *relationship* to other representations within a conventionalised conceptual scheme; and *also* by virtue of the fact that it is 'useful [rather than 'accurate'] for *believers* to believe' that it is true.[56] Here, a relational theory of meaning, in which there are 'no positive terms',[57] is linked to a pragmatist theory of truth and ethics, in which 'The true is only the expedient in our way of thinking, just as the right is only the expedient in our way of behaving'.[58]

In addition to a relational and pragmatist theory of knowledge, conceptual idealism also implies a commitment to both a considerable degree of 'conceptual relativism' or 'incommensurability' and a rejection of the 'correspondence' theory of truth. These two areas are often run together in the work of conceptual idealists. For example, Paul Feyerabend believes that notions of 'objectivity' are related to the needs of dominant power structures, as 'becomes apparent when different cultures with different objective views confronted each other'.[59] Similar attitudes concerning the relationship of foundationalist concepts to dominant power structures are also evident in the work of theorists such as Michel Foucault, Jean Baudrillard and others, who have had a more direct impact upon film studies. However, these two areas (conceptual idealism and the correspondence theory of truth) are, and should be kept, distinct, whilst conceptual relativism and incommensurability do not, in fact, refute or contradict the correspondence theory of truth. On the contrary, it will be argued that the correspondence model can accommodate a degree of conceptual relativism, and that 'there is no plausible alternative' to that model, whilst relational and pragmatist conceptualisations of truth, however fashionable they may be, 'face serious regress and epistemological objections'.[60]

Conceptual idealism and representational realism occupy hard by median points along a graded scale topped by solipsist ontological idealism at one end, and tailed by 'metaphysical realism' at the other. Whilst ontological idealism asserts that reality is the creation of mind, metaphysical realism asserts that reality exists entirely independent of mind, can be accurately represented, and – crucially – *can be considered to possess definite characteristics*. This means that:

> the aim of any conceptual system will be to draw the distinctions which actually exist in nature. Unless we wish to be conceptual idealists, it is quite wrong to think of nature, reality, things-in-themselves, or however we wish to characterize what there is, as having no definite characteristics before we apply our conceptual system.[61]

Representational realism is, and must be, a species of metaphysical realism, and both must also be forms of ontological realism. However, whilst representational realism accepts both the existence of external reality (it is a form of ontological realism) and the idea, in principal, that reality and representation *might* converge, it questions the 'hard' metaphysical realist epistemological proposition that the world can ever meaningfully be considered in terms of 'definite' 'distinctions which actually exist in nature'. Representational realism asserts that such a consideration is impossible, because an external existent can always be regarded from a number of different perspectives, as opposed to only one 'God's Eye View'.[62] Representational realism differs from 'hard' metaphysical realism also in placing emphasis upon the notion that the world can never be considered 'independent of any particular representation of it';[63] and argues that the 'objectivist' notion of 'One True Image'[64] stems from a seventeenth-century mechanistic viewpoint which too rigidly stresses the distinction between 'things in themselves – and sense impressions [representations, 'projections'] of them'.[65] Representational realism asserts that such a distinction cannot be made, and accepts the Kantian rejection of the idea that a concept-independent, perspective-independent reality can ever be meaningfully experienced or theorised.[66]

The rejection of a 'concept-independent' reality also implies a requisite degree of conceptual relativism. However, representational realism differs crucially from conceptual idealism in arguing both that correspondence between reality and representation can be legitimately theorised in more than merely conventionalist, pragmatist terms *and* that the compass of conceptual relativism can be properly restricted by diverse means. A metaphysical realist position consists, therefore, of two related parts: (1) a belief in the independence of reality from representation and (2) an epistemological system designed to both show how representation and reality can be thought to 'converge', and 'how the danger of divergence between thought and reality can be averted'.[67] Ontological idealism rejects both these propositions, whilst conceptual idealism rejects the second – and is highly guarded about acceptance of the first (or finds the question irrelevant). However, a representational realist position not only accepts both propositions but also adds a qualifying third, namely, that no epistemological system can ever fully 'converge' with reality, and that the 'danger of divergence between thought and reality' can never be fully averted.

One especially influential formulation of representational realism which will now be considered here in greater depth is Hilary Putnam's conception of 'internal realism'. In addition to being one of the most important of recent philosophers in the analytic tradition, Putnam is also particularly relevant for this book because of his endeavour to link aspects of the analytical and continental philosophical traditions, and because of his attempt to connect notions of realism to ideas of explanatory indeterminacy and limited conceptual relativism. All of this brings him closer to the spirit of Kracauer, Bazin, Grierson and Lukács than thinkers in either the metaphysical realist or conceptual idealist camps. In addition, Putnam is also strongly influenced by Kant in a way which enables us to reinterpret fruitfully some of the important Kantian influences upon Kracauer; particularly those concerning ambivalent meaning and its relationship to experience. The trajectory of Putnam's thinking leads him also to a conception of realism which embraces ordinary experience – and also leads him to reject what he calls the abstract 'craving for absolutes'.[68] His notions of 'realism with a human face' and 'realism with a small r' are also based on what he refers to as our 'commonsense image of the world', and embrace the Husserlian concept of the *Lebenswelt*, with its focus on 'ourselves-in-the-world'.[69] Putnam's emphasis upon the notion of 'human flourishing' also brings him in line with the humanist or modernist orientation of Kracauer, Bazin and Lukács (there is a particular resonance, for example, between Putnam's notion of 'human flourishing' and Kracauer's idea of the 'family of man');[70] whilst his methodological approach, which is, rather like Jacques Derrida's, based upon the purging of 'dichotomies',[71] also fits the intuitionist realist position more clearly than it does a structuralist, post-structuralist or postmodernist one. However, and as will be argued later, there are also important differences between Putnam's 'pragmatist' internal realism and the intuitionist realist tradition.

An internal realist epistemology is so called because, as Putnam argues, any theory concerning reality must, of necessity, be formulated *within* a particular conceptual scheme, and cannot transcend such a scheme in order to face 'external' reality *per se*.[72] This 'internalist' model (as Putnam also calls it) suggests that fundamental theoretical dichotomies between subjectivity and objectivity, convention and fact, reality and representation, truth and falsity, must be eradicated because what Putnam refers to as the 'cut' between subjectivity and objectivity cannot legitimately be made: 'the attempt to draw this distinction, to make this cut, has been a total failure. The time has come to try the methodological hypothesis that no such act can be made.'[73] In place of such a cut, Putnam proposes the adoption of a model based on a continuum of the 'relatively subjective' and the 'relatively objective'.[74] Nothing exists 'objectively' for us, and any attempt to know such a thing is also necessarily mediated. Hence, there is a continuum between an object which can only be known in a 'relatively objective' sense and a means of knowing which can transcend subjectivity only to a relative extent.

According to the tenets of internal realism, absolute truth claims are really justifications under ideal conditions – conditions that can never be met in the course of human experience, and we must abandon such a desire to know things as they are because such a desire makes us 'unfit to live in the common'.[75] This abandonment of any attempt to know 'The Way the World Is'[76] stems from Putnam's Kantianism and, particularly from the Kantian notion of the 'transcendental illusion'. In the opening paragraphs of the *Critique of Pure Reason* (1781), Kant argues that 'Human reason has this peculiar fate that in one species of its knowledge it is burdened by questions which, as prescribed by the very nature of reason itself, it is not able to ignore, but which, as transcending all its powers, it is also not able to answer'.[77] The 'species of knowledge' which

Kant refers to here is metaphysics, and Kant goes on to argue that the tendency towards 'metaphysics' exists in 'mankind' as a 'natural disposition', or *Naturanlage*; and that human beings are 'driven on by an inward need, to questions such as cannot be answered by any empirical employment of reason, or by principles thus derived'.[78] The 'transcendental illusion' is the delusion that these questions of ultimate knowledge can ever be satisfactorily dealt with and, more specifically, the chimera that 'the subjective necessity of a connection of our concepts, i.e. a connection necessitated for the advantage of the understanding', objectively exists in the 'determination of things in themselves'.[79] In other words, Kant is arguing that it does not follow that all things in themselves can be 'connected', or explained, through reason, though we can be misled by the transcendental illusion to think that this is so.

Following Kant, Putnam also argues that realism must resist the siren call of the transcendental illusion. However – and significantly – Putnam also pays relatively little attention to Kant's assertion that 'metaphysics' is a *Naturanlage*, 'inseparable from human Reason', and focuses, instead, on Kant's warning that metaphysical speculation 'will not cease to play tricks' on 'human Reason' and will 'entrap it' into 'aberrations'.[80] Taking this cue, Putnam contends that metaphysical realism has succumbed to the transcendental illusion, and that, in contrast, 'internal realism' should be more 'human'-oriented, and not attempt to go beyond what is understandable in terms of experience.[81] But this also seems to misinterpret Kant, because Kant argued that to exercise the transcendental illusion *was to be human*: 'metaphysics is real . . . there has always existed and will always continue to exist some kind of metaphysics'.[82] This is an important point, because, as we will see later, it bears upon crucial differences between Putnam's representational realism and the utopian aspirations underlying the cinematic intuitionist realist tradition.

At one level, Putnam's position on the transcendental illusion, and his concomitant belief in the need to avoid questions concerning 'the way the world is' and 'things in themselves', brings him near to the position adopted by philosophers such as Nelson Goodman and Richard Rorty and, in particular, leads him to reflect upon their charged submission that 'a world of unknowable "things in themselves"' [is] 'A world well lost'.[83] Goodman is unambiguous on this point, arguing that 'while the underlying world . . . need not be denied to those who love it [presumably metaphysical realists and the like], it is perhaps on the whole a world well lost'.[84] Rorty also adopts Goodman's phraseology and sentiment in an influential essay entitled 'The World Well Lost',[85] and in his equally influential *Philosophy and the Mirror of Nature*.[86] However, as a realist, Putnam cannot agree unequivocally with Goodman and Rorty on this point, because their positions deny all possibility of convergence, and thus lead to radical relativism. So, whilst Putnam is at one with Goodman and Rorty in agreeing upon the problems caused by the transcendental illusion, he cannot stomach their relativism, and this leads him to put clear blue water between their ideas and himself.

Nevertheless, Putnam's theory of internal realism, based, as it is, upon the elimination of dichotomies, does clearly imply a degree of meaning relativism and, in his *Realism with a Human Face*, Putnam explicitly argues for 'the importance of conceptual relativity'.[87] However, Putnam also makes what is for him a clear distinction between 'conceptual relativism' and 'relativism' proper – the latter of which he associates with Rorty and others. For example, Putnam insists that an 'inter subjective agreement' model of truth, such as that advanced by Rorty, where the idea of 'truth' is understood in pragmatist and conventionalist terms, inevitably severs the connection between reality and representation and, consequently, leads to 'self-refuting relativism'.[88] Internal realism, in contrast, is based, first, on the belief that there is no clear connection or distinction to be made between representation and reality but, instead, a continuum which involves the intersection of both; and, second, on the conviction that some representations are more important than others which are merely intersubjectively based, and are so because they are more *likely* to approximate to the truth.[89] Putnam's position here is based upon his desire to defend scientific reason and rational reflection against the inroads of 'cultural' or pragmatist relativism. It is important for him to argue, on the one hand, that scientific reason can accommodate a legitimate degree of conceptual relativism, whilst, on the other hand, asserting that such relativism should be limited by some sort of truth conditions. But what are these 'truth conditions'?

Putnam differentiates himself from both Goodman and Rorty, and positions himself closer to a philosopher such as W. V. O. Quine, by asserting that various theoretical versions of the world can be judged on the extent to which they possess 'rational assertability'. Here, Putnam puts forward a theory based upon the privileged status of rational procedures, and argues for the importance of 'canons and principles of rationality'. Although such 'canons and principles' do not confer truth-value absolutely, because such value can only be conferred in an unrealisably 'ideal' context, they set limits upon the remit, acceptability and potential array of interpretation.[90] These 'canons and principles', which Putnam believes possess high standing, interact with experience so that an 'explanation space' is created – a circumscribed area within which certain accounts of reality can be argued to be more justified than others, on grounds of warranted assertability – because they are, amongst other things, more 'instrumentally efficacious, coherent, comprehensive and functionally simple'.[91] What we have here is something on a par with Derrida's 'indispensable guardrail' (see later in this chapter), the rational procedures of enquiry which, according to Derrida, ensure that representation cannot just develop 'in any direction at all and authorise itself to say almost anything'.[92] Using similar language, Putnam also insists that 'Internalism is not a facile relativism which says that "Anything goes" '.[93]

Putnam's theory of truth is based upon a rationalist/pragmatist position, and a coherence rather than correspondence model: 'Truth in an internalist view, is some sort of (idealized) rational acceptability – some sort of ideal coherence of our beliefs with each other and with our experiences *as those experiences are themselves represented in our belief system* – and not correspondence with some mind independent or discourse independent state of affairs';[94] 'What makes . . . a theory or conceptual scheme – rationally acceptable is, in large part, its coherence and fit'.[95] At the same time, Putnam rejects the correspondence theory of truth, and welcomes 'the demise of a theory that lasted over two thousand years'.[96] The principles of warranted assertability which Putnam holds up are *useful*, rather than 'true' in an externalist sense and, because of this, can be said to be 'true for us': 'Objectivity and rationality humanly speaking are what we have; they are better than nothing'[97] . . . 'the suggestion which constitutes the essence of "internal realism" is that truth does not transcend use.'[98] This seems to suggest that truth is *relative to use-value*. However, Putnam argues that what makes something more than just relative to use-value is its adjudication by rationality. Truth does not transcend use but use-value is to be regulated by reason, and so rise above mere self-interest. However, Putnam's pragmatist position, and wish to sidestep the transcendental illusion, also stops him from awarding a privileged status to his 'warranted assertability' conditions, a status which would make them more than merely culturally relative. Nevertheless, there remains some ambiguity over this, and the extent to which these conditions *are* more than culturally relative, rather than, as Kant argued, 'an objective necessity in the determination of things in themselves',[99] remains unclear. The outcome is that there seems little to choose, in the end, between Putnam's rationalist, pro-scientist pragmatism and Rorty's discursive, cultural relativist pragmatism.

Realism is always, and will always be, a more difficult stance to defend than relativist, conventionalist, structuralist, idealist, pragmatist, post-structuralist or postmodernist positions. This is partly because the realist (unless he or she is a particularly 'hard' metaphysical realist') must argue against both relativism and absolutism, and yet still accommodate elements of each into what is effectively a limit position for both relativism and absolutism.[100] However, third-way theoretical positions such as this are also, perhaps necessarily, more problematic, qualified and tentative than those characterised by conceptual extremity and greater inner assurance. It may be that Putnam's arguments are, indeed, often 'tortuous', but his 'tightrope treading' is common amongst thinkers who hope to avoid total relativism while at the same time rejecting objectivism.[101] At the same time, there are also a number of problems with Putnam's model of 'internal realism', both in itself and in relation to its potential applicability to cinematic realism. Before addressing such problems however, two other concepts central to a philosophical realist position – those of 'ontological depth' and the importance of the empirical – will first have to be briefly addressed.

Philosophical realists believe that reality is characterised by an 'ontological depth', and that appropriate explanatory conceptual schemes, or representations, must be devised so as to represent such depth.[102] A realist scheme must, therefore, possess 'epistemological depth', by both positing and encompassing the existence and influence of abstract, intermediate and empirical determining factors, which also have a strong genetic and evolutionary dimension. This aspect of philosophical realist thought has already been addressed within the field of film theory, in Robert Allen and Douglas Gomery's *Film History: Theory and Practice* (1985), which draws specifically on the work of Roy Bhaskar, and in which the authors argue that, to the realist:

> reality is complex and only partially observable, even with the most sophisticated scientific tools. The level of observable phenomena is but one of a multilayered structure. The event the empiricist describes is the effect of processes and mechanisms at work in other layers of reality. Explanation for the realist consists of not only describing the observable layer of reality, but also the workings of the generative mechanisms that produce the observable event.[103]

One of the most important formulations of such a model of explanation is Rom Harré's notion of the 'open system', an epistemologically deep model, which conceives reality as existing simultaneously at a number of different interactive and evolving levels, and the role of representation as one of constructing a conceptual equivalent of such levels.[104] Unlike the 'closed system' of scientific experiment, the open system of realist analysis cannot account for all factors, but it can use a scaled model of empirical and logical categories, which can include some of Putnam's warranted assertability conditions, in order to arrive at a more legitimate 'epistemologically deep' conceptual account of the world. This is what Allen and Gomery attempt in their study, in which they apply the ideas of Bhaskar and Harré to an 'open system' reconstruction of the American *cinéma vérité* movement of the 1950s.

This approach to explanation and representation within philosophical realism is intended to improve upon an empirical mode of analysis which can only explain to a limited extent, or just 'describe', regularities and irregularities. Nevertheless, this approach also suffers from the general realist problem, in that the existence of causal entities which are relatively 'abstract', and not directly observable, can only be *postulated* as causal factors rather than be 'known' as such. As we will see, this problem often leads theorists to reject realist modes, and to adopt more empirical methodologies. That realists postulate the existence of entities which have not been observed – and cannot be

observed – [105] *is* a problem and leads to the kind of 'tightrope-treading' referred
to earlier. Nevertheless, the adoption of a substantively empirical methodology
is perhaps even more problematic, as it possesses abridged explanatory power,
and because there is no such thing as a 'theory neutral language of observation'
to begin with.[106] Any empirical study is laden with generally unacknowledged
suppositions. Realists recognise this, and conceive of empirical data in terms
of 'empirical concepts' which are part of an 'open system' containing both
empirical, and more theoretically weighted concepts.

Having said this, however, realism is also *premised* on the importance of the
empirical (as opposed to 'empiricism'). There are several reasons for this, but
perhaps the most important is that it is the empirical which provides the greatest apparent defence against relativism. In the end, Putnam's theory of internal realism does not actually provide such a safeguard, because Putnam is not
prepared to grant the warranted assertability conditions on which he places so
high a value any more than a culturally contingent status. Far from possessing
any 'noumenal' status, these conditions are 'connected with our view of the
world, including our view of ourselves as part of that world, and change with
time'.[107] But if this is so, why should the 'rationally acceptable' principles which
Putnam singles out for praise be given more credence than any other grouping
of 'culturally' derived principles?

Putnam's reluctance to award such a status to warranted assertability conditions or 'canons and principles of rationality' stems from a number of factors.
First, the basis of his theory of internal realism rests upon the view that everything is internal to a conceptual scheme, and this rules out the possibility that
certain principles of rationality might be endowed with a trans-scheme status.
Second, Putnam's theory of internal realism was formed partly (though to
what extent is far from clear) in response to a scientific world view which
had 'turned the external world' into 'mathematical formulas', therefore
making our own experience of the world a 'second-class' one.[108] Putnam claims
that he wishes to resist such a transformation, and confront the hegemony of
the scientific world view in order to raise up our everyday experience of the
Lebenswelt:

> I am concerned with bringing us back to precisely these claims which we do, after
> all, constantly make in our daily lives. Accepting the 'manifest image', the
> *Lebenswelt*, the world as we actually experience it . . . demands that we both
> regain our sense of mystery . . . and our sense of the common.[109]

The irony, or paradox, here though, is that, whilst Putnam's entire theory of
internal realism is based upon the advocacy of rationality, he also wants to warn
of the dangers of (not even metaphysical but 'internal') rationality. It is because
of this that Putnam does not wish to elevate one aspect of the *Lebenswelt* –
rationality – to a higher level than other aspects, as such an elevation would

contribute to the continuing subordination of those other aspects, and to a
further reinforcement of the scientific world view. Because Putnam thinks that
rationality is just 'one part of our concept of human flourishing, one part of our
idea of the good', he does not wish to elevate it in this manner.[110] Instead, and
as with a general trend within philosophy which includes the work of Duhem,
Hesse and others, he wishes to 'leave room for something else – whether religion, or art, or metaphysics, or a sociology whose claims to be a science have so
often been disputed'.[111]

One critic has argued that 'to write about "Putnam's philosophy" is like
trying to capture the wind with a fishing-net', and that this is so because of the
often contradictory positions which Putnam adopts.[112] Putnam's purgative
strategy in relation to 'dichotomies' often leaves him facing in different directions. For example, he is both a realist and a relativist, rejects – but sometimes
seems to adhere to – a correspondence model of truth, champions the importance of science, whilst also objecting to science's elevation over the arts, and
places great weight on rationality, whilst also warning of its dangers. In addition to such fence-sitting, a number of problems are also apparent in the above.
For example, although Putnam argues that rationality is just 'one part of the
good', he hardly mentions any other parts. Although he invokes the idea of the
Lebenswelt, he also draws no conclusions from the fact that Husserl's concept
defines an essentially non-cognitive realm of experience. This means that he
redefines the Lebenswelt as a realm of rational activity, and such a redefinition
appears to misrepresent the Husserlian idea. Nevertheless, Putnam's work on
realism remains amongst the most influential philosophical thinking on that
subject to appear since the 1960s, and this means that it must be considered
here as part of any attempt to understand, and rearticulate, cinematic realism.

Before closing this brief, and schematic account of philosophical realism it
will be necessary to return to a very important notion – the idea that the empirical can provide the basis of a convincing theory of realism. Whilst Putnam
does not give rationality an elevated status, he does come close to giving empirical experience such a status when he argues that all our representations are
part of a system designed in relation to sensory experience, and that our projections are, therefore, a 'field of force whose boundary conditions are experience'.[113] However, Putnam does not go beyond this to attempt to show how the
empirical can be theorised as the basis for the convergence between reality and
representation. One theorist who has attempted this, however, is Mary Hesse.
Hesse draws on the ideas of Duhem and W. V. O. Quine to develop a 'machine
analogy' for perception, in which she argues that there is a constant and invariant relationship between data reaching us from the external world, and our
cognitive and perceptual processing mechanisms.[114] This invariant relationship enables realism to hypothesise a symbolic equivalent between conceptual
schemes and forces, and phenomena in the external world. It is, then, the

invariant interface between external data and internal coding principles, and the cumulative information which results from this, which enables the possibility of postulating an indirect symbolic equivalence between external reality and conceptual schemes. Empirical experience may be the product of symbolic transformation, as perceptual data is transformed into what Hesse calls 'coded input', but it is also the phenomenal manifestation of the invariant factors involved in the interaction between our faculties and the external world. This gives the empirical an important status:

> There is, however, a relation between machine hardware and input that does remain constant during the process of data collection and theory building . . . This is the set of physical conditions under which input becomes coded input. These conditions [are] sufficiently stable to permit the assertion that a high proportion of statements in the C.I. [coded input] are true.[115]

Hesse's model may provide the basis for a future theory of realism, based on the importance of empirical data, where 'coded input' is regarded as isomorphically related to reality, and where our concepts map reality in an abstract manner. Putnam himself brings up this possibility, only to reject it.[116] But he may be wrong. In any event, such a theory cannot be developed further here. Instead, we must now turn to the second tradition of thought relevant to a consideration of cinematic realism, that of the 'pragmatist' school of film theory.

Realism, pragmatism and film theory

Writing in 2000, at the turn of the millennium, Bill Nichols presents a useful diagram of the wide range of positions which make up the field of contemporary and near-contemporary film theory, theoretical positions which, he believes, both possess 'sufficient explanatory power to account for most of cinema', and also have 'generated valuable results'. These include (in summary): (1) a Marxist concept of culture, (2) a semiotic theory of sign systems, (3) formalist and neo-formalist notions, (4) a psychoanalytic theory of the subject, (5) a post-structural theory of narrative, (6) a phenomenology of film.[117] Nichols's map is a helpful starting point for dealing with the 'conceptual frames' of major film theory, but, of course, one particular theoretical continent appears to have disappeared from the map altogether: the one which this book is concerned with. Any map betrays the orientation of the cartographer, and Nichols quite rightly discloses his own. However one also has to question whether it is justifiable to efface from such a chart traditions of film theory which pre dated the emergence of screen theory in the late 1960s. One is reminded here of the claim that the publication of Jean Mitry's *Esthétique et psychologie du cinéma* (translated into English in 1973) placed 'a full stop after the pre-history of film theory'.[118] In any event, this 'revisionist' study of 'prehistorical' classical cinematic realism will attempt to substitute a less definite form of punctuation for that full stop.

There is little point in attempting here what would be an inevitably schematic summary of the field of positions which Nichols indicates, and such recapitulations have, in any case, already been carried out in a number of other, admirably well informed textbooks on film theory. What will be attempted here, instead, is something far more germane to the study of cinematic realism which this book is centrally concerned with. Following the critique of pragmatist positions carried out in the preceding pages, this final section of the chapter will first move to an assessment of pragmatist influenced theoretical positions which have emerged within film studies relatively recently, and then to a further comparison between such positions and those associated with cinematic realism. Before that, however, it will, initially, be useful to have a measure against which the competing claims of cinematic pragmatism and cinematic realism (and also philosophical realism) can be evaluated. That measure will be provided by what is surely the *bête noire* for both sides, the screen theory tradition of the 1970s. However, it must be admitted from the outset that this measure will not be determined in an even-handed manner, as far as either cinematic pragmatism or screen theory is concerned. The more weighted and explicit intent here is to highlight problems within screen theory which are, it will be argued, likely to emerge again within contemporary pragmatist film theory, but which can also, it is hoped, be circumnavigated through adherence to the principles and tenets of cinematic realism.

The attempt to develop a general theory of cinema in the 1970s, based on the intersection of Marxism, psychoanalysis and semiotic theory, was motivated by high ideals. The objective was to utilise film, and film theory, in an effort to challenge the dominant capitalist or patriarchal order, and establish a 'counter cinema' within a 'counter culture'. However, whilst the committed idealism of screen theory cannot be faulted, the conceptual foundations which it relied upon can. The problems of screen theory are well known, but can be usefully summarised for present purposes as follows. (1) The screen theory tradition contains an implicit commitment to determinism, and preoccupation with the determining influence of 'deep', or 'innate' or 'self-regulating' internal structures. (2) This orientation leads to depleted conceptions of agency. (3) These lesser conceptions of agency, whilst problematic in themselves, also negate the overall objectives of the screen theory project, because such an account of agency implies that the attempt to develop a counter culture must be predestined to fail. (4) The screen theory answer to this question is, of course, based upon the Althusserian recourse to 'theoretical practitioners' who have access to knowledge, and who are, as a consequence, able to nurture a more enlightened form of subjectivity in others. However, as E. P. Thompson has argued in his critique of Althusserian Marxism, the notion of the theoretical practitioner rests upon an elitist model of the relation between an 'elect' of knowledge bearers, and the rest of the academic, intellectual and public community.[119] (5) The idea that realism, in the shape of the 'classic realist text', was intrinsically politically reactionary at the level of form led to a counterproductive rejection of an aesthetic form consumed by spectators the world over. Just as screen theory advocated a conception of agency which was insufficient to realise the objectives which the theorists desired, their advocacy of anti-realist film-making also ensured that an effective oppositional cinema would never become common. (6) Screen theory, particularly in its structuralist mode, often displayed a pronounced degree of essentialism, whilst viewing established notions of truth and reference in terms of ideological naturalisation. (7) Screen theory adopted a model of the relation between theory and evidence which subordinated evidence to theory. (8) Screen theory often employed unhistoricised accounts of subjectivity, determination, representation and agency. (9) Whilst screen theory was often able to describe representations in great detail – because it was based on a relational theory of signification – it was often unable to explain what such representations *meant* in a satisfactory manner. (10) The emphasis which screen theory placed upon interior structures and relations marginalised issues of reference, and externality.

As argued, this précis of the tribulations of screen theory is not meant to be even-handed, and makes no attempt to assess the more affirmative features of the tradition. Its purpose here is to provide a deliberately cautionary and caveat-leaning categorical scheme against which a more recent school of film theory can be assessed. The paradoxes inherent in screen theory led to the emergence of diverse responses during the 1980s, including the revival of empirical and historical approaches (again, missing from Nichols's map of modern film theory), an increasing emphasis upon a postmodernist rejection of master narratives and the continued influence of psychoanalysis, feminism and gay studies. However, the most pertinent response – in relation to to this study of cinematic realism – to emerge during the 1980s, and 1990s, was a body of work which, as has already been argued, will be referred to here as 'pragmatist' in orientation.

As has been indicated when discussing the ideas of Putnam, pragmatism is based upon conceptions of truth, knowledge and reality different from those adopted within philosophical realism. Such conceptions are premised upon the conviction that truth claims, for example, have their origins in whatever a community of believers believes to be the case. Such claims are not, therefore, viewed in terms of representations which may 'converge' with an 'external reality' for ever out of reach. The inherent relativism in such a stance is palpable, but also qualified to an extent by the endorsement of rational and logical procedures, such as Putnam's warranted assertability conditions, which provide the ground for establishing that one notion of truth is more coherent, or superior or 'useful' (if not 'truer') than another. In this kind of pragmatism, therefore, relativism is limited by the adjudicating power of rational principles and procedures. As a consequence of its adoption of such a median position on the grounds for truth claims, pragmatism also eschews discussion of 'absolutes', on the related grounds that such debate will, in effect, be about things which we can never know. Instead, pragmatists prefer to address areas of knowledge which can be more directly observed, measured, verified, classified, refuted, tested and evaluated. Pragmatism, therefore, steers well away from what Kant called the 'burden of questions' which human reason is 'not able to answer', and is content to arrive at more warranted, if circumscribed, forms of knowledge.[120]

There are, however, a number of apparent problems associated with such pragmatist inclinations. Some of these have already been touched upon in the earlier analysis of Putnam's internal realism; but it will be of help to provide a synopsis of them here again, this time with the ultimate objective of relating such a synopsis more directly to issues affecting film theory. First, the idea that something should be believed to be true because it is useful to believe such is undermined by the fact that it can hardly ever be said of anything that it is *universally* (or even substantially) useful to believe such a thing to be true in all cases. This means that notions of use-value lack the inclusivity that notions of truth-value possess. In addition, in arguing for the superiority of use-value over truth-value, pragmatism opens up a fissure between belief and truth, and this, in turn, also implies a commitment to a significant degree of relativism, because belief is contingent. Second, such a commitment also means that the crucial pragmatist article of faith that rational assertability conditions may legitimately adjudicate between different consensual belief systems is undercut, because such conditions are, themselves, subject to contingency. All that is left for pragmatism, once the idea that warranted assertability conditions are admitted to be just another product of a particular cultural belief system, *is*, in fact, the idea that truth can be defined in terms of 'usefulness'. But, at one level, 'use-value' is not much of a value at the end of the day, when the dark is drawing in; and is not, for example, as inherently laudable as 'goodness', or even 'truth'. Use-value can be defined in one of two ways: in an instrumental sense, and in an ethical sense. The former would seem to possess little intrinsic merit, in the sense that to 'use' something can also be to control or manipulate it. Where use-value is linked to notions of 'betterment', or to what Putnam calls 'human flourishing', on the other hand, it would appear to possess more inherent merit. However, there remains an ambiguity here, which is not clarified within much pragmatist discourse. In addition, the idea of 'human flourishing' still seems a little insipid, like a more contemporary version of the utilitarian doctrine of the 'pursuit of happiness'; a notion that feels rather insubstantial, and which Grierson felt to mark 'an aberration of the human spirit'.[121] Like Lukács, Kracauer and Bazin, Grierson preferred the idea of a more commited and intensely tracked quest for enlightenment to such a pursuit. The suggestion of the 'pursuit of happiness' also entails a degree of individualism, whereas the realists sought to 'act according to the light that is in us', for the benefit of the whole 'community of men'.[122]

Finally, at an ontological, rather than an ethical, level, 'use' also, and necessarily, implies the subsistence of that which is more than merely a relativist use-value. For what makes an idea 'useful' is related to the circumstances associated with that idea, circumstances which must have *actual* characteristics. In other words, what makes propositions about some things appear to be useful 'is (at least in part) what is the case concerning [those things], *not* what it is useful to believe about them'.[123] This, in turn, suggests realism, and the correspondence theory of truth, rather than pragmatism and, as a consequence, 'pragmatism runs aground here'.[124] As will be argued shortly, this issue of the difference between use-value and correspondence to reality is a problem for pragmatist-influenced film theory.

It is important, not only for philosophy but also for film studies, to recognise that pragmatist notions of truth, use-value, representation and reality have problems, as well as benefits, attendant upon them, because the underlying philosophical disposition of some of the work in film theory to emerge during the 1980s and 1990s was influenced by pragmatism. It will also be argued here that this pragmatist-based tradition is of particular importance because, unlike more subject-targeted forms of contemporary film theory, it touches on general epistemological questions (even if mainly to distance itself from such questions) concerning the nature of knowledge, the relationship between theory and evidence, and the scope for effective intervention within the field of study.

Pragmatist-influenced film theory follows on from pragmatism in eschewing a concern for abstract theory, and turns, instead, to more restricted inquiries into empirical or intermediate categories of concept and material. It is impelled to do so by the previously referred to pragmatist conviction that smaller-scale, 'lower-theory'-based studies, which explore more directly observable research materials, will provide more useful, classifiable, testable results. Pragmatism and pragmatist-influenced film theory are, therefore, linked, in their bracketing of abstraction. However, (whether consciously or unconsciously) this pragmatist practice has tended to secrete such a bracketing of high theory under the veil of an opposition to screen theory and, in particular, to the unifying imperative underlying screen theory. So, for example, David Bordwell argues against the need for a 'Big Theory of Everything', by which he means screen theory, or any contemporary facsimile of screen theory:

> you do not need a Big Theory of Everything to do enlightened work in the field of study . . . In the Post-Theory era. Sharply focused, in-depth enquiry remains our best bet for producing the sort of scholarly debate that will advance our knowledge of cinema. Grand Theories will come and go, but research and scholarship will endure'.[125]

However, what Bordwell calls 'middle-level theorising' and what Noël Carroll refers to as 'piecemeal generalizations'[126] does not stand just as an opposition to screen theory, or even to 'big' comprehensive theories, but also, as argued, as a general opposition to the predominant use of chiefly abstract theoretical categories within film research. The opposition set up here between a 'big theory of everything' and a whole number of smaller scale theories about particular things is also an erroneous one,[127] because it leaves out the possibility that theories, both big and small, may possess abstract, *as well as* intermediary and empirical, categories. For example, we can see Allen and Gomery's attempt to provide a theoretical model for the study of American *cinéma vérité* in the 1950s as one such model which attempts to unite empirical, intermediary and abstract categories (the latter derived from 'big theory' philosophers of science such as Harré and Bhaskar) within an approach which possesses 'epistemological depth'. It is not clear whether this would count as a 'big' theory or not in Bordwell's sense. On the one hand it does edge towards comprehensiveness; on the other, the subject itself (American *cinéma vérité* in the 1950s–60s) is relatively 'sharply focused', and not 'of everything'. Bordwell and Carroll's position on 'big' and little theories leads to four potential variations which might be realised in practice: (1) big theories about big subjects, (2) big theories about small subjects, (3) small theories about big subjects, and (4) small theories about small subjects. Of these four, it is the latter two which they favour. But this prompts the question as to why, just because screen theory was so problematic, we must abandon the first two categories. Of course, the bulk of research carried out in film studies will, and probably should, fall into the latter two categories, but there must always be a space for work falling into the first two, otherwise paradigms will not be challenged.

Bordwell also refers to the sort of research schemes which he favours as 'middle-level research programs'.[128] By this, Bordwell means programmes which avoid excessive abstract speculation. However, the term 'research programme' is also of interest here because it is reminiscent of Imre Lakatos' use of exactly the same phrase, and because both formulations share similarities with Thomas Kuhn's crucially influential notion of the 'paradigm',[129] a term which, as one critic has indicated, was 'once almost confined to grammarians [but has now] swept like a plague across the intellectual landscape', justifying all manner of autonomous positions on the basis that theoretical schemes must be treated as 'incommensurate'.[130] What is, perhaps, even more important is that both formulations return us to some of the central problems of pragmatism. Taking his cue from Kuhn, Lakatos puts forward the notion that a theory is a 'momentary abstraction from evolving theory families',[131] and, for Lakatos, as, possibly, for Bordwell, any particular theoretical exegesis is part of such evolving, semi-autonomous, discursive, 'theory families'. These theory families, or 'research programmes', are comprised of a set of interlocking structures of analogy, working models and practical metaphors about referents and other terms, which are employed because of their ability to account for directly or indirectly appropriatable data; *and* also because they have become acknowledged as part of a sanctioned 'paradigm' (a research programme must, it seems, necessarily be part of a paradigm). If this is also Bordwell's model, it can be argued that Bordwell merely goes some way beyond Lakatos' definition of theory here to suggest that research programmes should also eschew abstract theoretical categories and consideration in order to be better able to remain discursively coherent, 'sharply focused and in-depth'. If a research programme must be part of a paradigm it may as well be sharply focused, as, within such a programme, questions pertaining to internal relations will tend to be more apposite than those pertaining to external reference.

However, whilst such research programmes (whether middle-level or not) may indeed be particular articulations of more general theory families, they may also be largely intra-discursive and self-referential, as the notion of trans-discursive commensurability plays little part in the philosophy of Lakatos – and even less so in that of a thinker such as Paul Feyerabend. This suggests that there may be problems associated with a research programme which is markedly discursive and paradigmatically self-referential, and which does not address the sort of absolutes which might challenge paradigm consolidation. One of those absolutes is reality, and the possibility of 'projection convergence'. But any attempt to address that issue would move the debate away from pragmatism, and towards realism. The more fundamental philosophical problems of pragmatism are also evident here, and raise a number of questions. For example, in such a research programme, what notions of use-value are in play, and what kind of use does the research programme serve – an internal programme use, or one more 'humanly' valuable? How incommensurable are the 'sharply focused' models and principles which the research programme deploys? Advocates of pragmatist positions may not wish for incommensurability, but their preference for notions of use-value over ideas of truth-value may entail such a consequence.

It is also, anyway, the case that the Kuhnian notion of the paradigm was not initially meant to stand as a means of promoting paradigm insularity and autonomy, far less 'cultural pluralism'. The fact that this came to be so prompted Kuhn to write his 1968 'Postscript' to *The Structure of Scientific Revolutions*, in which 'Postscript' he argued that the idea of incommensurability should not be taken from its proper place in discussions over the nature of 'normal science' and applied to areas of the social sciences, or, even less, more 'cultural' practices and fields.[132] In addition, Kuhn also believed that incommensurability was bound to be *overcome* within science, as the accumulation of evidence eventually led to a scientific 'revolution' which would reconcile divergent accounts in an act of synthesis. Although arguments over Kuhn's 'pragmatism', 'anti-realism' or 'realism' abound, the tone of the 1968 'Postscript' makes it clear that Kuhn's views are distinct from the position of Lakatos, and even more so of Feyerabend, with the latter explicitly advocating cultural incommensurability. But even if, for present purposes, Kuhn's important counsel is overlooked, and we pursue the idea that discursive pluralism might be overcome within cultural fields, best models held up, and paradigms challenged – and even if, in addition, we pursue such an idea on the basis of conjectures concerning the greater value of use-value or coherence conditions – it still seems unlikely that a middle-level research pro-gramme could ever achieve such an outcome, because it would not be able to mobilise sufficient abstract categories. What would be preferable to such a pro-gramme, therefore, would be one which, whilst retaining the ability which middle-level programmes undoubtedly possess to describe and explain well at the micro and middle levels, could also challenge paradigms, hold out the prospect of achieving best-model status, and aim for the possibility of projec-tion convergence.

As previously argued, because pragmatist-based positions within film studies exclude abstract theoretical categories, they also have a reduced explanatory power. Such exclusion is a problem in itself, because any theory must have, at its core, a set of abstract conceptions and, like the philosophical realist 'open system', must be structured in depth, and contain a range of empirical, intermediate and abstract concepts. If it does not, it sets limits upon its explanatory scope. However, such limitations are also bound to be ulti-mately unsatisfactory because, as Kant foresaw, human beings will always be driven to employ such categories. As Putnam argues, their exercise 'is simply reflection at the most general; to put a stop to it would be a crime against reason'.[133] Although the pragmatist project in film theory played an important historical role in countering some of the excesses of screen theory, it is, there-fore, bound to eventually run out of steam, because middle-level or piecemeal theorising will never be felt to be sufficient.

Another problem with pragmatist positions within film theory lies within their capacity, or lack of it, for political engagement. Carroll rightly argues that it is mistaken to assert that any theory, or object of theory, must always, as a matter of doctrine, be accepted or rejected on the basis of its perceived politi-cal or ideological orientation (or lack of such).[134] Such blanket repudiations were one of the worst aspects of screen theory, and led to the marginalisation of, amongst other things, the entire tradition of film theory considered in this book. However, the general *orientation* of the pragmatist approach is largely to bypass the political, and focus more on relationships between intermediate determining influences, textual structures, and perceptual/cognitive faculties. Of course, as Carroll argues, pragmatist-oriented work may, and often does, address the political in particular instances. However, in general practice, it will tend not to do so.[135] This body of work may be politically neutral, but it is also largely politically risk-free.

Since the 1980s, a great deal of work has emerged in film studies which professes to call itself cognitivist or cognitivist-influenced, and much of this has achieved considerable results in applying methods derived from cognitive psychology and related disciplines to areas such as identification and spectator response. Such work includes the individual writings of Carroll and Bordwell, their co-edited *Post Theory* (1996), Grodal (1997), Smith (1995), Allen and Smith (1997), Plantinga and G. M. Smith (1999) and many others.[136] It is beyond both the scope of this present project and its aspirations for a study of cinematic realism to explore this body of work in detail. What will be attempted instead, as suggested earlier, will be a brief summary of cognitivism in relation to the preceding account of pragmatism. This section will also concentrate on the potential problems attendant upon a cognitivist approach, in so far as these problems relate to an understanding of cinematic realism. No attempt will be made to discuss the benefits of a cognitivist approach, though it should be clearly understood that such benefits do exist.

Firstly, the term 'cognitivism' is charged with a sizeable amount of historical baggage. Some contemporary cognitivist positions display the continued influence of behaviourism, a deterministic form of psychology. Second, cognitivism draws on areas such as information processing, cognitive psychology, neuroscience and artificial intelligence theory. These are areas of relatively 'hard' science, and the application of hard science-based methodologies to the arts has rarely been successful in the past. Third, what may emerge from this intellectual synthesis, in what has been referred to as a 'hard AI' (artificial intelligence) version, is a notion that central neurological processes in human beings are thought of as functioning in a computer like way;[137] and a view that the mind is to the brain as the programme is to the computer hardware.[138] The underlying imperative of cognitivism is thus, it is feared, to 'provide the blueprint for a machine' (the human mind and mental processes) based upon computer analogies. However, as one critic of cognitivism has noted, computer programmes cannot be used as 'blueprints' for the mind in this way because 'Programmes, in short, are not minds, and they are not by themselves sufficient for having minds'.[139] Fourth, cognitivist approaches – certainly hard AI approaches – may lead to a diminished account of agency. Even if cognitivists believe that people are not machines, or that the human mind is not a computer programme, 'pursuit of the programme analogy in our understanding of ourselves can still lead to a loss of status . . . because it promotes a form of psychology to do with showing how people can be replaced by machines'.[140] Finally, in cognitivism, as with pragmatism, the focus upon empirical and intermediate range categories also tends to exclude more abstract conceptualisations – though cognitivists often see this as a positive thing.

There are also some apparent similarities between cognitivism and screen theory which should be noted. Like screen theory, cognitivist film theory does not particularly promote the notion of agency, largely because of the extent to which it focuses on small-scale psychological and neurological processes. On the face of it, it would also seem that screen theory and cognitivist film theory share a degree of essentialism in assuming that concrete links between representation and spectator response can be uncovered. For example, one writer asks 'What characteristics of monsters make us respond with fear and disgust?',[141] as though such characteristics could ever be specified in a definite manner. Screen theory, in structuralist mode, was particularly effective at description and micro-explanation, but less so at more compelling, wide-ranging forms of explanation involving abstract concepts. The same may hold true of cognitivist-influenced film theory, (but, again, cognitivists may view this as a positive attribute of the approach). For example, in attempting to link the Kantian concept of the sublime with cognitivist approaches to the analysis of emotional responses, one critic concludes that cognitivism cannot easily cater for the abstract characteristics of the sublime,[142] even though what the writer calls the 'meta-emotions' of spectators necessarily involve the application of abstract concepts:

> because the meta-emotions of viewers involve not just our wiring and physiology, but our higher-level conceptions of value. We have these because we are humans using complex concepts that reflect our social organisation as beings who make artworks, interpret them, and can understand their moral visions. When we see and react to Joan's suffering we need to have thoughts about patriarchy, nationalism and religion, just as Aguirre requires conceptions of colonialism, incest and madness.[143]

An orientation towards 'higher-level conceptions of value' is, of course, characteristic of both philosophical realism and classical cinematic realism, and the lack of ability to cater for such 'complex concepts' forms the basis of the realist criticism of pragmatism and cognitivism. Cognitivists, on the other hand, would respond by claiming that the 'specificity' of a cognitivist approach allows highly detailed analysis of particular situations to take place, bringing about 'a clearer understanding of the emotional [in this case] processes of watching a film'.[144] Such specificity and detail has its place, as does cognitivism, and some of the work already carried out in this area has already achieved much. Similarly, middle-level research programmes in general will always make up the bulk of research carried out within film studies, and rightly so. On the other hand, if pragmatist cognitivism is to become a dominant paradigm within the field, key concerns of realism may be marginalised and, for realists, these concerns are more than academic, because they touch upon the nature of human subjectivity, and the possibilities for agency and acquisition of knowledge about reality. Only realism, and not middle-level cognitivism, will stop 'the chill winds of relativism and even nihilism blowing ever more strongly', because realism looks outwards.[145]

Conclusions

What has gone before should make it clear how the cinematic realist traditions explored here differ from the pragmatist schools just referred to. What remains, and is also of particular relevance to this project, is a need to assess the extent to which links can be drawn between cinematic realism and philosophical realism. In his *The Rise of the Novel* (1957) Ian Watt makes the point that it may not be possible to relate philosophical realism to cultural practices in a precise way: 'What is important to the novel in philosophical realism is much less specific: it is rather the general temper of realist thought, the methods of investigation it has used, and the kinds of problems it has raised.'[146] Similar, hesitant doubts concerning the feasibility of relating philosophical realism to the arts in an incisive manner have also been raised by other writers, whilst the application of philosophical realist principles within film theory, in Lovell (1980) and Allen and Gomery (1985), has also led to inconclusive results. Summary definitions always have their limitations, particularly in terms of what is included and excluded from the terms of definition. On the other hand, and as argued previously, it is important to connect traditions of realist film theory to larger theoretical positions, so that these traditions rise above their persistent isolation, and their voice is strengthened. With this in mind, a provisional categorisation of these cinematic realist traditions in terms of philosophical realism will be attempted. Such a categorisation is not meant to be conclusive, but to mark out a schema through which cinematic realism may be linked with philosophical realism in the future.

Lukácsian and intuitionist cinematic realism can be classed as a form of indeterminate, representational intuitionist realism, as opposed to direct realism or conceptual idealism. It is also based upon a conception of the importance of the empirical, active agency and the need for limited conceptual relativism. This tradition is not anti-rational, but is sceptical about the uses to which reason is put within modernity, and accents the importance of non-cognitive experience. It is committed to an abstract, rather than 'hard' metaphysical realist correspondence theory of truth, and is focused upon the nature of the modern experience, and its impact upon subjectivity. The tradition can also be distinguished from other approaches in its use of highly abstract concepts, its reliance on a continental idealist strand of philosophy and its utopian aspirations.

Having said this, though, many questions remain unanswered. Above all, the question of how these cinematic realist traditions can be developed into a more coherent and modified realist position, and how they can be related to other disciplines, such as philosophy and history. But that is a question for another project.

Notes

1 Auerbach, Erich, *Mimesis, The Representation of Reality in Western Literature* (Princeton: Princeton University Press, 1953), p. 556.
2 Malevich, Kasimir, 'Non-Objective Art and Suprematism', in Harrison, Charles, and Wood, Paul (eds) *Art in Theory, 1900–1990: An Anthology of Changing Ideas* (Oxford: Blackwell, 1992), p. 291.
3 Ibid.
4 Ibid., p. 297.
5 Frascina, Francis, Blake, Nigel, Fer, Briony, Garb, Tamar, and Harrison, Charles, *Modernity and Modernism: French Painting in the Nineteenth Century* (New Haven and London: Yale University Press, in Association with the Open University, 1993), p. 13.
6 Ibid., p. 14.
7 Greenberg, Clement, 'Towards a New Laocoon', in *Partisan Review*, vol. VII, no. 4 (New York: July–August 1940), pp. 296–310. In Harrison and Wood (eds), p. 558.
8 Greenberg, Clement, 'Avant-Garde and Kitsch', in *Partisan Review*, vol. VI, no. 5 (New York: fall, 1939), pp. 34–49. In Harrison and Wood (eds), p. 531.
9 Adorno, Theodor, 'Commitment', in Harrison and Wood (eds), pp. 763–4.
10 Greenberg, Clement, 'Modernist Painting', in *Art & Literature*, no. 4 (spring 1965), pp. 193–201. In Harrison and Wood (eds), p. 755.
11 Ibid., p. 754.
12 Ibid., p. 755.
13 Wollen, Peter, 'The Two Avant-Gardes', reprinted in his *Readings and Writings: Semiotic Counter-Strategies* (London: Verso, 1982), pp. 92–104.
14 Bürger, Peter, *Theory of the Avant-Garde* (Minneapolis: University of Minnesota Press, 1984).
15 Williams, Raymond, *Keywords: A Vocabulary of Culture and Society* (London: Croom Helm, 1979), p. 219.
16 Needham, Gerald, *Nineteenth Century Realist Art* (New York: Harper & Row Publishers, 1988), p. 95.
17 Hemmings, F. W. J., *Emile Zola* (Oxford: Clarendon Press, 1966), p. 200.
18 Lovell, Terry, *Pictures of Reality* (London: BFI, 1980), p. 81.
19 Holub, Robert C., *Jürgen Habermas, Critic in the Public Sphere* (London and New York: Routledge, 1991), p. 136.
20 Ibid., p. 135.
21 Jameson, Fredric, *Signatures of the Visible* (New York and London: Routledge, 1992), p. 156.
22 Needham, p. 42.
23 Becker, George J., *Master European Realists of the Nineteenth Century* (New York: Frederick Ungar Publishing Co., 1982), p. 95.
24 Frascina et al., p. 9.

25 Castagnary, Jules-Antoine, 'Naturalism', in Harrison, Charles, Wood, Paul, and Gaiger, Jason (eds), *Art in Theory, 1815–1900* (Oxford: Blackwell, 1998), p. 414.
26 Williams, Raymond, 'A Lecture on Realism', *Screen*, vol. 18, no. 1. (1977), pp. 64–5.
27 Auerbach, p. 554.
28 Nochlin, Linda, *Realism* (London: Penguin, 1971), p. 34.
29 Buchon, Max, 'On Courbet's *Stonebreakers* and *A Burial at Ornans*', in Harrison, Wood and Gaiger (eds), pp. 364–5.
30 Ibid., p. 365.
31 Andrew, Dudley, *Mists of Regret: Culture and Sensibility in Classic French Film* (Princeton: Princeton University Press, 1995), p. 104.
32 Faulkner, Christopher, *The Social Cinema of Jean Renoir* (Princeton: Princeton University Press, 1986), p. 55.
33 Lunn, Eugene, *Marxism and Modernism: An Historical Study of Lukács, Brecht, Benjamin and Adorno* (Berkeley, Los Angeles and London: University of California Press, 1982), p. 13.
34 Houlgate, Stephen, *Freedom Truth and History: An Introduction to Hegel's Philosophy* (London: Routledge, 1991), p. 39.
35 Királyfalvi, Béla, *The Aesthetics of György Lukács* (Princeton: Princeton University Press, 1975), p. 82.
36 Ibid., p. 117.
37 Taylor, Charles, *Hegel* (Cambridge: Cambridge University Press, 1975), p. 473.
38 Houlgate, p. 132.
39 Lukács, Georg, 'Tolstoy and the Development of Realism', in Craig, David (ed.) *Marxists on Literature: An Anthology* (Harmondsworth: Penguin, 1977), p. 303.
40 Kracauer, Siegfried, *Theory of Film, The Redemption of Physical Reality* (Princeton: Princeton University Press, 1997), p. 71.
41 Bazin, André, *What Is Cinema? Volume II* (Berkeley and Los Angeles: University of California Press, 1972), pp. 49–60.
42 Bazin, André, *What Is Cinema? Volume I* (Berkeley and Los Angeles: University of California Press, 1967), pp. 10–11.
43 Kracauer (1997), pp. 184–5.
44 Bazin (1967), p. 27.
45 Kracauer (1997), p. 40.
46 Ibid., p. 39.
47 Bhaskar, Roy, *A Realist Theory of Science* (Leeds: Leeds University Books, 1975), p. 33.
48 Hesse, Mary, 'The New Empiricism', in Marrick, Harold (ed.) *Challenges to Empiricism* (London: Methuen, 1980), p. 198.
49 Papineau, David, *Reality and Representation* (Oxford: Oxford University Press, 1987), p. x.
50 Russell, Bertrand, *History of Western Philosophy* (London: George Allen & Unwin, 1965), p. 20.
51 Schmitt, Frederick F., *Truth: A Primer* (Boulder, San Francisco and London: Westview Press, 1995), p. 217.

52 Putnam, Hilary, *Reason, Truth and History* (Cambridge: Cambridge University Press, 1981), p. 6

53 Russell, p. 20.

54 Rescher, N., *Conceptual Idealism* (Oxford: Blackwell, 1973), p. 167.

55 Lovell, pp. 64–78, 79–95.

56 Schmitt, p. 78.

57 Aitken, Ian, *European Film Theory and Cinema: A Critical Introduction* (Edinburgh: Edinburgh University Press, 2001), pp. 96–7.

58 James, William, *The Meaning of Truth: A Sequel to 'Pragmatism'* (Cambridge, MA: Harvard University Press, 1909), p. vii.

59 Feyerabend, Paul, *Farewell to Reason* (London: Verso, 1987), p. 5.

60 Schmitt, p. 147.

61 Trigg, Roger, *Reality at Risk, A Defence of Realism in Philosophy and the Sciences* (New York and London: Harvester Wheatsheaf, 1989), p. 111.

62 Conant, James, 'Introduction', in Putnam, Hilary, *Realism with a Human Face* (Cambridge, MA, and London: Harvard University Press, 1992), p. xlv.

63 Passmore, John, *Recent Philosophers: A Supplement to A Hundred Years of Philosophy* (London: Duckworth, 1985), p. 104.

64 Conant in Putnam (1992), p. xlv.

65 Putnam, Hilary, *The Many Faces of Realism* (New York: Open Court, 1987), p. 7.

66 Ibid., p. 27.

67 Papineau, David, *Reality and Representation* (Oxford: Basil Blackwell, 1987), quoted in Trigg, p. xxiii.

68 Putnam (1992), p. 131.

69 Conant in Putnam (1992), p. xlv.

70 Ibid., p. xv.

71 Passmore, p. 105.

72 Putnam (1981), p. 52.

73 Putnam (1987), p. 27.

74 Ibid., p. 29.

75 Conant in Putnam (1992), p. 1.

76 Ibid., p. 49.

77 Conant in Putnam (1992), p. xxviii.

78 Kemp Smith, Norman, *A Commentary to Kant's 'Critique of Pure Reason'* (Atlantic Highlands: Humanities Press Inc., and Basingstoke: Macmillan, 1984), pp. 12–13.

79 Ibid., p. 13.

80 Ibid.

81 Putnam (1992), p. 261.

82 Kemp Smith, pp. 12–13.

83 Goodman, Nelson, quoted in Putnam (1992), p. 262. Putnam does not provide a precise citation.

84 Ibid., p. 262.

85 Rorty, Richard, 'The World Well Lost', *Journal of Philosophy*, no. 69 (1972).

86 Rorty, Richard, *Philosophy and the Mirror of Nature* (Oxford: Oxford University Press, 1980).

87 Conant in Putnam (1992), p. x.

88 Putnam (1981), p. 216.

89 Ibid., p. 51.

90 Putnam, (1987), p. 34.

91 Putnam, quoted, uncited, in Passmore, p. 106.

92 Derrida, Jacques, *Of Grammatology* (Baltimore, MD: Johns Hopkins University Press, 1974), p. 158.

93 Putnam (1981), p. 54.

94 Ibid., pp. 49–50.

95 Ibid., pp. 54–5.

96 Ibid., p. 74.

97 Ibid., p. 55.

98 Putnam, Hilary, *Representation and Reality* (Cambridge, MA, and London: MIT Press, 1992), p. 115. Hereafter 1992a.

99 Kemp Smith, p. 13.

100 Putnam (1991), p. 107.

101 Passmore, pp. 106–7.

102 Keat, R., and Urry, J., *Social Theory as Science* (London: Routledge, 1975), p. 29.

103 Allen, Robert C., and Gomery, Douglas, *Film History, Theory and Practice* (New York: Alfred A. Knopf, 1985), pp. 14–15.

104 Harré, Rom, *The Philosophies of Science: An Introductory Survey* (Oxford and New York: Oxford University Press, 1972), p. 178.

105 Keat and Urry, p. 35.

106 Ibid., p. 37.

107 Putnam, Hilary, *Reason, Truth and History,* quoted, uncited, in Passmore, p. 105.

108 Conant in Putnam (1992), p. xlv, quoting from Putnam, *The Many Faces of Realism,* page number uncited.

109 Ibid., p. xlix–l.

110 Passmore, p. 107.

111 Ibid., p. 116.

112 Ibid., p. 92.

113 Putnam (1992), p. 264, quoting from Quine, W. V. O., 'Two Dogmas of Empiricism', in his *From a Logical Point of View* (Cambridge, MA: Harvard University Press, 1953), p. 42.

114 Hesse, in Marrick (ed.), p. 198.

115 Ibid., p. 206.

116 Putnam (1981), pp. 72–3.

117 Nichols, Bill, in Gledhill, Christine, and Williams, Linda (eds) *Reinventing Film Studies* (London: Arnold, 2000), p. 35.

118 Willeman, Paul, 'Editorial', in *Screen,* vol. 14, no. 1/2 (spring–summer 1973), p. 2.

119 Thompson, E. P., *The Poverty of Theory and Other Essays* (London: Merlin, 1978).

120 Kemp Smith, pp. 12–13.

121 Aitken (1990), p. 45.

122 Ibid., p. 25.

123 Schmitt, p. 93.

124 Ibid.

125 Bordwell, David, 'Contemporary Film Studies and the Vicissitudes of Grand Theory', in Bordwell, David, and Carroll, Noël (eds), *Post-Theory: Reconstructing Film Studies* (Madison and London: University of Wisconsin Press, 1996), pp. 29–30.

126 Carroll, Noël, *Theorising the Moving Image* (Cambridge: Cambridge University Press, 1996), p. 332.

127 Carroll, Noël, 'Prospects for Film Theory: A Personal Assessment', in Bordwell and Carroll (eds) (1996), p. 39.

128 Bordwell, in Bordwell and Carroll (eds) (1996), p. 29.

129 Harré, Rom, in Bhaskar, Roy (ed.), *Harré and His Critics* (Oxford: Basil Blackwell, 1990), p. 299.

130 Passmore, p. 95.

131 Harré, in Bhaskar (ed.), p. 302.

132 Passmore, pp. 96–7.

133 Conant in Putnam (1992), p. xxxv, quoting from Putnam, *Realism and Reason* (Cambridge: Cambridge University Press, 1983), no page number cited.

134 Carroll, in Bordwell and Carroll (eds) (1996), p. 49.

135 Ibid., p. 48.

136 Grodal, Torben Kragh, *Moving Picture: A New Theory of Genres, Feelings and Cognitions* (Oxford: Clarendon Press, 1997); Smith, Murray, *Engaging Characters, Fiction, Emotion and the Cinema* (Oxford: Clarendon Press, 1995); Allen, Richard, and Smith, Murray (eds), *Film Theory and Philosophy* (Oxford: Clardendon Press, 1997) and Plantinga, Carl, and Smith, M. Greg (eds) *Passionate Views: Film, Cognition and Emotions* (Baltimore and London: John Hopkins University Press, 1999).

137 Hamlyn, D. W., *In and Out of the Black Box: On the Philosophy of Cognition* (Oxford: Basil Blackwell, 1990), p. 3.

138 Searle, John, *Minds, Brains & Science* (London: Penguin, 1989), p. 28.

139 Ibid., p. 39.

140 Shutter, J., in Heil, John (ed.), *Perception and Cognition* (Berkeley; London: University of California Press, 1983), p. 44.

141 Plantinga, Carl and Smith, M. Greg, 'Introduction', in Plantinga and Smith (eds) *Passionate Views: Film, Cognition and Emotions* (Baltimore and The Johns Hopkins University Press, 1999), p. 3.

142 Freeland, Cynthia, A., 'The Sublime in Cinema', in Plantinga and Smith (eds), p. 82.

143 Ibid., p. 83. Freeland is referring to Carl Dreyer's *The Passion of Joan of Arc* (1928) and Werner Herzog's *Aguirre, the Wrath of God* (1972).

144 Plantinga and Smith, in Plantinga and Smith (eds), p. 3.

145 Trigg, p. iv.

146 Watt, Ian, *The Rise of the Novel: Studies in Defoe, Richardson and Fielding* (London: Chatto and Windus, 1957), p. 90.

Conclusions

Film theory has yet to acquire the substantial historical canon of critical assessment, and analysis which older disciplines within the humanities are blessed with. This means that film theory is faced with two, related requirements: (1) to extend the range of theoretical perspectives and core concepts available to the discipline, and (2) to connect with ideas from other fields. The juncture of film studies, and the field of history from the late 1970s onwards has been hugely productive, in terms of the number and quality of historically based works which have materialised. Another, recent, attempt to connect film studies to other disciplines involves the taking up of Anglo-American analytical philosophy. Here, prospects also appear excellent, with scholars such as Richard Allen, Murray Smith, Noël Carroll, Allan Casebier, Gregory Currie and Stanley Cavell making important contributions. The present book has also attempted to connect film theory to a branch of the analytical tradition, that of philosophical realism; but such a tentative enterprise, following on from the pioneering work of Lovell and Allen and Gomery, still has a long way to go. In addition to history and philosophy, other disciplines, including those of cognitive science, psychology, feminism, phenomenology, art history and ethnography, have also been drawn on by film theorists in recent years. In this process of connection with important intellectual disciplines and traditions, 'classical' realist film theory also has an important role to play, because the approaches developed by the classical realist theorists are directly linked to historically important traditions of thought, including those of Kant, Hegel, Weber, Bradley, Marx, the Frankfurt School, Bergson and Husserl.

Some recent works influenced by the fields mentioned above also touch upon the subject of realism. Allan Casebier's *Film and Phenomenology*, Richard Allen's *Projecting Illusion* and Gregory Currie's *Image and Mind* all fall into this category, as does some of the work of Cavell. Particularly important also, in relation to notions of realism and film, has been the work of scholars such as

Thomas Elsaesser, Miriam Bratu Hansen, Gertrud Koch, Heide Schlüpmann, Thomas Y. Levin, Patrice Petro, Sabine Hake and others, on theorists and theories connected with the Frankfurt School. In this respect too, the role of the journal *New German Critique* must also be singled out as exemplary. Other important contributions to the issue of realism and film also include the rehabilitation of the 'realist' psychologist J. J. Gibson by Joseph Anderson and Barbara Anderson in Bordwell and Carroll's *Post-Theory*. Other examples might be given.

And yet, the question of realism still remain a relatively unfashionable one. Why? At one level, realism is regarded as passé because it has been marginalised within a dominant teaching and research paradigm within which questions of realism and film are regarded as irrelevant, or to have been answered to the extent that little more needs to be said on the matter. The prevailing position here is one of support for the view that realism is a form of discourse, or rhetoric or naturalised ideology. However, the dominant paradigm's understanding of realism is an inadequate one, because, although the question of realism as an absolute rarely presents itself openly and overtly in everyday, or even everyday academic, activity, realism is actually of fundamental and everyday importance. All theory involves not only rhetoric but also the exercise of realist assumptions, because any account of causal explanation is premised upon the notion that 'something which is the case' exists. It is untenable to argue that theories and representations should only be thought of in terms of the cultural influences upon them, because, although such influences play a part in shaping theory, theories also posit real factors as the basis for the positions they adopt, and they are also engendered in relation to such factors. Whether we like it or not, we engage with the question, or the experience of realism, more or less continuously, and our daily movements within the life-world are premised upon assumptions concerning 'projection' and 'convergence'. Film theorists do not need to, and actually *cannot*, ignore this everyday reality of realism. Nor, either, should they turn away from the question of realism as an absolute, for, it is not defensible to argue that lack of observability should dictate that theory must not refer to highly abstract things.

For film studies to overlook the question of realism to the degree that it has done is a problem. However, what kind of projects involving realism might it be possible to imagine within the field of film studies, which might help to achieve redress? The first book in this series, *European Film Theory and Cinema*, explored relationships between intuitionist cinematic modernism and intuitionist cinematic realism. *Realist Film Theory and Cinema* attempts an overview of nineteenth-century Lukácsian and intuitionist realist film theory. The third planned book in the series will look at the relationship between film and philosophical realism. However, all the major theorists of cinematic realism are still in need of further, more detailed investigation. Much work has been carried out on Kracauer, but less on Grierson and Bazin, or Lukács's writings on film. The models derived from these theorists can also be applied to the analysis of particular films, as the study of *Senso* carried out here suggests. The idea of an intuitionist realist cinema and film theory itself also needs to be explored in more depth, contested or adapted. The relationship between philosophical realism and film theory needs to be explored further, as does the application of philosophical realism to the analysis of particular films. The background theoretical influences upon the major theorists of cinematic realism also need to be explored, and key concepts drawn from Kant, Hegel, Bradley, Husserl, Bergson and others, then applied to both films and film theory. The question of realism and the cinema also impinges upon other disciplines, including history, the philosophy and psychology of perception, gender theory, linguistics, phenomenology, information science, ethnography, artificial intelligence theory and branches of cognitivist research. All of these are capable of furnishing concepts which can be explored in relation to notions of cinematic realism. Realism can also furnish models of theory and evidence which may be particularly useful in the field of the documentary film. All of these constitute possible ways forward for future studies of cinematic realism, studies which may eventually come to establish a new paradigm.

Bibliography

Abel, Richard, *French Cinema: The First Wave 1915–1929* (Princeton: Princeton University Press, 1984).

Abel, Richard, *French Film Theory and Criticism: A History/Anthology 1907–1939* (vols 1 and 2) (Princeton: Princeton University Press, 1988).

Adorno, Theodor, 'Commitment' (1962), in Harrison, Charles, and Wood, Paul (eds) *Art in Theory, 1900–1990: An Anthology of Changing Ideas* (Oxford: Blackwell, 1992).

Adorno, Theodor, 'The Curious Realist: On Siegfried Kracauer', in *New German Critique* no. 54 (fall 1991).

Aitken, Ian, 'John Grierson, Idealism and the Inter-war Period', *Historical Journal of Film, Radio and Television*, vol. 9, no. 3 (1989).

Aitken, Ian, 'Distraction and Redemption: Kracauer, Surrealism and Phenomenology', *Screen*, vol. 39, no. 2 (summer 1998).

Aitken, Ian, *European Film Theory and Cinema: A Critical Introduction* (Edinburgh: Edinburgh University Press, 2001).

Aitken, Ian, *Film and Reform: John Grierson and the Documentary Film Movement* (London: Routledge, 1990, 1992).

Aitken, Ian, *The Documentary Film Movement: An Anthology* (Edinburgh: Edinburgh University Press, 1998).

Aitken, Ian, *Alberto Cavalcanti: Realism, Surrealism and National Cinemas* (London: Flicks Books, 2001).

Aitken, Ian, 'The Documentary Film Movement: The Post Office Reaches all Branches of Life', in Hassard, John, and Holliday, Ruth (eds), *Organization Representation: Work and Organizations in Popular Culture* (London: Sage, 1998).

Aitken, Ian, 'Pictorialist Naturalism and *La Terre*', in Fowler, C. (ed.) *Representations of the Rural* (New York: Wayne State University Press, 2005).

Aitken, Ian, 'The Documentary Film Movement', in Murphy, Robert (ed.) *The British Cinema Book* (London: BFI, 2001).

Allen, Richard, *Projecting Illusion, Film Spectatorship and the Impression of Reality* (Cambridge: Cambridge University Press, 1995).

Allen, Richard, and Smith, Murray (eds) *Film Theory and Philosophy* (Oxford: Clarendon Press, 1997).

Allen, Robert C., and Gomery, Douglas, *Film History, Theory and Practice* (New York: Alfred A. Knopf, 1985).

Allison, Henry E., *Idealism and Freedom, Essays on Kant's Theoretical and Practical Philosophy* (Cambridge: Cambridge University Press, 1996).

Andrew, J. Dudley, *Mists of Regret: Culture and Sensibility in Classic French Film* (Princeton: Princeton University Press, 1995).

Andrew, J. Dudley, *The Major Film Theories: An Introduction* (Oxford: Oxford University Press, 1976).

Andrew, J. Dudley, *André Bazin* (New York: Columbia University Press, 1978).

Andrew, J. Dudley, *Concepts in Film Theory* (Oxford: Oxford University Press, 1984).

Arato, Andrew, and Breines, Paul, *The Young Lukács and the Origins of Western Marxism* (New York: Seabury Press, 1979).

Armes, Roy, *Patterns of Realism* (London: Tantivy Press, 1971).

Armes, Roy, *French Cinema* (London: Secker & Warburg, 1985).

Arnheim, Rudolf, *Film* (London: Faber and Faber, 1933).

Arnheim, Rudolf, *Art and Visual Perception* (Berkeley and Los Angeles, CA: University of California Press, 1985).

Arnold, Matthew, *Culture and Anarchy* (London: Murray, 1869).

Auerbach, Erich, *Mimesis: The Representation of Reality in Western Literature* (Princeton: Princeton University Press, 1968).

Aumont, Jacques, *Montage Eisenstein* (London: BFI and Indiana University Press, 1979).

Bacon, Henry, *Visconti: Explorations of Beauty and Decay* (Cambridge: Cambridge University Press, 1998).

Balázs, Béla, *Der sichtbare Mensch oder der Kultur des Films* (Vienna and Leipzig: Deutsch-Österreichischer Verlag, 1924).

Barlow, D. John, *German Expressionist Film* (Boston, MA: Twayne, 1982).

Barnouw, Dagmar, *Critical Realism: History, Photography and the Work of Siegfried Kracauer* (Baltimore and London: Johns Hopkins University Press, 1994)

Bazin, André, *What Is Cinema? Volume I* (Berkeley Los Angeles and London: University of California Press, 1967).

Bazin, André, *What Is Cinema? Volume II* (Berkeley and Los Angeles: University of California Press, 1972).

Becker, George, J., *Master European Realists of the Nineteenth Century* (New York: Frederick Ungar Publishing Co., 1982).

Bernet, Rudolf, Kern, Iso, and Marbach, Eduard, *An Introduction to Husserlian Phenomenology* (Evanston, IL: Northwestern University Press, 1993).

Bernstein, J. M., *The Philosophy of the Novel: Lukács, Marxism and the Dialectics of Form* (Minneapolis: University of Minnesota Press, 1984).

Bhaskar, Roy, *A Realist Theory of Science* (Leeds: Leeds University Books, 1975).

Bhaskar, Roy (ed.) *Harré and His Critics* (Oxford: Basil Blackwell, 1990).

Bisztray, George, *Marxist Models of Literary Realism* (New York: Columbia University Press, 1978).

Boas, George (ed.) *Courbet and the Naturalistic Movement* (New York: Russell & Russell, 1967).

Bondanella, Peter, *Italian Cinema from Neorealism to the Present* (Northampton: Roundhouse, 1983).

Bordwell, David, *French Impressionist Cinema: Film Culture, Film Theory and Film Style* (New York: Arno, 1980).

Bordwell, David, *Making Meaning: Inference and Rhetoric in the Interpretation of Cinema* (Cambridge, MA: Harvard University Press, 1989).

Bordwell, David, and Carroll, Noël (eds) *Post-Theory: Reconstructing Film Studies* (Madison and London: University of Wisconsin Press, 1996).

Bordwell, David, and Thompson, Kristin, *Film History: An Introduction* (New York: McGraw Hill, 1994).

Bradley, F. H., *Essays on Truth and Reality* (Oxford: Clarendon Press, 1914).

Braudy, Leo, *Jean Renoir: The World of His Films* (New York and Oxford: Columbia University Press, 1989).

Brion, Marcel, *Art of the Romantic Era: Romanticism, Classicism, Realism* (London: Thames and Hudson, 1966).

Buck-Morss, Susan, *The Origin of Negative Dialectics* (London and Lincoln, NB: University of Nebraska Press, 1993).

Budd, M. *The Cabinet of Dr. Caligari: Texts, Contexts, Histories* (New Brunswick: Rutgers University Press, 1990).

Bürger, Peter, *Theory of the Avant-Garde* (Minneapolis: University of Minnesota Press, 1984).

Canudo, Ricciotto, 'Chronique du Septième Art: Films en couleurs', *Paris-Midi*, no. 4131 (31 August 1923).

Carr, David, *Interpreting Husserl: Critical and Comparative Studies* (Dordrecht, Boston and Lancaster: Martinus Nijhoff Publishers, 1987).

Carroll, Noël, *Theorising the Moving Image* (Cambridge: Cambridge University Press, 1996).

Casebier, Allan, *Film and Phenomenology: Towards a Realist Theory of Cinematic Representation* (Cambridge: Cambridge University Press, 1991).

Colletti, Lucio, *Marxism and Hegel* (London: New Left Books, 1973).

Congdon, Lee, *The Young Lukács* (Chapel Hill: University of North Carolina Press, 1983).

Copleston, Fredrick, *A History of Philosophy, Volume Six: Wolff to Kant* (London: Search Press, 1960).

Cortall, Alan, and Still, Arthur, Against Cognitivism: Alternative Foundations for Cognitive Psychology (New York and London: Harvester Wheatsheat, 1991).

Costall, Alan, and Still, Arthur, *Cognitive Psychology in Question* (London: Harvester, 1987).

Craig, David (ed.) *Marxists on Literature: An Anthology* (Harmondsworth: Pelican, 1975).

Crisp, Colin, *The Classic French Cinema, 1930–1960* (Bloomington: Indiana University Press, 1993).

Currie, Gregory, *Image and Mind, Film, Philosophy and Cognitive Science* (Cambridge: Cambidge University Press, 1995).

Derrida, Jacques, *Speech and Phenomena and Other Essays on Husserl's Theory of Signs* (Evanston, IL: Northwestern University Press, 1967).

Derrida, Jacques, *Of Grammatology* (Baltimore, MD, and London: Johns Hopkins University Press, 1976).

Deutscher, Isaac, *Marxism in Our Time* (Berkeley: Ramparts Press, 1971).

Dreville, Jean, 'Le Documentaire, aimé du cinéma', *Cinémagazine*, no. 2 (February 1930).

Eagleton, Terry, *Marxism and Literary Criticism* (London: Methuen and Co., 1976).

Eagleton, Terry, *The Ideology of the Aesthetic* (Oxford: Basil Blackwell, 1990).

Eisenman, Stephen F. (ed.), *Nineteenth Century Art: A Critical History* (London: Thames & Hudson Ltd, 2001).

Ellis, Jack C., *John Grierson: Life, Contributions, Influence* (Carbondale: Southern Illinois University Press, 2000).

Ellwood, C. A., *Cultural Evolution: A Study of Social Origins and Development* (New York and London: The Century Co-Social Science Series, 1927).

Elsaesser, Thomas, 'Cinema – The Irresponsible Signifier or "The Gamble with History": Film Theory or Cinema Theory', *New German Critique*, no. 70 (1987).

Elsaesser, Thomas, *Weimar Cinema and After: Germany's Historical Imaginary* (London and New York: Routledge, 2000).

Esslin, Martin, *Brecht: A Choice of Evils – A Critical Study of the Man, His Work and His Opinions* (London: Eyre Methuen, 1980).

Falkowska, Janina, *The Political Films of Andrzej Wajda: Dialogism in Man of Marble, Man of Iron and Danton* (Providence, NJ, and Oxford: Berghahn Books, 1996).

Faulkner, Christopher, *The Social Cinema of Jean Renoir* (Princeton: Princeton University Press, 1986).

Feyerabend, Paul, *Farewell to Reason* (London: Verso, 1987).

Frascina, Francis, Blake, Nigel, Fer, Briony, Garb, Tamar, and Harrison, Charles, *Modernity and Modernism: French Painting in the Nineteenth Century* (New Haven and London: Yale University Press, in Association with the Open University Press, 1993).

Frisby, David, *Fragments of Modernity: Theories of Modernity in the Work of Simmel, Kracauer and Benjamin* (Cambridge, MA: MIT Press, 1986).

Furst, Lilian, R. (ed.) *Realism* (London and New York: Longman, 1992).

Furst, Lilian R., and Skrine, Peter N., *Naturalism: The Critical Idiom* (London: Methuen & Co. Ltd, 1971).

Gay, Peter, *Weimar Culture: The Outsider as Insider* (Harmondsworth: Penguin, 1992).

Ghali, Noureddine, *L'Avant-garde Cinématographique en France dans les années vingt* (Paris: Editions Paris Experimental, 1995).

Ginsberg, Terri, and Thompson, Kirsten Moana (eds) *Perspectives on German Cinema* (New York and London: G. K. Hall and Co. and Prentice Hall International, 1996).

Gledhill, Christine, and Williams, Linda (eds) *Reinventing Film Studies* (London: Arnold, 2000).

Glover, Janet, *The Story of Scotland* (London: Faber, 1960).

Gluck, Mary, *Georg Lukács and his Generation 1900–1918* (Cambridge MA: Harvard University Press, 1985).

Green, Fredrick C., *French Novelists From the Revolution to Proust* (New York: Frederick Ungar Publishing Co., 1964).

Grierson, John, 'Better Popular Pictures', *Transactions of the Society of Motion Picture Engineer*, vol. 9, no. 29 (August 1926).

Grierson, John, 'Flaherty, Naturalism and the Problem of the English Cinema', *Artwork* (autumn, 1931).

Grierson, John, 'Preface', in Rotha, Paul, *Documentary Film* (London: Faber & Faber, 1952).

Grierson, John, 'Answers to a Cambridge Questionnaire', *Granta* (Cambridge: Cambridge University Press, 1967).

Grierson, John, 'The Challenge to Peace', in Hardy, Forsyth (ed.) *Grierson on Documentary* (London and Boston: Faber & Faber, 1979).

Grierson, John, 'The Documentary Idea', in Hardy (1979); reprinted in Aitken, Ian, (ed.) *The Documentary Film Movement: An Anthology* (Edinburgh: Edinburgh University Press, 1998).

Hake, Sabine (ed.), *The Cinema's Third Machine: Writing on Film in Germany 1907–1933* (London and Lincoln, NB: University of Nebraska Press, 1993).

Hamlya, D. W., *In and Out of the Black Box: On the Philosophy of Cognition* (Oxford: Basil Blackwell, 1990).

Hampson, Norman, *The Enlightenment: An Evaluation of Its Assumptions, Attitudes and Values* (London: Penguin Books, 1990).

Hardy, Forsyth (ed.), *Grierson on Documentary* (London and Boston: Faber & Faber, 1979).

Harré, Rom, *The Philosophies of Science: An Introductory Survey* (Oxford and New York: Oxford University Press, 1972).

Harré, Rom, *Varieties of Realism* (Oxford: Blackwell, 1996).

Harré, Rom, *Cognitive Science: A Philosophical Introduction* (London: Sage, 2002).

Harrison, Charles, and Wood, Paul (eds) *Art in Theory, 1900–1990: An Anthology of Changing Ideas* (Oxford: Blackwell, 1992).

Harrison, Charles, Wood, Paul, and Gaiger, Jason (eds), *Art in Theory, 1815–1900* (Oxford: Blackwell, 1998).

Hatton, Ragnhild (ed.), *A History of European Ideas* (London: C. Hurst & Co. (Publishers) Ltd, 1962).

Hauser, Arnold, *The Social History of Art: Three: Rococo, Classicism and Romanticism* (London: Routledge and Kegan Paul, 1951).

Hayward, Susan, *French National Cinema* (London: Routledge, 1993).

Hayward, Susan, and Vincendeau, Ginette (eds), *French Film: Texts and Contexts* (London: Routledge, 2000).

Hegel, G. W. F., *Introductory Lectures on Aesthetics* (London: Penguin Books, 1993).

Heil, John (ed.), *Perception and Cognition* (Berkeley and London: University of California Press, 1983).

Held, David, *Introduction to Critical Theory, Horkheimer to Habermas* (Berkeley and Los Angeles: University of California Press, 1980).

Heller, Agnes (ed.) *Lukács Revalued* (Oxford: Basil Blackwell, 1983).

Hemmings, F. W. J., *Emile Zola* (Oxford: Clarendon Press, 1966).

Hobsbawm, Eric, *The Age of Revolution: 1785–1848* (London: Cardinal 1962).

Holub, Robert C., *Jürgen Habermas: Critic in the Public Sphere* (London and New York: Routledge, 1991).

Honour, Hugh, *Neo-classicism: Style and Civilization* (Harmondsworth: Penguin Books Ltd, 1968).

Horkheimer, Max, and Adorno, Theodor W., *Dialectic of Enlightenment* (New York: Herder and Herder, 1972).

Houlgate, Stephen, *Freedom, Truth and History: An Introduction to Hegel's Philosophy* (London: Routledge, 1991).

Husserl, Edmund, *The Crisis of European Science and Transcendental Phenomenology* (Evanston: Northwestern University Press, 1970).

James, William, *The Meaning of Truth: A Sequel to Pragmatism* (Cambridge, MA: Harvard University Press, 1909).

Jameson, Fredric, *Marxism and Form: Twentieth Century Dialectical Theories of Literature* (Princeton: Princeton University Press, 1971).

Jameson, Fredric, *Signatures of the Visible* (New York and London: Routledge, 1992).

Jay, Martin, *Marxism and Totality: The Adventures of a Concept, from Lukács to Habermas* (Cambridge: Polity and Basil Blackwell, 1984).

Johnson-Laird, P. N., *The Computer and the Mind: An Introduction to Cognitive Science* (London: Fontana, 1988).

Kadarkay, Arpad, *Georg Lukács: Life, Thought and Politics* (Oxford: Basil Blackwell, 1991).

Kardarkay, Arpad (ed.), *The Lukács Reader* (Oxford: Basil Blackwell, 1985).

Kaes, Anton, *From Hitler to Heimat: The Return of History as Film* (Cambridge, MA, and London: Harvard University Press, 1992).

Kant, Immanuel, *The Critique of Judgement*, trans. J. C. Meredith (Oxford: Clarendon Press, 1978).

Keat, R., and Urry, J., *Social Theory as Science* (London: Routledge and Kegen Paul, 1975).

Kemp Smith, Norman, *A Commentary to Kant's 'Critique of Pure Reason'* (Atlantic Highlands: Humanities Press Inc., 1984).

King, Norman, *Abel Gance* (London: BFI, 1984).

Királyfalvi, Béla, *The Aesthetics of György Lukács* (Princeton: Princeton University Press, 1975).

Koch, Gertrud, 'Béla Balázs: The Physiognomy of Things', *New German Critique*, no. 40 (Winter 1987).

Koch, Gertrud, *Siegfried Kracauer: An Introduction* (Princeton: Princeton University Press, 2000).

Koch, Gertrud, ' "Not Yet Accepted Anywhere": Exile, Memory and Image in Kracauer's Conception of History', *New German Critique*, no. 54 (fall 1991).

Kolakowski, Leszek, *Main Currents of Marxism, Volume Three: The Breakdown* (Oxford: Clarendon Press, 1978).

Kracauer, Siegfried, *From Caligari to Hitler: A Psychological History of the German Film* (Princeton: Princeton University Press, 1974).

Kracauer, Siegfried, *History: The Last Things Before the Last* (Princeton, NJ: Markus Wiener Publishers, 1995).

Kracauer, Siegfried, *The Mass Ornament, Weimar Essays* (Cambridge, MA, and London: Harvard University Press, 1995).

Kracauer, Siegfried, *Theory of Film: The Redemption of Physical Reality* (Princeton: Princeton University Press, 1997).

Kracauer, Siegfried, *The Salaried Masses: Duty and Distraction in Weimar Germany* (London and New York: Verso, 1998).

Kracauer, Siegfried, 'Cult of Distraction: On Berlin's Picture Palaces' (1926), reprinted in *New German Critique* no. 40, (winter 1987).

Lapsley, Robert, and Westlake, Michael, *Film Theory: An Introduction* (Manchester: Manchester University Press, 1988).

Larkin, Maurice, *Man and Society in Nineteenth-Century Realism: Determinism and Literature* (London: Macmillan, 1977).

Larrabee, Harold A. (ed.), *Selections from Bergson* (New York: Appleton-Century-Crofts Inc., 1949).

Lefebvre, Georges, *The French Revolution: From Its Origins to 1793* (London: Routledge & Kegan Paul, 1971).

Lefebvre, Georges, *The Coming of the French Revolution 1789* (Princeton, NJ: Princeton University Press, 1947).

Lehman, Peter (ed.) *Defining Cinema* (New Brunswick: Rutgers University Press, 1997).

Leprohon, Pierre, *The Italian Cinema* (London: Secker & Warburg, 1972).

Levin, Tom, 'From Dialectical to Normative Specificity: Reading Lukács on Film', *New German Critique*, no. 40 (winter 1987).

Leyda, Jay, *Kino, A History of the Russian and Soviet Film* (London: Allen & Unwin, 1960).

Lichtheim, George, *Georg Lukács* (New York: Viking Press, 1970).

Liehm, Mira, *Passion and Defiance: Film in Italy from 1942 to the Present* (Berkeley and London: University of California Press, 1984).

Liehm, Mira, and Liehm Antonin, J., *The Most Important Art: East European Film After 1945* (Berkeley and London: University of California Press, 1977).

Lippmann, Walter, *Public Opinion* (New York and London: Allen & Unwin, 1922).

Livingstone, Rodney (ed.) *Georg Lukács: Essays on Realism* (London: Lawrence and Wishart, 1980).

Lovell, Terry, *Pictures of Reality* (London: BFI, 1980).

Löwy, Michael, *Georg Lukács: From Romanticism to Bolshevism* (London: New Left Books, 1979).

Lukács, Georg, *History and Class Consciousness: Studies in Marxist Dialectics* (London: Merlin Press, 1990).

Lukács, Georg, *The Meaning of Contemporary Realism* (London: Merlin Press, 1963).

Lukács, Georg, *Theory of the Novel: A Historico-Philosophical Essay on the Forms of Great Epic Literature* (Cambridge, MA: MIT Press, 1971).

Lukács, Georg, 'Tolstoy and the Development of Realism', from *Studies in European Realism*, reprinted in Craig, David (ed.) *Marxists on Literature: An Anthology* (London: Penguin, 1977).

Lukács, Georg, *Studies in European Realism: A Sociological Study of the Writings of Balzac, Stendhal, Zola, Gorki and Others* (London: Merlin Press, 1972).

Lukács, Georg, *Writer and Critic and Other Essays* (London: Merlin, 1978).

Lukács, Georg, *The Destruction of Reason* (London: Merlin, 1980).

Lukács, Georg, *The Historical Novel* (Harmondsworth: Penguin, 1976).

Lukács, Georg, *Essays on Thomas Mann* (New York: Grosset and Dunlap, 1965).

Lukács, Georg, *Solzhenitsyn* (London: Merlin Press, 1970).

Lukács, Georg, *Goethe and His Age* (London: Merlin Press, 1968).

Lunn, Eugene, *Marxism and Modernism: An Historical Study of Lukács, Brecht Benjamon and Adorno* (Berkeley, Los Angeles and London: University of California Press, 1982).

MacCabe, Colin, 'Realism and the Cinema: Notes on some Brechtian Theses', *Screen*, vol. 15, no. 2, (summer 1974).

McLennan, Gregor, *Marxism and the Methodologies of History* (London: NLB, 1981).

Macquarrie, John, *Existentialism* (Harmondsworth: Pelican, 1973).

Magraw, Roger, *France 1815–1914: The Bourgeois Century* (London: Fontana, 1983).

Marcus, Judith, *Georg Lukács and Thomas Mann: A Study in the Sociology of Literature* (Amherst: University of Massachusetts Press, 1987).

Marcus, Judith, and Tarr, Zoltán (eds), *Georg Lukács: Theory, Culture and Politics* (New Brunswizk: Transaction, 1989).

Marcus, Millicent, *Italian Film in the Light of Neorealism* (Princeton: Princeton University Press, 1986).

Marrick, Harold (ed.) *Challenges to Empiricism* (London: Methuen, 1980).

Martin, John, W. *The Golden Age of French Cinema 1929–1939* (Boston: Twayne, 1983).

Marx, Karl, *Karl Marx and Frederick Engels: Selected Works* (London: Lawrence and Wishart, 1968).

Mészáros, István, *Lukács' Concept of Dialetic* (London: Merlin Press, 1972).

Mukerji, A. C., 'British Idealism', in *A Dictionary of Eastern and Western Philosophy* (London: Allen & Unwin, 1953).

Natanson, Maurice, *Edmund Husserl, Philosopher of Infinite Tasks* (Evanston, IL: Northwestern University Press, 1973).

Needham, Gerald, *19th Century Realist Art* (New York: Harper & Row Publishers, 1988).

Nettl, J. P., *The Soviet Achievement* (London: Thames and Hudson, 1967).

Nochlin, Linda, *Realism* (Harmondsworth: Penguin, 1971).

Novack, George, *Pragmatism Versus Marxism: An Appraisal of John Dewey's Philosophy* (New York and London: Pathfinder, 1975).

Nowell-Smith, Geoffrey, *Luchino Visconti* (London: Viking, 1973).

O'Shaughnessy, Martin, *Jean Renoir* (Manchester: Manchester University Press, 1988).

Papineau, David, *Reality and Representation* (Oxford: Basil Blackwell, 1987).

Parkinson, G. H. R. (ed.) *Georg Lukács: The Man, His Work and His Ideas* (New York: London House, 1970).

Parkinson, G. H. R., *Georg Lukács* (London: Routledge, 1977).

Parmesani, Loredana, *Art of the Twentieth Century: Movements, Theories, Schools and Tendencies 1900–2000* (Milan and London: Skira Editore/Giò Marconi and Thames & Hudson, 2000).

Partridge, Colin, *Senso: Visconti's Film and Bioto's Novella, a Case Study in the Relation between Literature and Film* (Lampeter: The Edwin Mellen Press, 1992).

Passmore, John, *Recent Philosophers: A Supplement to A Hundred Years of Philosophy* (London: Duckworth, 1985).

Passmore, John, *A Hundred Years of Philosophy* (London: Duckworth, 1957).

Pauly, Rebecca M., *The Transparent Illusion: Image and Ideology in French Text and Film* (New York: Peter Lang Publishing, Inc., 1993).

Pinkus, Theodor (ed.), *Conversations With Lukács* (London: Merlin, 1974).

Plantinga, Carl, and Smith, M. Greg (eds), *Passionate Views: Film, Cognition and Emotion* (Baltimore and London: The Johns Hopkins University Press, 1999).

Poster, Mark, *Sartre's Marxism* (London: Pluto, 1979).

Purcell, Edward A., *The Crisis of Democratic Theory: Scientific Naturalism and the Problem of Value* (Lexington: University Press of Kentucky, 1973).

Putnam, Hilary, *Reason, Truth and History* (Cambridge: Cambridge University Press, 1981).

Putnam, Hilary, *Representation and Reality* (Cambridge, MA and London: The MIT Press, 1991).

Putnam, Hilary, *Realism with a Human Face* (Cambridge MA and London: Harvard University Press, 1992).

Putnam, Hilary, *The Many Faces of Realism* (La Salle: Illinois Open Court, 1987).

Ray, Robert B., 'Impressionism, Surrealism and Film Theory', in Hill, John, and Church Gibson, Pamela (eds), *The Oxford Guide to Film Studies* (Oxford: Oxford University Press, 1998).

Rescher, N., *Conceptual Idealism* (Oxford: Basil Blackwell, 1973).

Rockmore, Tom (ed.), *Lukács Today: Essays in Marxist Philosophy* (Dordrecht: Reidel, 1988).

Rodowick, D. N. 'The Last Things Before the Last', *New German Critique*, no. 54 (fall 1991).

Rodowick, D. N., 'On Kracauer's *History*', *New German Critique*, no. 41 (spring 1988).

Rorty, Richard, 'The World Well Lost', *Journal of Philosophy*, no. 69 (1972).

Rorty, Richard, *Philosophy and the Mirror of Nature* (Oxford: Blackwell, 1980).

Rorty, Richard, 'Feminism and Pragmatism', *Radical Philosophy*, no. 59 (autumn 1991).

Rudé, George, *Revolutionary Europe 1783–1815* (London: Fontana, 1965).

Russell, Bertrand, *History of Western Philosophy* (London: Allen & Unwin Ltd, 1965).

Sadoul, Georges, *Histoire générale du cinéma II: Les pionniers du cinéma (De Méliés à Pathé) 1879–1909* (Paris: Les Editions Denöel, 1973–7).

Salt, Barry, 'From Caligari to Who?', *Sight and Sound*, vol. 48, no. 2, (spring 1979).

Sartre, Jean-Paul, *Being and Nothingness: An Essays on Phenomenological Ontology* (London: Methuen and Co., 1969).

Saussure, Ferdinand de, *Course in General Linguistics* (New York and London: McGraw-Hill, 1966).

Sayers, Sean, *Reality and Reason: Dialectic and the Theory of Knowledge* (Oxford: Basil Blackwell, 1985).

Schifano, Laurence, *Luchino Visconti: The Flames of Passion* (London: Collins, 1990).

Schlüpmann, Heide, 'Phenomenology of Film: On Siefried Kracauer's Writings of the 1920s', *New German Critique*, no. 40 (Winter 1987).

Schmitt, Frederick F., *Truth A Primer* (Boulder, San Franscisco and London: Westview Press, 1995).

Searle, John, *Minds, Brains & Science* (London: Penguin, 1989).

Servadio, Gaia, *Luchino Visconti: A Biography* (London: Weidenfeld and Nicolson, 1982).

Sesonske, Alexander, *Jean Renoir: The French Films, 1924–1939* (Cambridge: Cambridge University Press, 1980).

Silberman, Marc, *German Cinema: Texts in Context* (Detroit: Wayne State University Press, 1995).

Singer, Peter, *Hegel* (Oxford: Oxford University Press, 1983).

Stam, Robert, *Film Theory: An Introduction* (Oxford: Blackwell, 2000).

Tallis, Raymond, *Not Saussure: A Critique of Post-Saussurean Literary Theory* (Basingstoke: Macmillan, 1995).

Taylor, Charles, *Hegel* (Cambridge: Cambridge University Press, 1975).

Thompson, E. P., *The Poverty of Theory and Other Essays* (London: Merlin, 1978).

Tonetti, Claretta, *Luchino Visconti* (Boston: Twayne, 1983).

Trigg, Roger, *Reality at Risk: A Defence of Realism in Philosophy and the Sciences* (New York and London: Harvester Wheatsheaf, 1989).

Vaughan, James C., *Soviet Socialist Realism: Origins & Theories* (London: Macmillan, 1973).

Weisberg, Gabriel, P. (ed.) *The European Realist Tradition* (Bloomington: Indiana University Press, 1982).

Williams, Alan, *Republic of Images: A History of French Film-making* (Cambridge, MA, and London: Harvard University Press, 1992).

Williams, Raymond, *Culture and Society 1780–1950* (London: Chatto & Windus, 1958).

Williams, Raymond, *Marxism and Literature* (New York: Oxford University Press, 1977).

Williams, Raymond, 'A Lecture on Realism', *Screen*, vol. 18, no. 1 (1977).

Willett, John (ed. and trans.) *Brecht on Theatre* (London: Eyre Methuen, 1979).

Wilson, Emma, *French Cinema Since 1950: Personal Histories* (London: Duckworth, 1999).

Winston, Brian, *Claiming the Real: The Documentary Film Revisited* (London: BFI, 1995).

Wittgenstein, L., *Philosophical Investigations* (Oxford: Oxford University Press, 1953).

Wollen, Peter, *Signs and Meaning in the Cinema* (London: BFI/Secker & Warburg, 1969).

Wollen, Peter, 'The Two Avant-Gardes', reprinted in his *Readings and Writings: Semiotic Counter-Strategies* (London: Verso, 1982).

Wollen, Peter, *Readings and Writings: Semiotic Counter-Strategies* (London: Verso, 1982).

Woolhouse, R. S., *The Empiricists* (New York and Oxford: Oxford University Press, 1988).

Zitta, Victor, *Georg Lukács' Marxism: Alienation, Dialectics, Revolution: A Study in Utopia and Ideology.* (The Hague: Martinus Nijhoff, 1964).

Index